Developing Adult Learners

Developing Adult Learners

Strategies for Teachers and Trainers

Kathleen Taylor
Catherine Marienau
Morris Fiddler

JOSSEY-BASS
A Wiley Company
www.josseybass.com

Published by

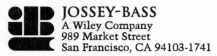

JOSSEY-BASS
A Wiley Company
989 Market Street
San Francisco, CA 94103-1741

www.josseybass.com

Jossey-Bass books and products are available through most bookstores. To contact Jossey-Bass directly, call (888) 378-2537, fax to (800) 605-2665, or visit our website at www.josseybass.com.

Substantial discounts on bulk quantities of Jossey-Bass books are available to corporations, professional associations, and other organizations. For details and discount information, contact the special sales department at Jossey-Bass.

 Manufactured in the United States of America on Lyons Falls Turin Book. This paper is acid-free and 100 percent totally chlorine-free.

Library of Congress Cataloging-in-Publication Data
Taylor, Kathleen, 1943-
    Developing adult learners : strategies for teachers and trainers /
Kathleen Taylor, Catherine Marienau, Morris Fiddler.—1st ed.
      p. cm. — (The Jossey-Bass higher and adult education series)
      Includes bibliographical references (p.   ) and index.
      ISBN 0-7879-4573-0 (alk. paper)
      1. Adult learning.   2. Learning, Psychology of.   I. Marienau,
Catherine. II. Fiddler, Morris. III. Title. IV. Series.
      LC5225.L42 T39 2000
      374'.13—dc21
                                                    00-008478

FIRST EDITION
HB Printing 10 9 8 7 6 5 4 3 2

The Jossey-Bass

Higher and Adult Education Series

This book is in memory of Beverly K. Firestone,
whose dedication to improving teachers
and teaching was an expression of her love
for learners and learning.

CONTENTS

PREFACE

Currently there are nearly as many undergraduates over the age of twenty-five as there are traditional-aged college students, and thousands of adults each year take advantage of workplace-based training opportunities. This "modern era" of adult learning can be traced to two major societal shifts that began in the 1960s and continue today. First, responding to radical critiques of higher education as elitist and exclusionary, educational innovators created programs that recognized and responded to the needs of more diverse learners. Second, in the workplace, blue-collar and manual labor have given way to "knowledge" workers, who increasingly require ongoing training and lifelong learning to avoid obsolescence. As a result, adult-focused programs continue to expand in community colleges and flagship universities and in corporate, public sector, and workplace training. Learning once reserved for the few is increasingly available to men and women of all ages and social strata, and the focus of learning has changed from preserving the past or maintaining the status quo to providing the tools needed to make sense of increasingly complex challenges now and in the future.

Training, Teaching, or Education?

The once clearly marked distinction between teaching and training has become an increasingly permeable boundary. Bridges (1988), for example, distinguishes between skills-based training and context-based training, which enables people to see and understand things differently and depends on imagination and dialogue rather than on memorization and programmed responses. Training associated with leadership development, in particular, has moved away from a framework based on skills development and behavioral objectives. Attention is now paid to attitudes and beliefs that may promote people's flexibility, capabilities, and effectiveness. There is also a new emphasis on creating learning organizations (Senge, 1990). Rather than simply react and respond to the external environment, people in such organizations create their own future through changing their mental models and learning to think systemically. To accomplish this, however, people need to understand how they currently think; they need to surface and examine the assumptions and attitudes that underlie their "knowledge" and behaviors.

Especially for executive leaders, workplace training increasingly focuses on learning activities. As Bennis and Goldsmith (1994) point out in *Learning to Lead,* people need more than skills development. They need to examine their experiences and beliefs and reflect on the underlying implications; they need to "[see] the world simultaneously as it is and as it can be" (p. 73). This analysis can, in turn, lead to shifts in attitudes and understanding that support more appropriate and effective behaviors. In a similar vein, Peter Vaill (1996) focuses on the need for modern managerial leaders to become systems thinkers and to "embrace complexity, contingency, dynamism, and even mystery" (p. 109)— capabilities unlikely to be developed in traditional, reductionist training environments.

In many institutions of higher education, ideas about teaching have also evolved. With more adults in the classroom, as well as more younger students who are already employed, there has been an expanding need for more experiential, more applied, and more self-reflective approaches to teaching and learning. Higher learning programs are focusing increasingly on learners actively making meaning, rather than passively accepting meaning made by others.

Given the similarities of these goals, many adult educators hold that it is no longer sufficient for professors to profess and trainers to train. Both have to *educe,* or to draw out, a term that comes from the same root as the word *educate.* Where they may once have emphasized information acquisition or behavior change, teacher-educators and trainer-educators have expanded their focus on learning. They attempt to draw out adults' experiences and reflections on experience as a major strategy toward learning that can lead to changes in attitudes, beliefs, understanding, and behaviors. We therefore refer to both practitioners simply as *educators.*

Purpose

Such education can help adults view themselves, their past choices, and their future possibilities in new ways. These new perceptual frameworks are described by adult learning theorists and practitioners (Mezirow, 1991; Candy, 1991; Brookfield, 1989) and adult development theorists (Kegan, 1994; Belenky, Clinchy, Goldberger, & Tarule, 1986) as among the potential areas of growth and change in adulthood. However, this literature is widely known only among psychologists or adult learning specialists. As a result, few teachers and trainers from other disciplines or professions realize that the possibility for developmental change in adults is enhanced when educators' practice is consciously informed by developmental intentions.

Our overarching aim with this book, therefore, is to influence adult educators to make more intentional choices toward developmental growth in their work with adult learners. As Kolb (1984) observes: "With the recognition that learning and development are lifelong processes, there comes a corresponding responsibility for social institutions and organizations to conduct their affairs in such a way that adults have experiences that facilitate their personal learning and growth" (p. 15). To encourage educators to assume this responsibility, we offer, first, a conceptual framework that links intentions and development; second, dozens of classroom- and workshop-tested activities framed by developmental intentions; and, third, an examination of developmentally focused educational practices. We intend in this way to enrich and expand the repertoires of experienced adult educators and those relatively new to adult learning and development.

Audience

This book is directed toward two major audiences. First, it is designed for the many adult educators who are being recruited, due to shifting enrollment trends, from the ranks of traditional educators and professionals or practitioners in other fields. A few have pursued the field of adult education as an intentional career choice, and some have been drawn to this work because it meshes with their values and instincts about learning. Still others, however, have focused primarily on their professional specialties or academic disciplines and only secondarily on their teaching or training and the process of learning, and now find themselves in a job they were not aspiring to as they began their professional careers. Our second audience is faculty developers and "train-the-trainers"—those whose task is to sharpen the skills of the front-line adult educators described above.

Because we expect our readers to come from such various disciplines and professional backgrounds, we assume little, if any, prior knowledge of adult learning or adult development theories. Detailed theoretical discussions have been kept to a minimum, since they are not requisite to trying the activities. For those who would delve deeper, we have provided five appendixes that contain glosses on some of the models that are central to this book.

In short, this book is addressed to the growing number of instructors and faculty members (full-time and adjunct), workplace educators, and leadership trainers working with adults whose continuing development rests on their ability to learn from experience.

Overview of the Contents

The book is divided into three parts. Part One provides a rationale for attending to the developmental growth of adult learners and a framework of intentions that encourage such development. The first chapter describes some of the salient characteristics of adults as learners, seen through the eyes of experienced adult educators. We link aspects of the changing nature of adults' lives to their potential for ongoing development and to choices adult educators can make to enhance that possibility. Chapter Two explores intersections between learning and development, drawing on constructive-developmental theory and theories of adult and experiential learning. The third chapter examines the notion of developmental intentions as a framework for educational practice. This framework was abstracted from descriptions of desired learning outcomes that skillful teachers and trainers shared with us and serves as a conceptual bridge to the strategies and activities.

Part Two contains nearly seventy activities. Some can be completed within one meeting; others take place over a series of meetings or an entire course. Discussion of these activities is divided among seven chapters, each focused on a particular strategy that incorporates developmental intentions: assessing, collaborating, experimenting, imagining, inquiring, performing-simulating, reflecting. All are described so that readers may adapt them to and use them in contexts other than those for which they were originally designed.

In Part Three we focus on issues related to implementing the strategies effectively. Chapter Eleven highlights assumptions implicit in the strategies. We use these to illustrate how experienced adult educators create developmentally supportive learning environments. The twelfth chapter turns the focus to the development of the educator and explores the importance of conscious reflection on practice. Chapter Thirteen examines possible costs of change and growth in the lives of adults and describes how a relationship of care may be essential for such growth to proceed.

What We Intend

We have tried to make this book accessible and useful in the following ways:

- By writing in a voice that is intended to be personal and engaging
- By introducing and using a conceptual framework of educational practice based on theories of development and deep approaches to learning
- By highlighting the powerful, compelling voices of learners describing their own experiences of learning, growth, and development, as well as voices of educators
- By limiting jargon
- By presenting a variety of teaching strategies and activities that can be used in many contexts
- By speaking to the broad group of adult educators that includes both teachers and trainers in a variety of settings

Who We Are

Knowing that the experiential frames we bring to this project undoubtedly color our perceptions, we identify ourselves as individuals beyond the usual author biographies.

> KATHLEEN: Having dropped out of college just before my junior year, I know firsthand the challenges faced by those who later try to drop back in. Faced with starting over from the beginning, with no acknowledgment of my maturity or experience, I very nearly gave up. Then I discovered a program that would allow me to petition for credit for my years of personal and professional extramural learning, as well as design my own program and learning agreements. I was delighted that I would not have to fit a thirty-seven-year-old square peg into a round hole designed for someone half my age, but I had no way of knowing that these learning experiences would also change my life. Now, twenty years later, I hardly recognize the person I was then.
>
> Once I began to understand the transformative potential of adult-centered learning, I changed careers and went on for graduate study specifically focused on the intersections between adult learning and adult development. For the last fifteen years I have been a change agent in two ways: by creating learning environments intended to support adults to develop as individuals and as shapers of our collective future, and by encouraging other educators to adopt developmental goals and practices.

CATHERINE: I entered the adult learning field in 1971 through the alternative higher education movement, wanting to make a difference in individuals' lives and to reform higher education. In the fashion of many adult learners, I worked full-time in my field while earning my advanced degrees in areas related to learning and development. I have made my professional home in individualized, outcomes-based degree programs for adults at undergraduate, graduate, and doctoral levels. As a practitioner, I was always hungry for theories and models that would help me understand more and act more effectively. One of my long-time goals has been to help translate theory so that practitioners can enhance their understanding and practice. As a practitioner, I have directed my teaching-mentoring, program administration, scholarship, and consulting activities toward fostering individuals' growth and development and toward creating learning environments to support that growth. The constant reward for me is working with individual learners and participating in various ways in their experiences of learning and growth. The constant challenge for me is working toward better aligning the ideals of adult learning with the structures and practices in educational settings to make higher education more hospitable for adult learners in every way.

MORRY: I come to this work with curiosity and respect for individual differences that I trace mostly to my training in human genetics and the values of my heritage. I have worn several professional identities: geneticist, entrepreneur, musician, and, for roughly fifteen years, fellow traveler with learning adults. When I turned to working full-time with adults in higher education, I did so with instincts, heart, and desire to shift how adults experience their relationship with educational institutions. How might the authority students vest in academia become subordinate to adults' authorship of their lives as creators of families, communities, organizations, businesses, and self? As my identity as an adult educator emerged, it brought with it a responsibility to understand better those adults with and for whom I was working. What contributes to the variation in how they learn? Why is each seeking education and training? What might development mean in addition to what I already understood and studied as a geneticist? I've come to know that this responsibility hasn't been only to learn what I could about adult learning and development to inform my

work, but also to give back to others in return. I came to this book with
a desire to consolidate what I thought I understood; what I've found, once
again, is how elusive my understanding can be as a developing adult and
as an adult educator.

Acknowledgments

Our vision of this book could never have been realized without the thoughtful and generous contributions of many colleagues. We would like particularly to thank those educators who shared their experiences and allowed us to use their observations: Patricia Brewer, Nancy Davis, Gloria Eive, Kate Farrell, Karen-Kelly Hicks, Mark Hoyer, John Kindar, Sam Lester, Lanie Melamed, Chuck Piazza, Rebecca Proehl, Paul Rea, Grete Stenersen, Don Stone, Phyllis Walden, and Kim Winkelman.

We are also grateful to those who provided conceptual feedback and other support at various stages of our work: David Boud, Stephen Brookfield, Arthur Chickering, Carolyn Clark, Sam Crooks, Larry Daloz, Velde Elliott, Tom Kalb, Rebecca Proehl, Joy Segal, and Pamela Tate.

We wish to also acknowledge the contributors of strategies, without whom this book would have no core; our editors at Jossey-Bass, Gale Erlandson and Melissa Kirk; and our family members, who have demonstrated saintly forbearance for far longer than they or we anticipated.

Most especially, to the adult learners whose voices, gathered formally and informally over our years of practice, grace and illuminate this work, go our heartfelt thanks for teaching us about learning.

March 2000   Kathleen Taylor
                                                            Catherine Marienau
                                                            Morris Fiddler

THE AUTHORS

KATHLEEN TAYLOR is a department chair and professor at Saint Mary's College of California. She returned to college to finish an undergraduate degree in her mid-thirties. For the last fifteen years, she has supported other returning adults as they encounter the challenges of transformative learning, believing that their changes in perspective will lead toward a more sane, safe, and just society. Her research and writing explore the intersections of adult learning and adult development, with an emphasis on women's development. She also examines the contributions of self-assessment, prior learning assessment, experience-based learning, and constructivist approaches to teaching and learning in encouraging developmental growth in adult learners, and consults on faculty development related to these topics. She earned a doctorate in adult higher education from Union Graduate School.

CATHERINE MARIENAU is professor and faculty mentor in the School for New Learning at DePaul University in Chicago, Illinois. She has worked in alternative higher education for adults for over twenty-five years as mentor, advisor, teacher, administrator, researcher, writer, and consultant. Her current research and writing focus on adult learning and development, particularly that of women, and on assessment of learning, including self-assessment and prior learning assessment. She earned a doctorate in adult higher education at the University of Minnesota. Marienau is a past president of the Alliance—Adult Higher Education Association.

MORRIS FIDDLER is associate professor and faculty mentor in the School for New Learning at DePaul University in Chicago, Illinois. He has worked with adult learners for twenty years as a mentor, advisor, teacher, administrator, researcher, writer, and consultant. His research interests and writing focus on competence-based learning, prior learning assessment, advising, Internet-mediated learning, adult development, individual differences, medical genetics, and genetic counseling. He earned a doctorate in human genetics at the University of Minnesota.

Developing Adult Learners

PART ONE

CONCEPTS AND FOUNDATIONS

Being in a learning environment seems to place adults "in grave danger of growing" (Kegan, 1994, p. 293). The three chapters in Part One explore this phenomenon from the perspectives of learning and development.

Chapter One begins by drawing on the voices of experienced adult educators to sketch a picture of adults as learners. The themes that emerge focus on internal and external changes that adults experience and suggest a relationship among these changes, development, and learning.

This initial examination is deepened in Chapter Two, which describes significant concurrence between constructive-developmental theories and some of the most widely known adult learning theories. This chapter also highlights three essential aspects of adult learning theory—experience, reflection, and meaning-making—that form a bridge between learning and development.

Chapter Three presents a conceptual framework synthesized from the views of adult educators in the United States, the United Kingdom, and Australia for using "developmental intentions" to guide practice.

CHAPTER ONE

LINKING LEARNING
WITH DEVELOPMENT

The proper aim of education is to promote significant learning.
Significant learning entails development. Development means
successively asking broader and deeper questions of the relationship
between oneself and the world.

—Laurent A. Daloz (1999)

Adults can be paradoxical learners. When adult educators walk into classrooms or workshops, they find a diverse group of learners who at one moment can draw on a rich store of life experiences and at the next may resist new ideas that challenge what they already know. Adults tend to be highly motivated to learn *yet* will sometimes focus on evaluations or grades rather than on learning. They think of themselves as "self-directed" *yet* they may feel shortchanged when an educator explains that she intends to be less a source of answers than a resource for learning. When entering or reentering college, many adults who have successfully managed their own professional development nevertheless sometimes revert to classroom strategies that worked for them in high school ("How many pages?" "Will this be on the test?"), generally trying to do "what the teacher wants." In the training environment, learners may seek to improve their job performance yet may deny themselves the practice it takes to develop the new skills.

The colleagues whose voices enliven this chapter are all experienced adult educators. They are workshop and seminar leaders and corporate trainers, full-time faculty and part-time adjunct faculty in programs designed for adults, and administrators in urban community and technical colleges. Their areas of expertise include English, religious studies, sociology, career counseling, technology conversion, strategic planning, philosophy, biology, business management, social work, women's studies, counseling psychology, and education. We will draw on their experience to outline the salient features, from an educator's perspective, of adults as learners.

Adults as Learners

Adults learn everywhere—in the workplace, at home, in their communities. They do so to function effectively in the changing world around them.

Patricia: Adults come with an agenda. I like to think that my assistance helps them to become "architects" of their own learning. My students don't know "how" but they often know "what"; I supply the "how" and [the learning] gets done through their efforts.

Chuck: [Adults] want to engage in learning that (re)sharpens their relationships, world, dreams . . . They can see that their lives are in transition and that the course, workshop, program, etcetera [are] facilitating that change.

Indeed, *change* is a major ongoing factor in adults' lives, hence in their engagement with learning. Although many people respond to change initially by trying to stay within existing patterns of behavior and frameworks of belief, others gradually recognize contradictions between *this* part of their lives and *that* part of their lives. Such discoveries may motivate adults to seek new learning in a formal setting.

Their learning needs often grow out of their larger life issues: *Do I stay in this secure but unsatisfying job, or try a new career path and risk my family's financial security? How do I respond to my spouse, who wants to restructure our relationship? How do I deal with a company initiative that I don't believe is sound? Where do I stand, as a voter, on issues such as legalizing euthanasia, ending affirmative action, requiring handgun registration, or requiring English-only classrooms and ballots?*

Whether building on something they already know or exploring new areas, adults want to learn things that seem relevant and applicable to their current lives, including work and family matters. Adults differ from younger learners in that a younger person is still anticipating most of the responsibilities in which an adult is fully engaged. Adults are therefore more likely than younger students to personalize learning. They want to relate the subject matter, whether business management, history, or philosophy, to themselves.

Sam: [Adults focus on] the "so what" of an idea . . . [and are excited when they] find examples from their life or recognize explanations for things they've experienced but didn't understand.

MORRY: In the midst of discussing dimensions of culture, a veteran police officer suddenly became aware of the tension between his increasing appreciation of collective decision making and the deeply embedded hierarchical structure of his organization, if not profession. Another student countered that she feels her desire to exert more personal power and influence is constrained by the highly consensual norms of her ethnic tradition. Dimensions of culture began to take on new meaning for these students and others in the group.

Though this can enrich discussions and enhance each person's learning, adults' desire to focus on what they feel is relevant can also be a limiting factor.

Mark: At times, they're so results-oriented that if they don't [see] an immediate tangible (and practical, that is, usable) result to what you're doing, they'll mentally "tune out" or otherwise resist the process.

Rebecca: [Some] managers . . . want "How to Be a Better Supervisor" in four easy steps, and [do] not necessarily [want] to do the work to recognize the complexities of being a more effective supervisor.

Although some adults reflect a belief that only work-related learning really matters, many go beyond that.

Phyllis: Adults are able to make meaningful connections that reflect diverse experience—that makes for more engaged and exciting learning and dialogue. . . . They appreciate learning and what the liberal arts [can] contribute to quality of life—and I would go as far as saying soul. Adult experience provides a context for liberal education that the eighteen-year-old does not yet have.

John: A thrill for me is seeing an adult learner apply what we're studying in class to her own life. I've seen students become active in supporting the homeless in their own neighborhoods and lobbying for antidiscrimination housing policies in their own towns.

Because what adults learn may have a more immediate impact on their lives, they bring a greater sense of urgency to their learning. Educators often note adults' seriousness of purpose:

Kate: I have found that adults have a willingness to learn that is quite remarkable. Their motivation is in gear; they are alert and focused on learning. . . . With these attributes, learning can be accelerated and often life-changing.

Don: I love teaching adults because they are highly motivated and mature in their expectations. I can generally count on them to do the [assignments] so we can have fruitful discussions. . . . Given all their work and family obligations, my adult students inspire me with their commitment.

Despite their high level of motivation, however, some adults feel a sense of inadequacy about performing and being judged in formal learning settings. Helping individuals acknowledge and work with their fears is also part of an adult educator's task:

Grete: Adults often believe (incorrectly) that they are not intelligent enough to complete their educational goals.

Chuck: [It is essential to] build their self-esteem and confidence that they can research material, critically analyze it, and present their own concepts. They often still don't trust themselves.

KATHLEEN: Many adults have had problematic experiences with learning—sometimes those experiences go back to a particularly insensitive (or unaware) teacher in elementary school! Early in my work with them, I encourage learners to revisit some of these memories and to work on challenging the feelings that might still haunt that person's belief about his or her ability to learn.

Though adults often gravitate to learner-centered environments, once there they may be unsure of what to do, as they are likely to have had little or no previous experience in such settings.

Kim: I tell my students at the beginning of each course, "Learning is not a matter of regurgitating information; learning is a process of *how* to think, not *what* to think." . . . [It's a challenge] to wean adults from the institutionalized process of what Freire so aptly identified as the "banking system" of education.

Rebecca: Particularly in the workplace, adults tend to be atheoretical: *Just give me the facts; don't bore me with theory.* . . . [They're also] concerned that if they actually do things differently, they'll become less productive while they're learning.

Fortunately, positive learning experiences can help develop adults' desire and capacities for deeper learning.

Chuck: If they have a supportive and honest traveling companion-mentor, [adults] are often ready (with a little nudge) to take responsibility for their learning and push the limits of their comfort zone.

CATHERINE: Adults' tendency to focus on learning that connects immediately to the workplace can be a challenge. I try to create ways to help them use real life situations and conflicts as a basis for identifying and solving problems. This problem-based approach tends to lead to a real integration of learning. For example, when a student experiences the need to create collaboration and ownership among members of a work team, this drives which theories and models are examined. I have found it less effective to introduce students to an array of theories and models that they do not apply to something concrete. The problem-based approach also helps students recognize the complexity and murkiness of their own real life problems and stimulates them to search for answers from among a wider sphere of information, ideas, and perspectives.

The major difference between adults and younger learners is the wealth of their experience. They have seen, been, and done. They have personal history: marriage and divorce or other long-term relationships, perhaps children and grandchildren, certainly births and deaths of people close to them. They have work history: various jobs, sometimes at impressive levels of responsibility. They also have social history: firsthand knowledge of the same historical period that their instructors have. These experiences are valuable—we would claim *essential*—contributions to the learning process.

Paul: [I enjoy] the sense of shared life experiences; a sense of being understood, [for instance,] of class members "getting it" when one refers to Anita Hill or whatever; a feeling of working among equals, with no "parental" dimension; and a feeling of being "met" emotionally when I express emotion.

Phyllis: Adults are able to make meaningful connections that reflect diverse experiences—[this] makes for more engaged and exciting learning and classroom dialogue.

Lanie: Adults bring rich life experience to the learning situation and can tie abstract ideas to concrete reality quite readily. They tend to be more sure of themselves and less impressionable. I really appreciate it when students speak up and disagree with what I have to say or with what they read.

Nevertheless, as Brookfield (1998) observes, using adults' experience as a basis for their learning requires careful facilitation. Some individuals may not be able to generalize from the particulars of their experience; others may not be able to see the relevance of experiences that are not their own.

Susan: Adults bring such rich and varied experiences to connect with the material. I keep wondering about and trying out ways to capitalize on their experience for the benefit of the student as well as the group.

Nancy: I certainly recognize the experience and competence in many areas that adults bring with them. . . . But when I start with people's experiences, they can get stuck there. And too easily, it seems, people want to tell their stories in great detail; and I'm left trying to make connections to a main point, to getting us back on track.

When everything comes together—when adults have been reassured that "they really do know something" (Belenky, Clinchy, Goldberger, & Tarule, 1986), yet can learn more, the potential for change exists.

Kelly: [It's important] for adults to find out how much they need to learn . . . meaning that, no matter the age, life experience, or resident knowledge, the humans we identify as "adults" are never too anything not to [learn] something new. And this in itself is exciting, seeing those already "grown," as they move through the developmental wonders of learning.

Don: [Adults'] experience is like ripe fruit—just ready to be noticed and analyzed and appreciated. It is a pleasure to facilitate their taking perspective on their experiences; a lot happens with relatively little effort on my part. I can really see the changes that the coursework facilitates—the transformations of their perspectives. They are open about acknowledging what they have learned. And grateful. And I know the changes are a direct result of our working together.

Given the complexity of adults' lives, and the variety of experiences, attitudes, and skills that they bring with them to learning environments, it is hardly surprising that our colleagues tell us working with these learners is both "exhilarating" and "a challenge"; that it can provide "more immediate gratification" and "fun" than working with younger learners yet still be "frustrating"; and that being an adult educator can be both "intimidating" and "a fascination and a joy"! Most experienced adult educators seem to find lasting satisfaction less in learners' successfully acquiring the subject matter of their courses or seminars than in those moments when they see evidence of adults' change and growth. And although they may express disappointment when learners back off from learning that holds the potential for growth and development, they realize that learning and growth can't be produced on demand.

Lanie: I think you have to create instances of disequilibrium. Open the door for them to see and appreciate complexity. . . . [As] much as we would like [to], I don't think the process can be rushed. As I grow older I realize that I can't "push the river"— that growth and development take time, despite the fact that I may be impatient.

Moreover, growth and development of this kind is a challenge to the adult's way of being in the world. And, as Bridges (1980) points out, beginnings start with endings. Before people can create a new life, or even just a new way of thinking about their current situation, they must first bring some kind of closure to the old life and the old way of seeing and thinking. The deeper the transformation, the more difficult the process of letting go.

In sum, despite the considerable variation in adult learners' lives, we find two overarching themes: Adults experience situations, problems, and changes that are opportunities for and the basis of learning; and development is one possible response to these internal and external changes. Because these themes inform our practice as adult educators, we will explore them more fully in the rest of this chapter.

Learning and Changing

Most adults who initially seek out formal learning to help them deal with external change do not realize that it is also likely to engender internal change. Similarly, they may not realize that seeking higher education or higher-level training is often an outgrowth of change that is already in process. If asked, most are likely to name reasons connected to job security or career advancement; a few come "just because" learning something new appeals to them for its own sake or, in the case of a degree program, to complete something left undone. For those whose primary attention has been devoted to supporting others, putting their own goals first is itself a dramatic shift in priorities. As one learner said: "All my life I've done for others—this is something I'm doing for *me*."

Though adults' expressed purpose is usually to work toward pragmatic goals, thoughtful self-reflection often reveals more complex desires as in the case of these three learners from diverse backgrounds:

In response to the Vietnam draft, my family moved to Canada, where I finished high school. I tried higher education but dropped out because I couldn't conform—I didn't want to listen to some stuffy professor, I wanted to change the world! But I finally realized I would have to have more education to make the kind of contribution to society that's important to me.

I am the first woman in my family to get a divorce and the first to pursue a college education—I don't know which is harder for my mother to accept. What I know is I must step outside the boundaries of my culture and learn to make my own way in the world.

After fifteen years as a manager, I thought I had a pretty good idea what management was. Then I started leadership training, and came up against all these new ideas. Pretty soon, I discovered that it wasn't really about the ideas, it was about me. I had to learn to think in a different way about what I meant by "being a manager."

Grappling with these complexities can bring about changes in how people understand aspects of their world and themselves; such changes become, in turn, the framework for new beliefs and actions. Vaill (1996) calls this "learning as a way of being" and claims that in today's world of constant challenge and change, which he terms "continuous white water," such substantive, lasting learning is essential. Indeed, in their longitudinal research on "learning that lasts," Mentkowski & Associates (2000) found that "when learners reflect on deeply held personal beliefs and assumptions, they embrace a transforming developmental challenge, pulling their self-reflection into an awareness of themselves in a wider world" (p. 202).

According to Eduard Lindeman (1961), whom many identify as the father of adult education, "Life becomes rational, meaningful, as we learn to be intelligent about the things we do and the things that happen to us. If we lived sensibly, we should all discover that the attractions of experience increase as we grow older. Correspondingly, we should find cumulative joys in searching out the reasonable meaning of the events in which we play parts" (p. 7).

Lindeman's description of learning as *seeking meaning in experience* is matched by current descriptions of adult development. Since the literature of adult learning and adult development frequently defines each in terms of the other (Bright, 1986), we will explore them as intertwined.

Adult Development

Though the modern study of adult development can be dated from the mid-twentieth century, since ancient times philosophers, poets, and other students of human nature have framed human development as a series of changes (for example, the sphinx's famous riddle to Oedipus; Shakespeare's "Seven Ages of Man"). Currently, development spans many disciplines, including biology, psychology, and philosophy (epistemology). *Development* can be broadly defined as *a process of qualitative change in attitudes, values, and understandings that adults experience as a result of ongoing transactions with the social environment, occurring over time but not strictly as a result of time* (Nemiroff & Colarusso, 1990, p. 98; Tennant & Pogson, 1995, p. 199; Weathersby & Tarule, 1980, p. 2).

Four aspects of development that cut across various models and theories provide a foundation for understanding adult learners:

- People develop through interactions with their environment
- Development follows a cycle of differentiation and integration
- Within individuals development is a variable, not uniform, process
- The ability to reframe experience serves as a marker of development

Environmental Interactions

According to John Dewey (1938/1963), experience is created by interactions between external conditions (what goes on outside of one's skin) and an individual's "personal needs, desires, purposes, and capacities" (p. 42). Development therefore takes place in a social context of environmental prompts as people act on the world and it, in turn, acts on them. However, how adults experience this interaction is influenced by how they perceive and make sense of the events that make up that experience. The norms of cultural practices, authorities, class, and racial identity, for example, shape how and what people know and thus the course of their development.

Differentiation and Integration

Development can also be thought of as an ongoing cycle of differentiation and integration. When adults encounter events that cannot be adequately interpreted through or assimilated into their existing frames of reference, the process of differentiation may begin. If so, they come to experience themselves, albeit unconsciously, as made up of parts that do not form a coherent whole. No wonder that adults can find certain learning experiences challenging and even, at times, traumatic when they find themselves at odds or dissatisfied with what they have believed, the boundaries of their socialization, or the values that have served as givens. Ideally, though, this disintegration becomes an opportunity to create a new kind of integration; but to successfully accommodate these new experiences requires a larger, more complex frame of reference. This accommodation is also a dialectical process, in that the resulting synthesis transcends the previous contradictions. This way of thinking about development—as a recurring cycle of differentiation and integration—contrasts with concepts of development as a culturally idealized, normative endpoint.

Variable Process

When people operating from one set of beliefs encounter others who operate from another set of beliefs, the potential exists to change one or both sets of ideas.

Particularly in circumstances that provide for thoughtful reflection and analysis, people may slowly come to see, feel, and understand things differently. However, these changes do not necessarily happen in concert, and some aspects of the developmental process may be "ahead" or "behind" as a more complex worldview, or perceptual framework, emerges.

Age may be a fairly good predictor of development in the lives of young people, but chronological maturity is not necessarily an indicator of adult development. Adults who are not afforded the necessary interactions and supports may never develop beyond the way of perceiving generally associated with early adolescence (Kegan, 1986). In addition, "the nature, timing, and processes of development will vary according to the experience and opportunities of individuals and the circumstances of their lives" (Tennant & Pogson, 1995, p. 197). Some of these circumstances may be random events in individual lives; others may be a product of socialization—for example, the experiences of Latina women are likely to be different than those of African-American men, and so forth.

Reframing Experience

Another way to conceptualize developmental change is in terms of how adults perceive and reframe their life themes. *Life themes* refers to beliefs that guide an individual's choices and self-understanding, such as *responsibility, success, competence.* These often originate in childhood and adolescence, though some may emerge during adulthood. These themes help interpret and bring order to the myriad perceptions, thoughts, actions, and feelings that constitute an individual's interactions with her environment. Other themes derive from cultural, racial, and gender identification, social class and position, and individual differences. How people interpret and reinterpret these themes affects their engagement with and perceptions of new experiences. However, such life-themes are often invisible to the person whose life they inform. Or to the extent that someone becomes conscious of these themes, she may perceive them simply as "That's the way I am."

When, however, someone can not only acknowledge but *reframe* these beliefs—can, for example, perceive them as "how certain experiences and my reactions to them have led me to be"—she has moved toward a more complex self-construction and the possibility to be some other way.

Learning and Development

These four aspects of development have in common elements also associated with learning. Through recurring cycles of interacting with their environment, people interpret what is going on either through their existing frames of reference or by constructing new ways of making meaning. Precisely how people engage in learning, or when they do it, will vary for individuals.

The dynamic intersection between learning and development concerns the fundamental change in how meaning is made or *how we know what we think we know.* Mezirow's (1996) definition of learning elaborates on this point: "Learning is understood as the process of using a prior interpretation to construe a new or revised interpretation of the meaning of one's experience in order to guide future action" (p. 162). Looked at from a learning perspective, development is a qualitative change, or transformation, in a way of knowing. Kegan (2000) emphasizes the significance of *form* to this concept of transformation: "At the heart of a form is a 'way of knowing' (what Mezirow calls a 'frame of reference'); thus genuinely transformational learning is always to some extent an *epistemological* change, rather than merely a change in *behavioral* repertoire or increase in the quantity or *fund* of knowledge" (original emphases).

Mezirow's (1991) description of transformative learning describes "a way of thinking that is increasingly inclusive, discriminating, and integrative of experience [as well as open] to alternative perspectives." Ensuing shifts in values, attitudes, and understandings are functions of this fundamental change in epistemology. People come to these new understandings because their very form of knowing—that is, the "rules" by which they construct meaning—is itself transformed.

Not all learning has this developmental potential. In-form-ative learning simply adds to the form as it is, whereas trans-form-ative learning "puts *the form itself at risk of change*" (original emphasis, Kegan, 2000). The new form is also *bigger* than the earlier one; it is the *larger mind* of which educational philosophers such as Newman and Whitehead wrote long before developmental psychology provided theoretical frameworks and empirical evidence to support their contentions.

Learning That Transforms

Among the transformations that such learning can engender is a qualitative shift in how adults understand both the task of learning and themselves as learners. In the least developed conception, learning is understood as increasing or acquiring "knowledge"—something that originates outside the self—primarily by memorizing or reproducing. *Reproductive learners,* according to Säljö (1982, p. 182), therefore take a surface approach and think in terms of "getting" and storing this knowledge. A second, somewhat more sophisticated, conception is *preparatory-to-action learning,* which focuses on a different kind of knowledge acquisition—taking in procedures and facts so they can be used in some practical way. The most complex conception, *reconstructive learning*, centers on the learner's abstraction of meaning; this is a *deep approach* to learning, "an *interpretive* process aimed at understanding reality," and most significantly from a developmental perspective, "*learning as changing as a person*" (Marton & Booth, 1997, p. 38).

Using phenomenographic methodology, studies have shown that if learners come to the learning environment expecting to accrue knowledge as discrete bits of information, and *if nothing is done to influence a change in that perspective,* reproductive learning will be the outcome (Richardson, 1999). Whether learners change their conceptions is, however, strongly influenced by *educators'* conceptions (Prosser & Trigwell, 1997). In an Australian study, for example, history instructors who thought about their task in terms of "delivering" the content of the course to their students encouraged surface approaches to learning. By contrast, instructors who supported deep approaches to learning were those who saw the study of history as a process of developing interpretations and shared with their students their own process of grappling with the content to abstract meaning (Marton & Booth, 1997, pp. 176–177).

Based on our practice as adult educators, our familiarity with theories of adult development and adult learning, and our understanding of phenomenographic theory and research, we suggest that reconstructive learning—learning in which adults construct or reconstruct meaning—is at the core of development. Given that connection, we propose that educators who wish to encourage development must intentionally focus on strategies that can be used to prompt deep approaches to learning. In this way, adults are supported to move beyond conceptions and practices related to learning as information (that is, "knowledge acquisition") toward conceptions and practices that focus on the possibility of learning as transformation (that is, "changing as a person").

Educating with Development in Mind

An educator who has read thus far may well think, "Why do I need to worry about development and 'deep approaches' now? I've been teaching biology [or business management, history, or organizational development] successfully for years." We acknowledge that most adult educators' primary focus is not simply to impart information, but also to create in learners an enthusiasm for thoughtful discrimination among conflicting ideas and to counter rigidity of belief. By extension, then, many adult educators are already, if tacitly, teaching or training for development. At the same time, however, we suggest that the definition of *successful* may need to be revisited in light of the potential for transformational learning in adults.

KATHLEEN: In my experience, many more learners are at the threshold of change than realize this fact. Even those who start out saying, "I just want a piece of paper" or "I need this for my job" often find that what they really wanted was to look at their life choices in new ways. I therefore see my task as more complex than simply providing information or skills training. How I approach the learner's *real* needs will affect what is *really* learned.

We also suggest (and research confirms [Schneps, 1989]) that information-focused approaches to learning often leave learners' underlying assumptions intact. Reproductive learning is unlikely either to challenge existing beliefs and interpretations or—of particular note to those involved in workplace education—to enable learners to use information in new settings. Learners may *appear* to "take in" the new information but in fact may "isolate [the] discovery in the world of academics alone and never allow it to raise questions about [their] own life and purposes" (Perry, 1970, p. 37). By contrast, when people actively engage with a topic, including drawing on what they already "know" (experience), thoughtfully critiquing both their experience of the present event and their previous assumptions about this or similar events (reflect), and attempting to arrive at understandings both rooted in the past and responsive to the present (make meaning), they are more likely to hold multiple perspectives, think flexibly, and deal with ambiguity—in short, they are not simply adopting new ideas but moving toward changing the ways in which they *construct* the ideas they hold.

Given the brief association many instructors have with adult learners, any given instructor may not see evidence of transformational learning nor of the deeper levels of personal transformation that tend to result from expansion of one's meaning-constructive system. One can, however, provide the environments within which changes are more likely to occur and be gratified to know that such development is an ongoing process of *becoming* rather than of arrival at some final destination. It is lifelong movement toward more complex ways of knowing and more sophisticated understanding of self and others.

Such changes—not just in *what* but in *how* one knows—can lead to changes in all the arenas of adult life. As Schommer (1989) found, the more developed adults' conceptions of knowledge, "the more likely they were to take multiple perspectives, be willing to modify their thinking, withhold ultimate decisions until all the information is available, and to acknowledge the complex tentative nature of everyday issues" (p. 138). Adults with these capacities are likely to be more deliberative, responsible, and competent in carrying out the work of society. They may also do a more effective job of wisely rearing the next generation. They are likely to be less reactive and more considered in personal, workplace, and political decisions, as well as better able to adapt to changing circumstances. They are also better able to recognize the need for more just, humane, and equitable economic and social structures and to work toward achieving those goals. They are more likely to act as stewards of the limited resources of our planet.

For all these reasons, we focus on development of the individual as an essential step toward creating a better society and therefore agree with contemporary educators and psychologists who hold that development should be a major aim of those who educate adults (Chickering et. al, 1981; Kegan, 1994; Kolb, 1984; Daloz, 1999; Hayes & Oppenheim, 1997; Belenky et al., 1986). This, then, is the central theme of our book: *Adult development is influenced by the educational environment, hence by choices and intentions of individual educators with regard to teaching, training, and learning.* The next chapter will therefore describe specific theoretical constructs that can inform our choices and intentions in order to set the stage for learning activities framed by those intentions.

CHAPTER TWO

KEY THEORIES THAT INFORM PRACTICE

*Experience is the necessary condition for development . . . [and] each
person's experience must be of a kind that presents genuine cognitive conflict.*
—HAYES AND OPPENHEIM (1997)

*The way in which we experience a certain phenomenon, the specific meaning it has
for us, is the most fundamental aspect of learning. Learning is learning to experience.*
—MARTON AND BOOTH (1997)

When adults realize that they *construct* their ideas and beliefs—and that they can, if they choose, *re*construct them—they experience themselves and the world around them differently. The possibility that knowledge is *constructed*, rather than coming from some external source, and that it is as much a reflection of the knower as of something that exists independently in the world are notions about human understanding that have emerged only recently in the history of ideas.

Constructivism Redux

Human beings have been trying to understand the world around them since the dawn of consciousness, but the most famous theories of knowledge have come from the classical Greeks. To Plato, sensory data was almost antithetical to grasping universal ideas. By contrast, for Aristotle, understanding began with individual perception; one could then project or discover the universal within it. Both, however, believed that knowledge was acquired and truth discovered through philosophical reasoning. Indeed, for nearly two thousand years philosophers were believed to hold the keys to understanding and knowledge.

With the Renaissance began a paradigmatic shift from philosophy to what has come to be called scientific method as the source of knowledge and truth.

Though there had been, certainly since Aristotle, an empirical thread in philosophy, Francis Bacon's new method, especially as employed by Sir Isaac Newton, emerged as the only means for discovering true knowledge. Furthermore, knowledge obtained in such "objective" fashion was understood as both an increasingly accurate picture of external reality and independent of the knower.

All along, however, there had been naysayers. In ancient Greece, sophists and skeptics, among others, had pointed to the impossibility of providing philosophical proofs of things that were known through individual perceptions. Fifteen hundred years later, Enlightenment philosophers Immanuel Kant and Giovanni Battista Vico similarly claimed that "knowledge" was a construction that followed interpretation of perception.

In the mid-twentieth century, these constructivist notions reemerged in what appears to be a third major paradigm shift in the history of ideas (Sexton, 1997, p. 7). From this perspective, which has been influenced by explorations of particle physics and quantum mechanics, how we know something affects what is known.

Constructivists hold that it is impossible to demonstrate that we know something as it *really* is, as opposed to how we perceive it. As Werner Heisenberg famously said, "We have to remember that what we observe is not nature in itself, but nature exposed to our method of questioning." Currently the scientific viewpoint increasingly embraces the "contextual and relative nature of reality" (Sexton, 1997, p. 8).

KATHLEEN: Some dismiss constructivist claims as *there is no reality*, or at least, *there is no reality outside our minds*. Contrary to these misperceptions, however, constructivism does not claim that the world does not exist, only that what we know of it is ultimately our own construction. Constructivism makes more sense to me when I think of it in concrete terms. For example, if all the people on a completely isolated desert island were color-blind, how would they ever find out? For that matter, what does *color-blind* mean in that context?

Contemporary Constructivists

In this century, Piaget (1954), Vygotsky (1978), and Kelly (1955) have advanced constructivist thought based more on empirical data than on philosophical speculation. Though they came to their researches from different fields (biology, education, and psychology), their ideas about how people know and understand have notable similarities.

First, they believe knowledge is gained through an *individual's interaction with social processes* and *contexts,* for example, the cultural milieu. In other words, people understand *contextually.* Of course, much of the context is so pervasive as to be "invisible," as in the old saying, "You can't ask a fish about water"; nevertheless, context affects what is known and how it is understood.

Second, rather than being *objective* (that is, independent of the thinking or perceiving self), knowledge is thought of as the best *creative construction* of which the individual, or active subject, is capable. Furthermore, how individuals make or construe meaning may change over time, perhaps in identifiable sequences of change.

> KATHLEEN: The principle of the "active subject" as construer of meaning has been misinterpreted and trivialized when people are indicted for circumstances over which they have no control, such as poverty and illness, because they have "made their own reality."

Clearly, ideas of learning that focus on the learner's discovery and creation of meaning owe much to constructivist ideas about knowledge. (This helps explain why Dewey is also often mentioned as a constructivist, though he is assigned to other schools of philosophy, as well.) One need not adopt the more radical tenets of constructivist philosophy (of which, for example, von Glasersfeld [1984] is a proponent) to see its relevance for creating effective learning environments for adults. As Candy (1991) describes it, "Constructivism in education is concerned with two things: how learners *construe* (or interpret) events and ideas, and how they *construct* (build or assemble) structures of meaning. The constant dialectical interplay between construing and constructing is at the heart of a constructivist approach to education" (p. 272).

> CATHERINE: Constructivism is not something I knew very much about. But as I learned about it, I discovered it was compatible with my educational beliefs and practices, and offered me an effective overarching concept for thinking about teaching adults. Even so, I wouldn't necessarily label myself *constructivist,* because my educational palette is broader than that. I have the advantage of working in a complex educational environment that calls on many other orientations to learning, as well.

Constructive-Developmental Theory

Constructive-developmental theories specifically link developmental growth in adults to their construction of meaning. Such theories posit that meaning is not absorbed or acquired from external sources; rather, that people create or construct meaning and that particular changes in one's constructions are identified with developmental growth. Furthermore, these changes in how we make (construct) meaning affect every aspect of our being: how we understand ourselves (our community, our society), respond to others (intimately, personally, professionally), make decisions (day-to-day, workplace, career, life), and how we learn and know (in formal and informal settings) (Belenky, Clinchy, Goldberger, & Tarule, 1986; Loevinger & Blasi, 1976; Perry, 1970; Kegan, 1982, 1994).

Much as a scientist does (Kelly, 1955), people respond to events in their environment, make assessments based on previous experiences and understandings, and change their ideas and actions to conform with the new discoveries. According to these theories, the ways in which people view events (their filters, or *lenses of perception)* change qualitatively in predictable ways throughout the life cycle. An early adolescent cannot hold two perspectives simultaneously if one of them is in contradiction to his own desires. For example, as Kegan (1994) notes, "I promised I would be home by midnight," will lose out to, "This is a great party and I don't want to leave." By contrast, a young adult, who has since internalized the significance of commitments made to others, may nonetheless be able to flip back and forth between contradictory perspectives without recognizing their inherent inconsistency; for example, "Killing is wrong; murderers should get the death penalty." A more mature adult who is capable of greater cognitive complexity cannot only see the merit of more than one perspective, but can also thoughtfully reconsider her commitment to the perspective she currently holds. For example, "I struggle with the conflict between free speech and what some deem pornography."

This journey of psychological or ego development is marked by paradigm shifts in people's meaning-constructive (epistemic) systems. Though some constructive-developmentalists, including Loevinger and Blasi (1976), Kohlberg (1981), and Piaget (1954), begin with childhood, we will limit ourselves to exploring the major changes in *adults'* ways of constructing meaning.

We will focus here on two transformations. The first is the move *into* psychological "adulthood," which seems to occur for most people around the end of adolescence. The second is probably associated in the popular consciousness with "mid-life change"—that is, a time of questioning established beliefs—however, there are no fixed age parameters.

Two Developmental Transformations Of Adulthood

Somewhere near the end of adolescence (and not a moment too soon for the young person's parents), the self-centeredness of childhood, in which others are valued extrinsically, for what they provide, tends to give way to mutuality, in which others are valued intrinsically, for who they are. At the same time, the young person begins to accept the rules of adulthood that, as he probably sees it, his parents and others (teachers, religious leaders, other respected authorities in the community) have been haranguing him with *forever*. Though different cultures may have different rules, the *essence* of the demand seems universal: To join the ranks of "adults," one must embrace (actually, *internalize*) adult values and attitudes (Kegan, 1982, 1994).

Along with this major shift comes the discovery that life is more complex than it seemed. Things can no longer be viewed in terms of simple dualities, such as *right-wrong, we-they, black-white,* and so on. Instead, the young adult finds himself or herself having to contend with various perspectives, many of which seem reasonable, even if in conflict with others equally reasonable (Perry, 1970). Though they may once have been content to hold opinions formed by listening to others, they now find they increasingly draw on their own store of experiences to make decisions (Belenky, Clinchy, Goldberger, & Tarule, 1986). Of course, not everyone who assumes adult roles and responsibilities has necessarily internalized associated values and ways of understanding. People who are chronologically mature, may not be developmentally mature (Kegan, 1986).

If they do, however, the potential exists for the second adult transition, which, if it occurs at all, is more likely to begin after people have experienced some stability in significant life roles. Most adults in workplace training programs and higher education settings are probably at the threshold of, or are already working through, this second transformation. Whereas the adolescent's task was to *internalize* what Jarvis (1987a) calls the socio-cultural-temporal surround, the adult's task is to bring to conscious awareness and to *question* what was earlier internalized.

For example, adults engaged in this change may find themselves asking not merely, "Am I in a job I really enjoy?" but also, "Does the kind of work I do reflect my values?" This may lead to, "What *are* my values?" and, "Are they really *mine*, or are they values I accepted unquestioningly from others before I was capable of formulating my own?" Other evolving questions might include, "How do I decide among the many points of view that I have come to recognize as worthy of consideration? Is 'everyone entitled to his or her own opinion,' or must I examine and evaluate ideas against some reasonable criteria, and then either accept, modify, or reject them? But how do I establish those criteria? And what do I do if the decisions I make turn out later to have been wrong?" (Perry, 1970). As Vaill (1996) points out, this ability to both recognize one's own perspectives and be willing to thoughtfully revise them is particularly relevant to the modern workplace, where change is not merely endemic—it is systemic.

People who earlier learned to trust their "gut instincts" may find their inner truth increasingly inadequate (Belenky, Clinchy, Goldberger, and Tarule, 1986). They may ask, "How can I integrate what authorities or my employer tells me with what I believe to be true? What is 'truth' anyway, and who decides?" Answers to such questions can be the "slippery slope" to the realization that one is responsible for one's own values, beliefs, and behaviors (Kegan, 1994).

We three are drawn to models that describe development in terms of changes in how people think and know (epistemic forms), because they offer educators a comprehensive way to think about teaching and learning. Constructive-developmental theories provide powerful analytic tools toward improving practice and developing strategies that encourage developmental growth in adult learners. (More detailed descriptions of these theories can be found in Appendix B.)

Developmental Dimensions Of Adult Learning Theories

The development theories just described explore the adult's process of change and growth from a psychological perspective; several learning theories also offer perspectives that illuminate adult development, notably those articulated by Kolb (1984), Mezirow (1991, 2000), and Freire (1992). These theories share certain premises about learning: that it is a process of *resolving contradictions in dialectical fashion,* in this way raising awareness of new possibilities and *multiple perspectives;* that it is also a process of moving toward more *complex ways of viewing* oneself and one's situation, potentially leading people to take a more *active responsibility* for the world in which they live; that *discourse is crucial* to the alteration of perspectives that is learning; and that such *transformed perspectives are developmental* in the lives of adults.

Rather than focus on psychological growth per se, these theorists focus on a variety of changes that may result when learning is viewed as having the potential to transform. Freire (1992), a Brazilian educator who worked in a context of illiteracy, poverty, and political repression, emphasized the relationship between liberation and education based on "critical and liberating dialogue [and] . . . reflective participation" (p. 52). Through *praxis* (reflection and action) people were empowered to overcome their oppression and work toward social change.

What Freire called *conscientization,* the emergence of consciousness, echoes the second epistemic shift described above. The person is no longer limited to beliefs "deposited" in her mental "account" by others, but can challenge and reconstruct these beliefs. The educator's role, therefore, is not to act as a *banker*, but as a *midwife*, facilitating at the birth of the learner's own ideas and understandings. Freire also claimed that education is never neutral—it either supports the dominant ideology or challenges it.

Freire's emphasis on the transformative potential of learning is echoed by Mezirow's (1996) focus on *emancipatory learning*, which frees individuals from limiting beliefs so that they may arrive at "an informed and reflective decision to act" (p. 164). Mezirow and Freire also agree that such learning is dependent on discourse, a form of dialogue that strives to recognize and set aside bias and looks toward consensus based on open and objective examination of assertions. When uncritically assimilated beliefs and assumptions (Mezirow: *meaning schemes*) are challenged in an atmosphere of rational discourse, people may become aware of distortions in the ways they view themselves and others. Both Freire and Mezirow emphasize moving beyond new meanings or consciousness to action, either internally or socially directed. Learning experienced this way engenders changes and growth not only in the intellectual realm, but also in feelings, behaviors, and perceptions.

Kolb (1984) also focuses on learning as a continuous, holistic, and adaptive *process*. He specifies four dimensions that mediate this adaptive process: affective, perceptual, symbolic, and behavioral. Through learning, people grow to have a greater range of emotions, increased awareness and capacity to "see," more sophisticated conceptualization schemes, and a more expanded repertoire of behaviors. However, people do not necessarily develop in all four dimensions at the same rate. For example, one can be emotionally mature yet not intellectually developed; the reverse is also true. Generally, though, development in one contributes to development of the others.

Learning from experience can help individuals understand that they construct knowledge. As a result, they are able to respond with increasing awareness to the complexities of adult lives, such as conflicts between their values and their current life choices. Kolb further echoes constructive-development theory in his claim that being able to hold complexities and resolve and integrate the dialectical in how one thinks, feels, sees, and acts is a mark of development. From the perspective of an educator working with developmental intentions, this implies maintaining a focus not only on learners' conceptions, but also on their feelings, perceptions, and actions.

Kolb's model is most widely known for his description of learning that includes experience, reflection, abstraction, and experimentation (Figure 2.1). With this multifaceted model, an educator can more effectively support learners in adopting deep approaches to learning. Embedded in the model is the premise that "knowledge results from the combination of grasping experience and transforming it"

Figure 2.1. Kolb's Learning Cycle.

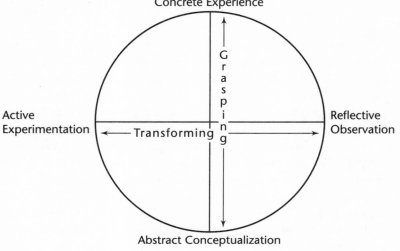

Source: Kolb, 1984.

(Kolb, 1984, p. 41). *Grasping* (the vertical axis) is the process of taking in information through either one's sensory or conceptual faculties. One also *transforms* (the horizontal axis) what has been taken in, through either reflection or action. In this way, the model integrates all four quadrants, or modes—experience, reflection, abstraction, and experimentation. Though learning often begins with the learner's current or prior experience, individuals may enter the learning cycle through any mode, depending upon their preferences and the particular learning situation.

The model helps educators recognize that learners vary in how they respond to each mode of the cycle, and in how they grasp and transform their experiences and observations. Attending to all four modes thus enhances learning and accommodates individual differences in approaches to learning, that is, *learning styles.*

In addition, adults often find the model useful in applications outside the learning environment. A policeman in his thirties noticed changes in his report writing.

In my most recent report about traffic conditions on a local street, I not only presented the facts about the collisions and enforcement activities, but I reflected on the previous attempts to solve the problem as well as the effects of those attempts. Having the ability now to generalize about the situation and the trends in traffic safety, I was able to identify new ideas and solutions to try and use to increase the level of traffic safety on this street. This process also allowed me to predict possible results, thus creating a sort of method of evaluation for further analysis in the future. In past movies depicting police officers you may have heard the officer saying, "Just the facts, nothing but the facts, that's all I need." This summarizes my writing style over the last ten years. I have been writing just the facts. This [model] is the reason I have changed.

Experience, Reflection, and Meaning-Making

Emancipatory and experiential learning models overlap with constructive-developmental theories in many particulars. Both the learning models and the psychological models are concerned with how adults know and understand. Both emphasize the importance of exploring one's current and past experiences through a critically reflective lens with the intention of reframing one's self-understanding while transforming one's ways of knowing. We therefore explore more closely these three essential aspects of adult learning theory: experience, reflection, and meaning-making.

Concerning Experience

"Experiences don't happen to us, events happen to us" (Brookfield, 1998, p. 129). An *event* is something that comes to us though the senses, all at once. It can come from within or without. An *experience,* however, is something one does, thinks, or feels. For an event to *become* an experience requires both *attending* (spending time "being present with" an event that just happened or recalling an event that happened in the past) and *affirming* (accepting and valuing the event, even if one's initial response is to dismiss or disregard it) (Kolb, 1984).

It is important for educators to understand how this process plays out in the learning environment. People do not notice everything that is available to their senses, as listening to a tape recording of an earlier conversation easily demonstrates. There are physical filters (one can process only so much input) and psychosocial filters (one interprets through existing assumptions and beliefs). People also vary widely in their comfort with and capacity for attending. It is common for adults to move swiftly to judgment based on unexamined criteria such as not wishing to dwell on what seems already familiar or, conversely, too foreign. Such premature judgment may also stem from the desire to feel in control and knowledgeable. Many people would rather assume they know something than explore the possibility that they do not know. Therefore, if the meaning of an experience is not immediately evident, there is an inclination to give up and move quickly on to something else.

> MORRY: If we want, as teachers, to draw on experience as a source and contributor to learning, we would do well to patiently help learners explore and describe it before moving, with intention, through the process of learning that makes it more complex and converts it to knowledge. Appreciating the nature of experience has nuances that are significant for understanding ourselves and for teaching that may stimulate a deep approach to learning.

Focusing on *appreciating* an event—taking time and taking it in—can counter this tendency. What would otherwise be an idiosyncratic event becomes an experience that can be articulated, connected to earlier experiences, and subjected to critical examination. In this way, appreciation helps realize potential for learning, whereas rushing past or sidestepping appreciation can close off this possibility.

A woman in her late thirties underscored the challenge of closely attending to and making meaning of experience.

Because I was in the habit of taking bits of information from other sources and building a [paper], I had a difficult time approaching a subject primarily from my point of view. . . . It took many attempts to unlayer my own feelings about a subject. . . . When I began writing the [assignments], they seemed rather useless in terms of learning, but I was wrong. . . . I thought, felt, and analyzed events that have happened in my life in a way I had not experienced before.

Marton and Booth (1997) describe this experience from a phenomenographic perspective: "In order to make sense of how people *handle* problems, situations, the world, we have to understand the way in which they *experience* the problems, the situations, the world. . . . You cannot act other than in relation to the world as you experience it" (original emphasis, p. 111).

Concerning Reflection

As John Dewey (1938/1963) observed, all genuine education comes through experience, but not all experience educates. "In addition to noticing or attending to an experience, we must also reflect upon it" (Merriam, 1994, p. 83). One characteristic of a deep approach to learning is *thinking about how and what* one is learning. This includes watching one's own process as a learner, questioning one's assumptions (old and new), checking out the new "knowledge" as it is being created, and seeing oneself, one's past choices, one's future possibilities, as central to what is being learned (Marton, Dall'Alba, & Beaty, 1993). In other words, for experience to lead to shifts of perception associated with meaningful learning and development, it is necessary also to include reflection and critical reflection. For Vaill (1996), the capacity to reflect on oneself *as a learner* is essential to "learning as a way of being," which is, in turn, essential to developing as a managerial leader.

In many instances, however, people do *not* reflect on experience. Many adults, says Brookfield (1998), "live a unitary existence in which the same emotions and perceptions occur in a self-confirming loop" (p. 127). Jarvis (1992) refers to this response to experience as "nonlearning" (p. 72). When something happens to challenge these emotions or perceptions, it is dismissed as irrelevant or rationalized to justify existing beliefs.

The woman quoted just above continued by examining her process of reflection:

I came to an understanding about occurrences in my life that I had not recognized before. When time has passed and we become removed from situations that have taken place in life, we often don't look back to explore these events. [These assignments] require you to do so. I found profound meaning and understanding in the occurrences that have taken place in my life.

Experience without reflection will engender only limited kinds of learning, which Jarvis (1992) calls "nonreflective learning" (p. 74). The outcome is mechanical rather than meaningful; for example, a change in practice or skills without a concomitant change in understanding. Such nonreflective learning is generally based on acquiring (perhaps memorizing) information or some process or sequence. Learners may change their performance without changing the way they *think about* the topic and their behaviors. For example, some people "learn" what to do on the computer by getting specific instructions for the sequence of mouse-clicks necessary to perform certain functions. Without reflection—such as looking for similar command patterns or thinking about the purpose of pull-down menus—their *understanding* of computer command sequences is unchanged. They need similar instruction for each new task, even though their ability to function has been enhanced.

Reflection can be defined as thinking and feeling activities "in which individuals engage to explore their experiences in order to lead to new understandings and appreciations" (Boud, Keogh, & Walker, 1985, p. 19). These changes can include a new way of looking at the experience, a new or altered behavior, or a commitment to action. Most models of reflection emphasize action, which can include the decision not to act, as the end product of the reflective process. Dewey (1944) underscored this: "No experience having a meaning is possible without some element of thought. . . . In discovery of the detailed connections of our activities and what happens in consequence, the thought implied in [trial and error] experience is made explicit. . . .[T]he quality of the experience changes; the change is so significant that we may call this type of experience reflective. . . . [Reflection accepts] responsibility for the future consequences which flow from present action" (p. 145).

Various models describe the process of reflection in terms of assorted elements: *What about this experience is uncomfortable or perplexing to me? What do I name the concern to clarify it? What new information am I taking in? What am I not considering? How might I look at this from a different perspective? In what ways am I trying on new ways of thinking, feeling, or behaving? How might I integrate these new ways of thinking or being into my life?* (Boud, Keogh, & Walker, 1996; Merriam & Caffarella, 1999). Awareness of these elements may enable an educator to draw on strategies that help learners engage in such reflections. The point of departure for reflection, as it is typically discussed in the literature, may be a specific event or problem. Or it might be simply something that is going on around or within an individual. Whatever the trigger for reflection, it will evoke certain thoughts, feelings, and behaviors that become the objects of one's reflection.

Critical reflection takes reflection to a higher level. When one thinks critically, one asks, "*Why* do I think this way?" Rather than thinking only *descriptively* about experience, the learner "goes *meta*" and thinks consciously and awarely about her *process of thinking*, learning, and understanding. This reflection includes conscious attention to values, assumptions, and beliefs that might affect one's current interpretations. And the process loops back onto itself as one's current understanding may be, in turn, the result of paying attention to one's thoughts, feelings, and behaviors. Such self-assessment is an important element in critical reflection (Marienau, 1999). When self-assessment involves making authentic, objective judgments about oneself, one may "gain a greater appreciation of the influences on [one's learning] and on the nature of [the] particular experience" (Boud, 1995, p. 19). A graduating adult student summarized her experience:

Before this program I never reflected—I just acted. The first exercise—of really examining what I had actually learned from previous college courses—made me aware that I have more knowledge about a variety of things than I ever thought I did. . . . Then I tried reflecting on my learning as it was happening and I become aware for the first time of some of my blind spots—you know, where I wasn't being at all objective about myself or open to someone else's ideas. This has been a huge awakening for me. Because of learning about reflection, and learning to do it, I am now willing to listen to another person's perspective and weigh it; I'm asking others for feedback about myself, especially at work, and I can do more generalizing—I'm not so concrete about everything. I just never thought I would have this kind of flexibility.

The complex process of critical reflection is iterative, as the individual progressively realizes the layers and connections among the influences on her thinking and actions. For example, if the computer user, above, was asked to reflect on why she was not more engaged with learning, she might realize that an early unsuccessful experience with less than user-friendly software had led her to assume, "I can't possibly learn this stuff." If further critical reflection was encouraged, she might realize that earlier experience was also influenced by social expectations about women and technology. This, in turn, could lead to her conscious assertion (not only in terms of computer commands) that she could choose not to be limited in these ways.

According to Brookfield (1998), this kind of critical reflection enables adults to critique the "sets of values, beliefs, myths, explanations, and justifications that appear self-evidently true and morally desirable" (p. 131). Discovering that these dominant ideologies are open to question may lead in turn to the disequilibrium that can serve as a stimulus to development; "development can be seen . . . as the natural outcome of attempts to make stable sense of a changing world" (Hayes & Oppenheim, 1997, p. 24).

Concerning Meaning-Making

"To make meaning means to make sense of an experience" (Mezirow, 1990, p. 1); in the process of reflecting critically on experience, people are engaged in making meaning. People constantly make meaning, in large and small ways, each time they·test a conclusion, make a judgment, "put two and two together," examine a feeling, explore a perspective, assign significance to an idea, and notice the importance of what had seemed inconsequential. These interpretations are influenced by "personal beliefs and values as well as norms and expectations derived from the sociocultural context" (Cranton, 1996, p. 85). An aspect of the meaning-making process is becoming aware of why people attach the meaning they do to their experiences.

CATHERINE: Typically, I ask learners first to recall and recount an experience, prompted by question(s) I pose connected to a concept we'll be considering. It's interesting how hearing about someone else's experience can jog a learner's memory, so that she might revise or embellish her own story. Then we add into the mix the relevant theories or concepts, which prompt learners to reexamine their experiences from new perspectives— some will help illuminate an individual's interpretation of her experience, while others will be at odds and stimulate questions about the "fit." Going

> through this process helps learners examine their experiences more fully, interpret them more meaningfully, and recognize that their script is pretty much always open to revision.

Meaning is not an intellectual endeavor alone; it is also emotional and even, in some sense, physical (Marton & Booth, 1997). Indeed, one knows something is meaningful when idea and emotion intertwine. "An event that is of no significance gives rise to no emotion. Feelings and emotions provide the best guides we have to where we need to devote our attention" (Boud & Miller, 1996, p. 17). In his description of the kind of learning that enables one to successfully navigate the permanent white water of the modern workplace, Vaill (1996) also claims that learning

> occurs as much at the level of one's feelings as it does at the level of ideas and skills. It has to be learning about meanings—how meanings are formed, how they are challenged or lost, how they can be sustained and revitalized. To know the *meaning* of something is not just to have impersonal ideas about it, but to know it deeply and personally [original emphasis, p. 46].

Creating meaning in these ways can lead to "a powerful and poignant sense *of pain*" when one's sense of self is challenged (Tarule, 1980, p. 26), or it can lead to the relief of an "aha" that comes from making sense of what previously seemed puzzling.

Because of the intricate connection between reflecting critically and making meaning, it is essential that we not overemphasize the finished product. As educators, we need to pay at least as much attention to how that meaning was constructed as to the outcome; that is, to the *process* whereby established values, ideas, and beliefs combine with critical reflection and new or prior experience. Furthermore, we must remember that the meaning currently being made is affected by all the meanings already made; meaning is never permanently fixed. As Mentkowski and Associates (2000) explain, "development extends immediate experience into broader purposes, meanings, and commitments. . . . . The distant future and past can seem immanent in the lived moment, making such moments pregnant with meaning" (p. 188).

Ultimately, learning to examine how one makes meaning and to accept responsibility for the meaning one constructs is the mainspring of adult development. "Meaning is, in its origins, a physical activity (grasping, seeing), a social activity (it requires another), a survival activity (in doing it, we live). Meaning understood in this way, is the primary human motion, irreducible" (Kegan, 1982, p. 18–19).

CHAPTER THREE

TEACHING WITH DEVELOPMENTAL INTENTIONS

The expansion of the self as a meaning-making system should be the proper aim of education.

—HAYES AND OPPENHEIM (1997)

Many educators, in many disciplines and learning settings, are incorporating some aspects of development into their repertoire—some by instinct, others by design. The theories offer us, as practitioners, framework and language to affirm and further guide our practice. In our own practice, we had been intuitively drawing on these connections even before we began fully exploring the theoretical underpinnings. However, many colleagues who also seemed to support the kinds of changes in adult learners that we defined as developmental appeared to do so tacitly while explicitly focusing on their field, discipline, or subject-matter. How then, we wondered, did experienced adult educators frame developmental objectives, and how did those objectives guide their practice?

To answer these questions, we sought out adult educators, some of whom have international reputations, as well as less renowned colleagues whose work we knew to be developmentally focused. These included educators in the U.S., Australia, and the United Kingdom. We asked: *What do you want your adult learners to walk away with, developmentally speaking, at the end of your time together?* We intentionally did not define *developmentally speaking.*

The responses ranged from three sentences to three pages. We analyzed these for common themes and found more than sixty. Over time, we clarified, combined, and ended up with thirty-six characteristics that we sorted into five overarching dimensions (see Exhibit 3.1). We sent this analysis back to the contributors, asking them to describe the strategies and activities they used to achieve these

Exhibit 3.1. Developmental Intentions Chart.

DEVELOPMENT IS MARKED BY MOVEMENT ALONG FIVE DIMENSIONS

I.   TOWARD KNOWING AS A DIALOGICAL PROCESS

1. Inquiring into and responding openly to others' ideas

2. Surfacing and questioning assumptions underlying beliefs, ideas, actions, and positions

3. Reframing ideas or values that seem contradictory, embracing their differences, and arriving at new meanings

4. Using one's experience to critique expert opinion and expert opinion to critique one's experience

5. Moving between separate and connected, independent and interdependent ways of knowing

6. Paying attention to wholes as well as the parts that comprise them

7. Associating truth not with static fact but with contexts and relationships

8. Pursuing the possibility of objective truth

9. Perceiving and constructing one's reality by observing and participating

10. Tapping into and drawing on tacit knowledge

II. TOWARD A DIALOGICAL RELATIONSHIP TO ONESELF

1. Addressing fears of losing what is familiar and safe

2. Engaging the disequilibrium when one's ideas and beliefs are challenged

3. Exploring life's experiences through some framework(s) of analysis

4. Questioning critically the validity or worth of one's pursuits

5. Exploring and making meaning of one's life stories within contexts (for example, societal, familial, universal)

III. TOWARD BEING A CONTINUOUS LEARNER

1. Reflecting on one's own and others' experiences as a guide to future behavior

2. Challenging oneself to learn in new realms; taking risks

3. Recognizing and revealing one's strengths and weaknesses as a learner and knower

4. Anticipating learning needed to prevent and solve problems

5. Posing and pursuing questions out of wonderment

6. Accepting internal dissonance as part of the learning process

7. Setting one's own learning goals, being goal-directed, and being habitual in learning

8. Seeking authentic feedback from others

9. Drawing on multiple capacities for effective learning

IV. TOWARD SELF-AGENCY AND SELF-AUTHORSHIP

1. Constructing a values system that informs one's behavior
2. Accepting responsibility for choices one has made and will make
3. Risking action on behalf of one's beliefs and commitments
4. Taking action toward one's potential while acknowledging one's limitations
5. Revising aspects of oneself while maintaining continuity of other aspects
6. Distinguishing what one has created for oneself from what is imposed by social, cultural, and other forces
7. "Naming and claiming" what one has experienced and knows

V. TOWARD CONNECTION WITH OTHERS

1. Mediating boundaries between one's connection to others and one's individuality
2. Experiencing oneself as part of something larger
3. Engaging the affective dimension when confronting differences
4. Contributing one's voice to a collective endeavor
5. Recognizing that collective awareness and thinking transform the sum of their parts

---

ends. From their responses we discovered that they did not see these characteristics as developmental *outcomes;* no one can "develop" anyone else. Several of our informants told us they were simply using methods that they had found worked well in helping learners gain certain capacities and skills.

We therefore began to refer to these characteristics as developmental *intentions.* However, we also saw that they could be used as *indicators,* by which we meant that a learner who became more proficient in demonstrating at least some of these characteristics had probably experienced growth.

Development as a Dynamic Process

In sorting the characteristics or intentions into categories, we were reminded of the essentially dynamic nature of development. Whereas most theories describe development in terms of movement along a continuum of growth, any individual's process defies linear organization. We found that the thirty-six discrete items interacted across the five dimensions. As a result, assigning characteristics to a particular dimension became, at times, a somewhat arbitrary exercise: some overlapped, some were sequential, and some seemed to enhance the potential for others to emerge.

To underscore the sense of movement, we chose to express the characteristics as *actions* (for example, reflec*ting*) rather than as *conditions* (for example, reflec*tion*). As people engage in these actions, they also develop the capacity to recognize the interplay of differentiation and integration in their own lives. They see themselves as made up of parts and yet a coherent whole, always in process, never arriving. Taken together, the five dimensions represent aspects of a self that is capable of sophisticated, ongoing engagement with the world of ideas and with learning from experience—a self that can examine its own biases and assumptions, make and carry out thoughtful commitments, and reach out to others for mutual enhancement. In short, a self that responds effectively and with increasing ease to internal and external changes.

In the following sections we examine the five overarching categories more closely as a springboard to the exercises and activities presented in Part Two that are designed around the developmental intentions.

Toward Knowing as a Dialogical Process

In dialogue, two or more people exchange ideas and beliefs. That exchange exposes them to ideas and ways of thinking different from their own, with the result that "individuals gain insights that simply could not be achieved individually" (Senge, 1990, p. 241). If their intention is to reach mutual understanding, which does not necessarily mean agreement, they examine the basis for the differences in order to surface and explore potentially distorting assumptions. Dialogue therefore becomes an essential feature of their making meaning and constructing knowledge.

Habermas's (1984, 1987) description of emancipatory knowledge provides a further rationale for relating dialogue and understanding. Unless people examine their own and others' ways of making meaning and reaching consensus, they can be at the mercy of distorted perspectives that block communication.

Mezirow (1985), who acknowledges Habermas's influence, is another proponent of "participat[ing] fully and freely" in dialogical learning to "test our interests and perspectives against those of others and accordingly modify them" (p. 27). It is only in dialogue that people can realize the extent to which assumptions affect what is known and how it is known. Such dialogue is not to be confused with aimless discussion in which participants take turns saying what they think they already know. Rather, learners *inquire into and respond openly to others' ideas,* at the same time thinking about and being willing to *surface and question assumptions underlying* their own and others' statements.

Similarly, learning from a text involves a dialogical approach when learners attempt to explore the meaning the author is trying to convey. In his study of approaches to learning, Säljö (1982) describes this communicative interaction in terms of a particular kind of "dialogue" (his term, p. 86), the contextual nature of which requires *paying attention to wholes as well as the parts that comprise them.* As Hounsell (1984) observed, "In a surface approach, what was to be learned was interpreted as the text itself. In a deep approach, the text was seen as the means through which to grapple with the meaning which underlay it" (p. 197). In effect, those who adopt a deep approach to learning engage in dialogue with the text and others by *using experience to critique expert opinion and expert opinion to critique experience.*

Brookfield (1985) also describes adult education as a "transactional dialogue between participants who bring to the encounter experiences, attitudinal sets, differing ways of looking at their personal, professional, political, and recreational worlds and a multitude of varying purposes, orientations, and expectations" (p. 41). The adult who engages in knowing as a dialogical process *associates truth not with static fact but with contexts and relationships* and is willing to take responsibility for *perceiving and constructing reality by observing and participating.* Meaning constructed in this way "is grounded in the capacity of people to communicate or to question the validity of each other's arguments" (Wildemeersch, 1989, p. 66).

Learners generally favor such dialogue and often see as positive the potential for changing their perspectives. As a man of forty observed:

The one-on-one discussions between students is a very good tool in learning. I do enjoy the four to five [person] group better. The reason I guess is there is more input. I came to the realization that I started listening to my "voice" around thirty. Same as another gentleman in the group. Other students had similar experiences. It is reassuring to know you were not the only one to have experienced something-or-other in your life. The topics in class are not topics I would normally discuss with someone else. This is the perfect place to discover and learn.

When learning focuses on mastery of factual material, however, there is no need to engage in a dialogical process. It is sufficient to read or listen, take notes, and store ideas and information. In a learning environment that depends primarily on educator-presented material (and meaning); a learner's question or comment is merely a temporary break in the flow of supplied information. This kind of education supports superficial approaches to learning, wherein learning is perceived as knowledge that can be transferred and memorized. As one man described it:

When I began this class, I saw myself as a good student. . . . I knew the ins and outs of the standard learning process. You know—read and repeat what you read.

By contrast, when we seek to foster deep approaches, where learning is perceived as constructed and context-dependent, dialogue is essential. Knowing as a dialogical process involves give and take among all the participants in pursuit of knowledge and its creation. Whether or not one agrees with the particulars of the following observation, this woman's description of her experience clearly captures the sense of discovery that can attend the dialogical process.

I would like to think that I have become more open-minded. . . . I am able to see things from other people's perspectives. I remember a discussion on whether or not large companies who offered their employees special benefits, like banks and post offices on [site], were taking time away from families. To me it seemed obvious that they were helping families because employees were able to get that kind of stuff done at work. . . . As the discussion wore on, I started to realize that maybe some of the other people in the class had valid points that differed from mine. *They believed that companies were offering these types of benefits so that the employee would spend more time at work and consequently less time at home* [emphasis added].

Her sense of discovery through dialogue illuminates Lindeman's observation that the adult's "education is a living intellectual interchange of the substance of thought" (Brookfield, 1987, p. 28).

The task of moving toward knowing as a dialogical process might be expressed in this way:

I want to become more aware of how I construct knowledge, to recognize the sources of the ideas I currently hold, and to engage with others in order to more effectively reconstruct knowledge as new experiences and reflection warrant.

Toward a Dialogical Relationship to Oneself

A mark of development is the capacity to see *oneself*, particularly one's beliefs and ideas, from multiple perspectives. Unfortunately, not only do existing biases and ways of thinking limit one's thinking, but these limitations are generally invisible. A dialogical relationship to the self can be a powerful tool in uncovering such limitations, as it encourages speaking to the self in much the same way as people dialogue with one another. Rather than seeing one's experiences exclusively from the "inside out," one is able to see them also from the "outside in." This ability is foundational to *exploring life's experiences through some framework of analysis,* and *exploring and making meaning of our life stories within contexts.* The capacity to hold multiple perspectives, to see beyond the "reality" that many may agree is "the way we do things around here," to propose and examine new possibilities, and to respond creatively as the work environment changes is increasingly important to survival, let alone success, in the modern world of work (Bridges, 1988, 1994; Vaill, 1996; Senge, 1990). As one of the research subjects of *Women's Ways of Knowing* (Belenky, Clinchy, Goldberger, & Tarule, 1986) explained: "I think it's important to see why I think the way I do. Some people seem to think that their ideas belong to them, but a lot of things people believe have a long tradition of belief. It helps you to understand your beliefs if you understand where they come from. And it helps you . . . examine them and say, "Well, do I really agree with this?" (p. 137).

The person not yet capable of a dialogical relationship to the self is likely to see herself as the totality of her experiences ("the way I am") rather than as someone capable of making choices about how to be. The following learner, a woman in her late thirties, poignantly describes having felt that way:

[For a long time] I was terribly afraid to look into the self as a person . . . because every time I had tried to express myself about what I wanted to do or what I wanted to be, I had always kind of been told that it doesn't matter: "You'll do or be whatever happens." I didn't know that I could change it and make things happen the way I wanted them to. Not just let it keep happening to me. I could kind of be playing a tennis game instead of on the sidelines just watching the ball across the net. I didn't know you could do that.

In what may seem paradoxical fashion, the capacity to take a perspective on one's ideas and behaviors, as though standing outside oneself, increases the likelihood of "placing standards within ourselves, recognizing that the goodness or badness of any experience or perceptual object is not something inherent in that object, but is a value placed on it by ourselves" (Kegan, 1994, p. 303). Because they accept this premise, such learners can more effectively *engage the disequilibrium* when their ideas and beliefs are challenged by others or themselves. As Daloz (1986) has observed, "Development is closely related to the enrichment of *inner dialogue*" (p. 124, emphasis added).

As one of this book's authors (Marienau, 1999) has written elsewhere, self-assessment is a powerful tool in support of dialogue with the self, as it helps learners "exercise keener attention to and reflection on their experience. . . . They . . . [are] *less likely to ignore the familiar or avoid the unfamiliar,* and more likely to expand their repertoire of experiences for critical reflection. Outcomes of their reflective process have included greater awareness and understanding of the self, new perspectives on their experience, changes in behavior, and deeper commitments to action, all of which are elements of learning from experience" (p. 143).

The etymology of self-assessment ("sitting beside the self") and learners' own descriptions of how they experience it emphasize its dialogical quality, as revealed by this woman in her mid-thirties (Taylor, 1995a):

I have learned how to watch what I think, what happens when I think different ways, and how to be more flexible in the thinking process. I now have more choices about what and how to think. I have begun to find a voice. An interesting thing along the way is that, once I was able to voice my thoughts, what I thought about something often changed and moved to a higher level (p. 23).

In addition, those who can engage in dialogue with the self are more likely to "perceive our standards as based on our own experiences (rather than upon the attitudes or desires of others)" and to "challenge and question our own basic values, our own thinking, so that we really think for ourselves" (Kegan, 1994, p. 303). *An Unknown Woman: A Journal of Self-Discovery* is Alice Koller's (1981) extended dialogue with her self in search of just this capability—to see herself through her own eyes, rather than "the endlessness of reflecting myself in other people's eyes. Turn a pair of eyes on me and instantly I begin looking into them for myself. I seem to believe there is no Me except in others' eyes. I am what I see in your eyes, whoever you are" (p. 113). Though he does not frame it in precisely those terms, William Bridges, a renowned corporate consultant, speaker, and author of several books on personal and organizational change, also calls for a dialogical relationship to the self, particularly when trying to survive the inevitable transitions of a world undergoing major economic transformation. He proposes a series of questions designed to encourage his readers to redefine their identities as workers; he adds, "only by making these mental shifts and *beginning to study yourself and your organization with new eyes* can you make change work to your advantage" (1988, p. 181, our emphasis).

The task of moving toward a dialogical relationship to the self might be expressed in this way:

I want to be able to recognize myself; to see who and how I am not only through the prism of my experience, but through reflection on that experience; to take responsibility for how I may choose to be in future. The self I discover is not the essence of who I am, it is my construction, and as such, subject to reconstruing.

Toward Being a Continuous Learner

As Dewey (1938/1963) noted, for experience to lead to learning, education must be viewed as "a continuous process of reconstruction of experience" (p. 87). A continuous learner recognizes the potential for learning amid the problems, changes, and flow of life's events. Vaill (1996) is even more specific: because *permanent white water* creates "an environment of continual newness . . . continual learning is a requirement of the modern [organizational] environment" (p. xiv); men and women who cannot continuously learn in ways that promote

imaginative flexibility, growth, and change are unlikely to be effective managerial leaders. Such learning requires approaching new situations willing to *pose
and pursue questions out of wonderment.* This is a habit of mind more than any con-
stellation of particular skills and includes *challenging oneself to learn in new realms;
taking risks* while also *accepting internal dissonance as part of the learning process,* as when
"world views confront and collide with one another" (Hounsell, 1984, p. 193)
because "continual learning entails the difficult psychological achievement of
open-mindedness" (Vaill, 1996, p. 80).

To become continuous learners requires that adults do not conceive of their
responsibility as "the acquisition of discrete packages of information" (Entwistle,
1984, p. 10), but as "finding [the internal] structure [of the material] in as deep a
sense as possible" (Dahlgren, 1984, p. 44). Rather than reacting, continuous learners *anticipate the learning needed to prevent and solve problems* (Botkin, Elmandjra, & Malitz,
1979). They seek out formal and informal learning environments to provide information, instruction in skills, and *authentic feedback from others.*

Though some continuous learning may be characterized as *self-direction* (see
Candy [1991] for extensive exploration of associated meanings, practices, and
controversies), this does not imply that the learner no longer constructs meaning
as a social, dialogical process. Rather, continuous learners will "take initiative; set
our own goals and standards; use experts, institutions, and other resources to pursue these goals; take responsibility for our direction and productivity in learning . . .
read actively (rather than only receptively) with our own purpose in mind . . . [and]
write to ourselves and bring our teachers into our self-reflection (rather than write
mainly to our teachers and for our teachers)" (Kegan, 1994, p. 303). Vaill (1996)
strongly echoes this when he asks, "Are we 'writing the book' as much as we are
reading someone else's book?" and contrasts *creative, active,* and *expressive* learning
with passive absorption (p. 88).

The task of moving toward being a continuous learner might be expressed in
this way:

*I want to focus on learning as what I do when I am interested in ideas or activities. Though I
may call on others for advice, input, expertise, or directions, I will decide my learning goals, seek
appropriate resources, and actively engage with the process. I also recognize that learning is likely
to lead to new ways of constructing myself, and I accept that challenge.*

Toward Self-Agency and Self-Authorship

As noted above, adults who have internalized the demands made of them by the
socio-cultural-temporal surround remain captive of those demands until they are
surfaced and challenged. Values, morals, and ethics are based on group, family,

and cultural imperatives; these norms and assumptions are invisible and therefore cannot be questioned. A woman in her late thirties described the assumptions that had kept her from college:

It was all right for my brothers to get their degrees and do wonderful things. But . . . [I] was sort of inadvertently taught that a woman has to do other things. And one of the other things was anything but going to school if that meant taking you away from being home and wife and mother.

Growth, however, leads to the capacity to perceive values and other cultural imperatives as contextual, situational, and constructed. Such assumptions can be examined and accepted or rejected. For example, another woman in her late thirties described changes in her appearance and personal style that signaled major changes in her sense of self:

I've just changed completely from when I first began [this program]. I used to take this little African body and force it into this European square peg. And you know, it just didn't work. I kept trying to do it and trying to change who I was and tried to fit in. . . . When I finally decided to be the person that I am, I started feeling more comfortable. . . . It's not easy. It's never easy being who we are. It's always easier just to buy into whatever [is going on and] for everybody to be blond and get [blue] contact lenses and that whole kind of thing. . . . There have been times when—just recently I've thought to myself: Would it be easier just to conform? . . . Would it be easier to just straighten your hair and do the [professional] suit and that whole kind of thing? . . . because I've been catching a lot of hell on my job about who I am lately. And I thought: Nah. [laughter]

Authority is the sense of being in charge of oneself, of being able to set one's own standards, establish one's own values, and make choices based on these self-constructed systems rather than continue to "be captive of the beliefs . . . of our psychological and cultural inheritance" (Kegan, 1994, p. 302). In Mezirow's (1991; 2000) terminology, these are "transformed meaning perspectives." Such transformed perspectives move individuals closer to autonomy as they become increasingly "conscious of the sources and consequences of meaning perspectives, and [increasingly] free from coercion, constraints, and distortions in those perspectives" (Cranton, 1994, p. 60). These changes in perspective can ultimately lead to a transformation of consciousness wherein people become the *authors* of their roles (for example, as workers, learners, and participants in a diverse society) rather than just adopting roles defined by others. This self-authorization strongly suggests a shift in the locus of control (Merriam & Yang, 1996) amid the ongoing transactions between the person and the environment.

A woman in her early sixties discovered that when schoolwork required that she make her own needs a priority, family dynamics changed:

Everybody [in my family] has had to change. . . . I was the one [who] recognized it and said, "Hey [laughter], this is not going to work for me [anymore]. . . . Then [my husband and children] realized it's not ever going to be like it was . . . easy for everybody to depend on [me]. . . .[Now] I have my life, too.

A divorced mother in her mid-thirties also discovered changes in her way of constructing relationships.

I'm much more willing to abandon relationships that aren't good, that don't feel right, that don't seem to be harmonious. I don't have the need to maintain the relationship. I have been enabled to really challenge my parents' view [of how relationship should be] . . .[and to allow] my own voice to come forward. I've expressed myself completely differently and I don't just say things anymore that I think people want to hear.

Agency is the increased capacity to act on one's own values and self-definition; some might call it a *sense of empowerment.*

[I feel] a strength and a calmness and an acceptance, a self-acceptance. The world is not going to shatter if I don't keep my fingers in the hole in the dike. It's not going to come apart. And yet it's not a "well, I don't make a difference, anyway" [feeling]. It's not like that. Yes I do make a difference. . . .[But] I don't have to hold that image or protect that image of being perfect.

As Kegan (1994) describes it, adults can "learn the psychological myths or scripts that govern our behavior *and reauthor them* (rather than just use insight for better understanding of why the script is as it is)" (p. 303).

The task of moving toward self-agency and self-authorship might be expressed in this way:

I want to acknowledge that I construct the choices I make and the values I hold and that I'm responsible to act on behalf of those values to the best of my abilities.

Toward Connection with Others

Much psychological theory has framed human development in terms of increasing individuality, further defined as separateness and autonomy (Erikson, 1959; Levinson & Associates, 1978). However, Miller (1976), Gilligan (1982), Peck (1986), and Jordan, Kaplan, Miller, Stiver, and Surrey (1991) have cogently argued that these definitions of psychological maturity are derived primarily from research on male experience and inadequately represent women's patterns of growth and development. In describing "women's growth in connection," Jordan and her colleagues (1991) make clear that a view of autonomy based on separation is *also* inadequate for men. Rather, development grows out of ongoing interaction among people. The outcome is that relationships are created or recreated in a new, more conscious, way. Autonomous people are not "indifferen[t] to the attitudes, opinions, preferences, or well-being of others" (Candy, 1991, p. 123), but at the same time, they "reach their understandings and make their own decisions without being unduly influenced by others" (Boud, 1989, p. 43).

Though establishing one's individuality is part of development, it need not mean separation; rather, connections are based on mutual support rather than the need for the other to somehow complete the self. It is therefore important to be able to *mediate boundaries between one's connection to others and one's individuality and* to respect, value, and *engage the affective dimension when confronting difference.*

In *The Place of Discussion in the Learning Process,* written in 1935, Lindeman described the essentiality of connection to adults' learning: "How does one rise above unreality? The surest method is, I believe, one which will relate the person to something outside the self. Obviously, the 'something' outside the self which is most important is the other person. All our perplexing problems are at bottom problems of human relationships" (Brookfield, 1987, p. 43).

People who have moved toward connection with others are also likely to *experience themselves as part of something larger.* Though they may not necessarily follow an activist social agenda, they are likely to be more aware of the ways in which human society is mutually interdependent (Daloz, Keen, Keen, & Parks, 1996). Along with this realization comes the desire to *contribute one's voice to the collective endeavor.* To Kegan (1994), however, this is distinct from simply "joining the community as participant . . . in a new conformity" (p. 288–289), which is the accomplishment of the transformation from adolescence to socially constructed adulthood. Instead, such adults are able to query the goals and assumptions of various collective endeavors, even as they uncover and examine their individual beliefs and assumptions.

Rather than view development as only an individual process, Vygotsky (1978) focused also on the role of the social context. He emphasized the role of culture and context, and focused particularly on the dynamic interplay between learners and those who would help them learn, and on the implications of such learning for development.

The task of moving toward connection with others might be expressed as follows:

In discovering the self-constructed, individual nature of myself, I nevertheless want to recognize and act on the essential connectedness of the human enterprise: Though we may be existentially alone, we find our most human expressions in community. I wish to engage in a form of connectedness in which I can, without loss of my selfhood, bring myself into relationship and community.

Developmental Intentions

A common theme among the intentions is their focus on *experience*—attending to experience, interpreting experience, relying on experience, using experience as a point of reference, and creating experiences. They also underscore the necessity that learners engage in *reflection* and *construct meaning*. In the next section, we present activities and exercises that use experience, reflection, and meaning making to encourage deep approaches to learning and to enhance the potential for developmental growth in adults.

PART TWO

STRATEGIES AND EXERCISES

We are generally the better persuaded by the reasons we discover ourselves than by those given to us by others.

—PASCAL

In this section, we showcase an array of activities that educators use with adult learners in college and workplace settings. The activities meet two criteria: They incorporate key elements that support deep approaches to learning, such as adults' reflection on their own and others' experiences, with a focus on creating meaning and meaningful learning; and they illustrate how educators incorporate developmental intentions in their practice.

With this common base, the learning activities also vary significantly. For example, they have been applied in undergraduate and graduate-level courses in community colleges, four-year colleges, and universities, as well as in corporate and workplace settings and other professional arenas. The subjects range from cross-cultural communication to physics and from autobiography to management.

Some of the activities are discrete (stand-alone) exercises contained within a single class session or workshop. Others extend over more than one session or inform the design of a whole course. Whereas some activities are specific to the subject or topic, others could be applied to several subjects or disciplines.

Organization of the Activities

Each activity has been keyed by its author to no more than five *developmental intentions* (Exhibit 3.1), though many incorporate additional intentions, as well. (See the Index of Strategies, p. 373 for a list of activities cross-referenced by intention.)

Strategies of Learning

What we are calling *strategies of learning*—assessing, collaborating, experimenting, imagining, inquiring, performing-simulating, and reflecting—shift the emphasis from the developmental intentions of the educator to the kind of learning activity in which learners will primarily engage. As is typically the case, most learning involves several such strategies. Furthermore, our definitions are somewhat arbitrary and may overlap. Nevertheless, we assigned each activity to one strategy according to what seemed to us most supportive of the educator's overall emphasis.

Presentation of the Activities

The template for the activities includes up to eight parts, starting with the *title* of the activity and a brief identification of the *contributor.* Most contributors have provided their e-mail addresses, thus inviting conversation about their activity. This is followed by the *list* of developmental intentions, identified by the same Roman and Arabic numerals as in Exhibit 3.1. The fourth part, *context,* describes the setting where the activity has been most frequently employed.

The *description of the activity* includes two components: a statement of *purpose* specific to that exercise as implemented in its usual setting; and detailed directions for "how to" in the *format-steps-process* component. Some contributors also include examples and additional suggestions to broaden the activity and make it more generic. *Processing tips* elaborate on some aspect of the exercise and answer typical questions that the contributor has anticipated.

The seventh part, *contributor's commentary,* adds depth and dimension; these comments are often reflections on or interpretation of the underlying meaning of the activity. The contributor also may include caveats about challenging aspects of the activity or may name other possible applications.

Finally, some contributors provide *references* not only to works related to the specific exercise, but also to their own publications that are relevant to an audience of adult educators.

Adopting and Adapting

Some exercises are described primarily in terms of process and could be applied to many subjects; see for example, Mark Tennant's "Rotating Groups" in Chapter Five. Others, though more focused on content, could still be adopted or adapted for various settings. Topics such as listening, cultural differences, and ethics are obviously relevant to college and workplace settings. Many of the processes would work in either setting simply by the user choosing an appropriate subject or exercise content; for example, Carolyn Clark and Deborah Kilgore's "Educational-Autobiographies" in Chapter Four could just as easily focus on *leadership* autobiographies. Still other activities could be adapted to purposes somewhat different from those suggested by the contributors by shifting the emphasis slightly. Ideally, readers of this book will modify and build on these exercises in keeping with their own settings, purposes, and participants.

Readers familiar with the literature of adult education may wonder at the absence of well-known experiential methodologies such as case study and problem-based learning. In fact, adaptations of these strategies are among the contributions (see Peter Reason's "Cooperative Inquiry" in Chapter Five and Don Margetson's "Problem-Focused Education" in Chapter Eight). However, those methodologies are already supported by a significant body of research and descriptions of practice, whereas the activities in this book draw on the creativity and experience of educators and practitioners who have, for the most part, designed their own activities with learners' development in mind.

Within each of the seven strategies of learning, the activities are further sorted into one of two categories. Presented first are those that can be carried out in a single session. These are followed by activities that extend over more than one session or that represent a multilayered approach. Within each of these subcategories, the activities are sorted alphabetically by last name of contributor.

With this introduction and these caveats, we invite you to explore the rich variety of activities in this section either as they are presented here by their contributors or with your own creative modifications.

CHAPTER FOUR

ASSESSING

The focus here is on having a set of criteria or a framework to examine something; that something may include the self. The criteria or frameworks may be provided by someone else (see Patty Brewer's "Learning Styles Assessment," p. 66) or they may be created by the learners themselves (see David Boud's exercise on "Development Through Self-Assessment," p. 63). Different processes are also represented, such as Morry Fiddler's "Novice to Expert Continuum," (p. 59) and Philip Candy's "Repertory Grids" (below) for assessing aspects of one's value system.

Activities that extend over more than one session begin with David Boud's "Development Through Self-Assessment" on page 63.

◆ ◆ ◆

Repertory Grids

Philip Candy, Ballarat, Victoria, Australia
E-mail: p.candy@ballarat.edu.au

Philip Candy is the academic vice president of the University of Ballarat. He has written extensively on aspects of adult and higher education.

Developmental Intentions

    I. Toward knowing as a dialogical process.
      2. Surfacing and questioning assumptions underlying beliefs, ideas, actions, and positions.
      3. Reframing ideas or values that seem contradictory, embracing their differences, and arriving at new meanings.
    II. Toward a dialogical relationship to oneself.
      2. Engaging the disequilibrium when one's ideas and beliefs are challenged.
    III. Toward being a continuous learner.
      1. Reflecting on one's own and others' experiences as a guide to future behavior.
    IV. Toward self-agency and self-authorship.
      1. Constructing a values system that informs one's behavior.

Context

Repertory grids have been used successfully in formal education programs (undergraduate and postgraduate), short courses on subjects ranging from organizational leadership to teaching, and consulting situations.

Description of Activity

Purpose. To raise to the level of awareness a learner's assumptions as a springboard to conscious analysis of those assumptions toward greater self-understanding.

Format-steps-process. The essence of this activity is exploring an aspect of one's value system. For purposes of this example, we will presume the learner has decided to explore how she relates to other colleagues in her workplace.

Creating the Grid

1. The interviewer ([I], who could be another learner) and the respondent ([R]) sit together. [I] has a preprinted grid form (Exhibit 4.1) and a number of small, blank cards. [I] asks [R] to note down, each on a separate card, the name, initials, or some identification for each person with whom she regularly comes into contact in the workplace. [I] writes the identifications (such as initials) for each person across the top of the grid.

2. To ensure that a range of elements is sampled, [I] also asks [R] to identify on other, separate cards various categories such as *the best colleague I have ever worked with, the worst colleague I have ever worked with, someone I dislike,* or *someone I admire,* as well as a card for herself.

3. [I] then shuffles the name cards, presents [R] with three chosen at random, and asks her to group them so that two are similar and one is different from the other two. When [R] has done so, [I] asks, "in what way are these two people similar to each other, and different from the third?" When [R] responds, [I] then asks her for a one- or two-word characterization, for example, *observes deadlines* and *ignores deadlines*. This is written on the grid form on one of the horizontal lines, with the paired identification on the left and the singleton on the right. (See Exhibit 4.2.)

4. All the name cards, including the one with her name, are now placed in front of [R] and she is invited to place them in a continuum between the two poles of this construct. If two or more people are indistinguishable with respect to this characterization, they can be placed together. Then each person is given a "score" from 1 to 7, with 1 representing the "positive" pole and 7 representing the "negative" pole. (It is not required that every number between 1 and 7 is used.) [R] also has to score herself ("me") with respect to this criterion, along with the others.

5. This process is repeated, from step 3, for about an hour. Each time [I] presents [R] with a different beginning triad and requests that [R] identify a bipolar construct. [I] then assists, but does not shape, [R]'s responses as she gives a score to each person in the array for each of the horizontal scales (characterizations).

Exhibit 4.1. Blank Repertory Grid.

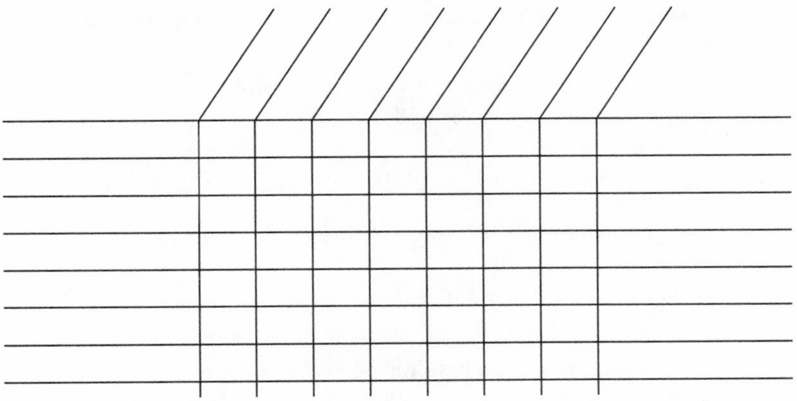

Exhibit 4.2. Sample Repertory Grid.

	Me	BB	CC	DD	EE	FF	GG	
Observes deadlines	1	7	4	3	1	5	5	Ignores deadlines
Helpful	3	3	2	1	7	1	4	Uninvolved
Reserved	6	1	5	4	2	3	7	Gregarious
Dull	6	2	4	4	3	1	6	Creative
Tidy office	3	3	2	1	7	1	4	Messy office
(Etc.)								

Interpreting the Grid

1. By the end of the session, a completed grid is ready for interpretation and analysis (see partial sample above).
2. Reading down the list of attributes assigned to each person in a narrative way, it is possible to gather a picture of [R]'s view of that person. Another area of discovery may be in how [R] has pictured *herself.*
3. Also notable are unexpected correspondences between elements of the grid. Reading across and down, the numbers may, for example, reveal that a construct such as *helpfulness* is consistently ranked along with *tidy office.* Perhaps [R]'s experience has taught her that people with tidy offices are more helpful. However, if she *anticipates* this in her dealing with people, she may subtly influence her relationships with people—especially those whose offices are not tidy when she make their acquaintance—leading perhaps to a self-fulfilling prophecy.

It is almost impossible for a respondent to generate construct labels or assign meaningful ratings to the elements in the array without critical reflection. The result is that a person will often have reconstructed some part of his or her universe in the process. Accordingly, if the grid were to be administered again, a slightly different but no less valid result is perfectly possible. The grid is entirely idiosyncratic; it is unlikely that anyone else at [R]'s workplace would rank people in precisely the same way.

Processing Tips

In step 3 of creating the grid, [R]'s identification is not a question of "truth" but of [R]'s construct. [I] does not have to agree. The "poles" of the line do not have to be dictionary opposites. For example, in Exhibit 4.2, *helpful* is not necessarily opposite in meaning to *uninvolved*—except in [R]'s construction of the moment.

As they proceed through the repetitions of step 3 through 5, [I] and [R] chat informally about relationships, experiences, and personalities. It is likely that as [R] becomes less self-conscious, constructs may start to "bubble-up" spontaneously. [R] may even identify significant bipolar descriptors before being presented with a new triad. [I] must be an active, aware interlocutor, alert to the comments and patterns that [R] may reveal in her discussion, yet careful not to impose his interpretation on her experience.

In an hour's interview, one might reasonably examine ten to twelve constructs (characterizations). More than that is likely to be redundant, as the interviewee would probably start to repeat himself or herself. Similarly, fewer than six discrete entities (in this case, colleagues in the workplace) may not offer enough scope to explore adequately the outcome space occupied by the relevant constructs, and more than ten may lead to the respondent making somewhat artificial or contrived distinctions that are not actually applied in reality.

Once the grid is complete, the elements and constructs may be reordered to highlight similarities or differences in the meanings attributed to the elements or the constructs. The "reordering" is done by moving the words and all related scores so they are closer to another column or row to which they are numerically most similar. In a classroom environment, this can be performed by "eyeballing" the data. (There are also computer programs that reorder quite complex grids on the basis of the numerical similarity of columns and rows.) What this maneuver achieves is a restructuring of the grid so that similar items (elements or constructs) are co-located, hence making the meaning of the grid clearer.

Grids can also be used to show changes in one person's constructs on successive occasions or to compare various people's views of the same array of elements. In the latter case, the grid can transcend individuals' frames of reference and highlight shared and divergent understandings and interpretations.

Although some experience in professional counseling can be helpful in [I]'s role, it is not a requirement, as much of this process is within the capabilities of anyone who can thoughtfully reflect, including [R] herself, once the grid is completed.

In the field of adult learning, grids can be applied in a variety of areas (Thomas & Harri-Augstein, 1985, pp. 344–352). For instance, learners might be asked to construe physical entities (such as geological specimens, photographs, or learning resources), people (colleagues, learners, teachers, subordinates), temporal events (learning experiences, interview situations, events in a family relationship), social entities (departments or units, political parties, roles in an institution), behaviors and activities (learning strategies, hobbies, activities for the unemployed), abstractions and evaluations (personal beliefs about learning, personal relationships, metaphors), or emotions and sensations (drug experiences, pieces of poetry, awareness-raising techniques).

Contributor's Commentary

Repertory grids, developed by George Kelly (1955) and based on personal construct psychology, enable learners to surface and examine hidden assumptions. They were originally used in psychotherapeutic situations to allow patients to examine their underlying assumptions about people, events, or ideas. They can also reveal ways in which learners have constructed meaning and can highlight inconsistencies by showing dominant and at times dysfunctional patterns of thinking, reveal implications of construing things in particular ways, and demonstrate alternative and perhaps preferable ways of understanding the world and relating to it.

The aspect of one's value system chosen as the subject of the exercise could be connected to the learning process itself, such as learning situations, instructional methods, or teaching styles. It could also be friends, colleagues, poems, works of art, cities, or virtually anything with a qualitative similarity in the range of elements. Even three-dimensional objects such as flower arrangements or sculptures and tactile or sense objects such as wines, cheeses, or textiles can be used to elicit the constructs that the learner uses to differentiate between them. Though a written grid is the most common process, it may be possible to present a person with, say, an arrangement of pieces of sculpture and ask him or her to arrange these items along an imaginary continuum, without necessarily naming or specifying the two poles of the construct (Neimeyer, 1979).

Whenever and however grids are used, two things in particular must be borne in mind. The first is that the constructs elicited are highly personal statements of people's beliefs and values that have implications for action. They are not mere abstractions or items of curiosity for a researcher and must accordingly be treated with respect. The second is that emancipatory education is inevitably predicated on some vision of a "better world" (Jarvis, 1987b, p. 307). Although the dominant focus of the repertory grid is with individuals transforming their own perspectives and worldviews, the end result can be a community where reflective self-awareness is the norm and where people, individually and collectively, are free to become masters of their own destiny (Armstrong, 1977).

References

Armstrong, A. K. (1977). *Masters of their own destiny: A comparison of the thought of Coady and Freire.* Occasional Papers in Continuing Education No. 13. Vancouver: Centre for Continuing Education, University of British Columbia.

Candy, P. C. (1980, August). *Adult learners' views of adult learning: Report of a pilot study.* Paper presented at a national workshop on Working with Adults: Strategies for Adult Learning, Macquarie University, New South Wales, Australia.

Candy, P. C. (1981). Mirrors of the mind: Personal construct theory in the training of adult educators. *Manchester Monograph* No. 16. Manchester: Department of Adult Education, University of Manchester.

Candy, P. C. (1990). Repertory grids: Playing verbal chess. In J. Mezirow & Associates (Eds.), *Fostering critical reflection in adulthood: A guide to transformative and emancipatory learning.* San Francisco: Jossey-Bass.

Candy, P. C. (1991). *Self-direction for lifelong learning: A comprehensive guide to theory and practice.* San Francisco: Jossey-Bass.

Fransella, F., & Bannister, D. (1977). *A manual for repertory grid technique.* London: Academic Press.

Jarvis, P. (Ed.). (1987b). *Twentieth century thinkers in adult education.* London: Croom Helm.

Kelly, G. A. (1955). *The psychology of personal constructs* (2 vols.). New York: Norton.

Neimeyer, R. A. (1979, July). *The structure and meaningfulness of tacit construing.* Paper presented at the Third International Congress on Personal Construct Psychology, Breukelen, Netherlands.

Pratt, D. D., & Candy, P. C. (1985, March*). The repertory grid in group oriented learning situations: Construing the constructions of others.* Paper presented at the Twenty-sixth Annual Adult Education Research Conference, Arizona State University.

Thomas, L. F., & Harri-Augstein, E. S. (1985). *Self-organised learning: Foundations for a conversational science of psychology.* London: Routledge & Kegan Paul.

Contradictions Workshop

David Dunn, Denver, Colorado
E-mail: icadunn@igc.org; website: www.mirrorcommunication.com

David Dunn has been an organizational development consultant using the Institute of Cultural Affairs (ICA) Technology of Participation™ in his facilitating practice. He writes, edits, and designs print and electronic publications primarily for nonprofit organizations.

Developmental Intentions

II. Toward a dialogical relationship to oneself.
1. Addressing fears of losing what is familiar and safe.

    3. Exploring life's experiences through some framework(s) of analysis.
V. Toward connection with others.
    2. Experiencing oneself as part of something larger.
    4. Contributing one's voice to a collective endeavor.
    5. Recognizing that collective awareness and thinking transform
       the sum of their parts.

Context

This activity helps a workgroup discern and name present impediments to its future vision. It is a brainstorming and analyzing process.

Description of Activity

Purpose. To discern and name the underlying patterns, structures or limiting beliefs in the present circumstances—that is, the *contradictions,* that block a group's vision—so that strategic, corrective action might be taken.

    Format-steps-process.

1. After a group has delineated its vision, I ask each person individually to brainstorm his or her blocks, issues, irritants, or other impediments to that vision. From this brainstorm, each person selects his or her top ideas and writes them on cards with felt-tip markers. The "cards" are often half-sheets of standard paper, and people are asked to write so the words can be read by everyone in the room.

2. I collect one card from each person. (At each successive round I may suggest a new criterion—for example, *most important, most insightful, most contributive to the problem, clearest*—whatever selection criteria make sense to the outcome that the group and I have negotiated.) I randomly post these on the wall; for example, onto a large piece of butcher paper or a sticky surface. (This process can be simplified by using a commercially available spray-on product that allows material to be repositioned as often as necessary.)

3. The group begins the organizing process when I ask them to identify pairs of cards that stem from the same underlying cause or *root cause.* I reposition the cards according to their responses. On successive rounds, each person provides another card for posting. The group continues to advise me in forming new pairs and, as needed, larger clusters, until thirty to forty cards (see Processing Tips) have been posted and positioned.

4. I direct the group's attention to the largest cluster first, asking them to look for one or more of three factors, that is, *patterns, structures,* or *limiting beliefs* that

inadvertently block movement toward their vision. I ask them to focus on patterns, not problems; on factors that actually exist (not factors they "lack"); on factors in which they participate (there is no one to blame); and on factors that, once identified, may suggest effective, corrective action. I illustrate these four points with an example or story from my consulting practice.

5. I help the group watch or listen for the "aha"—the flash of insight when a new perspective breaks through from the discussion of the items in that particular cluster. The group then crafts a name for this underlying obstacle or *contradiction.*

Closure. After all the clusters are named through a similar process, I ask the group to reflect on their discoveries, including asking how they might address the contradictions they identified.

Processing Tips

The first key to this activity is that a contradiction workshop is used only within a larger strategic context; that is, it presumes that a group has a vision—an aspiration they hope to achieve—and intends some form of response to remove obstacles to that vision. In other words, it depends on the group's commitment to a larger process in which the contradictions workshop plays a pivotal role.

The second key is that the group works with its own experience in a way that creates safety for discussion and analysis. The data for the contradictions workshop come from the life experience of the group's members and must be honored. After people contribute their input (brief phrases on cards or half sheets of paper), questions of clarity are allowed but not criticisms of content. A person with a different perception is invited to contribute a different card.

A handy rule of thumb is that the total number of cards posted to the group brainstorm should be between thirty and forty. With fewer than thirty, some insights may be omitted. With more than forty, duplication begins to occur. However, once that number are up on the wall, I always ask the group to check that all their pertinent insights have been covered by at least one of the cards on display, and to add any ideas that might have fallen between the cracks.

When all the data have been displayed, the question shifts to, "What is beneath these data?" The search for contradictions—that is, *underlying causes, root causes*—is driven by two questions: (1) "Why do these obstacles, blocks, or irritants that emerged during the brainstorm remain?" and (2) "What is the dysfunctional underlying pattern, structure, or limiting belief?" Continually asking, "Why?" and continually asking people to look through their experience to what underlies it takes them out of the anxiety of the present and below the surface to a deeper level. When that happens, anxieties about personal problems, interpersonal conflicts, or the limitations of life (not enough time, money, or personnel) suddenly become quite beside the point in light of the group's collective search for the patterns, structures, or limiting beliefs that block them.

Given a vision and an intent to act, and with a rich data set based on personal experience, a contradictions workshop can lead to insights about the present that are startlingly fresh and that genuinely illuminate future actions.

Contributor's Commentary

The trick is to wean people from the old image that issues, obstacles, and blocks are negatives and problematic. The concept of *contradiction* is a positive, system-oriented approach that invites people to find in their present situation factors that are inadvertently dysfunctional with respect to their aspirations. The discussion that takes place when a group names the underlying patterns, structures, or limiting beliefs blocking their vision can become an exciting quest for what amounts to a secret doorway to the future, currently hidden within the baggage and idiosyncrasies of the present arrangements of a group's worklife. This is described further in Spencer's (1989) *Winning Through Participation*.

When a group joins this quest and discovers how they inadvertently thwart their hopes, a huge weight is removed. Their situation is no longer their problem. The problem, which is their challenge, becomes instead how they relate to their situation. They had supposed that personal problems or lack of resources or too little time were the real problems they faced. Instead they find that beneath these limiting givens are other, more fundamental factors with which they've unwittingly been complicit that are the real obstacles to be overcome, but these factors are ones they can control or transform. There is no one to blame and there is no reason to be a victim of circumstances. By naming these knotty and previously invisible complexities, the group gets handles on the tasks to which they must address themselves. The potential for concrete action is released as people take a proactive, constructive relationship to their situation.

People are helped to look beneath the surface, adopt a larger perspective, trust their experience, and use their intuitive insights to analyze what they discover. Einstein said something to the effect that no problem can be solved from the same consciousness that created it; we must learn to see the world anew. The contradictions workshop helps people create an enlarged and deepened context that permits them to see factors that had previously been hidden. The contradictions workshop helps people overcome the distraction caused by the superficial artifacts of what are in fact deeper, systemic variables. When they look through the surface data of issues, obstacles and blocks to the underlying patterns, structures and limiting beliefs, they gain control over these deeper factors by seeing, naming, and then systematically acting on them.

A footnote about patterns, structures, and limiting beliefs: We all have mental images of how work should be conducted, how life should be lived, what organizations should look like, and so forth. We call them *mindsets, mental sets, images*. *Limiting beliefs* is another name for limiting, dysfunctional mental images. *Pattern* is a name for the institutionalized residue of old images in interpersonal relationships. *Structure* is the name for the institutionalized residue of old images in organizational systems. In any case, the contradictions workshop deals in the realm of images or the institutionalized residue of images. And since images can be evaluated, adjusted, discarded, or transformed, so can the institutional arrangements that flow from them. Organizations and workgroups become expressions of our minds, and like our minds, they can be enlarged, illuminated, and recreated continually.

Reference

Spencer, L. J. (1989). *Winning through participation: Meeting the challenge of corporate change with the Technology of Participation*. Dubuque, Iowa: Kendall-Hunt. (Also available from the Institute of Cultural Affairs at www.ica-use.org)

Novice to Expert Continuum

Morris Fiddler, Chicago, Illinois
E-mail: mfiddler@wppost.depaul.edu

Morris Fiddler is a faculty mentor to undergraduate and graduate students pursuing individualized programs at the intersections of liberal learning and professional development in the School for New Learning, DePaul University. He also works with graduate students in genetic counseling at Northwestern University Medical School.

Developmental Intentions

    II. Toward a dialogical relationship to oneself.

        3. Exploring life's experiences through some framework(s) of analysis.

    III. Toward being a continuous learner.

        7. Setting one's own learning goals, being goal-directed, and being habitual in learning.

8. Seeking authentic feedback from others.
IV. Toward self-agency and self-authorship.
2. Accepting responsibility for choices one has made and will make.

Context

This activity is used regularly in an individualized degree-planning course for graduate students pursuing diverse areas of professional study.

Description of Activity

Purpose. To help students begin to characterize differences between novices and experts, and to encourage students to situate themselves along a continuum with respect to their profession generally and to discrete competencies more specifically.

Format-steps-process.

1. At a point relatively early in students' exploration of their goals and self-assessment of their capabilities and learning needs, I introduce the concept that movement from being a novice to becoming an expert has a variety of characteristics. One of these characteristics is how novices and experts respond differently to new information and experiences. Drawing on Kolb's conception of experiential learning, Sheckley (1989) posited these differences as a relationship between *grasping* the content of new information or experiences and *transforming* it. Novices, because they lack sophisticated interpretive frameworks and mental models, are in a predominantly grasping mode. According to the model, as the novice builds a foundation of information and through application builds a conceptual architecture, he or she increasingly adopts a predominantly transforming mode—one in which new information becomes expert knowledge. The contexts into which new information "fits," or the relationship of new information to the web of cognitive associations, lead the expert to make meaning more quickly and more frequently.
2. One of the ways these ideas emerge is through a *fishbowl activity,* in which one person is the subject of the group's attention. I ask for a volunteer to do the following:

   Identify an area of competence (for example, managing a project, doing an organizational needs analysis).

   Trace back the process through which she arrived where she is now with respect to her capability or area of knowledge. I use some prompting questions to help the student attend to her early learning experience, such as, "When you first were interested in this area, what was the context? Did you need to learn or develop this competence? Describe your first efforts or activities. What did you do to learn?"

3. Following the volunteer's story, I hand out to everyone a one-page novice-to-expert continuum sheet (see Table 4.1). I say a few words about it, and respond to questions to get the group oriented to the ideas.

4. I then return to the "fish in the bowl" and ask her to relate aspects of her story to points along the continuum. This concludes the first example.

5. I then ask for a second volunteer who would like to work through the evolution of a capability in similar fashion. This time, however, I provide prompts in greater detail and attention to the continuum as a way to help frame the story. I draw on questions that slow down the speaker in the telling, such as, "What were you thinking when X happened? What did you do, think, feel next? How quickly did you find yourself analyzing the situation? What sort of information were you looking for?"

Table 4.1. From Novice to Expert: Level of Competence, Developmental Path, and Learning Processes.

Level of Competence	Developmental Path	Learning Process
Novice: Can assess and adapt to deviations from basic rules and procedures	No distinction between rules and context in which rules are applied	90 percent grasping 10 percent transforming
Advanced beginner: Can assess and adapt to important aspects of a situation	Shifting from actions dictated by rule to actions dictated by situation	70 percent grasping 30 percent transforming
Practitioner: Can assess and adapt to deviations from a plan	Shifting from actions dictated by situation to actions dictated by a general plan	50 percent grasping 50 percent transforming
Professional: Can assess and adjust to deviations from the pattern	Shifting from actions dictated by general plan to actions dictated by intuitions	30 percent grasping 70 percent transforming
Expert: Can assess and focus on critical factors in a situation	Actions and situation are synonymous	10 percent grasping 90 percent transforming

Source: Adapted from B. Sheckley, *Experiential Learning Theory: Implications for Workplace Learning.* Philadelphia: Council for Adult and Experiential Learning International Assembly, 1989.

Grasping (taking in the content of new information or experiences) and *transforming* (putting information into interpretive contexts or acting on it) refer to learning processes of the experiential learning cycle as described by Kolb (1984). See Figure 2.1, page 24.

6. Members of the group also participate in the questioning of "fish" number two. I diminish my "presence" and let the activity eventually move into a more general dialogue on the continuum model; for example, its details, value, viability to explain their experiences and observations of people considered experts in the participants' lives, and its uses in planning a degree program. The "fish" simply rejoins the group.

Processing Tips

I have found a couple of things that have helped students initially grasp the information and move toward transforming the ideas into a meaningful framework. For example, I ask the group to write down the characteristics of people whom they deem to be experts and collectively organize their observations into themes. This frequently elicits some insights into the meaning of the language involved in the continuum (derived from experiential learning theory) and the qualities of expertise each person values. It is also helpful to provide prompts that are framed in simple terms to begin with, and to move progressively toward more complex ways of interpreting the ideas; for example: "What did you do? What were you thinking? As you recognized your own evolution of expertise, was there a shift in the *locus of control* of determining what actions to take? Did your comfort level with the unexpected change?" Weaving back and forth among the person's story or experiences, the ideas contained in the continuum handout, and applications of these ideas to planning and future action also helps keep the discussion flowing among the participants who are at various stages of their professional development and may have different levels of comfort with the abstract and the concrete.

The fishbowl technique also provides to people telling their stories the initial safety of having a framework and structure within which to do so. Positioning myself in the mix of the group, rather than in front of it, seems to encourage a discussion that moves between the members of the group and the "fish" without people looking to me for "permission" to speak.

Contributor's Commentary

The ideas connected to the continuum form the backdrop to asking students to do a variety of things: assessing themselves in the various arenas and skills of their professional work, raising awareness of where they are in their learning and what mode is in effect; using the ideas themselves as part of the planning process for what and how they want and need to learn and at what level.

The idea of the continuum provides some bearings for what individuals and the group are expecting to gain through a graduate program. Creating a learning plan for their studies helps many students move along the spectrum and progressively take ownership of their learning. Learners comment on the value of the idea for providing a frame of reference for interpreting the capabilities of managers and colleagues and better understanding distinctions of authority.

I have found that some students become adept at differentiating between learning goals that they want to attain at a high level of expertise and those that they are willing to accept at a level of adequacy of their degree programs. Goals and desired learning outcomes become framed less in terms of knowledge and more in terms of realistic movement along the continuum without a felt need to master everything. Students have frequently commented that they see themselves differently as professionals, particularly when we return to the continuum at later points in their programs.

Reference

Sheckley, B. (1989). Experiential learning theory: Implications for workplace learning. Philadelphia: Council for Adult and Experiential Learning International Assembly.

Development Through Self-Assessment

David Boud, Sydney, Australia
E-mail: David.Boud@uts.edu.au

David Boud is professor of adult education and associate dean (research) in the faculty of education at the University of Technology, Sydney. He has written extensively on teaching, learning, and assessment in higher and adult education.

Developmental Intentions

    II. Toward a dialogical relationship to oneself.
        4. Questioning critically the validity or worth of one's pursuits.
   III. Toward being a continuous learner.
        3. Recognizing and revealing one's strengths and weaknesses as a learner and knower.
        8. Seeking authentic feedback from others.
   IV. Toward self-agency and self-authorship.
        2. Accepting responsibility for choices one has made and will make.
        7. "Naming and claiming" what one has experienced and knows.

Context

This activity has been used in graduate courses for adult educators and in undergraduate courses in law. It has also been used at all undergraduate and graduate levels other than in introductory courses.

Description of Activity

Self-assessment involves a range of different practices in which learners take responsibility for making their own judgments about their work. Self-assessment does not occur in isolation from others; learners need to draw upon teachers, practitioners, and peers. What characterizes self-assessment is that learners themselves make decisions. In formally accredited courses, self-assessment has been used as part of a mix of assessment activities, which includes teacher-determined, self-determined, and negotiated assessment, depending on the context.

Purpose. To involve students in the process of actively engaging with what counts as "good work" and to apply these ideas to their own assignments. (The assignment may be a paper, a research proposal, or the report of project work. The process works well in each case.)

Formats-steps-process.

1. A few weeks after students have identified a topic for their major assignment, I mention that the following week we will spend some time in class focusing on what constitutes good assignments and that they should come prepared with ideas of their own.
2. I start the next class by discussing the notion of self-assessment, giving a rationale for its use in the present context. I then invite each student in turn to offer one idea about what distinguishes good from not-so-good work with regard to their assignment. The round continues until all criteria are covered. (I write these on large sheets of paper, so that all can see and I have a record.) Once all the ideas have been displayed and numbered, I seek clarification from the class on any item that is unclear. Some items are thus modified or reworded, and identical ideas are collapsed together.
3. I then pose a question: "Are there clusters or groupings of items?" Invariably there are, and I create a list of major headings as identified by the students, with the numbers of the specific items that they associate with each.
4. I then ask: "Would you be happy to have your work judged on the basis of the criteria before us?" Normally there is rapid assent, but occasionally discussion arises when students believe that some criteria are relevant in certain circumstances but not in others. These items are starred and marked "only as relevant."

5. In classes where students are graded, students commonly say, "It may be OK for us to use these criteria, but which criteria are you going to use when you make your judgments?" I normally have no difficulty in agreeing to use their criteria, as they are often more thorough than I would have adopted anyway.

6. Following the class, I take the paper and transcribe the list of criteria into the following format: major heading, list of criteria under that heading (using the exact words from class discussion). A large area of blank space is included so that students can later add their own comments on the extent to which they have met these criteria in their assignment.

7. An optional stage is for students to exchange drafts of their assignments and use the criteria to provide qualitative feedback to each other prior to final revision.

8. Students finish their assignments and return their completed self-assessment sheets on the due date.

Processing Tips

It is vital that the teacher does not intrude her or his own views about criteria or make judgmental remarks during the generation stages (steps 2 and 3). When I think that important criteria may be overlooked, however, I will join in at the end of each round and add a statement to the list in the same way as any other member of the group.

Contributor's Commentary

Self-assessment in adult and higher education involves much more than self-administered and self-marked tests. Self-assessment skills of learners are developed when learners are more actively involved in understanding and formulating the criteria used for judgment. My experience, and that of colleagues in other disciplinary areas who have used this approach, is that the quality of students' work improves. The reason for this is simple: Students have a ready-made checklist in their own language that they can use to judge the quality of their work. In addition, they have engaged in a process of questioning what counts as good work, thus becoming involved with deeper questions of academic standards in the subject area and standards of presentation.

A single exercise involving systematic self-assessment does not in itself foster the development of the skill, but it can lay the foundation for its development if reinforced elsewhere. If the self-assessment is repeated in different ways in other classes, it is likely to lead to habits of questioning criteria for performance and noticing the extent to which one's own work meets these criteria.

The process described is effective in classes of up to forty; it is less effective in groups of less than six to eight, as the group may be too small to generate ideas of sufficient diversity.

This activity is but one of many self-assessment activities. Experience shows the importance of designing self-assessment to fit the particular context (discipline, nature of group, class size, degree of sophistication in self-assessment) and to introduce it in ways that illustrate the educational value of the process. Self-assessment involves a set of complex educational skills. Development of these skills needs to be embedded in classes in diverse ways. Further discussion and many examples of using self-assessment in higher education contexts can be found in my book on self-assessment (Boud, 1995).

Self-assessment can be used to

- Self-monitor and check progress
- Promote good learning practices (learn how to learn)
- Self-diagnose and self-remediate
- Practice alternatives to other forms of assessment
- Improve professional or academic practice
- Consolidate learning over a range of contexts
- Review achievements as a prelude to recognizing prior learning
- Achieve self-knowledge and self-understanding

References

Boud, D. (1995). *Enhancing learning through self-assessment.* London: Kogan Page.

Boud, D., & Miller, N. (Eds.). (1996). *Working with experience: Animating learning.* London: Routledge.

Boud, D., Cohen, R., & Walker, D. (1993). *Using experience for learning.* Buckingham, England: Society for Research into Higher Education and Open University Press.

Learning Styles Assessment

Patricia Brewer, Dayton, Ohio

E-mail: pbrewer@sinclair.edu

Patricia Brewer coordinates adult degree programs at Sinclair Community College, including an accelerated weekend college and a student-designed, interdisciplinary program. She has served as president of the Adult Higher Education Alliance.

Developmental Intentions

I. Toward knowing as a dialogical process.
    6. Paying attention to wholes as well as the parts that comprise them.
II. Toward a dialogical relationship to oneself.
    3. Exploring life's experiences through some framework(s) of analysis.
III. Toward being a continuous learner.
    1. Reflecting on one's own and others' experiences as a guide to future behavior.
    3. Recognizing and revealing one's strengths and weaknesses as a learner and knower.
    7. Setting one's own learning goals, being goal-directed, and being habitual in learning.

Context

This activity is used in a degree planning seminar for adult learners in a community college.

Description of Activity

Purpose. To enable students to become more aware of the process of learning and to provide a framework for reflection and analysis of self-directed learning experiences.

Format-steps-process.

1. At the beginning of the term, I ask each student to develop a self-designed learning project as part of the course requirements. Students begin with an outline, then do iterative drafts until the student and I agree that the documentation of learning is acceptable.
2. In-class content includes the study of learning-style preferences and the completion and interpretation of various learning-style instruments (a personality descriptor [Myers-Briggs Type Indicator], an information processing instrument [Kolb Learning Style Inventory], a short hemispheric preference scale, and a modality indicator [auditory, visual, kinesthetic]). Some students also elect to complete a CD-ROM exercise that focuses on Gardner's multiple intelligences model.
3. In a written analysis of the inventories, students describe the various components of their individual styles and reflect on what seems true (or not true) about the preferences indicated.

4. Finally, students are asked to *double-loop* the learning. Each student reviews her or his project in light of the learning-style information and indicates how, where, and if the preferences indicated in the inventories are reflected in the self-designed project. This analysis is included with the final draft of the project.

Contributor's Commentary

Community colleges attract a variety of adult learners. Students who attend my class may be reentering college with an existing degree (often above the associate level) or they may be recent recipients of the G.E.D. The flexibility of the self-designed learning project is important to this activity, for almost any project will provide a sufficient context for the final learning-style analysis. Many of the students select a project that focuses on instrumental learning, but the reflection and analysis components are equally applicable for projects that develop communicative or transformative learning (Mezirow, 1996). Regardless of the content and type of learning, asking the student to rethink the learning behavior, as it is documented in the project and reflective of learning style, is an activity that challenges the student cognitively.

I am persuaded that self-knowledge of how one learns increases the capacity for self-direction in learning. Students report that the double-loop analysis portion of this activity increases reflective learning skills and enhances the capacity to develop learning strategies in subsequent courses.

Other Applications

Faculty who complete in-service learning-style workshops are asked to provide a similar analysis of a successful teaching activity and to focus the reflection on the connection between their preferred learning style and their teaching style.

References

Association for Supervision and Curriculum Development. (1997). *A conversation with Howard Gardner: Exploring our multiple intelligences* [CD-ROM]. Alexandria, VA: Association for Supervision and Curriculum Development.

Carbo, M. (1987). *Increasing reading achievement.* Alexandria, VA: National Association of Secondary School Principals.

Gardner, H. (1993). *Frames of the mind: the theory of multiple intelligences.* New York: Basic Books.

Kolb, D. A. (1985). *Learning style inventory.* Boston: McBer Company.

Kolb, D. A. (1984). *Experiential learning.* Englewood Cliffs, NJ: Prentice-Hall.

Mezirow, J. (1996). Contemporary paradigms of learning. *Adult Education Quarterly, 46,* 158–172.

Myers, P. B., & Myers, K. D. (1987). *Myers-Briggs Type Indicator.* Palo Alto, CA: Consulting Psychologists Press.

Educational Autobiographies

M. Carolyn Clark and Deborah Kilgore, College Station, Texas and Ames, Iowa
E-mail: cclark@tamu.edu; dkilgore@iastate.edu

M. Carolyn Clark is associate professor of adult education at Texas A & M University. Her research focuses on transformational learning and identity development of marginalized women. Deborah Kilgore is assistant professor of adult education at Iowa State University.

Developmental Intentions

   I. Toward knowing as a dialogical process.
      4. Using one's experience to critique expert opinion and expert opinion to critique one's experience.
  II. Toward a dialogical relationship to oneself.
      3. Exploring life's experiences through some framework(s) of analysis.
 III. Toward being a continuous learner.
      8. Seeking authentic feedback from others.
 IV. Toward self-agency and self-authorship.
      6. Distinguishing what one has created for oneself from what is imposed by social, cultural, and other forces.
      7. "Naming and claiming" what one has experienced and knows.

Context

This activity has been used in a five-week summer session course for women graduate students.

Description of Activity

This approach evolved from a single reflective exercise to a structured modality for the entire course.

Purpose. To encourage learners to identify and reflect on specific life events, in this case, educational experiences; construct a cohesive interpretation of those experiences in an integrated way and present it authoritatively as text for use by others; critically assess their own interpretations by bringing them into dialogue with other texts (both from class participation and from the formal texts); and be in dialogical relationship with their own growth and the process of their ideas.

Format-steps-process.

1. We begin by each of us writing our educational life history. In this particular course we had nine students (all women) and two instructors, so there were eleven educational life histories to read. No page limits were given. Histories ranged from approximately eight to fifteen pages, single-spaced.
2. We post our document on our FirstClass site (a Website) and each of us reads all the other documents.
3. We next read the texts for the course (Aisenberg & Harrington, 1988; Belenky, Clinchy, Goldberger, & Tarule, 1996; Goldberger, Tarule, Clinchy, & Belenky, 1996; Middleton, 1993).
4. The students write several short papers in which they identify key ideas in each text and put them in dialogue with relevant themes within the educational life histories. These are posted on FirstClass and read by everyone, with their comments posted. (It should be noted that this class met face-to-face twice each week for three hours and that there was extensive and on-going discussion of the on-line dialogue as it unfolded.)
5. At the end of the course, each student revisits her educational life history and writes an addendum that assesses the course's impact on her interpretation of her educational life experiences.

Processing Tips

We gave only sketchy guidelines for the first step (writing the educational life history), as we want each person to have maximum freedom to construct this narrative in the way that makes the most sense to her.

Contributors' Commentary

The process generates new insights into the self (a core developmental goal), but it also generates insight into the nature of knowledge constructions. Learners enter into dialogue with their experience, begin to explore the complexities and ambiguities of that engagement (for example, as shaper and shaped), and begin to put their experiences in dialogue with the experience of others. To frame this for women specifically enables them to recognize the impact of particular sociocultural forces on the lives and consciousness of women. The self-assessment further enhances the concept of personal and group knowledge construction, further underscoring the provisional nature of knowledge construction, its tentativeness, and the need for ongoing review and critique.

Editors' note. This exercise could easily be adapted for leadership development training by focusing on one's life history as a leader and the themes that emerge, for example, and by drawing on texts such as Senge (1990), Bennis and Goldsmith (1994), and Vaill (1996) (see main Reference section at the back of the book).

References

Aisenberg, N., & Harrington, M.(1988). *Women of academe: Outsiders in the sacred grove.* Amherst, MA: University of Massachusetts Press.

Belenky, M. F., Clinchy, B. M., Goldberger, N. R., & Tarule, J. M. (1996). *Women's ways of knowing.* Boston: Basic Books.

Goldberger, N. R., Tarule, J. M., Clinchy, B. M., & Belenky, M. F. (1996). *Knowledge, difference, and power.* Boston: Basic Books.

Middleton, S. (1993). *Educating feminists: Life histories and pedagogy.* New York: Teachers College Press.

Translating Personal Experience into Experiential Essays

Gloria Eive, Fremont, California
E-mail: geive@stmarys-ca.edu

Gloria Eive is a musicologist and instructor at Saint Mary's College in the liberal and civic studies program and the School of Extended Education.

Developmental Intentions

II. Toward a dialogical relationship to oneself.
    1. Addressing fears of losing what is familiar and safe.
III. Toward being a continuous learner.
    8. Seeking authentic feedback from others.
IV. Toward self-agency and self-authorship.
    5. Revising aspects of oneself while maintaining continuity of other aspects.

Context

This activity is used to create an experiential learning portfolio in a course entitled "Personal and Professional Assessment" for undergraduate adult learners.

Description of Activity

Students create a dialogue with the self that will lead to writing an experiential essay implementing the Kolb cycle (Kolb, 1984).

Purpose. To translate personal experience into generalizations or "universal" principles that apply to other similar problems and situations, and to discuss the results of this analysis in an experiential learning essay.

Format-steps-process (advance preparation). Students are familiar with the school's articulated criteria for preparing experiential learning essays, Kolb's learning cycle, and samples of experiential essays. Further, students have practiced analyzing essays or excerpts from them in terms of the learning cycle, and they have completed at least one essay. Students engage in a multitiered process; three of several exercises are presented here.

Elements of Kolb's learning cycle (see Figure 2.1) include the following:

- CE (concrete experience)—the experience itself.
- RO (reflective observation)—the evaluative reflections on the experience that will lead to a broader analysis of the experience and its implications.
- AC (abstract conceptualization)—the insight developed by reflection; the student identifies the "moral" or universal principle in this experience (CE + RO) that can be applied, constructively, to other similar experiences or problems.
- AE (active experimentation)—I interpret this as *applied experience,* meaning that the student identifies other situations (actual or potential) in which the insight developed in conceptualizing the experience can be applied to solving other, similar problems.

For purposes of this exercise, students should be able to *identify* situations in which the insights they have gained may be applied, even if they have not actually had an opportunity to test these insights.

Exercise A: Personal Kolb Cycle Game. The object is to analyze a personal experience to identify its component parts and derive, through abstraction, a moral or universal principle.

1. With a completed essay (and blank three-by-five cards provided by the instructor), each student selects one subtopic that she has fully developed and discussed in her essay (individual activity).
2. Each student identifies elements of the Kolb learning cycle in that section of her essay (individual activity).
3. Each student writes a summary on the blank index cards of each of the Kolb elements as reflected in her essay, using a different card for each element of the cycle (individual activity).
4. In dyads or triads (formed by the instructor to bring together students writing on similar topics), students report on their self-analyses, discussing the

necessary modifications and corrections revealed from designating the elements of the learning cycle.

5. As a follow-up homework assignment, students evaluate their essays according to the model established in class, and revise it as necessary via the following process: They prepare a set of Kolb cards for each subtopic of the essay to create an outline for the essay and determine the sequence of their discussion. *Clue:* Students often find that although they may have a rich description of the experience (CE—concrete experience, RO—reflective observation), they have failed to include a universal (AC—abstract conceptualization) or to elaborate on it sufficiently.

Exercise B: Let's Pretend. The objective is to understand one's own experiences in terms of universal principles and general sociocultural practices.

1. Each student selects a subtopic or a passage in her essay that she has found difficult to relate to the larger context of the subject she is writing about (individual activity).

2. One at a time, a few (three or so) students volunteer to read their own problematic passage aloud to the group and to articulate the difficulties they have encountered.

3. I make a point of modeling an example of "Let's Pretend" and invite discussion and participation in assessing the AC component.

4. These "fishbowl" students (the volunteers) then imagine themselves as someone else with different needs and perspectives but who would also need the universals (AC's) implicit in this topic and its applications. For example, a person writing about personal finance from the viewpoint of a young parent might consider the needs of an older adult who is considering retirement, or the needs of a single parent.

5. Upon completion of the demonstrations (steps 2 and 3), all the students move to small groups, where they repeat the process they have seen modeled by the volunteers.

6. Students (still in small groups) spend fifteen minutes working individually to outline the requirements of this imaginary person in managing personal finances, for example, and identify the subtopics that would be discussed from this new perspective.

7. Students (still in small groups) read their old and revised outlines to their classmates and discuss the differences and their implications.

Exercise C: Peer Review. Students bring a completed essay to class with two extra copies.

1. Students group into dyads or triads matched according to subject area.
2. Students exchange papers and read each other's essays aloud (or large portions of the essays if the paper is quite long). (*Note:* The student does not read her own essay; rather she listens as her colleague reads it to her. Readers are encouraged to pause only at the end of a major section or large passage of subtopical discussion. Authors follow the text on their own copies, annotating as necessary.)
3. Discussion of a student's essay is limited to content and focuses on coherence, the author's comprehensive treatment of the subject, the extent to which Kolb's principles are applied, and the standard for such essays as modeled in school materials. Discussion of difficulties in grammatical structure and phrasing is permitted only when the reader cannot understand what the author is trying to convey.

Contributor's Commentary

Students seem to appreciate exercise C almost more than any other exercise during the course. The discussions produced by this reading exchange are usually salient, very lively, and extremely productive in clarifying the author's insights and perspectives on the essay topic.

Reference

Kolb, D. A. (1984). *Experiential learning.* Englewood Cliffs, NJ: Prentice-Hall.

Charting Our Inner Courses: Developing Students' Edu-Autobiographies

Christine Nevada Michael, Brattleboro, Vermont
E-mail: cnevadam@aol.com

Christine Nevada Michael is the director of the Certificate of Advanced Graduate Study program of Vermont College of Norwich University.

Developmental Intentions

II. Toward a dialogical relationship to oneself.
1. Addressing fears of losing what is familiar and safe.

5. Exploring and making meaning of one's life stories within contexts (for example, societal, familial, universal).
III. Toward being a continuous learner.
   1. Reflecting on one's own and others' experiences as a guide to future behavior.
   3. Recognizing and revealing one's strengths and weaknesses as a learner and knower.
   6. Accepting internal dissonance as part of the learning process.

Context

This activity has been used with undergraduate adult learners over the life of their degree program (eighteen to twenty-four months).

Description of Activity

Beginning with their enrollment and throughout their program, students engage in the process of examining key educational experiences they are undergoing and their affective impact.

Purpose. To stress the relationship between educational and personal development, decrease feelings of isolation that students may experience when going through transitions, share strategies that students feel have assisted them in their growth, encourage multiple ways of expressing personal knowledge, and give students data to use as part of their final self-evaluations required at graduation.

Format-steps-process. Students' edu-autobiography may take the form of a journal, scrapbook, collage, or other medium chosen by each student. Into this "container" students put writings, symbolic objects, artistic depictions, or other means of documenting the developmental issues that they confront during their course of study.

1. It is useful for the mentor to begin the first session by discussing a developmental model or schema or several salient adult developmental issues that commonly attend adults' experiences of beginning any educational journey. In doing so the mentor can introduce concepts that may be useful in encouraging reflection—concepts such as developmental crises as *turning points* or Mezirow's (1990) notion of the *disorienting dilemma*. I have found even more traditional stage models such as Erikson's (1959) to be wonderful jumping-off points for fostering consideration of education as a developmental process. The mentor also may assist students in imagining the various domains in which personal growth and transformation take place. For example, Fowler's work on faith development has

been extremely interesting to students, as many have not thought of the possibility that education may have a spiritual dimension as well.

2. At key points in their program, their mentor may ask questions designed to stimulate thinking about certain aspects of the educational-personal experience. I might ask, for example: "Has there been any time in your program in which you were faced with an educational hurdle that you thought you might not be able to get over?" The student is encouraged to write about the incident in detail (or depict it visually) and describe how he or she overcame the obstacle.

Other types of questions might lead students to describe the forces that motivated their enrollment in the program, depict what it feels like to leave their intense educational residencies and reenter the "real world" of work and family responsibilities, or find metaphors to symbolize their sense of personal and academic growth at different times in their program. Students themselves may wish to generate questions for the sessions and for self-guided activities. Writing activities based loosely on Brookfield's (1990) "critical incident" have been extremely successful.

3. In this program, students and mentors meet every few months. At those times, students may volunteer to share something from these autobiographical projects.

Processing Tips

A valuable role for the mentor is to identify commonalities of experience among students. Similarly, it is important to highlight strategies that learners have used to navigate particularly turbulent waters. For these purposes, developmental literature may prove a rich resource for information and a spark for discussion. For example, students have found research on human resiliency especially helpful in identifying traits, attitudes, and behaviors that characterize *thriving* under difficult circumstances. *Note:* I remain amazed at how frequently adult students express their pleasure in working with different media—particularly crayons and clay.

Contributor's Commentary

This continuous exercise permits students the luxury to examine their ongoing experiences in educational and personal developmental realms. It also suggests some key questions toward accomplishing this examination. In asking such self-directed questions, students probe the developmental issues that they face in their educational and personal worlds, especially when those worlds collide. They may come to appreciate better the heroic nature of the transformation, as well as the risks that they have taken to move forward in their educational journeys. Their own stories and symbols will contain clues to making meaning from their experiences and will point them toward strategies that have helped them conquer personal and academic fears and doubts. As they move toward the end of their program, they will have a complex narrative to study that documents their progress along that continuum of growth. They may also admire some of their own qualities as learners and feel emboldened to see themselves as mentors to others who are novices in the learning process.

References

Brookfield, S. D. (1990b). Using critical incidents to explore learners' assumptions. In J. Mezirow & Associates, *Fostering critical reflection in adulthood: A guide to transformative and emancipatory learning.* San Francisco: Jossey-Bass, pp. 177–193.

Erikson, E. (1959). *Identity and the life cycle.* New York: International Universities Press.

Fowler, J. (1981). *Stages of faith: The psychology of human development and the quest for meaning.* New York: Harper Collins.

Mezirow, J. (1990). *Fostering critical reflection in adulthood: A guide to transformative and emancipatory learning.* San Francisco: Jossey-Bass.

Michael, C., & Young, N. (1999). New traditions of the calling: Progressive practitioner education in Vermont college's graduate program. *CAEL Forum and News, 22* (3), 9–10, 24.

CHAPTER FIVE

COLLABORATING

Collaboration is the heart of the activities included here. "Group work" was an insufficient condition for inclusion; either the exercise is about collaboration, or major attention is paid to the process of collaboration. An example is Gail Feigenbaum's activity on "Structured Cooperative Learning" (p. 83). Activities that extend over more than one session begin with Meg Bishop and Graeme Gibson's "Learning Circles for Informal Adult Education" on page 80.

Rotating Groups: A Discussion Technique

Mark Tennant, Sydney, Australia
E-mail: Mark.Tennant@uts.edu.au

Mark Tennant is a professor of adult education in the faculty of education, University of Technology, Sydney, and has written widely on adult development and learning.

Developmental Intentions

   I. Toward knowing as a dialogical process.
      1. Inquiring into and responding openly to others' ideas.

  II. Toward a dialogical relationship to oneself.
      2. Engaging the disequilibrium when one's ideas and beliefs are challenged.
  III. Toward being a continuous learner.
      1. Reflecting on one's own and others' experiences as a guide to future behavior.
  V. Toward connection with others.
      2. Experiencing oneself as part of something larger.
      4. Contributing one's voice to a collective endeavor.

Context

This activity can be used in workshops, classes, and in almost any setting that would benefit from the exchange of ideas and views.

Description of Activity

Purpose. To engage all participants' views, provide a feedback loop for modification of a group consensus, and locate one's position in relation to a consensus.

    Format-steps-process.

1. I choose a topic for discussion that I expect participants will have the capacity and motivation with which to become involved.
2. I then form groups so that the number of groups is *one more* than the number of people in each group (see Processing Tips).
3. We divide the topic into subtopics—expressed as a question, a problem, or a heading for discussion—and allocate each subtopic to a group.
4. We discuss and agree on a common set of points to make as well as a time frame for the small group discussions and reporting stage.
5. Here is the distinctive part of this process: During the reporting stage, each member of the first group joins one of the other groups and reports their group's findings. The first group then reforms and the second group reports in the same way; each member reports to one of the other groups. The process continues until all groups have reported.
6. Each group reconvenes to consider any changes to their points as a result of feedback during their reporting.
7. The facilitator collates the outcomes, comments on the reports, and supplements where necessary.

Processing Tips

The technique works best in groups of twelve (four times three), twenty (five times four), and thirty (six times five). Any more than five reports becomes a little repetitive. Where the numbers are not easily divisible, ask one or two people to double up and report together. It is important in the reporting stage to ensure that all groups stop and start at the same time; this requires careful monitoring and timing.

Contributor's Commentary

This process can incorporate many developmental intentions, depending on the particular task set. Every person in a group has the responsibility for reporting, but it is done in the relative safety of a small group. This strategy offers a broader participation than the normal group work followed by a plenary format, and it takes no more time. This participation is important for group identity and especially when it involves group decision making. The nature of the outcomes will depend on the nature of the material being discussed.

The technique can be used to pool experiences, generate new ideas, clarify issues or questions, plan activities, or reach a consensus or decision on some matter.

References

Tennant, M. (1997). *Psychology and adult learning* (2nd ed.). London: Routledge.
Tennant, M., & Pogson, P. (1995). *Learning and change in the adult years.* San Francisco: Jossey-Bass.

Learning Circles for Informal Adult Education

Meg Bishop and Graeme Gibson, Downer Australian Capital Territory, Australia
E-mail: gandmee@dynamite.com.au

Meg Bishop and Graeme Gibson are the directors of Real Options International, an adult and community education consultancy.

Developmental Intentions

    I. Toward knowing as a dialogical process.
       2. Surfacing and questioning assumptions underlying beliefs, ideas, actions, and positions.
       4. Using one's experience to critique expert opinion and expert opinion to critique one's experience.

V. Toward connection with others.
 4. Contributing one's voice to a collective endeavor.
 5. Recognizing that collective awareness and thinking transform
 the sum of their parts.

Context

Much of the work is based on the development of learning circles for informal adult education in Australia. For example, the "Aboriginal Reconciliation Kit" is a learning circle kit that has been used by more than three thousand groups since its release in 1993. Learning circles are more traditionally known as study circles.

Description of Activity

Purpose. To exchange information and beliefs; attend to how people learn; consider bringing about change; and discuss, learn about, and consider action on an issue of concern.

Format-steps-process. The length and frequency of meetings will be chosen and agreed to by the group members; typically groups meet weekly for two hours. The group may meet at a workplace, someone's home, a community meeting room, or other convenient place.

Discussion for each meeting is centered around concise information and is facilitated by a group leader whose role is to assist in lively but focused discussion. The leader is not expected to be a teacher or subject expert.

Materials. Good quality, authoritative resource materials give confidence to members where matters of fact are concerned, and can give structure and direction to the discussion process. In some cases a specially prepared kit may be provided by sponsoring organizations. In other cases, a group may prepare their own resource material. This can be done simply and without a great deal of expense. Care is taken to ensure that different points of view are presented in the material.

A learning circle kit is not a text, as such, but rather a guide or resource at the disposal of the group. That is, the group's purpose is not simply to follow and absorb the kit or resource material, but to engage with it and one another, thus bringing to the circle the "text" of each person's experience and ideas. Learning-circle resources often focus on print material, but there are obvious advantages to including video, audio, and graphic support material when it is available.

A useful metaphor for a learning circle is a tourist map that leads people on a journey. Along the way there are lots of interesting and challenging things to explore or places to visit. But if the group has been there before or feels something will not be of interest, they can continue on. The group may also wish at times to backtrack to revisit an issue that has become more interesting as the trip has progressed.

Contributors' Commentary

Learning circles are based soundly on adult learning principles, including action learning and critical reflection. They are socially and educationally reinforcing (learner-friendly) in using and valuing the learners' existing knowledge and experience and providing a forum where people feel OK about what they don't know. Learning circles take a holistic approach; problems or issues are placed in a broad social, economic, and political context. Learning circles are intended to have action outcomes that are not prescribed; a range of possibilities is presented for a group to consider and decide upon.

Much of what we know about learning circles is anecdotal, and feedback from different programs varies in format. However, we can make some statements about specific programs with which we have been involved. As previously noted, the "Aboriginal Reconciliation Kit" has been used by more than three thousand groups since its release in 1993. A random snapshot analysis of group evaluation forms revealed that the majority of participants had taken some action as a result of the learning circle. For around three-quarters of the participants, the action was making contact for the first time in their lives with an Aboriginal or Torres Strait Islander person or organization. Other actions included speaking out knowledgeably and more confidently against racism, challenging stereotypes, and writing letters and lobbying the media and politicians. Around 96 percent of the groups were interested in using this approach to learning about other issues.

Some people are uncomfortable with the learning circle, at least initially; but once they become accustomed to the process, it works and people enjoy it. The kind of facilitation is particularly important; it must invite everyone's opinions and ideas and also encourage participants to use the kit and resources. Learning circles do not work easily with people who expect an authoritarian, didactic style of learning and are unable to cope with a different process. People with literacy problems may have difficulty; although learning circles may be supplemented by graphic resource material and video and audiotapes, the process relies to a large extent on the written word. A single learning circle isn't likely to change deeply held opinions and attitudes any more than one trip to the gym will convince us of the benefits of regular exercise. But those who have been through a number of learning circles say that they start reading or listening to the news more and in a different way, looking for options and their consequences. They also report that they are more confident in talking about and understanding complex issues.

Other applications of this exercise could include work teams.

Structured Cooperative Learning

Gail Feigenbaum, Albuquerque, New Mexico
E-mail: feigport@wans.net

Gail Feigenbaum is a self-employed adult learning and cooperative learning facilitator and consultant who prepares cooperative learning-based workshops for professional conferences, such as New Ways of Learning and Leading in the Classroom, Workplace, and Community.

Developmental Intentions

    I. Toward knowing as a dialogical process.
       7. Associating truth not with static fact but with contexts and relationships.
       9. Perceiving and constructing one's reality by observing and participating.
   IV. Toward self-agency and self-authorship.
       7. "Naming and claiming" what one has experienced and knows.
    V. Toward connection with others.
       2. Experiencing oneself as part of something larger.
       5. Recognizing that collective awareness and thinking transform the sum of their parts.

Context

The activity can be used in courses or workshops for adult learners in corporate and academic settings.

Description of Activity

The activity highlighted here is the *jigsaw*, a form of cooperative learning best used when learners are more fluent in the topic or discipline and have more confidence in the process, and when the instructor is more experienced with the cooperative-learning construct.

Purpose. To help learners become more fluent in the language of a particular discipline or topic as they gain more comfort in the cooperative-learning process, enable learners to see individual ideas as part of a larger picture, and empower individuals with more responsibility and control in the activities.

Format-steps-process.

1. Learners form groups in a particular manner (that is, I might group learners by interest, at random, or by similar or diverse professional positions). Once in these *home groups,* learners each take a number.
2. People with identical numbers form new *expert groups* (for example, all fives form a cluster).
3. I assign each expert group a different topic related to a central, typically inter-disciplinary, theme. I give each group a particular task to complete within a time limit; the task might be brainstorming reactions to a scenario, understanding a particular topic, or determining the essential elements of a certain concept.
4. At the appointed time, the expert groups disband and members return to their home groups. Each person in turn shares his or her expertise with the home group. Again, I designate a time frame for this portion of the activity.
5. I then invite the home groups to engage in group processing, whereby they reflect on reactions to the activity completed or to individual and group functioning or respond to additional questions posed by the instructor.
6. In a closure session, all groups come together as an entire community. Various group insights are shared; I might clarify or insert relevant ideas that did not surface or help learners synthesize the knowledge gained and conclusions drawn.
7. *Optional:* The session might be extended in various ways; for example, by asking for papers on individual or group reactions, a reflective journal entry, or a one-minute paper on "what stood out for me" or "one issue that is still unclear."

Processing Tips

Although I always provide task directions and remain an active, supportive resource person throughout the exercise, I refrain from offering learners many details about task goals initially. Instead, I assist learners in synthesizing insights, drawing conclusions, and making theoretical connections. This is done after the tasks are completed, thus providing the opportunity for learners to construct knowledge that is not merely parroting of my own perspective. Finally, I always give them some opportunity to connect the cooperative learning to their personal or professional contexts.

Contributor's Commentary

The jigsaw encourages a dynamic, connected way of knowing that grows out of and synthesizes individual perceptions. Learners see beyond bits and fragments—beyond a solitary, isolated self. One especially salient aspect of the activity is the vision of facts, disciplines, and people as being interlinked. This systems vision is the groundwork for developing portable skills that transcend diversity and offer a framework for lifelong learning.

Other Applications

Cooperative learning is adaptable to many organizational constraints, diverse learner backgrounds and characteristics, various teaching and managing philosophies, and open-ended and more fixed topics.

Cooperative learning is also a useful framework for facilitating committee and staff meetings, trouble-shooting interpersonal conflicts, and building community in diverse settings. The jigsaw is a process used by many practitioners and is thus well known in cooperative and collaborative learning circles. The original development of the jigsaw can be credited to a primary school application (see citation); however, there are many modifications to the process, as practitioners tend to adapt the jigsaw to their own settings. Many use the process in adult and postsecondary settings as well.

Reference

Aronson, E., Blaney, N., Stephin, C., Sikes, J., & Snapp, M. (1978). *The jigsaw classroom.* Beverly Hills: Sage.

Cooperative Inquiry

Peter Reason, Bath, England
E-mail: P.W.Reason@bath.ac.uk

Peter Reason is Reader in Organizational Behavior and director of the Centre for Action Research in Professional Practice, Director of the Postgraduate Programme in Action Research, and core staff member for the master of science in responsibility and business practice at the University of Bath. He has written widely on inquiry and action research.

Developmental Intentions

   I. Toward knowing as a dialogical process.
      9. Perceiving and constructing one's reality by observing and participating.
  III. Toward being a continuous learner.
      7. Setting one's own learning goals, being goal-directed, and being habitual in learning.
  IV. Toward self-agency and self-authorship.
      1. Constructing a values system that informs one's behavior.
      3. Risking action on behalf of one's beliefs and commitments.
   V. Toward connection with others.
      5. Recognizing that collective awareness and thinking transform the sum of their parts.

Context

Cooperative inquiry is a way of working with other people who have similar concerns and interests; for example, a patient's group, a women's or minority person's group, a professional interest group. Groups of up to twelve members can work well; groups of under six are usually too small. A cooperative inquiry often engages in some six to ten cycles of action and reflection. These can take place over a short workshop or may extend over a year or more, depending on the kind of questions that are being explored.

Description of Activity

Purpose. To engage in research as co-researchers and cosubjects; understand one's world, make sense of one's life, and develop new and creative ways of looking at things; and learn how to act to change things one may want to change and find out how to do things better.

Format-steps-process. There are four phases, each of which has several steps:

Phase one: The co-researchers explore an agreed upon area of activity by talking about their interests and concerns, formulating an initial focus for their inquiry, and developing together a set of questions or propositions they wish to explore. They also agree to undertake some action or practice that will contribute to this exploration and agree to a set of procedures by which they will observe and record their own and each other's experience. *Example:* a group of health workers in southwest England formed an inquiry group to explore the stresses of their work. They decided to explore the stress that comes from the "hidden agendas" in their work, such as depression, child abuse, and drug taking in the families they visit.

Phase two: The group applies some agreed upon actions to their everyday life and work: They initiate actions and observe and record the outcomes of their own and each other's behavior. They may at first simply watch what happens to them so they develop a better understanding of their experience; later they may start trying out new forms of action. *Example:* The health workers first explored among themselves their feelings about these "hidden agendas" and how they managed them at present. They then decided to experiment with confronting them. They practiced the skills they thought they would need through role play and then agreed to try raising their concerns directly with their client families.

Phase three: This phase is, in some ways, the touchstone of the inquiry method. The co-researchers become fully immersed in their experience. They may become more open, may see their experience in new ways, may go deeper into the experience and elaborate new understandings, or they may be led away from the original ideas and proposals into new fields, unpredicted action, and creative insights. It is also possible that they may get so involved in what they are doing that they lose awareness of being part of an inquiry group: they may encounter a practical crisis, they may become enthralled, they may simply forget. *Example:* The health workers' experience of trying out new ways of working with clients was both terrifying and liberating in ways none of them had expected. They felt they were really doing their job; they were concerned about the depth of the problems they would uncover and whether they had adequate skills to cope with them. They found they had to keep in contact with each other to provide support and reassurance as they tried out new behaviors.

Phase four: After an agreed period engaged in phases two and three, the co-researchers reassemble to consider their original questions in light of their experience. They may change their questions in some way, or they may reject them and pose new questions. They then agree on a second cycle of action and reflection. They may choose to focus on the same or on different aspects of the overall inquiry and to amend or develop its inquiry procedures. *Example:* The health workers came back together and shared their experience, helping each other understand what had taken place and developing their strategies and skills at confronting hidden agendas. After several cycles they reflected on what they had learned and wrote a report that they circulated to their managers and colleagues.

Some Practical Issues

Contracting: This may be the most important part of establishing a group. It is necessary to define the inquiry agenda and establish what the group process will be. Early discussions should explore the initiating research interests and introduce the process of cooperative inquiry. This might include paired discussions followed by questions and answers as a group, a decision by each person to participate (or not), and identification of dates, times, and financial and other commitments.

Roles: There are several roles that individuals may fill or the group may agree to rotate among them: group facilitation, inquiry facilitation, management of differences, working with distress.

Ground rules: These can be far-reaching, but issues such as equality of contribution and preservation of confidence are typical areas needing to be addressed.

Writing: Who is the audience for the research? If a written report is to be created, it is worth determining early who will write it. Do all members of the group have to see and agree to what is written? Is it acceptable for individuals in the group to write from their own perspective? One approach is to adopt the rule that anyone can write whatever she or he wants to about the group as long it is clearly stated who the author is and whether the group members have seen and approved the text.

Contributor's Commentary

Good research is research *with* people rather than *on* people. Ordinary people are quite capable of developing their own ideas and working together in a cooperative inquiry group to see whether these ideas can make sense of their world and work in practice. The outcome of good research is not just books and academic papers, but is also the creative action of people to address matters that are important to them. Cooperative inquiry is thus a form of what is called *action research:* It is concerned with revisioning our understanding of our world, as well as transforming practice within it.

In cooperative inquiry a group of people come together to explore issues of concern and interest. All members of the group contribute to the ideas that go into their work together and are also part of the activity that is being researched. Everyone has a say in deciding what questions are to be addressed and what ideas may be of help; everyone contributes to thinking about how to explore the questions; everyone gets involved in the activity that is being researched; and finally, everybody has a say in whatever conclusions the cooperative inquiry group may reach. In cooperative inquiry the split between "researcher" and "subjects" is done away with, and all those involved act together as co-researchers and as cosubjects.

References

Reason, P. (1988). *Human inquiry in action.* Thousand Oaks, CA: Sage.

Reason, P. (1995). *Participation in human inquiry.* Thousand Oaks, CA: Sage.

Reason, P., & Rowan, J. (1981). *Human inquiry.* Chicester, U.K.: Wiley.

CHAPTER SIX

EXPERIMENTING

I n this strategy, the subject to be learned is approached by trial and error. The focus is on the reiterative process of observation, hypotheses, and testing the outcomes with the new information gained. Morris Fiddler's "DNA Modeling," this page, is a single-occasion activity. Chris Chiaverina's "Exploratories in Physics," page 93, extends over more than one session.

◆ ◆ ◆

DNA Modeling

Morris Fiddler, Chicago, Illinois
E-mail: mfiddler@wppost.depaul.edu

Morris Fiddler is a faculty mentor to undergraduate and graduate students pursuing individualized programs at the intersections of liberal learning and professional development in the School for New Learning, DePaul University. He also works with graduate students in genetic counseling at Northwestern University Medical School.

Developmental Intentions

I. Toward knowing as a dialogical process.

8. Pursuing the possibility of objective truth.
III. Toward being a continuous learner.
9. Drawing on multiple capacities for effective learning.
V. Toward connection with others.
4. Contributing one's voice to a collective endeavor.

Context

This activity has been used in an undergraduate course for adult learners that engages students in exploring emerging genetic information and some social and personal implications and issues that accompany it.

Description of Activity

Purpose. To visualize the invisible and experience the social nature of science.

Format-steps-process.

1. Within the first two hours of the first meeting of the class, I present all the data (in lay terminology) that Watson and Crick had available to them when they proposed a structure for the DNA.

2. Then I ask students, working in groups of three to five for about twenty minutes, to reconcile the data and come up with a model of DNA. I provide them with markers and flip-chart paper, ball-and-stick "toys" for modeling chemical structures, and humorous encouragement to imagine the possibilities.

3. Each group reports on its proposed structure of DNA (and I make reference to the Watson-Crick model for the entire class as it begins to take shape from one or more of the groups; however, the details of the Watson-Crick are a subject for later sessions). Note: Even though the students are newcomers to this topic, the DNA models and proposals that emerge consistently replicate the different versions that were being discussed and debated in the late 1940s and early 1950s.

4. I then turn the groups' attention to the process of how each group came to decide on their model.

5. We make reference to the discarded models and their shortcomings periodically in the ensuing weeks as students learn more details of how DNA and genes seem to function.

Processing Tips

Because there are two agendas here—model building and group interactions—I find that weaving them together makes more lasting sense to the students than attending to one and then the other. When focusing on the group process, I tend to raise questions such as, "Did an 'expert' surface within the group? How did individuals experience and then negotiate the various media they were working with and their unsolicited immersion in unfamiliar territory? Did discussion about taking individual or group credit for the ideas enter into the post-activity conversations?" These and other issues become points of reference for discussing perceptions of how "scientists" go about their business.

To help the model building, I tend to serve as the memory for the "data" as I wander among the groups pointing out details they may not notice. Saying little, however, is my overall approach.

Contributor's Commentary

This process of model building and reconciliation of data with the groups' generalizations is used repeatedly as students encounter other questions, including those for which consensus in the literature has not been reached. It is a constructivist approach: introduce the idea, reconcile data and observations through model building, then return to the models to determine whether the models can assimilate additional observations and data. I raise questions regarding whether perhaps there is a "truth" to be recognized and pursued through an interactive and tentative process. The nature of models and metaphors as visualizations of reality become a topic for discussion.

This process of using phenomena and data that have been previously interpreted by others can be tricky because it appears to imply that there is eventually a "right" answer, even though the process is supposedly constructivist. Including and revisiting lesser-confirmed models keeps the pursuit more open and less dependent on the instructor (or currently accepted theory) for validation of the outcome. We can still keep open the question of an eventual truth as a continued motivator for continued inquiry and experimentation.

The model-building efforts are supposed to involve all members of the small groups. However, this rarely happens, especially at first, since few students are willing to express their ideas and risk being wrong. I therefore use this exercise as a jumping-off point for an assessment of the "collectiveness" of the effort and a look at how the scientific community functions in collaboration, competition, and the pursuit of curiosities and ideas.

The use of drawings, ball-and-stick chemical models, and other alternatives to auditory exchanges seem to work for those who are more comfortable with the kinesthetic or visual "intelligences." These alternatives also give others a chance to draw on and develop these capacities for learning.

Exploratories in Physics

Chris Chiaverina, Winnetka, Illinois
E-mail: Fizzforfun@aol.com

Chris Chiaverina has taught physics for thirty years and employs interactive exhibits to demonstrate interdisciplinary linkages.

Developmental Intentions

    I. Toward knowing as a dialogical process.
        8. Pursuing the possibility of objective truth.
        9. Perceiving and constructing one's reality by observing and participating.
    II. Toward a dialogical relationship to oneself.
        3. Exploring life's experiences through some framework(s) of analysis.
    III. Toward being a continuous learner.
        5. Posing and pursuing questions out of wonderment.
    V. Toward connection with others.
        5. Recognizing that collective awareness and thinking transform
           the sum of their parts.

Context

The activity is used in an undergraduate course, "An Interactive Introduction to Physics," for adult learners.

Description of Activity

Purpose. To help adult students who probably will not become scientists benefit from a knowledge of physics in this increasingly technological world and to understand and apply basic physical principles.

Format-steps-process. Many view the discipline of physics as an exercise in memorizing arcane theories and manipulating equations rather than a dynamic process capable of providing humankind with an ever deeper understanding of the physical universe. As a teacher of physics, I attempt to alter this perception.

The learning cycle approach is used to maximize student involvement in the study of physics. This application to physics was developed by California physics professor Robert Karplus. This pedagogy puts the phenomenon first; each major topic (for example, forces, energy, optics, waves, electrical circuits) begins with an exploratory activity. During this "exploratory," students perform a number of experiments that they may not be able to explain with their current knowledge.

1. The exploratory activities provide a smorgasbord of interactive physics experiences relating to a single topic. For example, our unit on optics illustrates how we employ the learning cycle to help our students proceed from the concrete to the abstract. The unit begins with a "light smorgasbord," a collection of stations that feature manipulatives relating to optics. A variety of hands-on materials invite students to explore color, reflection, refraction, diffraction, interference, polarization, sources of light, and various optical instruments. The activities may be done in any order. Student-size kaleidoscopes, large concave reflectors, phosphorescent screens, colored spotlights, visual illusions, and a giant soap film apparatus are a few of the props that allow students to have an enjoyable, nonthreatening introductory experience with optics. Included at the different stations are suggestions for using the manipulatives and thought-provoking questions to guide exploration.

Whenever possible, I include discrepant events in the exploratories to force students to question their existing beliefs regarding the physical world.

2. I engage students in class discussion only after hands-on exposure to the phenomena. At this stage of the cycle, I draw on the students' experiences and questions to introduce pertinent concepts and terminology relating to phenomena encountered in the exploratory. One component of the discussion phase is large-scale demonstrations dubbed "people demos." These demonstrations use students themselves as the apparatus of the physical system, thus offering an opportunity for kinesthetic learning.

3. During the application stage of the learning cycle, students return to the laboratory where they engage in real-life applications of their newly acquired knowledge. However, this time the laboratory activities may take place in some rather unorthodox venues. Students may push cars with bathroom scales in a parking lot to quantitatively examine Newton's Second Law of Motion, experience an acoustical interference pattern in an auditorium, or travel to an amusement park to experience the law of conservation of energy, centripetal force, weightlessness, frictional forces, and many more physical principles operating on a grand scale. During this final stage of the cycle, unexplained phenomena may arise, thus initiating a new learning cycle.

Processing Tips

Based on the belief that mathematics is the concise language rather than the substance of physics, I use graphical techniques whenever possible to obviate the need for the mathematics usually associated with the study of physics.

Contributor's Commentary

"Students have to have the opportunity to ask, 'what will happen if. . . .' They can't just read. They have to have props to see, handle, and understand what's happening. Otherwise, teaching science is like teaching swimming but not allowing anyone near the water" (Frank Oppenheimer, physicist-educator and founder of San Francisco's Exploratorium).

As students proceed through the optics exploration cycle, they are allowed a closer look at phenomena they have encountered all their lives but perhaps did not understand or were not even aware of. Students begin to construct their own meaning while developing an experiential foundation that will later be mined in subsequent class discussions. During these discussions, I try to ferret out students' misconceptions about light while helping them construct more accurate understandings. Only after they master the underlying physical principles are students presented with mathematical relationships that convey the physics they have witnessed. With these relationships, presented in both algebraic and graphical form, students solve traditional problems relating to mirrors, lenses, interference, and diffraction. Their study of optics concludes with a lesson on holography and an opportunity for them to make holograms. Since holography is current, exciting, and involves virtually every aspect of optics, it provides our students with the perfect culminating activity.

Exploratories are powerful instructional tools for a number of reasons. They provide students with a common experiential foundation. Exploratories have the potential to stimulate interest, nurture curiosity, and mitigate science anxiety. The activities encourage students to work in cooperative groups in which they can learn from each other. Comments and responses to exploratory questions reveal students' misconceptions that may be addressed during a subsequent class discussion. By incorporating common objects (for example, mirrors, household light sources, eyeglass lenses, toys) in exploratory investigations, linkages between physics and everyday life are demonstrated. Finally, through directed exploration, students are given an opportunity to construct their own understanding.

CHAPTER SEVEN

IMAGINING

Imagining involves visioning at a deeper level than reflecting (see Chapter Ten). It might include reexperiencing something that happened earlier (see Karen-Kelly Hicks' "Symbols Circle," p. 102), projecting into the future (see Rebecca Proehl's "Creating a Shared Vision," p. 122), or transforming someone or something through action learning (see Judy O'Neil and Victoria Marsick's "Action Learning," below). Imagining can include projecting into a particular situation, trying really to "be there" and to work with what one finds; for example, see Toby Glicken's "Anzio Effect," p. 100.

◆ ◆ ◆

Action Learning

Judy O'Neil and Victoria Marsick, Warwick, Rhode Island
E-mail: jaoneil@aol.com; vjm5@columbia.edu

Judy O'Neil and Victoria Marsick are principals in Partners for the Learning Organization, which works with organizations to design and implement strategic learning initiatives that build competitive advantage and drive business performance. Victoria Marsick is also a professor of adult and organizational learning and director of adult education graduate programs at Columbia University Teachers College.

Developmental Intentions

    I. Toward knowing as a dialogical process.
        2. Surfacing and questioning assumptions underlying beliefs, ideas, actions, and positions.
   III. Toward being a continuous learner.
        1. Reflecting on one's own and others' experiences as a guide to future behavior.
        6. Accepting internal dissonance as part of the learning process.
        7. Setting one's own learning goals, being goal-directed, and being habitual in learning.
        8. Seeking authentic feedback from others.

Context

Action learning is an intervention process that promotes development, change, and transformation in individuals, groups or teams, and organizations. It can be used in organizational, academic, and societal settings.

Description of Activity

Purpose. To promote development, change, and transformation in individuals, teams, and organizations; help individuals learn how to learn; and solve real problems for which there is no obvious solution.

Format-steps-process. The action learning process is not a packaged program of predetermined methods, steps, or ideas (Marsick, Cederholm, Turner, & Pearson, 1992). The key elements in the process are working in a small group and working on a real problem. A learning coach works with the group to help them learn how to learn from their work without compromising the work itself (O'Neil, 1999). Action needs to be taken on the problem, followed by reflection on that action. Each application of action learning is designed differently based on the needs of the participants and organization.

There are some specific considerations involved in the design stage (O'Neil & Dilworth, 1999).

- Should the problems worked on be familiar or unfamiliar?
- Should problems be group or individual problems?

- How will participants be chosen?
- If the process takes place in an organization, should it be in a familiar or an unfamiliar setting?
- How much time will the participants or the organization be willing to invest in the initiative?
- Will content learning be provided, and if so, what and how?

The following examples demonstrate some of the potential developmental outcomes:

Example 1. In designing a program in which teams worked on an unfamiliar group problem, but within their own familiar organization, participants were invited to join the team and could decline if not interested. The teams met one day a month over the course of four to six months. Individual and team development exercises were a part of the design. One of these teams faced a problem of improving employee satisfaction. They began by looking at extrinsic rewards. They examined these in light of their Total Quality culture and realized that *meaningful work* might be a stronger motivator. Further help from the learning coach with problem posing led them not only to recognize that respect was part of meaningful work but that the typical interruptions at work demanding immediate information and attention demonstrated lack of respect (O'Neil & Marsick, 1994). In this group's work, *inquiring into one another's ideas, surfacing and examining assumptions,* and *reframing the problem* served to create a dialogical process.

Example 2. An organization designed a program to help one of their departments learn how to be successful in the new competitive environment that was quickly replacing their former regulated, hierarchical world. The objectives established for the program were

- Enhance the way people communicate and interact with one another.
- Weave quality tools and behaviors into the fabric of the organization.
- Develop and use problem solving and coaching skills.
- Develop an environment of openness and trust and get conflict out on the table.

Each session averaged twenty-eight participants formed into four teams. Participants were chosen to be on teams. The teams addressed team projects sponsored by senior leaders in the organization. Each team met for a minimum of six and one-half days over a six-week period with a learning coach and additional days on their own. Content learning included processes for experiential learning and critical reflection.

Two sponsors assigned a problem to a group to merge two departments. The group—comprising representatives from both departments—began their data gathering to determine the most effective way to bring the merger about. The group found very quickly that they were unable to accomplish even the smallest step toward their goal without conflict. Their learning coach suggested they examine the cause of their conflict before proceeding. Through their reflections as individuals, and as the group, they realized their conflict was deeply rooted in past issues between the departments. This recognition led them to reframe their problem to deal first with these past issues before any movement toward a merger could take place. Said one participant, "I have gained insight into my resistance. I realize I have a fear of not being needed anymore if control of the process is taken away from my department." These participants demonstrated movement toward *being continuous learners* through their ability to *reflect as a guide to their future behavior* and their *acceptance of the resultant internal dissonance.*

Example 3. From participants in another group in the same program, "One of my teammates asked me a question about my personal learning goal that made me rethink the action I was taking. I'd never thought about it from that perspective." "Learning is ongoing, it never ends. I've learned how to learn." These participants are moving toward being continuous learners through setting their own learning goals, seeking feedback, reflecting on their own behavior, accepting the resultant internal dissonance, and explicitly recognizing the importance of ongoing learning.

Processing Tips

It is important to involve the organization and participants in the design of any action learning process. Particularly in the critical reflection practice, the changes and transformation in individuals can result in significant "noise" in the organization. Being a part of the design is one way to help leaders in the organization prepare for the potential challenges to the organizational norms.

Contributors' Commentary

Action learning is an approach to working with and developing people that uses work on a real project or problem as the way to learn. It is a nonexpert-based developmental process that is based instead in the idea that the best way to learn is through real work with one's peers.

Action learning is practiced differently depending on how various practitioners view the learning that occurs. O'Neil (1999) categorizes the practice of action learning into four schools—scientific, experiential, critical reflection, and tacit. We advocate critical reflection in our practice. Mezirow (1990) defines critical reflection as "the process of learning through critical self-reflection, which results in the re-formulation of a meaning perspective to allow a more inclusive, discriminating, and integrative understanding of one's experience. Learning includes acting on these insights" (p. xvi).

The role of the learning coach is important in helping participants learn the skills of learning how to learn from real work and in helping participants learn how to learn from one another. It is crucial, however, that learning coaches not end up being considered "expert" but instead work toward transferring their skills to participants, thereby intentionally making themselves redundant.

References

Marsick, V. J., Cederholm, L., Turner, E., & Pearson, T. (1992). Action-reflection learning. *Training and Development, 46*(8), 63–66.

Mezirow, J. (Ed.) (1990). *Fostering critical reflection in adulthood.* San Francisco: Jossey-Bass.

O'Neil, J. A. (1999). *The role of the learning advisor in action learning.* Unpublished doctoral dissertation, Teachers College, Columbia University, New York.

O'Neil, J., & Dilworth, L. (1999). Issues in the design and implementation of an action learning initiative. In L. Yorks, J. O'Neil, and V. J. Marsick (Eds.), *Management development and organizational learning through action learning* (pp. 41–70). San Francisco: Berrett-Koehler.

O'Neil, J., & Marsick, V. J. (1994). Becoming critically reflective through action reflection learning. In A. Brooks & K. Watkins (Eds.), *The emerging power of action inquiry technologies* (pp. 17–30). New Directions for Adult and Continuing Education, No. 63. San Francisco: Jossey-Bass.

The Anzio Effect

Toby Glicken, Chicago, Illinois
E-mail:tglicken@condor.depaul.edu

Toby Glicken is currently developing and teaching life science courses for non-science majors at the School for New Learning of DePaul University.

Develpmental Intentions

    I. Toward knowing as a dialogical process.

        3. Reframing ideas or values that seem contradictory, embracing their differences, and arriving at new meanings.

9. Perceiving and constructing one's reality by observing and participating.
II. Toward a dialogical relationship to oneself.
3. Exploring life's experiences through some framework(s) of analysis.
5. Exploring and making meaning of one's life stories within contexts (for example, societal, familial, universal).
III. Toward being a continuous learner.
1. Reflecting on one's own and others' experiences as a guide to future behavior.

Context

This strategy promotes an integration of concepts from biology and psychology as part of a course entitled "The Senses: Our Links to the Environment." This exercise examines biological and psychological factors that contribute to the perception of pain and uses the concept of *mood, meaning, and morale—the Three M's* as a framework.

Description of Activity

Purpose. To develop an understanding of the complex integration of biology and psychology in the perception of and response to pain; and to use an understanding of the perception of pain to analyze one's own reactions to pain, past and future, and to better understand reactions of others to pain.

Format-steps-process.

1. I introduce "The Anzio Effect" (named for the infamous World War II battle fought in Anzio, Italy), which attempts to explain why American soldiers hospitalized with wounds inflicted during that battle required much less morphine to relieve their pain than did civilians back home in hospitals recovering from physically similar (or less severe) surgical wounds.
2. Before the class breaks up into groups of four to six people for discussion, I give them the following instructions: "Drawing on your own experience (or your imagination), describe two pain events that share a similar biology (similar stimulus, similar neural pathway, similar area on the cortex that receives the pain message) but have divergent Three M's (mood, morale, and meaning). How do the Three M's differ in each case? How would the total pain perception engendered by these two pain events be expected to differ?"
3. Learners reflect back on pain events from their own lives and examine how the Three M's surrounding an event affected their pain perception and their reaction to that pain. Learners compare and contrast their personal "pain

stories," and create appropriate "complementary" pain events to answer the questions posed.

4. After approximately fifteen minutes, each group, through a spokesperson, reports one to two composite pain stories back to the whole group. Responses have included contrasting the pain following a "nose job" with that of a nose broken in a mugging; contrasting surgical pain following Caesarian section birth versus that following a hysterectomy; contrasting the pain of a sports injury associated with a "win" with a similar injury associated with a "lose."

Contributor's Commentary

The explanation for the Anzio Effect? Total pain perception is dependent on the combination of *pain* and *suffering,* a combination of biological and psychological factors. And the psychological contribution to total pain perception is dependent on the Three M's that are associated with the pain event. (The soldiers were *heroes,* they spilled blood for a *good cause,* they were *alive,* and they were *going home.)*

This is just an example of the more interesting process of asking adult learners to examine together their experiences via a framework to help guide what they pay attention to and interpret. It is most interesting when that framework is not bounded by the limitations of any one discipline or analytic lens.

Symbols Circle

Karen-Kelly Hicks, Weed, New Mexico
E-mail: sevens777@aol.com

Karen-Kelly Hicks, a journalist before becoming a returning adult learner, has since been a college educator. She facilitates workshops focused on women's growth and development.

Developmental Intentions

   I. Toward knowing as a dialogical process.
      9. Perceiving and constructing one's reality by observing and participating.
  II. Toward a dialogical relationship to oneself.
      3. Exploring life's experiences through some frameworks of analysis.
 III. Toward being a continuous learner.
      8. Seeking authentic feedback from others.
 IV. Toward self-agency and self-authorship.

6. Distinguishing what one has created for oneself from what is imposed by social, cultural, and other forces.
7. "Naming and claiming" what one has experienced and knows.

Context

This exercise has been used in small group workshops focused on self-expression, growth, and understanding.

Description of Activity

Purpose. To help individuals define, own, name, and claim their own experience; and to challenge the larger worldview while shoring up their own, particularly if it's marginal or unsupported by the larger community.

Format-steps-process.

1. Prior to the event, I ask each participant to identify something tangible that she associates with some part of herself, and then to bring to the group a representative object, picture, poem, or other token to share.
2. Sitting as part of the group in a circle, each person introduces herself in turn by displaying her chosen object, describing it (perhaps reading the poem, and so on) and then describing how she identifies with it.
3. After each person speaks individually, she is asked to contribute her item to a common display—for example, central altar, display case, or wall space—for collective presentation.
4. Then each woman is asked whether there is anything she would wish to add, change, or expand upon, now that she sees her own representation presented as part of a collective grouping. Each person shares this with the group by again going around the circle, one by one.
5. However, during this part of the dialogue, each other woman is invited to provide feedback to the presenter. They may wish to comment on their associations with what the woman has said (perhaps a parallel experience), how she has likened the object to herself, or any other observations. So the process is that as each woman speaks about her object the second time, others comment, if they wish.

Processing Tips

This kind of self-disclosure requires a deep sense of safety that depends on everyone's commitment to maintain personal privacy within the group in attendance. Participants also need to feel that they can be open and "received" in this type of group process—the kind of "listening" that Nelle Morton has named "hearing into speech."

Another way to frame people's self-description, rather than using physical objects, is for participants to name archetypes, such as characters from literature or popular culture, with whom they identify. Then they are asked to make up a *self-archetype* based on things they know about themselves or would like to realize. When I use this exercise with women, we use *archetypal associations* to build a similar archetype of *self.* For example, a woman who lives in Weed, New Mexico becomes Weed Woman. Because she just read *Women Who Run With the Wolves,* and studies feminist theology, she becomes Wild Weed Woman; because she writes, she becomes WiWeWriWoman, and she builds upon that.

One can then have learners shift into imagining what this archetype might look like—to create an image of Wild Weed Woman. This phase of the process works best when combined with some kind of art or movement—ideally both—interspersed with the verbal activities.

Contributor's Commentary

Talking "who you are" through symbols feels safer to many people than beginning simply with words; people are less likely to censor what they say about themselves. In addition, even after the exercise, participants will go on to process more about themselves as they reflect on the feedback they received from others. Furthermore, once they identify with the more expanded and creative view of themselves developed in the self-archetype, they often find further reflections, associations, and imagery that speaks to the ways they present themselves in the world. For example, they may see ways in which they might be limiting themselves. Also, by naming these characteristics they might be able to tap into them more effectively. Once these strengths are identified and symbolized, it may be easier to emphasize these qualities while more clearly identifying aspects of themselves that they now wish to make less prominent. However, this is different from self-deprecation based on formerly internalized and largely unconscious beliefs about themselves. Even qualities considered negative can be examined with better focus, less projection, and a better possibility for correction or change.

Clustering: Moving from the Simple to the Complex

Lanie Melamed, Montreal, Canada
E-mail: melamed@vax2.concordia.ca

Lanie Melamed is retired after twenty-six years of college and university teaching, most recently from Concordia University and the Adult Degree Program at Vermont College.

Developmental Intentions

   I. Toward knowing as a dialogical process.
      3. Reframing ideas or values that seem contradictory, embracing their differences, and arriving at new meanings.
      6. Paying attention to wholes as well as the parts that comprise them.
      7. Associating truth not with static fact but with contexts and relationships.
    10. Tapping into and drawing on tacit knowledge.
  V. Toward connection with others.
      5. Recognizing that collective awareness and thinking transform the sum of their parts.

Context

Clustering is a multipurpose tool that can be used by an individual in the early stages of organizing thoughts for a writing task or by groups involved in problem solving or decision making. It is useful in helping students and citizens' groups understand the multifaceted economic, social, and cultural factors that influence their lives.

Description of Activity

Purpose. To bring to the foreground knowledge that is often buried in the subconscious where past experiences lie; gain skills and enthusiasm for dealing with complexity in lieu of reductionist and compartmentalized thinking; and learn to acknowledge conflicting ideas, experiences, and opinions and to incorporate these into larger contexts and systems.

Format-steps-process. Clustering, also called mind-mapping (or "concept webbing"), is a nonlinear thinking process that helps bypass logical, orderly, left-brain functions toward those of the intuitive, metaphoric, sensory, and imagic. It is also a means of acknowledging the multiplicity of ideas and perspectives found in groups wherever they are.

   1. I suggest that one begin with a key word or the kernel of an idea placed in the center of a circle on a large page of paper. *Example:* For someone interested in exploring diversity in the classroom, a good starting point might be to write

the word *diversity* at the center of the page. An individual can do this on a sheet of notebook paper. For a group, a sheet of flip-chart paper is recommended. More paper may become necessary.

2. In a state of relaxation, the learner gathers ideas that flow into her head (or the heads of group members) from the initial word or concept. Each new word or idea is written in its own circle, and these radiate outward from the original circle in the center. Unlike squares and rectangles, walls and windows that box us in, the circle is a natural, flowing organic shape. As in brainstorming, critical assessment and judgmental comments should be avoided at this stage. More than likely, numerous overlaps and contradictions will become evident as the ideas accumulate.

3. If a new word or phrase seems to be related to one already on the page, they can be grouped together. The more ideas, the merrier, at this point. The circles around related ideas can be linked by lines.

4. When a different spin on the original idea appears it can be placed close to the central nucleus. It, too, may develop radiating spokes from its core. In this manner themes begin visibly to emerge. During the processing period, entries that are malplaced can be relocated.

5. The mapping process continues until all contributions to the map have been exhausted.

Processing Tips

After a break or at the next class session, students review the map and are encouraged to share their reactions. More than twenty people should probably be divided into smaller subgroups for more fruitful discussion (six to eight is a good number). When using smaller groups, each should be asked to choose a scribe to take notes and a person to report on the group's learning. At the end of the map analysis and review, a writing assignment can tap each individual's learning. This could range from a five-minute writing time to a lengthier assignment. In total, about fifteen minutes should be allotted to creating the visual map and an hour or more to harvesting the learning.

The following questions might be asked to generate discussion and could be included among writing prompts:

- What surprised you most about this exercise? In what way?
- What contributions appeared that you would never have thought of?
- What significant themes emerged as this exercise unfolded?
- Do you feel enlightened or confused as a result of doing the exercise?

- Which ideas don't seem to fit well together, or are outright contradictory?
- Are these ideas really opposing or can we find ways to include them in a broader, more complex statement?
- How can the various themes be synthesized into new ways of making meaning?

Contributor's Commentary

This clustering approach to thinking makes tangible the value-added accumulation of information from multiple sources. Clustering recognizes that it is OK to start writing, planning, or analyzing without first having all the information neatly in place. It requires, however, that participants remain open to the unexpected and to the unexamined. The result is a visual representation of an extensive range of ideas, some clearly compatible, others in need of continued dialogue and analysis. Northrop Frye (1963) suggests that any word can become "a storm center of meanings, sounds, and associations, radiating out indefinitely like ripples in a pool" (p. 28). Gradually the separate or disconnected ideas connect and form patterns of meaning. Clustering helps to propel, deepen, and expand thinking.

Editors' Note: See exercises by Paula Horvath-Neimeyer, p. 170 and Barbara Jaworski, p. 214, this volume, for further examples of concept-webbing.

References

Frye, N. (1963/1993). The educated imagination (p. 28). *Massey Lectures.* Toronto: Canadian Broadcasting Corporation.

Seeing Your Emerging Future

Lois Morton, New York, New York
E-mail: LMorton511@aol.com

Lois Morton is a Gestalt psychotherapist and the former director of lifelong learning at the YWCA of the City of New York.

Developmental Intentions

II. Toward a dialogical relationship to oneself.
1. Addressing fears of losing what is familiar and safe.
2. Engaging the disequilibrium when one's ideas and beliefs are challenged.

4. Questioning critically the validity or worth of one's pursuits.
III. Toward being a continuous learner.
   9. Drawing on multiple capacities for effective learning.
IV. Toward self-agency and self-authorship.
   5. Revising aspects of oneself while maintaining continuity of other aspects.

Context

This activity has been used in short-term psychoeducational workshops.

Description of Activity

Purpose. To expand one's reality by use of a structure to envision interruptions and boundaries more clearly.

Format-steps-process.

1. Although I often play a tape of relaxing music during the following guided imagery exercise, it is not required. In any case, I begin by saying, "I'm going to suggest something; do it if you like, or if you prefer, use this time to relax."
2. Then, speaking more slowly and with pauses, I guide participants by telling them to make themselves comfortable in their seats and, if they'd like, to close their eyes. I continue leading by saying, "See whether you can block out what is around you. If interfering thoughts come along, just let them go by."
3. I ask them to *move inside themselves*. My directions would sound like this: "Now, think—see yourself five years from now. What will you be doing? [Pause] Notice the details. Where are you? [Pause] What are you wearing? [Pause] What is the temperature in the room or wherever it is that you find yourself? [Pause] What do you see around you? Allow yourself to be in that moment. Observe everything that is happening."
4. I also do a variation on the same exercise that begins with the same introduction but has the following guides: "Take a deep breath, relax, and let the imagery come. In your left hand you are holding a Polaroid picture that is completely blank. The picture has not yet emerged, and as you watch it is slowly emerging. It is a picture of you, in your ideal job. Notice the details—notice what you are wearing, where you are. Is anyone with you? What do you see outside the window, if there is a window? Are there any sounds?"

Processing Tips

If the group is small, everyone can share what the exercise was like for them. Alternatively, in a larger group, I have people share with a partner or with two others in groups of three, followed by a description to the larger group.

Contributor's Commentary

Guided imagery or visualization is a strategy adapted from the school of transpersonal education. It helps us bridge the gulf that has long existed between cognitive and affective modes of education and break through the boundary that separates conscious from unconscious knowing.

Self-discovery, the exploration of unconscious beliefs and desires (a key factor in transformational learning), can be facilitated through various types of guided visualization. Participants have the opportunity to become aware of their core beliefs in order to question them critically. The strategy presented here reflects the type of visualization that Naparstek (1994) calls *end state:* visualizing your desired future. This type highlights concrete, short-term goals and is widely used in sports, medicine, career advancement, performance, and neurolinguistic programming.

In my studies of what was possible in personal transformation in short workshops, the role of visualization emerged in unanticipated ways. Half of the people I interviewed who had been in workshops in which the presenter used some form of guided imagery or visualization said that their most significant moment in the workshop took place during a visualization, and many incorporated changes based on these learning experiences. Participants reported gaining insight and a clearer sense of choices open to them. With other types of visualization techniques, people reported that they visualized an image as a metaphoric way of seeing themselves (see Samples, 1976).

References

Naparestek, B. (1994). *Staying well with guided imagery.* New York: Warner.
Samples, R. (1976). *The metaphoric mind: A celebration of creative consciousness.* Reading, MA: Addison Wesley.

Discovering True Perceptions

Lois Morton, New York, New York
E-mail: LMorton511@aol.com

Lois Morton is a Gestalt psychotherapist and former director of life-long learning at the YWCA of the City of New York.

Developmental Intentions

II. Toward a dialogical relationship to oneself.
    4. Questioning critically the validity or worth of one's pursuits.

IV. Toward self-agency and self-authorship.
    2. Accepting responsibility for choices one has made and will make.
    5. Revising aspects of oneself while maintaining continuity of
        other aspects.
    6. Distinguishing what one has created for oneself from what is imposed
        by social, cultural, and other forces.

Context

This exercise has been used in short-term psychoeducational workshops.

Description of Activity

Purpose. To increase awareness of one's perceptions and views of life and to assess what may be "holding one back."

Format-steps-process. I use two visualization techniques to help people experience imagery and to engage in a potentially transforming process built on imagery. The first is designed simply to introduce the concept of imagery.

1. I ask participants to "visualize a container of any kind—glass, pottery, metal, and so on."
2. I pause and then ask each participant to fill it to the level of the satisfaction she feels in her present job, and to have some way of indicating or measuring the relative amount.
3. I then ask participants to describe to the group the type of container each visualized. Each participant will usually have a completely different type of container.
4. I then highlight the range of difference among the·participants (for example, beaker, earthenware pot, snare drum, measuring cup) and we go on to discuss the power of imagination as well as derived words: *image, magic, magi* (wise men), and so on.
5. This can segue into a discussion of right-brain versus left-brain functions—the imaginative and creative right brain versus the logical, analytical, judgmental left brain. We explore that it is possible to have a "dialogue" between the two sides of the brain.

(The imagined level of job satisfaction is not, in itself, important to this introduction to the imaginal process, but it often becomes a serendipitous discovery, or insight, for the participants.)

The second visualization technique involves transformation.

1. It can be done as a visualization with eyes closed, or, alternatively, as a drawing. I take them through in the following manner: "Close your eyes, and feel the emotional reaction when you want to say something, speak up for yourself, and are blocked. Imagine the block. Give it a form, a shape. [Pause] If you lose touch, close your eyes again."
2. I then invite people to talk about their experience. "What was it like to get in touch with that?" People may also wish to write down some of their reactions.
3. I then explain that the imagination is very powerful, creating pictures and images for ourselves all the time. Even dreams are like a set of moving pictures. But in your imagination you can create a different scenario. We explore the question: "How would you change the picture you saw into something else?"
4. I go on by asking them to "think back to the situation, visualize the scene. Now move out of the left brain, the intellectual thinking side, and send awareness into the right brain where we keep emotion, art, creativity, intuition, and laughter."
5. At this point, I ask participants to share and converse about some of the changes they experience. Consistently there is laughter, as well as supportive comments.

Contributor's Commentary

Guided imagery and visualization is a strategy adapted from the school of transpersonal education. It helps us bridge the gulf that has long existed between cognitive and affective modes of education and to break through the boundary that separates conscious from unconscious knowing.

Self-discovery, the exploration of unconscious beliefs and desires (a key factor in transformational learning), can be facilitated through various types of guided visualization. Participants have the opportunity to become aware of their core beliefs in order to question them critically. (See further information about guided imagery, including citations, in "Seeing Your Emerging Future," p. 107.)

Perspective Shift

Susan Munaker, Chicago, Illinois
E-mail: smunaker@mcs.net

As an organizational development consultant, Susan Munaker helps individuals and organizations define and achieve their strategic visions. She works with corporate, educational, nonprofit, and broad-based leadership clients.

Developmental Intentions

    I. Toward knowing as a dialogical process.
       9. Perceiving and constructing one's reality by observing and participating.
   III. Toward being a continuous learner.
       6. Accepting internal dissonance as part of the learning process.
       7. Setting one's own learning goals, being goal-directed, and being habitual in learning.
       9. Drawing on multiple capacities for effective learning.
    V. Toward connection with others.
       4. Contributing one's voice to a collective endeavor.

Context

Two examples are offered that employ a similar process to help shift perspective. The first is used when working with an organizational change problem; the second is used when teaching graduate students about personal change models and processes.

Description of Activity

Purpose. To introduce a strategy for an individual or members of the group to "stand above" or outside both their rational and intuitive selves (that is, engage in metacognition), and to help a learner tap his or her tacit knowledge.

    Format-steps-process (organizational change context). As one example, I worked with a 255-person regional office of a government agency that was seeking help in defining roles and responsibilities. Shortly after the work began, I noticed problems related to a lack of trust among members of the group and an inability to hold efficient meetings. For example, as participants reviewed their stated agenda, conversations would suddenly become heated, obtuse, and ramble aimlessly for ten to fifteen minutes, with repeated references to obstacles to organizational change. Any discussion would be diverted to the most difficult example and resolutions were consistently avoided. After several attempts at engaging the participants in an analysis of these dynamics (I would stop the interaction and attempt to focus on "what was going on"), I brought the technique into play.

1. With the group sitting at the discussion table, I place a chair at a little distance from the table; someone sitting in that chair (the *metachair*) would be able to see the entire group. I invite group members to sit in the chair any time they wish to observe the group process.

2. In all subsequent meetings, I continue to place the metachair there, and repeat the invitation for anyone to sit there at any time. That individual could simply observe the group process or, if he or she wished, stop the ongoing discussion to focus on group process. However, if the person in the chair wishes to rejoin the discussion, he or she would have to return to the table. At any time, however, anyone could switch again to the chair.

3. It is unusual for someone to actually get up from the table to sit in the chair; nevertheless, metalevel comments will begin to emerge, *as though* the person were sitting there. For example, "I imagined myself sitting in that chair for the last fifteen minutes and what I saw us do as a group was . . ."

4. It can take considerable time and multiple contexts for people to articulate *metaknowing* observations. One indication that this skill is developing is described just above: the person not only experiences the metaperspective, but is also self-awarely able to describe the experience.

Processing Tips

Metaknowing skills are most easily developed when they are sorted out from other skills and from each other. Participants will begin to catch on, "When I am thinking like this, I am in metaposition." Or, "I am really confused; how can I think about this from a metaposition?" It is important to distinguish between metacomments, which are made from (literally or figuratively) the metachair, and discussion comments, which are made at the table. In other words, the discussion comments are about the *topic* under discussion; the metacomments are about the *process* the participants are engaged in, or the individual's examination of the *foundation* for his or her own beliefs.

Format-steps-process (personal change context). I call this exercise "Nemesis." The person engaged in the activity rotates among three positions, or chairs:

1. In the first chair, the person experiences the world through his own eyes, experiences, and feelings. *Example:* Gary chose as his nemesis his son, a teenager who was focused on his music and did not want to do his homework. Gary, however, was working hard to give his son an education and was at his wit's end about how to get through to his son.

2. In the second chair, he identifies with a nemesis, someone with whom he has a pattern of unsatisfying discussions. *Example:* Gary sat in his son's chair and positioned himself in his son's posture. Sitting in the same way as his son sat during their unsuccessful conversations, Gary remembered sitting that way himself when he was younger.

3. The third position, or chair, is the place of the observer. From the observer position, the learner views himself, his nemesis, and their interaction. *Example:*

Gary recalled having had this same conversation with *his* father when he was younger. He now realized—knew at a visceral level—that he had the information he needed to speak more effectively with his son.

Processing Tips

It is important to distinguish clearly each position *(chair)* from the other. Since getting into the physical position of the nemesis is key to gaining access to kinesthetic memory, it is essential that the participant who is about to switch chairs first prepares for a different posture by getting up, looking around, and shaking his or her arms and legs.

During the "Nemesis" exercise, new and different information is gleaned as the person rotates several times through the positions. In Gary's case, the information he needed was in the pattern of the way his son sat during their unsuccessful conversations. This led him to realize the cost of dismissing his son's desires, a realization that eventually led to a transformed relationship.

Contributor's Commentary

The intent of highlighting metaknowing as a transformational skill is to tap into a natural human capacity. Metaknowing is possible because humans are multidimensional and have the ability to *parallel process*. We can, with practice, simultaneously feel our own emotions, imagine someone else's response, and remain a neutral observer of both.

The Institute of Cultural Affairs Kaleidoscope™ Teaching and Learning Strategy

Keith Elaine Packard, Chicago, Illinois
E-mail: icachicago@igc.apc.org

Keith Elaine Packard is codirector of program development for the Institute of Cultural Affairs in Chicago. She designs staff development workshops for teachers and administrators in the United States and abroad.

Developmental Intentions

I. Toward knowing as a dialogical process.
   2. Surfacing and questioning assumptions underlying beliefs, ideas, actions, and positions.

5. Moving between separate and connected, independent and interdependent ways of knowing.

6. Paying attention to wholes as well as the parts that comprise them.

III. Toward being a continuous learner.

9. Drawing on multiple capacities for effective learning.

V. Toward connection with others.

5. Recognizing that collective awareness and thinking transform the sum of their parts.

Context

This strategy has been used to help participants design course curricula, projects, lesson plans, meetings, and learning environments in formal and informal learning settings, including corporations, not-for-profit organizations, and schools.

Description of Activity

Purpose. To enable a group of teachers and learners to participate actively in the teaching and learning process; maximize learners' use of resources and enhance the outcomes in the learning process; and construct new insights, inventions, and social forms that are needed in our ever-changing, complex, and global society.

This is an overarching framework that can be applied to a variety of teaching, learning, and planning situations. For purposes of illustration, I will focus on an example: helping high school teachers design a unit for Spanish I. However, this design tool has also been used to plan or design meetings, celebrations, Web pages, and capital campaigns.

Format-steps-process.

1. Place the title of the primary subject matter in the center of the Kaleidoscope diagram; for example, "Teaching Verbs in a Spanish I Class." Based on this subject, form your intents or objectives, considering the cognitive and affective domains, the skills that you want to develop in yourself and in your students, the outcomes that you are aiming for, and the images that you want to shape in the learning environment with reference to that subject. These objectives can be stated as

RO (rational objective); for example, "The students will understand that verbs are conjugated in patterns."

EO (experiential objective); for example, "The students will experience effective team work."

EC (enhanced capacities); for example, "The students will be able to use the patterns to conjugate families of verbs."

OC (outcomes); for example, "Students will be able to use correctly conjugated verbs in dialogues."

IS (image to shape); for example, "Students as problem solvers."

2. With the objectives as *goalposts* for your thinking, use the Kaleidoscope framework to brainstorm actions (what you might do) in each of the *facets* (large circles in the center) and *mirrors* (oblong spaces around the central form). Your actions should relate to your subject matter and be influenced by your objectives.

Figure 7.1. The Kaleidoscope™ Teaching Strategy: A Framework for Lesson Planning.

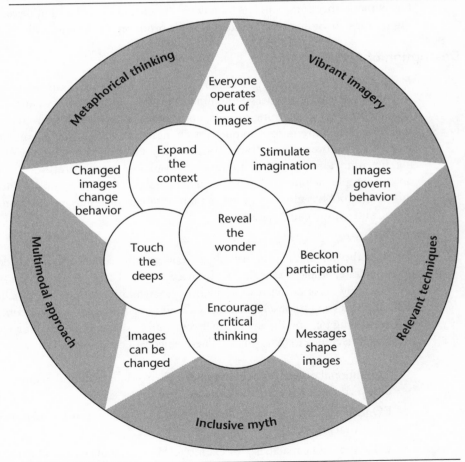

Copyright © Institute of Cultural Affairs. Reproduced by permission.

The following description of the process begins with the facets. However, you may begin anywhere; this is a nonlinear, interrelated model, so it makes no difference where you begin your brainstorming.

The Facets (large circles in the center)

- *Beckon participation:* Get participants involved through conversation, game, problem solving, song. For example, ask students to work in pairs to brainstorm as many verbs as they can. This activity will get them involved.
- *Touch the deeps:* Connect information with what participants care most about through stories, poetry, simulations, drama, and other art forms. For example, ask pairs of students to imagine that they are in a restaurant in Mexico. Ask them to write down in English what they would like to say in order to purchase lunch for themselves and their American guests. Ask them to underline all the verbs that they would need to use. Compare their underlined words with the verb lists that other pairs of students have brainstormed. What verbs would they need to know that do not appear on the lists?
- *Expand the context:* Broaden frames of reference through information via videos, time lines, verbal presentations. For example, ask students to find population figures for all the countries in which Spanish is the dominant language and then come up with an approximate number of people in the world who speak Spanish. Have them explore the value of communicating effectively in a variety of places and situations.
- *Stimulate imagination:* Apply information in a unique way; for example, through building models. Ask "What if?" For example, one could ask students working in small teams to pick a country from the list that they have created and then to decide a setting for dialogues they would design in which at least five verbs were used. The dialogue teams could also stage their dialogues with props and costumes.
- *Encourage critical thinking:* Ask participants to think reflectively—to draw connections and see implications and meaning through asking questions. For example, students could look at the brainstormed list of verbs and group them into "verb families" based on how they are conjugated.

The Mirrors (oblong spaces around the central form)

- *Vibrant imagery:* Think of how the use of color, texture, and multisensory imagery can be used to enhance your subject matter and achieve your objectives. For example, hang in the room artifacts from various Spanish-speaking countries and take time to locate on the map the place of origin of each and to relate the roots of culture embedded in each.

- *Multimodal approach:* Consider in what ways you will employ movement as well as asking yourself and the participants to share, receive, and process information through the visual and auditory pathways (including, where appropriate, smell and taste). For example, ask the students to put the conjugation of verbs to a rap beat, use minidramas that use the verbs in several conjugated forms, or make posters or other visual aids that relate the "families of verbs" based on how they are conjugated.

- *Relevant techniques:* What makes a technique relevant is its capacity to effectively address the participants' needs and achieve the objectives. Learning-focused techniques include super learning, whole-language learning, and cooperative learning. For example, in the brainstorming suggestions offered so far, team-based work, art expression, personal research, and student presentations are most relevant because the students are active and engaged in learning by being personally involved.

- *Inclusive myth:* The term *myth* is used to describe a journey story. As a teacher and learner, I can decide what journey story to adopt, adapt, or invent to motivate myself and others as learners in relationship to the subject matter (or as participants working toward some other collaborative goal). Because images are powerful in determining behavior, this model encourages teachers and learners to be inclusive in the images and stories chosen to illustrate subject matter. For example, employ teaching strategies that actively involve all students, thus enabling each student to feel that he or she is essential in the learning process of the class.

- *Metaphorical thinking:* Metaphor makes possible immersion into a participative experience. For example, name the classroom after a village, city, or country where the language of instruction is spoken; ask the students to choose a personal name, as well. A student might choose to be called Juan Carlos; the classroom might be called "la plaza del sol."

3.   Having filled out all facets and mirrors in the Kaleidoscope, as an individual or as a group, review what you have done. Look for overlapping information and repetition. Knowing that this is not a rational or sequential format, ask whether a suggested content item or activity falls into more than one category for good reason, or whether it would be more helpfully held in one distinct category. Decide how you will use the palette of suggestions that you have for your chosen context. Eliminate ideas that might not be helpful in achieving your guiding objectives; do not, however, eliminate any one facet or mirror. It is the complexity that provides the richness of this approach.

Processing Tips

When the brainstorm described above is over, the group chooses, from the multiple possibilities generated, items that would seem to be most effective given the parameters within which they are working (time, space, budgets).

An individual can use this process for his or her own planning; it usually requires about thirty minutes of focused thinking. For a facilitator working with groups of two to eight persons, the exercise requires about one hour.

Contributor's Commentary

The effectiveness of this strategy depends on having a clear focus on the desired outcomes and an understanding of how image theory affects learning. Briefly stated, images relate emotions and information and have the potential to powerfully govern behavior. For example, the image "Women are not as good as men at math and science" for years determined the study experiences and career plans of half the world's population. It has taken multiple role models and abundant research information to slowly replace this image. Furthermore, images that govern behavior are created by messages. When these messages change, there is a potential of changing an image and thereby changing behavior.

We have taught this approach to teachers in Institute of Cultural Affairs (ICA) learning labs in Chicago and in San Jose, California. It was particularly effective for coordinated efforts such as block scheduling and team teaching. We have also introduced the strategy in our two-day training for facilitators, "The Power of Image in Facilitation: Tools for Creative Facilitation." Facilitators in a variety of professions have used the Kaleidoscope process to design events, as well as plan sessions, meetings, and learning environments.

Examining Your Paradigms

Rebecca Proehl, Berkeley, California
E-mail: rproehl@stmarys-ca.edu

Rebecca Proehl is an associate professor of management, Saint Mary's College of California. As a management consultant, she helps public sector agencies work through the challenges of organizational change.

Developmental Intentions

    I. Toward knowing as a dialogical process.
        2. Surfacing and questioning assumptions underlying beliefs, ideas, actions, and positions.
        3. Reframing ideas or values that seem contradictory, embracing their differences, and arriving at new meanings.
   II. Toward a dialogical relationship to oneself.
        3. Exploring life's experiences through some framework(s) of analysis.
        4. Questioning critically the validity or worth of one's pursuits.
  IV. Toward self-agency and self-authorship.
        6. Distinguishing what one has created for oneself from what is imposed by social, cultural, and other forces.

Context

I frequently lead workshops with individuals who are working in large bureaucratic environments—the kind of settings that stifle creativity, openness, and change. The constraints are so powerful that the employees are generally not even aware of how limited their perspectives are. I use the following activity to help the participants *begin* to see other perspectives as they engage in a process of organizational change.

Description of Activity

Purpose. To recognize the power of paradigms in guiding thoughts and patterns, examine one's paradigms that affect attitudes and work values, and share with others one's basic assumptions or paradigms about work.

    Format-steps-process.

1. With a blank sheet of paper in front of them, I ask participants to draw a line creating two columns.
2. I provide a list of words (see Exhibit 7.1) and then ask that each person list, in the left-hand column, "What comes to mind when you first read each word?"
3. I then direct their attention to the right-hand column and ask that everyone list some alternative paradigms—*even if they do not believe in them.*
4. Once the worksheet is completed, I ask all participants to share their paradigms with someone else in the group and discuss the following questions:

"What similarities and differences exist between you and your partner with regard to your paradigms? What shifts, if any, are occurring in organizations today with regard to these concepts?"

Exhibit 7.1. Example of Categories and Columns.

Word List	Response Worksheet	
Work	A way to make a living	An outlet for my energy and talents
Coworkers	•	•
Leaders	•	•
Customers	•	•
Change	•	•
Bureaucracy	•	•
Restructuring	•	•
Teams	• (etc.)	• (etc.)

Processing Tips

Prior to this activity, I often show a video or have a discussion on the power of paradigms. Excellent examples exist of how individuals, going against the dominant paradigm of their time, changed the way the world is today.

After having the participants identify alternative paradigms, it is helpful to have them discuss the following questions:

- How would your organization be different if you operated on the basis of an alternative paradigm?
- What existing organizational structures and systems support your old paradigm?
- How would your role be different if you operated on the basis of an alternative paradigm? How would you be perceived by your colleagues? Your supervisor?

Contributor's Commentary

There has been a great deal of research on paradigms and their influence over how we see the world. This activity, coupled with a brief conceptual overview of this research, can help the participants see that they have a role in creating (and changing) their own paradigms.

Creating a Shared Vision

Rebecca Proehl, Berkeley, California
E-mail: rproehl@stmarys-ca.edu

Rebecca Proehl is an associate professor of management, Saint Mary's College of California. As a management consultant, she helps public sector agencies work through the challenges of organizational change.

Developmental Intentions

IV. Toward self-agency and self-authorship.
   3. Risking action on behalf of one's beliefs and commitments.
V. Toward connection with others.
   1. Mediating boundaries between one's connection to others
      and one's individuality.
   2. Experiencing oneself as part of something larger.
   4. Contributing one's voice to a collective endeavor.
   5. Recognizing that collective awareness and thinking transform
      the sum of their parts.

Context

This activity has been used in public sector organizations as part of organizational development efforts.

Description of Activity

Purpose. To help participants understand the vital role that visioning plays in organizational change and to experience the challenges of creating an organizational vision.

Format-steps-process. There are four progressive, interlinking exercises. I start by having the group break into smaller groups and identify a facilitator, recorder, and timekeeper. I then assign the groups a case (see Contributor's Comments) to which they can apply the principles of visioning; this activity can also be slightly modified and used with an organizational change project. We then move into the four exercises.

Exercise I: The Present (30 minutes duration)

1. I ask the groups to review their case that describes a proposed change. In doing this review, the members of each group should answer the following questions

as though they were members in that organization: "What disappoints us most in our organization? What are our greatest shortcomings?"

2. I ask the groups to spend no more than fifteen minutes on this task and to have the group record its ideas on flip-chart paper.

3. I then ask the groups to follow the same procedure in answering these questions: "What are we proud about in our organization? What have been our great successes?"

Exercise II: The Future (60 minutes duration)

4. I set out the following scenario: Imagine that it is the year 2005 (or some appropriate year three to ten years in the future) and your agency has just won the National Award for the Organization of the Year. The organization has been successful beyond your wildest dreams in implementing change. You are being contacted by newspapers all over the country asking for more information about the changes that you have instituted. These are the questions and the information they are interested in:

What has made you successful?

What is your reputation all about?

What kinds of services are you providing?

What do your customers or clients think about you? Why are they so satisfied?

How are people relating to one another in your organization?

What does it feel like to be working there?

What contributions are you making to the organization?

What values are important to everyone working there?

5. My instructions to the smaller groups are to have everyone in that group tell about the organization by addressing the above questions. I ask them to spend forty-five to sixty minutes on this exercise and to capture the ideas on a flip chart. Once the ideas are recorded on the flip-chart paper, I ask them to hang the results on the wall.

Exercise III: Summarizing the Vision (30 minutes duration)

6. I now instruct the groups to spend thirty minutes drafting a summary statement of the ideal vision for their organization. I let them know that each group will briefly present the vision statements of the desired future to the class.

7. I ask them to use the following statements in drafting their organizational vision:

When our proposed change is fully implemented two years from now, it will have the following features . . .

When our change is implemented, our organization's reputation will be improved because we now are able to . . . As a result of the change process, the values that guide our relationships will have changed from . . . to . . .

Exercise IV: What did we learn about visioning?

8. As a concluding activity, I ask members of the group to reflect on the simulation and discuss what they learned about visioning. I suggest that they address what each person would do the same and what each person would do differently if completing the visioning process in his or her organization.

Processing Tips

This activity can be an extremely powerful learning experience for the participants if they become engaged in the visioning process and if the facilitator ties the experience back to a conceptual framework. To assist with the former, the case must be relevant and appropriate for the participants in the group. There has to be sufficient detail in the case so the participants can answer the questions, yet it has to be short enough that it is not inordinately time consuming to read. Of course, this problem is resolved if the group chooses an actual organization and change project for this activity.

The cases might be prepared by the instructor from his or her consulting experience, created with one of the participant's organizations, or written from information obtained from the Internet or other published sources. Excellent material for cases can be obtained from the following Internet sources: public sector—Innovations in American Government; private sector—Hoover's Online; nonprofit sector—The Drucker Foundation.

To prepare participants for the visioning activity, it is also helpful to look at future trends. A brief handout or small lecture could help "prime the pump." An excellent source for this information is *The Futurist* magazine.

There are many resources available on visioning. Two that I would suggest are Peter Senge's (1990) *The Fifth Discipline* and John Kotter's (1996) *Leading Change.* Senge discusses the value of creating a shared vision within organizational settings; Kotter discusses the role of vision in leading change.

Contributor's Commentary

Organizations today are continually faced with organizational change. The change may be incremental or dramatic, proactive or reactionary, welcomed by employees or resisted. In any event, change will only be successful if the leaders are clear about what the future will be like if the change is successfully implemented. The leaders must clearly define and articulate the vision for the change.

Though the activity itself is simple to set up and easy to process, it sometimes works extremely well whereas other times does not. I believe that the differences are probably not due to the activity itself or the facilitator's skill. Rather, the variation can be attributed to the participants' ability to envision. [Editors' note: This may be a function of participants' development.] I have come to realize how difficult it is for some (and in certain organizations, *most*) participants to think creatively, see the big picture, and anticipate changes in the future. In addition, many adults have had less than positive experiences with vision statements within their own organizations. Though the organization may have a formal vision statement, there is enormous cynicism among the rank-and-file or middle managers because the organizational leaders do not "live the vision." Even so, I am utterly convinced that the differences between successful and unsuccessful organizations can be attributed to vision, so I continue to use this exercise.

References

Kotter, J. P. (1996). *Leading change.* Cambridge, MA: Harvard Business School Press.
Senge, P. M. (1990). *The fifth discipline: The art and practice of the learning organization.* New York: Doubleday.

Drawing Theory

Grete Stenersen, El Cerrito, California
E-mail: gsteners@stmarys-ca.edu

Grete Stenersen is an instructor in the School of Extended Education of Saint Mary's College of California and teaches adult development theory to adult learners.

Developmental Intentions

I. Toward knowing as a dialogical process.
   4. Using one's experience to critique expert opinion and expert opinion to critique one's experience.
II. Toward a dialogical relationship to oneself.
   3. Exploring life's experiences through some framework(s) of analysis.

III. Toward being a continuous learner.
    9. Drawing on multiple capacities for effective learning.

Context

"Personal and Professional Assessment" is the first course taken in a bachelor degree completion program. Students write an autobiography and five experiential learning essays to petition for college credit for their prior learning from previous life and work experiences. The students go through the program in a cohort model, so a lot of group-dynamic exercises are included in the curriculum. In this course students also focus on critical thinking skills, learning adult development theory, and adjusting to being back in college after what has been for some a prolonged absence.

Description of Activity

Purpose. To identify experiences that relate to theories and critique the validity of the theories.

    Format-steps-process.

1. Prior to class I have asked students to read several authors' theories of adult development.
2. In class I ask each student to identify which theory he or she likes best or which one best describes his or her own experience.
3. Based upon the students' own choices, students then work in groups to draw a picture or an illustration of the theory they have selected. I allot about forty minutes for the groups to come up with an idea, construct the drawing and prepare to present their drawing to the rest of the group. I also tell them that each student will need to talk about some part of the drawing during the group's presentation to the class. I provide newsprint paper and marking pens in various colors. Students often want to include words in their drawings; I urge them to keep text to a minimum.
4. During the presentations, students regularly offer concrete examples from their own lives that support or illustrate the authors' theories.
5. I encourage them to express disagreements and refinements of the theories, something that they are eager to do.

Contributor's Commentary

To illustrate the theory of adult development that they have chosen, the students go through a process of *naming and claiming* what they have already experienced and know. As I work with adult students in the area of adult development theory, I realize that I am not offering them new content; rather, I am giving them a framework to describe to themselves something that they already know to be true. This process of naming and claiming may bring strong feelings to the surface as they reconnect with important periods of transformation in their lives.

This exercise is also very helpful with group or team-building experience in the classroom. For example, adults who are accustomed to being in charge and dominant in their workplaces may not shine so easily in this exercise, since it uses an entirely different set of skills; they may have to rely on people less professionally accomplished than they. It also encourages adults to try something new; it certainly isn't a common method of reviewing reading material in the classroom. Since part of what we want our students to achieve at our school is to "take hold" of their own educational process, this exercise and all of the work that they do with development theory leads them in that direction.

Journal Dialogue

Phyllis A. Walden, Chicago, Illinois
E-mail: waldenp@morton.cc.il.us

Phyllis A. Walden is an administrator in an urban community college and regularly teaches a course entitled "The Personal Journal" for DePaul University's School for New Learning, which is designed to enable learners and instructors to use journals as a tool toward becoming life-long, continuous learners.

Developmental Intentions

   I. Toward knowing as a dialogical process.
      7. Associating truth not with static fact but with contexts and relationships.
  II. Toward a dialogical relationship to oneself.
      5. Exploring and making meaning of one's life stories within contexts (for example, societal, familial, universal).
  III. Toward being a continuous learner.
      6. Accepting internal dissonance as part of the learning process.
  V. Toward connection with others.
      3. Engaging the affective dimension when confronting differences.

Context

I have used the journal dialogue method in a variety of courses, including liberal arts philosophy courses, writing courses, and educational planning and assessment courses.

Description of Activity

Purpose. To assist journal writers to become more actively engaged in writing that deepens their thinking and learning processes; to bring to awareness the context of a relationship; and to examine these contexts from a variety of perspectives.

Format-steps-process. Prior to my introducing the dialogue process, students have practiced using free writing, list making, unsent letters, and a visually oriented strategy such as mind-mapping (see "Clustering," p. 104). Students write their first journal dialogue as an in-class activity.

1. In preparing to do a journal dialogue, students make a list of possible people, concepts, or events for the dialogue. To prompt students' selections, I find it can be helpful first to describe some specific ways of using the technique, such as a dialogue with an author, a historical figure, a concept or ideal, a work in progress, an inner teacher or mentor, or a work of art.

2. After they choose one for a focus, I ask students to list the key steps in the development of the relationship between the student and the *object* or *partner* in the dialogue. This summary of the history of this relationship is a key step in setting the context for the dialogue with the individual or concept.

3. Next I guide students through writing a focusing statement on how this relationship is now. I ask students to relax and consider the partner in the dialogue in a way that feels comfortable to them. Prompts include suggesting visualization, noticing memories that they are aware of, and allowing themselves to feel the presence of this dialogue partner. Students begin the dialogue by greeting the other, perhaps noting a question or issue that prompted the dialogue. They write this greeting down in the journal, and write the response. They record the dialogue script in their journals.

4. After completing the dialogue, I ask students to reread what they have written in this exercise and write a brief reflective statement on the experience. This might include reactions to the process, any insights that stand out, additional questions, and possible future directions for the dialogue.

Processing Tips

I allow time for processing this activity in class. I first invite students to share their observations on the process of doing a journal dialogue. Many comment on how awkward the dialogue felt, and this is a frequent comment of persons who are new to the dialogue process. Some wonder about who the other voice in the dialogue really is, and the source of insights and information. Most acknowledge it is not "really" the other person and some begin considering a deeper part of themselves as a source of knowing. I suggest that students use these questions in future dialogues. They are assigned additional dialogue work and I sometimes repeat this in-class dialogue later in the term and ask students to assess their use of this tool. Even those who do not readily use this technique without prompting comment on the increased ease and fluidity with practice.

Contributor's Commentary

The journal dialogue is a tool that helps learners further their skill in engaging deeply in their learning and using observations and insights to generate more questions and connections. When they experience dissonance with their partner in a dialogue, they are able to move through this sense of disequilibrium by expanding the dialogue.

Most students need specific writing strategies to create a journal that contributes to productive learning. Often a novice experiences keeping a journal as "writing in circles." The journal dialogue is a tool that helps move writing to a deeper, reflective level. I have adapted this process from Ira Progoff's (1975) *At a Journal Workshop*. His elaboration of the dialogue dimension of journal writing is a valuable contribution to the use of journal writing as a tool that empowers and transforms people.

I have used this tool for many years in my own journal writing and learning. I share my experience and draw on examples in my own writing. I try to give students many examples of how they can use this tool. In courses emphasizing learning and educational planning, we may focus on dialogues with influential teachers, mentors, and authors or creators. In courses that focus on ideas and concepts, I suggest dialogues with authors and ideas or issues.

Reference

Progoff, I. (1975). *At a journal workshop.* New York: Dialogue House Library.

CHAPTER EIGHT

INQUIRING

Inquiring centers on pursuing a question—the question may be the learner's own, or it may be set by the educator. The emphasis is on something to be investigated, to be found out about. For example, Paula Horvath-Neimeyer's exercise "Through Another's Eyes: Using Concept Mapping in Cross-Cultural Training" (p. 170) focuses on exploring questions through the eyes of another culture, whereas Steven Stahl's exercise "Working with Parents as 'Expert' Copresenters" (p. 150) helps early childhood service providers inquire deeply into the thoughts and feelings of parents of disabled children. The subject of inquiry is personal experience in Stephen Brookfield's exercise, "Using Personal Experience to Critique Expert Opinion" (below).

Activities that extend over more than one session begin with Xenia Coulter's "Psychology Tutorial" (p. 155).

◆ ◆ ◆

Using Personal Experience to Critique Expert Opinion

Stephen Brookfield, Minneapolis, Minnesota
E-mail: sdbrookfield@stthomas.edu

Stephen Brookfield is Distinguished Professor at the University of Saint Thomas. He is a three-time winner of the Cyril O. Houle World Award for Literature in Adult Education.

Developmental Intentions

    I. Toward knowing as a dialogical process.
        2. Surfacing and questioning assumptions underlying beliefs, ideas, actions, and positions.
        4. Using one's experience to critique expert opinion and expert opinion to critique one's experience
    II. Toward a dialogical relationship to oneself.
        3. Exploring life's experiences through some framework(s) of analysis.
    III. Toward being a continuous learner.
        1. Reflecting on one's own and others' experiences as a guide to future behavior.
    IV. Toward self-agency and self-authorship.
        1. Constructing a values system that informs one's behavior.

Context

This activity has been used in workshops and courses on reflective practice for teachers, graduate students in adult education, leadership, and other professional education and development contexts.

Description of Activity

Purpose. To encourage critical analysis of experts' ideas and to emphasize the validity of participants' own experiences.

    Format-steps-process.

1. I ask participants to read three or four interpretations of the same idea or concept; I include one of mine in the mix.
2. After participants move into small groups, I ask them to summarize briefly the central arguments of each piece.
3. I then ask them to select those elements that they feel

    Have some validity

    Are ambiguous, confusing, and poorly presented

    Are contradicted by their own experiences

    (These are the same requirements I have set for the participants' written work.)

4. Once the members of the groups have shown that they have understood the central ideas in the body of work, I ask that a critical analysis of the ideas be undertaken. I prompt this with the following instructions:

Identify the hidden assumptions underlying the writers' central ideas

Identify any ethical questions that have not been addressed by these writers

Highlight ambiguities, fallacious reasoning, and lack of clarity in these writers' expressions of their idea

Identify contradictions in these writers' works

Examine whether or not these writers' ideas take account of the practical realities of facilitating learning that have become evident in course members' own experiences

Processing Tips

I have found it important when setting up this assignment to stress that critical analysis entails positive elements as well as negative appraisal. This seems to make it considerably easier for some people to engage in criticism; they can balance what they see as negative comments with positive ones. I think there is fear that they will be perceived by the authority figure (me) as being engaged in a demolition of "expert" work, and this relieves that concern.

Contributor's Commentary

Recognizing one's faults can be difficult in almost any organizational setting, whether in academia, business, or industry. Acknowledging that one is having problems functioning effectively in a particular work environment can be a very threatening public admission. I believe that the only way that employees and managers will be willing to admit publicly to error, doubt, and anxiety—and be willing to ask for assistance from colleagues in scrutinizing their actions critically—is when people in positions of considerable power model these behaviors.

It is critical in this activity that I include my own published work(s) on the topic I or we choose. By encouraging participants to read others' critiques of ideas along with my own, I hope that I send a clear message that criticism of self and others is perfectly acceptable and appropriate in my sessions.

References

Brookfield, S. D. (1986). *Understanding and facilitating adult learning.* San Francisco: Jossey-Bass.

Brookfield, S. D. (1989). *Developing critical thinkers: Challenging adults to explore alternative ways of thinking and acting.* San Francisco: Jossey-Bass.

Brookfield, S. D. (1990a). *The skillful teacher.* San Francisco: Jossey-Bass.

Brookfield, S. D. (1998). Against naïve romanticism: From celebration to the critical analysis of experience. *Studies in Continuing Education, 20* (2), 127–142.

A Surface-to-Depth Discussion Method, Nicknamed "ORID"

David Dunn, Denver, Colorado
E-mail: lcadunn@igc.org; Website: www.mirrorcommunication.com

David Dunn has been an organizational development consultant using the Institute of Cultural Affairs' Technology of Participation™ in his facilitating practice. He writes, edits, and designs print and electronic publications for nonprofit organizations.

Developmental Intentions

I. Toward knowing as a dialogical process.
    10. Tapping into and drawing on tacit knowledge.
III. Toward being a continuous learner.
    1. Reflecting on one's own and others' experiences as a guide to future behavior.
    5. Posing and pursuing questions out of wonderment.
V. Toward connection with others.
    4. Contributing one's voice to a collective endeavor.

Context

This is a format that a group leader, trainer, teacher, or facilitator can use to craft and sequence questions so that a group is drawn into a topic. "ORID Lite" is useful for brief transitional discussions; for example, a five- to ten-minute reflection on a common experience such as a lecture, movie, or demonstration. A more lengthy discussion can draw out insights in depth about a chapter, an assignment, a period of time, and the like. In organizational planning workshops, the ORID surface-to-depth discussion method is a powerful tool to help a group become self-conscious about their experience as employees and coworkers charged with managing change strategies.

Description of Activity

Purpose. To foster a train of thought in a group discussion that leads to illumination or significant discovery.

Format-steps-process. ORID is the acronym for Objective, Reflective, Interpretive, Decisional, the four steps or stages in an ORID discussion, which more or less parallel the levels of cognitive processing. Whatever the focus of the discussion, this progression of questions allows me to move a group from surface information to depth insight. The four levels of questions that I pose to groups are as follows:

1. One or more *objective*-level questions that solicits surface level data, information, and facts—any information that can be gathered by the senses; I encourage everyone to respond and contribute brief answers.
2. One or more *reflective*-level questions to draw out associations that the group members experience with the data; examples of this type of questions are, "What was surprising? What touched you? What were you most interested in? What feeling did you experience?" I hope these questions will elicit subjective, intuitive, "gut" reactions, and I encourage people to respond with affective content.
3. One or more *interpretive* questions to solicit insights about the significance or meaning of the data. My intent here is to engender thoughtful and analytic responses; for example, "What's the learning here? What's the point of this for us? What really happened? What story do you tell from your point of view?"
4. One, probably, *decisional*-level question to solicit comments about the implications of the discussion, next steps, consequences, or requirements in light of the discussion. These questions involve some kind of *choice* or *will*.

Closure: I use a simple, affirming statement to close the discussion and acknowledge the group's insights.

Processing Tips

The leader sets the stage with a context that connects the group's expectations and the leader's reason for a discussion. Sometimes telling a story does the job, sometimes focusing a topic intellectually, sometimes posing a problem or issue. In any case, the group is helped to warm up if the leader begins with a simple, objective-level question, asking for a brief answer from each person in turn. In this way, each person has "broken the ice" of contributing to the group discussion; however, the question requires only recall, not processing.

If any of my questions cause furrowed eyebrows, I rephrase the question. But if people are thoughtful and not confused, I simply restate the question, after a pause. I understand that silence usually indicates that processing is taking place and that all I need do is to help keep people's minds focused by restating the question. Open-ended questions keep the conversation progressing; yes-no questions tend to shut the conversation down.

The time allotted to each level of the questioning sequence will vary depending on the objective of the discussion and the leader's aim with respect to what the participants are to experience. A typical twenty-minute discussion about an intellectual topic might flow as follows: objective-level questions, three minutes; reflective-level questions, four minutes; interpretive-level questions, twelve minutes; and decisional-level questions, one minute. If, by contrast, the point of the discussion was to explore implications or to elicit commitment, the flow might be objective, three minutes; reflective, four minutes; interpretive, five minutes; decisional, eight minutes.

A typical, brief transition or closure discussion (after the major ORID session), lasting five minutes, might be, for example, objective ("What do you recall [about the session itself]"?), one minute; reflective ("What was most engaging?"), one minute; interpretive ("What insights will you take away from this encounter?"), two minutes; decisional ("How will your point of view be different?"), one minute.

The leader can be quite informal and conversational about posing the questions, without bothering to announce the level of the question or the intent of the discussion. The magic is in the sequence. Because it reflects the levels of our mind's cognitive processing, it is a natural flow, built on a foundation of shared information. Often a group member spontaneously answers the next-level question. If I feel that the group has entertained enough data at the present level, I'll take such a response as an indicator to ask the next-level question.

Members of a group skilled in using the ORID method will remember the steps in the thought process and remind each other if they need more data at any given level. Or they will request to move to the next question if they feel they have exhausted the possibilities of the question currently before the group.

It is my experience that there are four skills required to use the ORID method powerfully. The first involves being self-conscious about the purpose of the discussion and the hoped-for experience of the participants. The second is thoughtfully crafting open-ended questions so that they build on each other. The third is trusting that the questions themselves, put repeatedly to the group, will elicit rich content. The fourth is the ability to enter intuitively into a natural flow state with the group to capture and build upon the insights of the moment in light of the aims of the discussion. Anyone can begin to practice the ORID method. It takes years of practice for it to become second nature and natural and to consistently achieve occasions of discovery and wonder.

Contributor's Commentary

The skillful crafting of the questions and the flow of thought that leads from surface impressions to depth of understanding may draw out a group into an unsuspected moment when a discovery is made. The discovery can be mundane or transcendent, depending on the topic and the point of the discussion. Wonder and awe don't break loose all the time, but when they do, they are a strong indicator that a *break-loose* insight has just occurred that can be noted and used in some important, practical way. But the point of the method is to invite the group to look beyond the surface and see what they discover: an insight, an implication, whatever. The movement of the four levels, that is, the flow that "gets somewhere," releases energy because it occasions insight or action based on a joint exploration.

The times that I have used this method in connection with a workgroup's planning have been most consistently the occasions for break-loose thinking. For example, when a group is analyzing the barriers to their vision for their future, I'll use an informal ORID discussion to help them process the brainstorm of issues, obstacles, and irritants on a flip chart or a wall chart. The questions would typically be as follows: objective [I read the data from the flip chart]; reflective ("Which of these issues and obstacles do you personally experience most powerfully?"); interpretive ("What gives these obstacles power over us?" or "What keeps these from being removed as barriers?"); and finally, decisional ("What name would you give to the underlying pattern that keeps these barriers in place?").

Groups that thoughtfully address these questions discover aspects of their culture or their approach to work that inadvertently thwart their best intentions and most cherished hopes. For example, a group of gifted architects discovered that the very perspective they bring to their craft tends to separate them from the other players in projects with whom they need to collaborate most effectively. Or in another case, the staff of an important human service agency discovered that the patterns of care that enabled them to serve their clients effectively had seduced them into dysfunctional patterns in their supervisory relationships with each other. In both of these real life instances, the ORID method allowed people to explore the evidence of their own life experience and together to look at it in new ways. When the interpretive questions focus on "Why?" the group frequently has an "aha" discovery that sheds new light on real predicaments. These moments are very energizing and stimulate creative brainstorming about natural and effective solutions to the real, underlying problems facing people in their work together.

As Stanfield (1997) points out, other uses of the method include informal, light occasions when it's fun or useful to review a period of time or an accomplishment; supervisory or disciplinary interactions requiring a disciplined, reasoned train of thought; occasions when it's important for people to discover what they know together or what they have experienced in their lives.

Reference

Stanfield, B. (1997) (Ed.). *The art of focused conversation: 100 ways to access group wisdom in the workplace.* Toronto, CA: Institute of Cultural Affairs. (Available from the Institute of Cultural Affairs at www.ica-usa.org or www.web.net/~icacan)

Insight by Surprise

Joe Luft, Berkeley, California
E-mail: jljlj@flash.net

Joe Luft is the "Jo" half of the "JoHari" window, a model used widely in organizational development. A retired professor, he is currently adjunct faculty at University of California, San Francisco, and a professional member of the National Training Laboratories, where he facilitates process-oriented workshops.

Developmental Intentions

    I. Toward knowing as a dialogical process.
        2. Surfacing and questioning assumptions underlying beliefs, ideas, actions, and positions.
        9. Perceiving and constructing one's reality by observing and participating.
    III. Toward being a continuous learner.
        1. Reflecting on one's own and others' experiences as a guide to future behavior.
    IV. Toward self-agency and self-authorship.
        1. Constructing a values system that informs one's behavior.
        6. Distinguishing what one has created for oneself from what is imposed by social, cultural, and other forces.

Context

This exercise can be used effectively in both higher education and training settings. It is an excellent beginning exercise for a group that is going to work on communication, multicultural, or other interpersonal issues. However, it must take place very early in the group's activities, as it works only when most of the participants do not know one another.

Description of Activity

Purpose. To raise to awareness people's unarticulated assumptions, challenge stereotypes, and experience seeing others with fresh eyes.

Format-steps-process.

1. Everyone in the room stands in a big circle in a cleared space. I ask everyone to think of this as a safe space. I also ask people to remain silent until I give instructions to the contrary.
2. I ask for a volunteer. When he or she steps forward, I ask that individual to scan the room and pick another person. I then ask these two people to continue choosing others in the room until they have chosen half the people there, first allowing the two of them a moment of conversation to negotiate how they will approach this task. (Having two people choose saves time over having one person do all the choosing. The people chosen can congregate in the middle of the room.) No criteria for their choices are provided—it is up to them. I also remind people that all this takes place in silence.
3. I then ask the participants to form two circles, one inside the other; the members of the inner circle, the people who were chosen, face the members of the outer circle.
4. The people in the inner group are asked to move around in a circle, slowly and silently, so that they pass the members of the outer group, looking carefully at each person as they pass. However, I provide no directions as to what they should pay attention to or look for. This takes about five minutes; each person in the inner group passes each person in the outer group two or three times.
5. I then ask the people in the inner circle to gather in a close knot in the center of the room. For a minute or two, still in silence, they continue to observe everyone in the outer circle. Then people in the inner circle are asked to choose someone in the outer circle who is different from them in every way they can think of. It is up to them to decide what criteria they will use—probably just "intuition." I wait a moment, allowing the group's uncertainty and confusion, before I reassure people that, "You cannot make a mistake—whatever you decide about someone being 'different from' or 'opposite to' you is correct."
6. I then ask them to move toward and once again stand opposite the person whom they think is as different from themselves as possible. Occasionally

two or more people will pick the same person; they are encouraged to quickly find someone else and assured that it will not affect the outcome of the exercise.

7. They then face the person in the outer circle and look at one another in silence for about fifteen seconds.

8. Then I tell them they may talk freely to one another, but only to one another, about their experiences during this exercise.

9. After three to five minutes (I judge by the sound in the room; when there is a pause in the intensity of the conversation) I ask for silence again. Then I ask the group as a whole: "Well, so how did it go?"

10. People are usually bursting to share their experience. Though I do not *require* that people debrief in pairs, when someone participates, I invite that person's partner to share his or her own impressions. For example, "How was the experience for you?"

11. About fifteen minutes is spent debriefing everyone's experiences with the entire group.

12. Depending on the context, various follow-up exercises will make the meaning more concrete. For example, if this exercise was an introduction to a course in social psychology, the next step might be to write a paper about the experience, integrating theoretical analysis. Or if it was used at the beginning of a community or organizational development retreat, participants could focus specifically on ways to integrate the discoveries made during the exercise in those settings.

Processing Tips

It is obviously essential that most people do not know one another. The silence is important to creating tension and drama. Because adults are uncomfortable in situations where they aren't sure what they're supposed to do, the tension within them builds to a point where, when they are finally invited to speak, their dammed up impressions and feelings burst out and tend to lead quickly to surprisingly intense discussions.

The essence of this exercise is allowing for maximal individual response to an ambiguous situation. It may be difficult, at first, for the facilitator to "trust the process," but it is best not to intervene toward a particular outcome. In the debriefing, the conversation will most likely turn to the reasons for choosing someone as "opposite" and the discrepancy between that and the reality. It is likely that the term *stereotype* will come up, and perhaps even *prejudice*. Others will discover that who they chose as "opposite" were in fact very much like them.

Contributor's Commentary

We all grow up making instantaneous judgments. Socialization into adulthood is, in part, learning to control and modify these perceptions. This activity is unusual in that it freezes such an instantaneous perception for further examination.

Although this is behavior that everyone engages in all the time, it can be risky to acknowledge and discuss it with others. It is therefore essential that the group feel safe in order to mitigate the risk. Providing this safety can be somewhat challenging when a facilitator also wants to provide minimal direction and information and where the participants are, for the most part, strangers to one another. However, the facilitator's attitude and verbal and nonverbal behaviors throughout the exercise can contribute to a sense that "this is a safe place." The institutional setting—whether academic, corporate, or community—is likely also to encourage a sense of security.

It may be important, as the debriefing begins, to remind people that their experiences are valuable *exactly as they experienced them* and are, in all likelihood, shared by everyone in the room to some extent. It is important to avoid any pejorative attribution about the phenomenon. No part of what anyone says is "wrong." It may be useful to ask, after initial revelations, "How many other people thought or felt something similar?" Many hands will shoot up, reassuring that speaker (and those to follow) that they are not alone in their feelings.

The point is not, of course, to affirm prejudice, but to raise to consciousness how pervasive are our instantaneous judgments. This is a powerful exercise for thinking about the role of unexplored assumptions of every kind and how things going on in unawareness affect our perceptions, hence our lives. Even people who have considerable experience with multicultural environments find themselves drawing on unexpected biases.

References

Luft, J. (1984). *Group processes: An introduction to group dynamics* (3rd ed.). Mountain View, CA: Mayfield.

Luft, J. (1969). *Of human interaction: The Johari awareness model.* Mountain View, CA: Mayfield.

Understanding Critical Thinking Through Tic-Tac-Toe

Sigrin T. Newell, Minneapolis, Minnesota
E-mail: snewell@waldenu.edu

Sigrin Newell is a member of the education division at Walden University, a graduate-level distance learning institution. She also teaches at the State University of New York at Albany.

Developmental Intentions

    I. Toward knowing as a dialogical process.
        6. Paying attention to wholes as well as the parts that comprise them.
       10. Tapping into and drawing on tacit knowledge.
  III. Toward being a continuous learner.
        1. Reflecting on one's own and others' experiences as a guide to future behavior.
        7. Setting one's own learning goals, being goal-directed, and being habitual in learning.

Context

I use this technique as part of an orientation workshop during a residency weekend for a distance-delivery graduate school. Specifically, I use this most often in a session that serves as an introduction to critical thinking. It models questions that students should be asking about materials they read and social systems they analyze. Almost any idea or author can substitute for the "Whatzit."

Description of Activity

Purpose. To define critical thinking in operational terms, help new students get a sense of how to incorporate critical thinking into their graduate work, and surface learners' assumptions about a topic or idea.

    Format-steps-process.

1. I begin with a short lecture about critical thinking, using the following points of reference on an overhead:

      Critical Thinking—How Do You Do It?

      Connect to prior knowledge

      Ask thoughtful questions

      Identify relevance

      Look for analogies

      Understand how topic fits others

      Honor multiple perspectives

     Identify key and unusual purposes

     Identify examples

     Evaluate how well it works

     Create applications

     Think creatively about improvements

2. Then I distribute a grid handout (Exhibit 8.1), asking pairs of participants to play the game as if it were a tic-tac-toe game. Each player must try to answer three blocks satisfactorily. Usually students end up answering all the blocks. The particular focus of this exercise is the graduate program itself, to which these learners are being oriented. It can be used in any number of other applications, however.

3. This is followed by a whole-group discussion in which students describe their answers and connect them to the critical thinking points on the overhead. I expand on these answers, pointing out other aspects of the institution and clarifying misconceptions. As a secondary benefit to the critical thinking focus of this exercise, the graduate program's orientation session arises out of this student work and their questions, rather than being a lecture.

4. At close, I point out that this matrix of questions can be used when studying almost anything. "Whatzit" could focus on the ideas of a theorist, such as Freud, or it could be a construct such as "social change" or "academic writing." The questions on the grid should be used on a regular basis to make critical thinking a habit.

Exhibit 8.1. The Whatzit.

The Whatzit is: _____

List three important features of the Whatzit	List three not-so-important (trivial or superficial) features of the Whatzit	List two very different kinds of features of the Whatzit
Identify a hidden feature of the Whatzit—a feature most people would not notice or think of	What is one feature without which the Whatzit would be entirely different?	Which feature of the Whatzit is hardest to understand? Why?
Which of the Whatzit's features do you find most interesting? Why?	Think of something you know about that is very different from the Whatzit. List two ways it is different and one way it is similar.	Think of something you know about that is very similar to the Whatzit. List two ways it is similar and one way it is different.

Source: Tishmon & Andrade, 1997. Used with permission.

Contributor's Commentary

The Whatzit game was developed by Project Zero at the Harvard Graduate School of Education. It can be found in a book with five other games designed to encourage critical thinking. These games focus on causes, connections, and reflection. Although these were originally developed for grades three to twelve, I find that they are very effective activities for adult learners.

Educators often say they want their students to engage in critical thinking but find it difficult to tell their students how to do it. The questions in the Whatzit game model questions that students should learn to use routinely.

Reference

Tishman, S., & Andrade, A. (1997). *Critical squares: Games of critical thinking and understanding.* Englewood, CO: Teacher Ideas Press.

Exploring Our Culture

Mary T. Parish, Moraga, California
E-mail: drmandb@pacbell.net

Mary T. Parish is an assistant professor at Saint Mary's College, where she teaches in the graduate counseling, multiple subject, single subject, and special education programs in the School of Education.

Developmental Intentions

    I. Toward knowing as a dialogical process.

      2. Surfacing and questioning assumptions underlying beliefs, ideas, actions, and positions.

    II. Toward a dialogical relationship to oneself.

      3. Exploring life's experiences through some framework(s) of analysis.

      5. Exploring and making meaning of one's life stories within contexts (for example, societal, familial, universal).

    IV. Toward self-agency and self-authorship.

      7. "Naming and claiming" what one has experienced and knows.

    V. Toward connection with others.

      5. Recognizing that collective awareness and thinking transform the sum of their parts.

Context

This strategy is based on part of an HIV Training Workshop sponsored by the University of California AIDS Health Project in San Francisco.

Description of Activity

Purposes. To explore personal norms by reflecting on current beliefs and past experiences for oneself, family, and friends; discuss how comprehension of one's beliefs and values regarding cultural and ethnicity can shape who we are personally and professionally and prepare us to counsel clients from backgrounds different than ours; and develop awareness of one's own beliefs and values concerning specific elements of culture and identity.

Format-steps-process.

1. Preparation: I post fourteen pieces of easel paper around the room, each headed with one of the following topics:

Religion	Ethnic background
Death	Family
Work and money	Education
Sexuality	Sexual orientation
Illness	Alcohol use and abuse
Gender	Drug use and abuse
Class	Other (to promote categories not considered)

   I divide each sheet of easel paper into three sections, labeled 1, 2, and 3 so that participants may easily respond to the three activity questions described in step 3.

2. Framing:

   (a) Several minutes are spent with students discussing a definition of culture and why the students would want to explore their own beliefs and values regarding the above topics, or

   (b) We view the film *The Color of Fear.* When I use the film, I engage the participants in a discussion of what they have seen and heard; this serves as a "warm-up" for looking at aspects of culture and their impact personally and professionally.

3. Process: I give participants a copy of the following questions:

   (a) In the culture in which you grew up, how was this topic (from the list in step 1) viewed? What were the acceptable norms? What were your family's views on this topic?

(b) What are your ideas on this topic today? What are your important beliefs relative to this topic today? What are your norms?

(c) Describe the difference between your family's view and yours or how your views differ from others. What feelings surface for you when you consider the difference between your values and beliefs and those of your friends, family, or colleagues?

4. I ask participants to respond to the three sets of questions (3a, b, c, above) on the category easel sheets posted around the room. It is helpful to demonstrate with brief phrases on a sample sheet how a person might answer the questions. For example, in talking about how death was viewed, the answer might be "not dealt with," "hidden," or "feared." I hand out felt-tipped markers so that the comments can easily be read by someone standing a few feet from the sheet, but not necessarily across the room. I allow twenty to thirty minutes for this part of the exercise. Since there are so many easel sheets, people do not have to wait long, if at all, to add their comments.

5. I request that the participants complete the assignment in silence. When they have completed answering all questions on all easel sheets, they are encouraged to return to their seats and wait in silence for the next instruction.

6. After *all* participants have completed entering their data on the sheets, they are asked to move about the room to review all the comments posted by their colleagues. Adequate time must be allowed for this part of the activity. The usual period is ten to fifteen minutes; again participants are asked to review in silence.

7. We then engage in a discussion by drawing from observations of the group's writings as well as the comments participants have about the exercise. Some suggestions for discussion follow:

What was it like to approach these particular topics and write on the sheets information that may be very personal?

Was any particular topic more difficult to write about than others? Were certain topics easier? What might these differences in ease or difficulty reflect?

Were there any surprises for you as you responded to, or tried to respond to, any of the topics?

Does this exercise suggest anything about the types of issues that you will need to keep in mind when working with clients who are culturally different from you?

8. Closure: Do you have any remaining personal feelings or concerns?

Processing Tips

Materials needed include easel paper prepared with headings (see above), one marker for each participant, and activity questions for each participant.

In facilitating discussion and reflection on *The Color of Fear,* I introduce the film by discussing the history and events that prompted the film's production. I then frame the exercise by asking participants to discuss the importance of understanding and valuing other cultures, beliefs, and norms that are different than our own. I then distribute the reflective questions for individual journal preparation and the discussion questions for postfilm discussions.

Reflective Questions for Individual Journal Writing

How do you identify culturally or ethnically?

How does your cultural and ethnicity identification effect your work as a counselor?

Discussion Questions for the Period Following the Film

What impact did the film have on you cognitively and emotionally?

How does the message of this film live in you?

What strategies can you add, delete, or modify to enhance your role of counselor?

Contributor's Commentary

Often, participants are frustrated because they do not feel they have had enough time to explore these issues as fully as they would like. Facilitators need to be aware of this frustration. *Facilitators must also have completed the activity in advance of facilitating it for others.*

Reference

Wah, L. M. (Producer and Director), Hunter, M. (Co-producer). (1994). *The Color of Fear.* Oakland, CA: Stir-Fry Productions.

Cultural Economic Values Activity

Cheryl A. Smith, Cambridge, Massachusetts
E-mail: csmith1@mail.lesley.edu

Cheryl Smith is an assistant professor working in the intensive residency program in Lesley College's adult baccalaureate program. She was an American Association of University Women American Dissertation Fellow for 1998–1999.

Developmental Intentions

I. Toward knowing as a dialogical process.
1. Inquiring into and responding openly to others' ideas.
II. Toward a dialogical relationship to oneself.
3. Exploring life's experiences through some framework(s) of analysis.
5. Exploring and making meaning of one's life stories within contexts (for example, societal, familial, universal).
III. Toward being a continuous learner.
1. Reflecting on one's own and others' experiences as a guide to future behavior.
IV. Toward self-agency and self-authorship.
6. Distinguishing what one has created for oneself from what is imposed by social, cultural, and other forces.

Context

This activity has been used in an interactive workshop on "Multiculturalism and Entrepreneurship Education and Practice" for entrepreneurship educators, adult educators, program planners and administrators, and leaders; it may also be used with adult entrepreneurship students.

Description of Activity

Entrepreneurship is an applied economics discipline that is influenced by many factors, including culture and context. However, entrepreneurship education, and to a somewhat lesser extent, adult education, does not readily acknowledge or examine those dimensions in their scholarship or practice. This activity provides a vehicle through which entrepreneurship practitioners and educators can address culture and context in a nonthreatening but illustrative manner. To do this, I have participants look at the way in which money was viewed, handled, and used in their families. We start with the family because it is the basic unit of society and the earliest transmitter of cultural values.

Purpose. To examine the roots of economic behavior among diverse groups of people and to explore how the learning acquired may be applied in their practice.

Format-process-steps. This process works best with four to six groups of three participants. The entire process takes approximately two and one-half hours.

1. Participants group themselves in triads, preferably with people who differ from them in at least one dimension (for example, race, gender, age, geography). I ask them to work with people they do not already know.

2. Participants spend the first ten minutes answering the questions below *individually.*

    (a) Who handled the money in your family (paid bills, budgeted, shared out)?

    (b) How was money viewed (as a means to an end, survival, status, other)?

    (c) What was money used for (meeting basic financial obligations, savings, education, leisure, things, sent to or shared with others, other)?

    (d) If saved, what vehicles were used (mattresses, banks, investments, family or group savings plans)?

    (e) How was credit and borrowing viewed (to be avoided, used a great deal, used as little as possible)?

    (f) Were there any gender-related economic roles in your family (men were sole breadwinners, women stayed home; women didn't work outside the home; both partners worked outside the home; women did the outside work, men stayed home; other)?

    (g) Was anyone in your family an entrepreneur, formally or informally? Who was it? When was it? What kind of business was it?

    (h) How did your family view entrepreneurship versus employment?

    (i) What constituted *wealth?* What did it symbolize (power, status, class, success)?

3. Students then share their answers with the members of the triad and record their summary as follows. First, each circle is identified as 1, 2, or 3, one for each member of the triad. Then, if all three have substantially similar answers to a question, the letter associated with that question (from the preceding list) is located within the intersection of all three circles. If two people had similar responses and the third had a different response, however, the letter would

be entered in two places: at the intersection of the two circles of the pair who agreed, and in the individual circle of the person with a different answer (see Exhibit 8.1).

4. Each small group then places their diagram on the wall and open discussion within the large group ensues.

Processing Tips

1. In processing in the triads, each person is encouraged to tell why they answered the way they did. This provides an opportunity to compare and contrast their answers.

2. In processing in the large group, questions can be raised by the instructor or facilitator if they do not come automatically from the group. "What can be said about differences occurring within like groups and across dissimilar groups (on any dimension)? Who did you assume would agree and disagree and why? What might happen when lenders and potential borrowers meet and have differing experiences, views, or behaviors with regard to money and business?"

3. Of course, how this is processed will be dependent upon the group, the context, and the facilitator's style.

4. Transfer of learning to practice can be raised by asking how their experience in the workshop could be used in their work settings.

5. Stephen Brookfield's "Classroom Critical Incident Questionnaire" was used to determine participants' feelings about the activity. Some form of evaluation is suggested at the end of each workshop or session.

Contributor's Commentary

Participants often state their surprise at the many commonalities among different cultural groups, contrary to their assumptions. At the same time, however, chronological age seems to account for more commonalities than differences. That is,

Figure 8.1. Cultural Economic Values Activity.

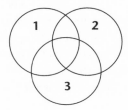

thirty-year-olds from different cultures are likely to have more in common with each other than they are with fifty-year-olds from their own cultural background—and the same is true of the fifty-year-olds. Nevertheless, participants report a heightened awareness of the impact of factors that they had not earlier considered on economic and business decisions and behavior.

This activity provides a lens through which life stories (economic behavior) can be examined as well as entrée to making meaning by examining multiple and cultural contexts—historical, societal, and universal. The richness that most participants discover by using these different lenses and angles of vision makes a case for the value of different perspectives and a multicultural approach to any field or discipline.

Other Applications

This activity can be adapted to other fields and areas, such as the study of adult education, and can focus on experiences with education, teaching, and learning instead of economic behavior.

Working with Parents as "Expert" Copresenters

Steven Stahl, Northfield, Vermont
E-mail: sstahl@together.net

Steven Stahl is an instructional technologist and courseware designer at Norwich University, vice president of Consultants for Innovative Instruction, and provides consulting for the Family Center of Washington County (Vermont).

Developmental Intentions

I. Toward knowing as a dialogical process.
  1. Inquiring into and responding openly to others' ideas.
  7. Associating truth not with static fact but with contexts and relationships.
II. Toward a dialogical relationship to oneself.
  1. Addressing fears of losing what is familiar and safe.
  5. Exploring meaning and making meaning of one's life stories within contexts (for example, societal, familial, universal).
V. Toward connection with others.
  3. Engaging the affective dimension when confronting differences.

Context

This activity is used in an undergraduate, special education course for early childhood service providers. I have used it face to face and via interactive television. Parents of children with various disabilities serve as copresenters along with the instructor.

Description of Activity

Purpose. To introduce early childhood caregivers to the realities of what is involved in parenting a child with disabilities; prepare them for gathering information about a client and having open discussion with any parent who may be looking for child care in an inclusive setting (one in which children with disabilities are included perhaps with accommodations); and encourage dialogue and engagement so that providers of care may move from a position of fear of the unknown to a feeling of empathy with parents.

Format-steps-process.

1. I begin the class with a warm-up activity that is directly related to the subject at hand. The warm-up activity should clearly have no wrong answers and provide an opportunity for each class member to participate and speak up. *Example:* I ask students to work in small groups around the question, "What are your greatest concerns about including a child with disabilities in your child-care setting?" This question can be easily modified to address any concerns that students would have dealing with any client with a difficult situation. The students create lists of their concerns in their small groups, which I then ask them to share with the large group. The parents who are serving as copresenters hear and see these concerns; they are thus informed of resistances they may encounter.

2. A second small group activity is assigned to decide what questions students would want to ask of parents before deciding whether they felt comfortable in accepting the child into their setting; for example, "What would you want to know?" In this second activity, the results are *not* shared with the large group. Again, participants are assured that there are no "wrong answers" (or in this instance, questions).

3. At this point, the parent or parents are introduced briefly. One parent takes on the role of a parent seeking to find quality child care for her child. One student in the class is asked to volunteer to begin an interview process with the parent, using some of the questions generated by the small group process just completed. The interview may be conducted between geographically distant sites connected by video conferencing.

4. After about five minutes, the instructor thanks the interviewer and asks whether another student would be willing to step in and continue the interview. A variation of this process is simply to open the interview process to the whole class. In that case, each student may ask only one or two questions. The information that the parents share is very real; it is often quite intense for students to hear parents talk about their daily life with their child, the support they need, and the stresses they deal with.

Processing Tips

There is no need to share the results of the second small group activity, since the questions will be asked in the context of the interviewing that follows. I encourage parents to bring photographs of their child so the child will be more real to the students. I let the parents know in advance some of the topics that students will no doubt want to cover in the interview, such as previous good and bad experiences working with care providers.

The instructor in this type of activity should not mold the discussion but can be prepared with questions to assist the interview process if it gets stuck or fails to address areas that the instructor feels are important. Usually this is more for the security of the teacher, however, as students generally have more questions than there is time for.

Contributor's Commentary

This activity can work in any course in which it is important to address affective issues relating to customer service or human relations. It is often beneficial to include clients or customers as part of a class. Since it is just as important to address affective issues of learning as well as cognitive ones, it can be extremely beneficial to expose students to the perceptions of those on the other side of the service provider–client-customer relationship.

This activity works because the copresenter speaks from experience. There are no fictitious scenarios, except the pretense that the parent is seeking placement for her child. Each student approaches from the perspective of his or her actual child-care setting, and parents speak about their true experiences, wishes, and concerns.

The two preparatory activities are important to the success of the process. First, they tap into the students' real fears and concerns. Second, they create safety for the volunteer interviewers, who, having generated questions as a group, know that what they want to know is reasonable and important to ask. One cannot, of course, expect to overcome all the fears and concerns of service providers in one session. This activity should be part of larger sequence. Ideally, it will be followed with reflective activities and classes that address specific situational concerns from a practical perspective. For example, students concerned about meeting the needs of a child with severe physical disabilities would need to see how easily effective accommodations could be made.

Issues of confidentiality should be addressed prior to the activity. This exercise requires a very respectful and noncompetitive classroom environment and is probably best used with a program in which such an atmosphere has been previously established, rather than making an attempt to create it specifically for this event. The activity also requires the instructor to step back and let the process take on a life of its own.

Interdisciplinary Tree Exercise

Robert Weiner, Oakland, California
Web: http://www.creativityandbeyond.com

Robert Weiner is a writer, teacher, and creativity consultant, formerly chair of liberal arts at John F. Kennedy University and coordinator of liberal studies at Saint Mary's College.

Developmental Intentions

    I. Toward knowing as a dialogical process.
       7. Associating truth not with static fact but with contexts and relationships.
    II. Toward a dialogical relationship to oneself.
       2. Engaging the disequilibrium when one's ideas and beliefs are challenged.
    III. Toward being a continuous learner.
       5. Posing and pursuing questions out of wonderment.
    V. Toward connection with others.
       4. Contributing one's voice to a collective endeavor.
       5. Recognizing that collective awareness and thinking transform the sum of their parts.

Context

This activity can be used in a workshop or course segment for adult undergraduate students or faculty.

Description of Activity

Purpose. To illuminate the differences and commonalities of the academic disciplines and the relationship of those disciplines to the greater world.

Format-steps-process. As a group, we walk outside and approach a tree. We then ask and try to answer the following questions:

- How might each individual academic department examine this tree? Art? Anthropology? Biology? Business? And so on.
- Do these disciplines represent different perspectives? Are they equally important? Can we prioritize them? What determines their relative importance?
- What are some ways these different perspectives overlap or intersect? Are there syntheses that are greater than the sum of the parts?
- What approaches are ignored by our academic departments? What if we look at a dictionary or the Yellow Pages to help categorize or identify the tree?
- What are some of the ways you and others might use the tree?
- Have you had any memorable experiences with trees? Are there any important family or community traditions about trees you can recall?
- Does it matter if we know the name of the tree? Does our view change if we call it a *bush* or *cactus* or *plant* or by a foreign name, instead?
- Do we see the tree more clearly by walking around it, looking from a distance, standing above or below it? Do we "see" it better by closing our eyes and touching it, smelling it, listening to it, dancing around it, meditating under it?
- Have we in any way gotten to the "essence" of the tree? Is there such a thing? Is there a central meaning to the tree regardless of the approach we take?
- Does this exercise change if we use an artificial tree or a picture of a tree? Does it change if we focus on a person or an abstraction, instead of a material object like a tree? Does the exercise change if we ask the questions in a different order?
- How do the answers to these questions change with the age, race, gender, class, professional interests, or moods of the participants?
- What is the environmental context of this tree—urban plaza, dense forest, desert? What season is it? What is "going on" around the tree? Traffic? People? Birds? Insects? What kind of parasites? What is the soil like? The climate? Are there scratches in the tree? Wires, strings, lights, signs on it? How do these factors alter our understanding?
- How do the perspectives indicated in the above questions coalesce when we address a concrete policy issue about a tree, such as whether or not to cut it down? Which of the questions increase and which decrease in significance?

- How important is it that we come to agreement about the tree? Have we achieved integration in any way—regarding our concept of the tree, our relationship to it, or our mutual ability to relate our different perspectives?

Processing Tips

At the conclusion of the exercise, I pose an open-ended question about what the participants have learned and allow for group discussion.

In some cases, I assign a follow-up writing exercise. Participants are asked to attempt a similar analysis directed toward something other than a tree. I read the papers, and the participants subsequently share ideas from this effort, especially regarding the new ways in which they have to come to understand their chosen subject.

I sometimes ask participants to reflect in their journals about how this exercise relates to their learning styles.

Contributor's Commentary

When I do this with newer students, I ask them to study the university catalogue beforehand. The more knowledgeable (academically or in terms of life experience) the participants are, the more interesting this is and the longer the exercise takes (anywhere from twenty to ninety minutes). The more interdisciplinary the facilitator is, the better this should work.

Aristotle contributed significantly to the formation of the academic disciplines in the West by arguing that each field has different content and different methodologies. The interdisciplinary tree exercise presents us with one common content and approaches it with a host of traditional and nontraditional methods and perspectives.

Psychology Tutorial

Xenia Coulter, Ithaca, New York
E-mail: xenia.coulter@esc.edu

Xenia Coulter is a faculty mentor with Empire State College and offers independent study tutorials in an individualized degree program for adults.

Developmental Intentions

I. Toward knowing as a dialogical process.

2. Surfacing and questioning assumptions underlying beliefs, ideas, actions, and positions.
4. Using one's experience to critique opinion and expert opinion to critique one's experience.
7. Associating truth not with static fact but with contexts and relationships.
III. Toward being a continuous learner.
2. Challenging oneself to learn in new realms; taking risks.
7. Setting one's learning goals, being goal-directed, and being habitual in learning.

Context

This activity is used as one of adult undergraduate students' first courses in an independent study (tutorial) program in psychology.

Description of Activity

Purpose. To assess the student's strengths and weaknesses and encourage cognitive, intellectual, and academically relevant personal development.

Format-steps-process.

1. With beginning students (in psychology), assuming that we have decided to use a textbook, I lend them a half dozen or so texts and ask them to select the one or two they like best. *Objectives:* to begin weakening their belief in the absolute truth of a particular text; begin sharing the responsibility for (and increasing their confidence in) making decisions about what and how to learn; strengthen their evaluative skills (for example, in comparing and selecting texts).

2. Throughout the course, I provide opportunities for students to collect data from friends and family that illustrate various basic psychological concepts (for example, problem solving, Piagetian principles, memory, test validity) and describe in writing what they have found. With each successive assignment I ask for more information so that by the end of the study they are able to write an abbreviated "research report." *Objectives:* to integrate their academic work into their personal lives (and encourage them to find people with whom they can share their new insights); appreciate the "messy" quality of data; provide a painless (and nonthreatening) opportunity for displaying quantitative information in graphs and tables; acquire the logic of research reporting; and encourage them to think about individual differences.

3. In some assignments, I explicitly require analysis; for example, providing students with case studies of "abnormal" behaviors for which they are asked to provide prognoses based upon a number of factors, some more important than others; or asking students to describe a known (and not necessarily liked) person's personality in terms of three theories. *Objectives:* to provide realistic opportunities to break down a whole into constituent parts as a way of thinking about a topic and helping students move beyond their reliance upon global opinions, and to encourage greater tolerance of and compassion for different behaviors.

4. I also ask students to examine some topic they feel strongly about and about which psychologists hold a particular position contrary to the student's. Some examples have included psychology's general opposition to drugs as the sole means of dealing with psychological problems, how extrasensory perception (ESP) and related phenomena are viewed in the field, and the nature-nurture issue. *Objectives:* on the one hand, to encourage students to take their own views seriously and not to be intimidated by what might be written in a text; on the other hand, to encourage them to examine why the discipline might take a contrary position and encourage them to wonder whether there is some way by which these controversies can be transformed.

Processing Tips

Every assignment can be completed successfully at various levels of sophistication so that failure is a near impossibility. For beginning or returning students, it's important to determine what a student can do, and then start there. I want to allow students some experience with success and at the same time provide them with new goals that they are likely to achieve.

Contributor's Commentary

At step 1, students are initially surprised, even shocked, by my request to have them select a book. After they have explored the texts from that perspective, however, by the time we next meet they are confident about their ability to do the work and clearly able to explain why they selected the text(s) that they did. At step 2, students are excited about their experiences with data collection and what they are able to understand (for example, how their children think or remember) and do (for example, display results). At step 3, they are surprised at how their acquaintance's personality can be interpreted in different ways, and they almost always become less judgmental. At step 4, the goal is to start a dialogue. A student's ability to accept different positions on topics in which they are emotionally vested is likely to take more time to develop than may be allotted to a particular assignment. We throw the stone and must have faith that it will have a ripple effect.

Adding Dimensions

Morris Fiddler, Chicago, Illinois
E-mail: mfiddler@wppost.depaul.edu

Morris Fiddler is a faculty mentor to undergraduate and graduate students pursuing individualized programs at the intersections of liberal learning and professional development in the School for New Learning, DePaul University. He also works with graduate students in genetic counseling at Northwestern University Medical School.

Developmental Intentions

   I. Toward knowing as a dialogical process.
      2. Surfacing and questioning assumptions underlying beliefs, ideas, actions, and positions.
      6. Paying attention to wholes as well as the parts that comprise them.
   II. Toward a dialogical relationship to oneself.
      3. Exploring life's experiences through some framework(s) of analysis.
   III. Toward being a continuous learner.
      4. Anticipating learning needed to prevent and solve problems.

Context

This activity has been used in Internet-based, independent study for adult students. Most interactions are through e-mail, with occasional meetings via telephone or in person.

Description of Activity

Purpose. To expand one's sense of self and the nature of being human, assess relative contributions of genetics and environment to human traits and states of health, recognize interactions among multiple variables, and recognize changes in perspectives that can come with new knowledge and its application.

Format-steps-process.

1. In a Web-based asynchronous format, I ask students to begin by identifying some of their existing beliefs. Each person is asked to name three traits she believes are governed exclusively by genetics and three governed exclusively by environment. (Later on, we return to these as reference points to determine whether her initial beliefs are being reinforced, changed, or becoming less clear or certain.)

2. I then ask students to take a closer look at a Nutrasweet package and explain the warning label that people with phenylketonuria should be aware of its contents. This is the beginning of considering genetic and environmental contributions to individual differences in ways that most of us don't usually do. I provide a link to a Website that serves as a resource for information on this question.

3. To further expand learners' thinking about individual differences, I ask students to read some articles that consider questions such as, "Why don't all smokers develop lung cancer? Why might some people be resistant to HIV infection?" and to read some relatively recent work that draws implicitly on a model they will encounter next.

4. At this point, I introduce a model—through readings, a page or two on the study's Website, and conversations—that distills how we might look at human traits as the outcomes of genes, environment, and their interactions. Frequently the common model of nature versus nurture becomes a point of dissonance for conversation, as does the idea of genetics as a source and study of variation and not determinism.

5. To this point, I have been treating the ideas as "out there"—external to the learner as an individual. Often, however, learners start offering comments on some shifts in perspective they are experiencing. I then raise the questions, "What relevance, if any, do these ideas hold for you at this point? Do you see indications that your thinking about yourself or human characteristics is changing? Are there ideas you are more or less sure of compared with when you began?"

6. I then ask the student to propose ideas for a specific question she would like to pursue on her own using the gene-environment model with which she is becoming familiar. I have two criteria for the question: first, that it focuses on a human trait or aspect of health; second, that the student cares about and is interested in the question or topic.

7. Meanwhile, I provide various questions that encourage increasingly sophisticated applications of the model. For example, students may select some of the following: "Is it true that every body needs milk? Admission to medical school

often follows a classical pattern of inheritance—how would you study whether there is genetics involved? What do you think accounts for variation in body weight, and what is being said by researchers on this topic? If you have children, how might you explore differences in their temperament?"

8. At the end of the course, we return to the student's initial ideas about various traits and then look at ways in which new ideas generated during the class may have changed her interpretation of others and herself.

Processing Tips

Using the student's initial beliefs as the starting or reference point, I sequence the learning toward increasingly complex activities and more sophisticated meaning-making. I also ask the learner to use her initial beliefs as a reference point for her final self-assessment.

The syllabus, on the Web, prompts a series of activities focused more on content—such as increasing knowledge of genetics and using a genetic-environment model—than on the meaning of the material to the student. However, our one-on-one interactions are directed primarily toward relationship building as a platform for conversations focused primarily on the student's self-awareness of shifts in perspective that emerge as she gains facility with the complexity of the material. To help me determine how best to use each medium, I ask myself, *What is done most effectively through interacting with me? What can the learner do on her own?*

The substantial structures I provide for the early activities taper off as the student gains confidence and facility with both the content and the process of inquiry. These structures include examples, questions, and readings to help the learner gain familiarity with the territory of genetic and environment interactions. I frequently serve as the student's memory for something she recognized in prior activities until she is more adept at converting ideas into knowledge.

Once she becomes familiar with the territory and the analytic framework, she can explore further using case(s) from her own experience by asking herself, for example, "What, if any, are known contributions of genetics to *x* phenotype? What, if any, are known environmental contributions?" Eventually, the questions shift to, "What do we know? How do we, or might we, find out more?" Somewhere in this process, doubt of her original ideas—if not outright change—almost always sets in. We can then explore underlying perceptions and beliefs that may not at first seem related to the subject matter of genetics.

Contributor's Commentary

The learning process becomes a point of explicit discussion between the student and me. Together we explore the challenges of engaging in independent study and working at a distance through an electronic medium, using progressively less-structured problems and inquiry, interacting with each other largely through our words, and moving at one's own pace with one's own discipline. Rather than focus on the logistics of being physically separated from the instructor (me), I nudge the learner toward thinking about how to effectively manage her own learning, as well as the strengths she has gained or weaknesses she has encountered.

As the adults begin to transform the ideas into knowledge, a common observation is framed generally in this way, "I am not who I thought I was but I'm not sure what to make of that. I'm looking at aspects of myself and my family differently but not with certainty." If and when a student starts to think about human nature and her own nature, the ideas of the study and their meaning begin to become more integrated.

Demystifying Modes of Inquiry

Beverly K. Firestone

Our colleague and friend, Beverly Firestone, who died during final manuscript preparations, was a faculty mentor and teacher in the School for New Learning at DePaul University, an individualized, competence-based degree program for adults.

Developmental Intentions

    I. Toward knowing as a dialogical process.
        5. Moving between separate and connected, independent and interdependent ways of knowing.
        6. Paying attention to wholes as well as the parts that comprise them.
        8. Pursuing the possibility of objective truth.
   III. Toward being a continuous learner.
        2. Challenging oneself to learn in new realms; taking risks.
        9. Drawing on multiple capacities for effective learning.

Context

This activity was developed for graduate or undergraduate courses on research methods, emphasizing nonparticipant observation, for adult learners.

Description of Activity

Purposes. To introduce learners to observational analysis (participant and nonparticipant observation), acquaint learners with the simplicity and complexity of issues when using people as sources of data, acquaint learners with methodological steps in acquiring data that can describe phenomena or eventually categorize or explain behaviors, and dispel the myths surrounding field and applied research and inquiry by demystifying it through creating an atmosphere of fun and a system of detective-like investigation.

Format-steps-process.

First session: The session presents the in-class preparation and out-of-class assignment for students. As background, students have already discussed the nature and purpose of research questions and how to determine in what sources the answers to these questions can be found. They may have noticed the shortage of studies that observe people's actions and activities though many of the questions that they are attempting to answer require people as subjects.

The "Famous Firestone Spaghetti Eating Observational Analysis Protocol" is then introduced to the class. They are given the following instructions verbally, on overheads, and in the form of a handout that is organized as it would be for a research investigator or assistant who is part of a team at the beginning a pilot phase. The instructions to the student for the first session include

1. Choose a restaurant in the greater Chicago area where spaghetti is served as a *major menu choice.* Describe your choice demographically (location, type of community, size of establishment, usual clientele, variety of cuisine, economic scale, and so forth). Obtain menus from the restaurants that you considered and be prepared to describe your reasons for choosing your observational site.

2. Ask to be seated at a corner table where you can have a good view of the majority of tables and diners.

3. Allow at least two hours for your observation. This will permit you to observe at least two seatings of diners during two periods. (You may want to inform your waiter that you are going to be there for that time.) It also gives you a warm-up time as an observer. You will see more as the session progresses.

4. Bring a notebook or journal with you. Record information on the spaghetti-eating behavior of the diners. Include age, gender, physical description, dress, relationships among diners (or your assumption, and how you arrived at it). Describe the ways that they actually eat the spaghetti and any other interesting information you observe in the process.

Session two: In *preparation* for this session, I instruct students as follows: After you have completed your observations and before you come to class, re-read your collected observations and write a report (make enough copies for *each* member of the class) that includes

1. A demographic analysis (the restaurant, location, cuisine, etc. as described in the "reasons for choice") and an analysis of the types of people you observed
2. Three to five *general statements* that summarize and categorize your observations on eating behaviors
3. Two or three possible *theories* to explain these generalizations (you may want to reflect on your own learned and preferred spaghetti-eating behavior to see whether it informs these explanations)
4. Some of the raw data—words, phrases that you used in your descriptions; for example, most unusual person, neatest
5. Three to five *questions* that have arisen from this experience (ideas for future observations; questions that grow from what you have seen)
6. Several ideas as to how you might approach a second round of observations (Does what you want to know inform how you observe and record information? If yes, how? If not, why not? Does what you want to know inform the methods of data collection that you might want to add to your study? If yes, how? If not, why not?)

To facilitate in-class processing of the observational assignment and reports, the instructor should

1. Distribute copies of *each* student's report to *all* class members.
2. Form groups of four to five members; ask them to select a spokesperson who will report their work to the large group.
3. Ask the students to look for similarities, differences, and points of interest in *all* the reports, not just those of their own group members. Ask them to construct a group-consensus summary of the observational reports by following the same format as the homework assignment: Determine three to five common themes; determine several assumptions or issues; construct several questions about the experience or for further investigation; determine two to three strategies, methods, or procedures that they might employ to gather information necessary to answer the new questions or test the assumptions. Ask the group also to keep track of where they were unable to reach consensus or agreement and of the process they used to form generalizations and categories.
4. Then ask each group to create a summary *visual presentation,* to be presented by their spokesperson. (Flip charts and colored markers work well for the presentations.)
5. Have all groups report to the large group on the results of their group analysis. As they do, keep track of each group's findings through a mind map or

some other recording or tracking method that will enable you to summarize these findings and continue the analysis by moving it to a whole-class level.

Mind mapping is a non-linear method of generating ideas by associating key words, ideas, images and impressions. A key idea or image is placed in the center of the mind map; through free association, related words or images are drawn on a line radiating out from the center, which may generate additional lines with new words. Major themes or patterns become evident in examining all the words spread across one page (Gelb, 1998, pp. 169-191).

6. When all the reports are done, process with the whole group what they have learned from this experience and how this learning positions them to pose research questions and design methods to answer them. Helpful questions might include

What have you learned from this experience?

What was the most interesting part of this protocol-analysis?

Which part did you find the most confusing or difficult?

What does a pilot contribute to a methods design?

What kinds of strategies and methods would be most appropriate for gathering the type of information needed to answer your questions or test your assumptions?

How would you chart or design a plan or course of action for that strategy of data collection?

What would be the advantages and disadvantages, points of access and blocks?

Processing Tips

Some students may express discomfort at the idea of watching others eat and then recording this behavior. I explain that this can be done very unobtrusively, and that it is hardly different from observing and commenting to others on what someone is wearing. The information gathered will be used only for in-class analysis, and the subjects are not affected by the observation.

The observation results can be processed quickly, during one postobservation meeting, or they can be processed throughout the term as an ongoing experience as a resource for the class. When appropriate, I teach content analysis and categorical analysis as a sublesson. This requires preparation of some analysis sheets with the process steps that the students would need to follow to analyze the all-class data sets.

Contributor's Commentary

At the completion of this exercise, students have performed a complete *naturalistic inquiry loop*. Their nonparticipant observation is the first step, similar to a pilot, that raises questions that will help them design future studies. They have learned to see connections between observations and real questions and issues that can arise from the data or the phenomenon being observed. This helps focus students' attention on research measures that spring from informed questions rather than simply from hunches or biases.

In addition to courses on research methods, this exercise could be used in psychology courses with sections on human behavior, in theatrical acting and directing classes to add physical behavior and gesture study to the Stanislavski creation of character, and in communications courses that contain units on meta and nonverbal communication.

Circular Questioning in Adult Learning

Thomas Hodgson, Syracuse, New York
E-mail: tomhodgson@hotmail.com

Thomas Hodgson is a counseling psychologist who has taught and advised adult learners at the University of Massachusetts at Amherst, the University of Minnesota, SUNY-Empire State College, and Vermont College of Norwich University.

Developmental Intentions

   I. Toward knowing as a dialogical process.
      3. Reframing ideas or values that seem contradictory, embracing their differences, and arriving at new meanings.
      5. Moving between separate and connected, independent and interdependent ways of knowing.
      9. Perceiving and constructing one's reality by observing and participating.
  II. Toward a dialogical relationship to oneself.
      3. Exploring life's experiences through some framework(s) of analysis.
      5. Exploring and making meaning of one's life stories within contexts (for example, societal, familial, universal).

Context

This model of inquiry is useful for promoting critical thinking skills in a variety of undergraduate and graduate subjects in both classroom teaching and mentoring one-on-one or in a group. This method can be applied to many learning activities in formal courses of study; however, the examples cited are directed at adult learners engaged in prior learning portfolio development.

Description of Activity

Purposes. To stimulate and facilitate discussion and critical thinking and to identify and give definition to learning from prior experience.

Format-steps-process.

1. During the initial steps of prior learning assessment, I ask students to gather personal documentation of all kinds, such as photographs, scrapbooks, diaries, journals, autobiographies, resumes, work samples, certificates of achievement, training records, and job descriptions. The students then discuss or write (freely and noncritically) about the activities associated with these records to begin identifying those life experiences that might be appropriate sources for prior learning assessment.

2. In the succeeding step, I ask learners to elaborate and expand on these preliminary accounts of their experience by introducing them to the process of *circular questioning* as discussed by Kassis (1987), Nelson et al. (1986), Penn (1982), Palazzoli et al., (1980), and based on the cybernetic thinking of Bateson (1979).

   In brief, circular questioning encourages examination of multiple views on a subject. Working either one-on-one, or modeling the process with the whole group, I pose questions derived from the categories below to help students discuss fully how past, present, and future or hypothetical realities are perceived, explained, and assigned meaning by themselves and others. This form of critical analysis involves three levels of inquiry, each of which contains multiple perspectives:

   Information gathering involves detailing the facts associated with a topic as derived from the learner's experience, the learner's perception of others' experiences, and official texts. Students operationally define their job responsibilities and common terminology; describe the methods and procedures they followed; and cite the outcomes of their activities.

   Context-across-time questions expand these perspectives by reframing the information gathered in the context of what was known (individually and collectively) about the particular endeavor in the past, how it is regarded today, and how it will or might be understood in the future.

Critical reflection and meaning-making questions deepen the study of the topic by pursuing the following distinctions:

Inquiring into the differences revealed in data gathering

Identifying the areas of agreement or disagreement among various perspectives about the topic

Actively considering from multiple perspectives (self and others) the explanations for and significance of truths revealed through this process of inquiry.

Processing Tips

To offer an example of circular questioning in support of prior learning portfolio development, the following is the inquiry I might pose to a student whose experiential learning essay concerns her work in the mental health field. Once I have worked through a sequence of such questions about one aspect of a learner's experience, the learner (or the group) can usually begin to pose their own questions of themselves and of one another. (It is important to note that I do not expect students to respond to *all* of the questions suggested below; rather, once they become familiar with the model, I encourage them to focus on the areas of inquiry about their experience that are most personally meaningful and substantive to analyze for academic credit.)

Sample Circular Questions

Information Gathering

1. Describe the primary functions and duties of your job as a mental health worker.
2. Detail a typical sequence or process you follow that reflects the depth and breadth of your knowledge and skills in that field.
3. What outcomes can you cite that are a direct result of your involvement in mental health work?

Context Across Time

1. How might you describe the typical functions or duties of your job in mental health when you first began this activity? In what way will the duties of your job be defined in the future?

2. What were the sequences or procedures you followed when you first began this work? How might these processes be accomplished in the future?
3. What were the outcomes or the impact of your work in the mental health field in the past? What outcomes are being sought in your work in the future?

Critical Reflection

Differences and Similarities

1. What differences do you notice between how your role in mental health was defined when you began and what you do now? What is similar about your work then and now?
2. What differences have you observed between the public and private practice of mental health care? How are the systems of care similar? How similar or different were they when you entered the field?
3. How were the therapeutic goals or outcomes different between what you were introduced to in the past and now? In what way are they similar?

Agreement and Disagreement

1. Would others in our society agree or disagree with how mental health care is being delivered now, in the past, or will be in the future?
2. How might other mental health workers (now, in the past, in the future) comment about the medication practices you follow in doing your job? In what specific ways would they agree or disagree with how you complete various steps along the way toward reaching a specific goal or outcome in your work? How would people in other cultures comment about the methods used in this country to address mental health concerns?
3. Is there agreement or disagreement in the field about the quality of inpatient care you have observed or contributed to in your work in mental health?

Significance or Meaning

1. How significant is your role in mental health to the overall activities of your agency? How valuable was your work considered to be in the past? How will its value be considered in the future? What does that mean to you as a mental health professional?
2. What are some of the reasons for the uncertain future of the mental health field, and how will substantial changes in the procedures you currently follow affect you? How do you explain the differences in the definitions of

effective mental health care established by employers and managed care providers compared to those developed by the clinical community?

3. What meaning is assigned by other cultures to the work you do as a mental health worker? How significant is it to you that other cultures may strongly disagree with the way that mental illness is identified and treated in this country?

Contributor's Commentary

There are many conceivable avenues for reflection when dimensions of experience are explored in this recursive way. Circular questioning fosters a continual series of dialectical tensions between what is known to the student and what may be of comparable or contrasting nature in the world. It follows that inherent to the process is the consideration of multicultural and multidisciplinary perspectives. Within the particular activity of writing about experience, this teaching strategy helps prior learning portfolio writers merit advanced levels of academic credit by moving them beyond merely describing what they have done in their lives to actively discovering, identifying, defining, and constructing meaning about what they have learned.

This method of inquiry finds support in the pedagogy of Paulo Friere (1986), a Brazilian educator and philosopher who saw the search for knowledge as a collaborative activity on the part of the student and the teacher. Circular questions posed of both agents in the learning process foster deeper meanings and nonhierarchical determinants of truth. Moreover, professionals in adult education who practice hypothesis formulation and reformulation in and about their teaching will find circular questioning methods to be invaluable tools which benefit both their students and themselves.

References

Bateson, G. (1979). *Mind and nature: A necessary unity.* New York: Dutton.

Freire, P. (1986). *Politics of education.* Greenwich, CT: Bruner-Mazel.

Kassis, J. (1987). Personal communication. Family Therapy Training Program: Crossroad Community Growth Center, Holyoke, MA.

Nelson, T. S. , Fleuridas, C., & Rosenthal, D. (1986). The evolution of circular questions: Training family therapists. *Journal of Marital and Family Therapy, 12(2),* 113–127.

Palazzoli Selvini, M., Boscolo, L., Cecchin, G., & Prata, G. (1980). Hypothesizing-circularity-neutrality: Three guidelines for the conductor of the session. *Family Process, 19,* 3–12.

Penn, P. (1982). Circular questioning. *Family Process, 21,* 267–280.

Through Another's Eyes: Using Concept Mapping in Cross-Cultural Training

Paula S. Horvath-Neimeyer, Gainesville, Florida
E-mail: phorvath@unf.edu

Paula S. Horvath-Neimeyer is an assistant professor of communications in the department of communications and visual arts of the University of North Florida.

Developmental Intentions

    I. Toward knowing as a dialogical process.
       1. Inquiring into and responding openly to others' ideas.
       6. Paying attention to wholes as well as the parts that comprise them.
    II. Toward a dialogical relationship to oneself.
       5. Exploring and making meaning of one's life stories within contexts (for example, societal, familial, universal).
    III. Toward being a continuous learner.
       2. Challenging oneself to learn in new realms; taking risks.
    V. Toward connection with others.
       1. Mediating boundaries between one's connection to others and one's individuality.

Context

I use concept mapping in my mass communication and interpersonal communication classes to provide students with a concrete technique for comparing their own world perspectives with those of other cultures.

Description of Activity

Purpose. To heighten people's knowledge and awareness of other cultures and to develop a conceptual framework that can be used to understand the world.

Format-steps-process. This is a multiphase process that begins with having students learn how to construct a concept map and then apply that process to an interview assignment. I will explain the process by first describing the steps of mapping and then merging that with the interviews.

Concept Mapping

1. I begin by introducing students to the notion of cognitive concepts by pointing out the idiosyncratic nature of concepts. I ask them to describe the men-

tal picture they have when thinking of concepts such as dog, tree, or game. I use these idiosyncratic views of a concept as examples of one reason people misunderstand messages. I also point out that such misunderstandings are especially prevalent during cross-cultural communication when individuals interpret messages in accordance with not only idiosyncratic personal concepts, but with different culturally based concepts as well.

2. I then provide students a list of features of a multidimensional phenomenon and ask them to arrange them hierarchically and connect them with lines labeled with linking phrases. I ask the students first to place them in order from the most to the least inclusive and then transcribe the features on a map.

3. Finally, I ask students to construct phrases that serve to connect the linked features. This gives them practice in concept mapping. *Example:* I might give them five features of the oceans—water, fish, plankton, waves, and coral reefs—and ask them to arrange the features hierarchically. I would then ask the students to draw lines to show the relationships among these various features, and finally to label the lines (for example, water contains fish, coral reefs support fish, plankton feed fish, and so forth).

Interview Assignment

4. I ask the students to select as the subject for the assignment a cultural group with which they have had little personal experience.

5. The students then interview a member of the selected cultural group. To help prepare them for meeting this person, I ask students to complete a concept map (as described previously) that indicates their own understanding of the culture selected.

6. Students conduct the interview during the following week and then complete a report that describes their experience.

7. During the classroom session following the interview, I ask students to concept map the culture as viewed from the *interviewee's* perspective.

8. The session culminates with students summarizing the two concept maps—their own and the one they developed from their interviewee's perspective—and emphasizing the differences.

Closure: These activities culminate in a discussion of students' observations regarding the maps and what they gained from the experiences.

Contributor's Commentary

The two concept maps highlight distinct differences between their own prior cultural concepts and the concepts of their sources of information. The students' maps are generally much less complex, whereas the maps based on the sources' concepts of their own cultures contain both more features and more linking phrases.

When I ask students to talk about this exercise they often describe how it has altered their concepts of their *own* culture. For example, many report that if they were to now construct concept maps of their own current cultural perspective they would be very different from the maps they might have drawn prior to the exercise. Others say that concept mapping helps them externalize cultural concepts, thus making the concepts more understandable and better integrated. In addition, mapping both sets of perceptions (their own and their interviewees') appears to have long-term effects for some learners. "The differences in the maps made me realize I rarely stop and think about others' perceptions," wrote one student. "It made me think I should be more understanding."

Responsibility for promoting and enabling the cross-cultural awareness of students has created special challenges for educators. Many approaches are limited, however, if they don't relate the students' personal experiences to information provided in the classroom. Although concept mapping has been used most often in science classrooms, it is very useful in the setting of cross-cultural education. Because meaning is not contained within events but assigned to events by people, it is important to understand how students are attaching meaning to cross-cultural experiences. Concept maps provide a way to articulate and negotiate those meanings, as well as highlight how people from various cultures interpret an event in common.

Problem-Focused Education

Don Margetson, Brisbane, Queensland, Australia
E-mail: d.margetson@mailbox.gu.edu.au

Don Margetson is senior lecturer in the School of Vocational, Technology, and Arts Education, Griffith University. He has written widely on problem-focused education (problem-based learning) within the context of ethics, being, and knowledge.

Developmental Intentions

I. Toward knowing as a dialogical process.
6. Paying attention to wholes as well as the parts that comprise them.
10. Tapping into and drawing on tacit knowledge.

III. Toward being a continuous learner.
1. Reflecting on one's own and others' experiences as a guide to future behavior.
7. Setting one's own learning goals, being goal-directed, and being habitual in learning.
V. Toward connection with others.
5. Recognizing that collective awareness and thinking transform the sum of their parts.

Context

This activity has been effective in university-based adult and vocational education with undergraduate and postgraduate students.

Description of Activity

Purpose. To foster a community of learners (teachers and students) around their roles as *inquirers* rather than in the relationship of transmitters and receivers of information; and to experience and give expression to knowledge, understanding, feeling, thought, critical reflection, and action as it develops in relation to a reality.

Format-steps-process.

1. I introduce the problem and context through a written study guide that includes some general suggestions on how to proceed through the six-item structure. I have found it important to emphasize that the components of the process indicate what needs to be done but not a necessary order in which they need to be done—apart from the first and last items.
2. I provide descriptions of the six items of the process that speak to the remainder of the method:

Problem-focus: The formal process of study begins by identifying clearly what the problem, or problems, seem to be in the situation that is being considered.

Initial inquiry: The problem is investigated, including suggestions by participants, prior to reading of possible explanations of the problem and tentative prioritization of multiple problems for attention. A vital requirement is the identification as clearly as possible of what participants need to learn to understand better the problem and possible responses to it.

Consulting resources: Reading and studying are necessary to develop, revise, extend, and deepen knowledge and understanding related to the problem. Selections of the resources are guided by what is identified in *the initial inquiry* component as what is needed to be learned to work with and solve the problem(s). Reading around the topic and issues is not passive but an active exploration of resources to help resolve the problem.

Critical reflection: An explicit, systematic consideration is required along the lines of, "In light of what has been learned so far, does the problem—together with any tentative solutions that may have been contemplated—as initially identified and formulated remain as framed or is revision necessary? Has an unforeseen problem emerged that requires a reformulation of the entire effort?"

Iteration: This stage reminds participants that revisiting (questions, information, explanations), revising, and rethinking are necessary throughout.

Conclusion: This involves articulation of the solution to the problem or acknowledgement of the intractability of the problem, including the extent to which a "learning to live with it" lack of solution should be acknowledged. An explicit conclusion helps acknowledge that the quality, breadth, and depth of conclusions will often depend on the time and resources available to reach them.

Example of a problem. During a three-week period, we looked at potential conflicts that may arise when an educational institution hires a job search and placement service to work with students. In the particular problem used, the firm was under pressure to give preferential treatment to students likely to be placed successfully (the more competent, locally encultured, and so forth) because it was paid on a results basis. Through the three-week educational process, we investigated ethical concerns centering on conflicts among educational value, social justice, and commercial viability.

Processing Tips

The role of the educator in this context is that of a guide helping students learn through inquiry, not as a didactic instructor. Helpful questioning is vital; simple telling (information transmission) undermines the educative process. The intent is to help students see that they need to guide their own learning by ensuring that they learn to ask themselves. For example: "What do we need to know in order to understand—and, if possible, solve—the problem we're working on, and how can we best find and learn what is needed?"

Contributor's Commentary

Critical reflection is essential and is used throughout the process. It is identified as a discrete item only to ensure that the importance of systematic critical reflection is recognized and undertaken.

Experience has shown that despite great pains to explain that the six items are a crutch to be thrown away as soon as one feels able to proceed independently, some participants and, surprisingly, staff persisted in seeing the items as some kind of straitjacket. This may be due to the difficulty some people find in changing from a passive, information-transmission mode of learning to a more active mode in which one seeks deeper understanding.

References

Boud, D., & Feletti, G. (Eds.). (1997). *The challenge of problem-based learning* (2nd ed.). New York: St. Martin's Press.

Margetson, D. B. (1994). Current educational reform and the significance of problem-based learning. *Studies in Higher Education, 19* (1), 5–19.

Margetson, D. B. (1996). Beginning with the essentials: Why problem-based learning begins with problems. *Education for Health: Change in Training and Practice, 9* (1), 61–69.

Margetson, D. B. (1998). What counts as problem-based learning? *Education for Health: Change in Training and Practice, 11,* (2), 93–201.

Margetson, D. B. (1999). The relation between understanding and practice in problem-based medical education. *Medical Education, 33* (5), 359–364.

Developing Media Literacy

Ann M. Taylor, Highland Heights, Kentucky
E-mail: taylorann@mail.nku.edu

Ann M. Taylor has taught in adult-focused educational environments for twenty years. She is principal and director of a nonprofit organization "Touching Kids' Lives" that provides educational enrichment services for young people, their caregivers, and teachers.

Developmental Intentions

    I. Toward knowing as a dialogical process.
        1. Inquiring into and responding openly to others' ideas.
        2. Surfacing and questioning assumptions underlying beliefs, ideas, actions, and positions.

III. Toward being a continuous learner.

    2. Challenging oneself to learn in new realms; taking risks.

IV. Toward self-agency and self-authorship.

    7. "Naming and claiming" what one has experienced and knows.

  V. Toward connection with others.

    5. Recognizing that collective awareness and thinking transform the sum of their parts.

Context

The activity can be used in undergraduate courses on communications, women's studies, multicultural issues—any course for which media literacy would be among course objectives.

Description of Activity

Purpose. To examine how the mass media treat race and gender issues, develop methods for evaluating media representations of women and people of color, and integrate personal experience with analysis of text.

Format-steps-process. The first four steps are repeated throughout the course, in iterative fashion, with each set of readings.

1. Students first read articles and essays from assigned texts. I use Biagi and Kern-Foxworth (1997) and Chisom and Washington (1997).
2. Students then write a reaction essay. The focus questions: How well does this match your own knowledge and experience? Why do you think this is so?
3. Then students come together in small groups to discuss their reflection on their individual experiences and to look at the variety of experiences within the group. The focus: How does our combined knowledge change or confirm our initial reflection on the readings?
4. In the next step, each small group reports back to the large group on their reflection and reaction to the readings. This sparks further discussion about differences and similarities between individuals' experiences and the readings.
5. In addition to reading, reflecting, reacting, and reporting on the assigned readings, students also engage in action research. For example, they watch certain TV programs, maintain an observation log for several days, and report. Their analysis focuses on content, context, and themes. This process continues throughout the course. Students can brainstorm a list of likely issues to examine, or the instructor can provide prompts, such as the following:

    Does the program support or refute the readings?

    How do we usually react to TV programming?

How much do we rely on our own experience to evaluate what we see on TV?

What effect does our increased awareness, as a result of this course's activities, have on our reactions?

Alternatively (or in addition), they read and compare a variety of newspaper and magazine accounts of a particular incident (current or historical):

What differences and similarities are observed among different print sources?

How might these be explained, given the kind of publication, its probable audience, editorial policy, and so forth?

6. The culminating project is the symposium. Each small group selects a topic sparked by the course discussion and readings for further exploration. The members of the group work together to research and report on their topic; for example, women in the news, the beauty machine, minorities and sports, and so on. They gather additional information to complement the readings and include personal experience as further illumination. Their research may support, refine, or contradict the text. In the final week of class, the groups present their findings to the class as a whole. Groups are encouraged to use examples from the media that support their analysis; for example, films, slides, video clips.

Processing Tips

Depending on the length and frequency of the class meetings and the amount of reading material, the first four steps can be repeated over several days or several weeks. The action research can be introduced at any time. The symposium is a final presentation and may take place over more than one session, if needed.

It is important to establish "safety" early in the course, since people will be discussing issues that may touch them personally. I begin by speaking about the likelihood that people will have strong reactions, and asking that students be sensitive to one another. I emphasize that everyone wants to be heard; therefore, everyone must also listen, even when their classmate's experiences are different from their own. At the same time, I urge people not to avoid all conflict, but to handle it with thoughtfulness and care, since major learning often happens when we hear someone's experience and perspective that is different from our own.

I also keep the small group members constant, so that trust and safety builds over time. We also occasionally stop and debrief our experience of the process: How does it feel to discuss this issue at this time?

Contributor's Commentary

When the focus of the course is media, race, and gender, we closely examine portrayals in the mass media of women and four ethnic groups: African Americans, Native Americans, Latinos, and Asian Americans. An additional or different focus could also explore the influence of politics and economics on such portrayals. Students are usually surprised to discover subtle sexist or racist portrayals in TV shows that they may have formerly enjoyed, and to see how differently print publications may frame issues that touch on gender and race.

Further aspects of study could include the effects of discriminatory hiring practices in mass media, communication education, and alternative media (which have provided additional opportunities for women and people of color to be heard). This last topic can be a topic of some interest, particularly if contrasted with portrayals in the dominant media.

Though the focus of this course as described here is media's portrayal of race and gender issues, the process could be used to explore any topic around which learners have sufficient experience. Although this exercise is designed as an entire course, pieces of it could be integrated in other courses to take place over one or a few class meetings.

References

Biagi, S., & Kern-Foxworth, M. (1997). *Facing differences: Race, gender, and mass media.* Thousand Oaks, CA: Pine Forge Press.

Chisom, R., & Washington, M. (1997). *Undoing racism.* New Orleans, LA: People's Institute Press.

Providing a Learning Culture

Kim Winkelman, Gilford, New Hampshire
E-mail: kwinkelman@tec.nh.us

Kim "Little Bear" Winkelman is director, Extended Learning and Virtual Campus, New Hampshire Community Technical College. He is a tribal enrolled Native American.

Developmental Intentions

I. Toward knowing as a dialogical process.
10. Tapping into and drawing on tacit knowledge.

   II. Toward a dialogical relationship to oneself.
      5. Exploring and making meaning of one's life stories within contexts (for example, societal, familial, universal).
   IV. Toward self-agency and self-authorship.
      2. Accepting responsibility for choices one has made and will make.
      6. Distinguishing what one has created for oneself from what is imposed by social, cultural, and other forces.
   V. Toward connection with others.
      4. Contributing one's voice to a collective endeavor.

Context

This exercise has been used in courses in sociology and social problems for diverse learners at a community college and in social science courses (sociology, science of society, race, and ethnic relations) at a private four-year liberal arts college.

Description of Activity

These techniques are applied during the life of a given course.

Purpose. To provide a learning culture, stimulate development of students' conceptual understanding, permit students to transform the acquired material to their value system in terms of relevance and concern, and prompt students' judgment of new knowledge that brings about change and ultimately action.

Format-steps-process (for the class as a whole).

1. I assign a reading (for example, a chapter) from the required text and pose a topic question connected to that reading.
2. In the class session we begin with an open discussion of the material: I initiate by talking about my own confusion or problem I had with the material (to help "level the playing field"). They, likewise, respond with their concerns, or what I call the *muddy points*. We discuss those points and how the author or text might have presented the material differently. *Objectives:* From students' responses I gain a better knowledge of their understanding of the material, and through their explanations, a better understanding of their background experiences—valuable information for mentoring the student.
3. We then move on to the topic question handed out at the end of the last class. I use their responses to mentor the class into synthesizing the material; that is, applying the material to their life and the greater society to which they belong. *Objectives:* Through this interaction students provide each other with a foundation for perceiving experiences, and thus they approach meaning making from a different perspective.

4. Following our class discussion students gather into groups (they must form new groups each session). At this step, they begin the process of formulating new questions and discuss what they have learned from the text and discussions. Each group must articulate what they have learned by the next class (that is, outcomes). *Objectives:* Here I am most interested in the common patterns that people are seeing and their concepts of understanding and learning from each other.

5. At the next class we list these outcomes and discuss them. Occasionally, I will present the class with a video, film, or documentary related to the topic of the day to further stimulate thought or to reinforce a point made in class. *Objectives:* Here I am most concerned with change in perspectives of personal values in the aftermath of the learning process.

6. Once this cycle is set we open each class with a discussion of group outcomes and the topic question from the previous class, present and discuss new material, and work in small groups for more in-depth feedback and reflection. *Objectives:* Here I look for a growth pattern in the student through her or his understanding and articulation of the material. It is the integration of the content of the subject matter, the comprehension and usage of the professional concepts, and the application of the acquired knowledge to the student's life-cycle that provide a learning culture to future development.

Format-process-steps (for independent research projects). Each student selects a question or topic to explore that is important to him or her. I provide basic parameters—the project must be concerned with a social issue pertinent to the course material; the methodology may be quantitative or qualitative. *Objectives:* I am most interested in how students develop their question(s) (their pursuit of interest) and how they connect their present understanding of the issue to what others have said about it.

Processing Tips

Regarding step 5, the film, video, or documentary presents real-life experiences of people described in their own words and focuses on contemporary issues. The sight and sound techniques enhance students' acquired knowledge through multiple intelligences (relating to others, transforming and connecting the whole, arriving at new meaning derived from different context and content).

Contributor's Commentary

My specific technique of teaching is derived from several sources, including Freire (1997), Gardner (1993), Norman (1982), and Gilligan (1982). To me, learning is a developmental process often tainted by social conditioning. How one gains knowledge is as important as the knowledge itself. Learning involves the convergence of a self-process (relationship to oneself) and the interrelationship of others to a context over time.

At each step, the student guides the scope and priority of the material as well as his or her experience. As a teacher, I see my role as facilitator and mentor. Since students enter the class or course at different levels of development, I provide them the tools and opportunities to pursue their interests, hence offering a space for their growth and development. I am always exploring the students' interests, assessing their understanding of material, and guiding them to formulate new questions. This process either validates their value system or, more often, challenges preconceived ideas; this challenge, in turn, requires that they attempt to reconcile their new ideas in relation to their previous ideas and others' ideas.

Along the way they learn the competencies outlined in the course syllabus in order to pursue the ideas or questions that animate them, such as, for example, the language, theories, and issues of sociology or race relations. They *become* by doing and by being mentored to analyze information instead of merely respond to questions of fact. It is a dynamic process that involves dialogue at the individual and interactive group levels.

References

Freire, P. (1992). *Pedagogy of the oppressed*. New York: Continuum.

Gardner, H. (1993). *Frames of the mind: The theory of multiple intelligences*. New York: Basic Books.

Gilligan, C. (1982). *In a different voice: Psychological theory and women's development*. Cambridge: Harvard University Press.

Norman, D. (1982). *Learning and memory*. San Francisco: Freeman.

CHAPTER NINE

PERFORMING-SIMULATING

This strategy is about *doing*—not performing *arts* but performing a *task*. For example, Don McCormick's "Field Study Reflection" (p. 224) involves doing something in the field. In the case of simulation, it is doing something that is as close to "real" as possible; for example, Susan Timm's "And Your Point Is? A Listening Experiential Exercise" (p. 207) and Rita Cashman's "Executive Coaching Practice" (p. 187).

Activities that extend over more than one session begin with Rosemary Caffarella's "Learning Activity Project" on page 211.

◆ ◆ ◆

Creating a Western Town

William Bergquist, Oakland, California
E-mail: WbergQ@aol.com

William Bergquist, president of the Professional School of Psychology, consults to collegiate institutions, corporations, human service agencies, and churches.

Developmental Intentions

I. Toward knowing as a dialogical process.
    7. Associating truth not with static fact but with contexts and relationships.
III. Toward being a continuous learner.
    9. Drawing on multiple capacities for effective learning.
V. Toward connection with others.
    1. Mediating boundaries between one's connection to others and one's individuality
    4. Contributing one's voice to a collective endeavor.
    5. Recognizing that collective awareness and thinking transform the sum of their parts.

Context

This exercise can be used virtually in any organization as part of a team-building, training, or other organizational development initiative.

Description of Activity

Purpose. To help participants become acquainted with one another before starting a new project, class, or retreat; and to help participants create a humorous, yet thought-provoking, metaphor for their own working relationship and the appropriate distribution of roles and responsibilities in their group/team.

Format-steps-process. This exercise is best used as an opening activity for a newly formed group or team.

1. In addition to having participants provide their names and something about what they do and who they are in their "back-home" job, ask them to envision the role that they would like to take in a "class B" Western movie. The instructions go something like this: "In addition to offering us your name and a little bit about what you do back at work, I would like you to imagine that we are about to create a brand new town somewhere in the Wild West. Imagine that this town looks a whole lot like all of the really bad Western movies you saw as a child on TV or at the movies. I would like you to choose the job that you would like to take on in this town. Who would you like to be? When you used to watch those Westerns on TV or at the theater, what role did you always want to play?"

2. There is usually some initial awkwardness, given that this is not the type of assignment that most of us are confronted with on the job and the norms of the group are not yet established. Participants are probably wondering: "Is this serious or humorous? How fanciful can I be? What if I don't want to participate?"

The facilitator's active participation at this point is essential. Offer several interesting and "off-the-wall" suggestions of the possible roles to be played: "One of us can play the role of sheriff, or dance hall floozy, or rakish outlaw, or even town drunk. What about the parson or the shopkeeper? The worldly bartender? The hermit or gold prospector who comes down from the hills once a month? What about the cattle baroness who owns everything in town?"

3. After allowing a few seconds for people to decide on their role, model the next step in the process by providing your own name, something about your background (very brief and low key), and the role you would like to play in this Western town. The facilitator's role should be rather central to the functioning of the town, but should also be a bit off-center (for example, the town doctor or the medicine man or woman in a local tribe). Then say a few words (very brief and more suggestive than definitive) about why you chose this role ("I want to be the barmaid so that I can find out what people are really feeling about this town." "I love to work with other people in an educational context. So I want to be the local school teacher.").

4. Invite other participants to offer their name, briefly describe their back-home job, and indicate the role they want to play in the Western town. This exercise tends to intrigue participants, so rather than talking about (or subtly bragging about) their real job, they move right into the exercise of creating a Western town. This attention to the fanciful task is constructive for most groups, as it diverts attention away from competitive and ego-gratifying introductions of self toward the playful creation of a new community.

It is not necessary to go around the circle in a regimented manner. People can be invited to make their brief presentation when they are ready, in any order. This way, those who are more comfortable, brave, or outgoing speak first, setting the tone (as well as establishing the initial norms) for the group. The facilitator may remain inactive during this process or can serve as *encourager, inquirer,* and *connector.*

- *Encourager:* The facilitator can encourage quiet members or serve as a cheerleader for members who take a bit of a risk. If a participant wants to take on a role that another member of the team or group has already chosen, I may provoke a brief discussion among all the participants about how the town is going to accommodate two or more people taking the same role (two preachers, three bartenders, a bunch of bandits, perhaps three hookers). I also support each member's contribution: A "thank you" after each completed self-presentation not only sets an appreciative tone but also serves as a marker for the next participant to begin.
- *Inquirer:* As they make their presentations, the facilitator can ask participants why they chose a particular role (if an explanation is not forthcoming). It is

important, however, not to be too probing or too psychoanalytic. Explanations should be taken at face value and not subjected to excessive interpretation.

- *Connector:* The facilitator (and other participants when they see patterns emerging) can begin to link various roles as they are being presented. This might initially be done in a humorous way, then often in a more thoughtful manner (as these linkages relate to the purposes and concerns of the group or team). The facilitator, for instance, might note that the local shop owner will probably have to do business with the local banker, or that the preacher will probably find many prospective converts among all participants who have taken on the role of town drunk, bandit, or hooker.

5. After each participant has self-identified, I offer a few comments about the jobs that are being done in the real world as well as the roles being played in the fanciful Western town. What roles are missing? There often is no one selling groceries or raising crops or managing the town bank. How will this town stay alive? What additional roles might have to be played by group or team participants? As this discussion proceeds, it will often turn easily from the fictional town to the formation of this team or group. What role should each member play and how do we ensure that this team or group will stay alive? The discussion is often rich and open, having been aided by the playful introduction of the Western town. The exercise at this point comes to an end (usually after about twenty to thirty minutes).

Processing Tips

When the facilitator chooses his or her initial role (step 2), a good move is to pick roles that are typically played by someone of the opposite gender. As a male I often select the role of the seasoned (and wise) barmaid or local schoolmarm. By shifting gender roles, the facilitator opens the vista to a much wider exploration of roles and resources in the group.

When the exercise as described above comes to an end, the facilitator and, in particular, group or team participants can continue to use the discoveries made during construction of the Western town throughout the course of the meeting, training program, or retreat. This opening exercise usually serves one of five bridging functions:

- *Clarifying Group or Team Roles.* Since each person takes on a role in the Western town, the facilitator and other participants can readily make references back to these "fantasized" roles. These comments should encourage reflection and discussion rather than serving as "got ya's." For example, "You seem to be taking over the role of sheriff in this group—I thought Sue had that job." "I see the 'school teacher' in you coming out. What is it that this group or team needs to learn from you . . . and do we all accept you as our teacher?" It is important to keep the metaphoric comments light and not too psychoanalytic.

• *Clarifying Group or Team Expectations.* When participants are identifying desired roles in the Western town, they are often indicating something about the kind of environment in which they would like to work—though admittedly their preferences are being taken to the extreme in this exercise. They might like the town to be exciting, or to be unregulated, or to be orderly. Connections back to the original statements made by participants are often helpful in the identification of personal preferences regarding work environments: "I remember that you chose to be a merchant because you like to bring order to a community, while providing service. You seem to be playing that role in this group as well and seem to want our group to be a bit less chaotic than it is now. Am I correct in this observation?"

• *Broadening the Base of Group or Team Participation.* Some participants "come alive" during the Western town exercise. They more freely interact with other members and talk about themselves when they are in this playful setting. The Western town metaphor may thus prove to be of value in bringing out quiet members: "We haven't heard from our bartender for awhile. Maybe you can pour up a couple of drinks, [Steve/Sally] and comment on what you have observed in this rowdy dance hall." "If I'm not mistaken, [Burt/Betty] is the only storekeeper in this town. What do you think [Burt/Betty] about how we might make this whole venture more viable in terms of both marketing and pricing these educational services?"

• *Providing a Safe Place for Addressing Group or Team Frustrations.* The Western town metaphor can provide a safe haven not only for quiet group members but also those who might become frustrated with the processes or outcomes of the group. The facilitator might note that a group member seems agitated regarding something happening in the group and, as a result, might suggest: "We seem to be in need of a gunslinger right now. Can you lend us a hand?" Or "Maybe the town needs a parson to keep peace or heal the wounds. What do you think [Marc/Melissa]? Are you available for this job?"

• *Identifying Collective Themes and Learning of the Group or Team.* Finally, the metaphor can be used in a collective sense to identify broad themes that have emerged in the group or team: "We seem to have moved away from the bar and dance hall into the town's school house and church. Why do you think we made the move and what do you think are the benefits and costs associated with becoming a more respectable town?" The Western town can also provide a context in which members of a group might reflect on lessons they have learned in the process of struggling with a process or content issues: "We seem to have finally brought 'law and order' to our town. How did we do it?"

Contributor's Commentary

This activity seems to be very light, even frivolous. However, it can provoke serious discussion—especially after the meeting, training session, or retreat is under way and people start to focus on the issues around which the event was instituted. The Western town becomes a safe place for the group or team to go when it wants to begin discussing these more serious matters. They may start with the metaphoric town and the roles they play there, then turn the discussion to the real world. The metaphoric town becomes a testing ground (even a sanctuary) for group analysis, planning, and action.

References

Bergquist, W. (1993). *The postmodern organization: Mastering the art of irreversible change.* San Francisco: Jossey-Bass.

Morgan, G. (1997). *Imaginization: The art of creative management.* San Francisco: Berrett-Koehler.

Morgan, G. (1999). *Images of organizations* (2nd ed.). Newbury Park, CA.: Sage.

Wheatley, M. (1992) *Leadership and the new science: Discovering order in a chaotic world* (2nd ed.). San Francisco: Berrett-Koehler.

Executive Coaching Practice

Rita Cashman, Oak Park, Illinois
E-mail: racashman@aol.com

Rita Cashman has been an independent consultant for over twenty years. For the last fifteen years, she has specialized in providing wholistic individualized coaching to high-performing executives and professionals.

Developmental Intentions

    I. Toward knowing as a dialogical process.
        1. Inquiring into and responding openly to others' ideas.
        3. Reframing ideas or values that seem contradictory, embracing their differences, and arriving at new meanings.
        4. Using one's experience to critique expert opinion and expert opinion to critique one's experience.
      10. Tapping into and drawing on tacit knowledge.
   III. Toward being a continuous learner.
        8. Seeking authentic feedback from others.

Context

This activity is used as part of a three-day workshop for coaches and as part of an ongoing supervision group that meets periodically for half-day sessions. Group members are select, experienced coaches who help corporate and professional clients achieve high performance and work and life satisfaction.

Description of Activity

Purpose. To develop, refine, and practice advanced coaching skills such as deep listening and rapport, identification of issues, generation of choices for intervention, and reframing of ideas through practicing on "live" personal or client cases.

    Format-steps-process.

1. Setup (five to fifteen minutes): In a group of six, two members volunteer, one to coach, the other to be coached, with regard to a real personal or professional challenge or a client case. The *coachee* may select by whom she would like to be coached; at times, two or more people rotate as coach, or the whole group serves as coach. In some instances, the coachee will choose to role-play a client, in which case the coachee briefs the group and the coach on the background of the case or situation. *Example:* "The CEO at X corporation wants me to help his vice president of marketing become a better leader and prepare to succeed him. The VP is not sure he wants coaching, the CEO is part of the problem, and the whole company seems very dysfunctional. I feel overwhelmed, unwanted, and not sure I want this job."

2. Practice coaching session (usually up to thirty minutes; however, it may take longer if there are pauses for input from group): The coach and coachee conduct a practice-coaching session with other group members observing. The practice conversation may run unbroken to a natural stopping point, or the coach may call time-out to ask for help from the group.

3. Processing (up to thirty minutes): Typically, the sequence is as follows:

> The coachee reports on the experience of being coached, what helped, what else might have helped.

> The coach comments on what she experienced as coach, what she felt worked, where she felt stuck.

> The group comments on items such as quality of rapport and what enhanced it, important cues or clues the coach noticed and used, critical choices the coach made, effective interventions and what made them work.

Group members use their own coaching skills to offer alternative possibilities, other issues that could be explored, other directions the practice coaching session might have taken, and other options for intervention (especially regarding places the coach got stuck).

The focus is on unpacking and analyzing what the coach did well intuitively, thus helping her gain conscious awareness of her own intuitive capabilities.

Contributor's Commentary

This coaching process is centered on the client rather than on models or techniques. The coach seeks to listen and attend to the client while integrating intuitive and analytic skills and processes.

The participants are experienced corporate coaches and have a grounding in various models, in particular neurolinguistic programming. These coaches are often working with clients on issues such as self-management, leadership style and presence, communication, conflict resolution, life balance, stress, and burnout. Ideally, the coach helps her clients become more congruent and to achieve their desired outcomes through the alignment of desired behaviors, necessary skills and competencies, beliefs and values, personal identity, and larger mission.

The coaching practice exercise provides multilayered learning opportunities, as the group is coaching the coach who is coaching a coach. It gives learners the opportunity to use their own experience to critique other talented coaches and to draw on the expertise of others to critique themselves.

The practice exercise requires a skilled facilitator to set frames that provide ample safety and support as learners receive feedback and suggestions. Important frames include

- We are all learners here.
- There is no one right way to coach.
- None of us, if we could repeat a session, would do it the same way.
- Each of us has our own unique blend of skills and experience, and we must draw from that source as we work.
- Our goal is to develop humble trust in our own coaching skills and to expand these through modeling other approaches.

The facilitator guides the group in discovering underlying structures and modeling what is effective, thereby helping participants gain mastery.

This exercise may be a model for practicing other skills whereby learners must draw upon a whole body of cognitive and intuitive skills and are more intent upon exploring options than right answers. It allows learners to exercise tolerance for low structure and ambiguity, which are essential competencies for coaching.

Lifeboat Allegory

Toby Glicken, Chicago, Illinois
E-mail: tglicken@condor.depaul.edu

Toby Glicken is currently developing and teaching life science courses for non-science majors in the School for New Learning, DePaul University.

Developmental Intentions

    I. Toward knowing as a dialogical process.
       2. Surfacing and questioning assumptions underlying beliefs, ideas, actions, and positions.
   III. Toward being a continuous learner.
      1. Reflecting on one's own and others' experiences as a guide to future behavior.
   IV. Toward self-agency and self-authorship.
      6. Distinguishing what one has created for oneself from what is imposed by social, cultural, and other forces.
    V. Toward connection with others.
      4. Contributing one's voice to a collective endeavor.

Context

This exercise has been used in an environmental science course, "Human Impact on the World," for undergraduate adult learners.

Description of Activity

Purpose. To help students develop global thinking and critical thinking on global issues.

   Format-steps-process.

1. I introduce Garrett Hardin's "Lifeboat Allegory" and pose this question: Is Garrett's "ten men in a lifeboat surrounded by thousands of men drowning in the sea" a meaningful metaphor for "the developed world surrounded by the undeveloped-developing world?" That is, if one concludes that "compas-

sionate sharing" is irresponsible in the first case, is it then irresponsible in the second case?

2. The class then breaks up into groups of four to six for 15 minutes of discussion. Each group should elect a reporter or spokesperson. First, I give the groups the following instructions: "Don't discuss what is *fair,* or what is *kind* or *good* or *godly.* Don't discuss your *feelings* about this. Don't talk about what *one should do.* We all know that sharing is good, drowning, hunger, and poverty are all tragic, and people should help one another. We came here tonight already *knowing* this. We're here for *new* learning. You will first focus on the lifeboat (the small picture) and compare it—feature by feature, thought by thought, idea by idea—to the bigger picture, the *worldview,* with these two questions in mind: How do these two pictures or perspectives differ? Given these differences, does this allegory work? Then, based on your answers to these two questions, evaluate Garrett's assertion that compassionate sharing is irresponsible."

3. Each group reports to the class and discussion ensues.

Processing Tips

Despite careful instruction, as the first groups report, it is common to hear a few "How can one possibly turn one's back . . . ," or conversely, "People just take advantage . . ." types of responses. This provides an opportunity for the facilitator to ask the reporting learner to examine his response. "Where did that statement come from? Did it come from thoughts and feelings you came in with, or is it based on new insights about how the two perspectives we've been talking about differ?" This prompting moves learners from old thoughts and feelings to responses such as, "In the small picture there is only one possible way to share; there are multiple ways in the world picture." Or, "The boat picture is a snapshot in time; the world picture has a past, present and future." As discussion ensues, new thinking, critical thinking, and global thinking is evidenced.

Contributor's Commentary

Most groups conclude that the allegory just doesn't cut it. Compassionate sharing might be irresponsible in the lifeboat story, but that does not preclude rational compassionate sharing in the worldview.

Nevertheless, I have found it difficult for many adult learners to move beyond their ingrained knowledge that *good people share* to reflect on and respond to a question that invariably, upon first hearing, evokes a "gee whiz, that's a given" type of response. But when they really begin to think about a question, that is, actually think new thoughts rather than rethink old thoughts and reexperience familiar feelings, learners open themselves up to new learning. They construct new knowledge as they reach a conclusion that they have generated for themselves. By requiring that they examine what they already know so that they might learn, this exercise also helps develop skills that enhance possibilities for future learning.

Aligning with the Organization's Mission

Susan Munaker, Chicago, Illinois
E-mail:smunaker@mcs.net

As an organizational development consultant, Susan Munaker helps individuals and organizations define and achieve their strategic visions. She works with corporate, educational, nonprofit, and broad-based leadership clients.

Developmental Intentions

    I. Toward knowing as a dialogical process.
        3. Reframing ideas or values that seem contradictory, embracing their differences, and arriving at new meanings.
        5. Moving between separate and connected, independent and interdependent ways of knowing.
  III. Toward being a continuous learner.
        6. Accepting internal dissonance as part of the learning process.
    V. Toward connection with others.
        1. Mediating boundaries between one's connection to others and one's individuality.
        2. Experiencing oneself as part of something larger.

Context

This simulation can be used with senior managers (administrators or executives) who are ambivalent about a new organizational mission. The activity has been used in situations in which some participants will lose their jobs as the new mission is achieved over time.

Description of Activity

Purpose. To provide participants with a schema that relates mission, beliefs, and behaviors so that they may discern the degree to which they are able to support the mission; have participants tap their tacit knowledge by using physical movement and spatial sorting; experience the equilibrium of alignment or the disequilibrium of a misalignment among mission, beliefs, and behaviors and learn how relative balance can be achieved; and draw on multiple senses for knowing.

Format-steps-process. The exercise is based on an already existing organizational mission. I begin by explaining that there are three system levels that each person in the group will explore.

Three Levels

- Mission. *Either* "This is my mission. I believe in it. It is mine." *Or* "This is not my mission."
- Belief. *Either* "I believe this is the necessary strategy to follow at this time. It follows from the mission." *Or* "Although this is not my mission, I believe this is the necessary strategy to follow at this time. My support is conditional but full."
- Behavior. *Either* "Because this is my mission and I believe that it is the correct strategy at this time, my behavior is X, reflecting my full support." *Or* "This is not my mission and I do not believe that it is the best thing to do at this time. However, as a leader of this organization, I will act 'as if' I support it. As leader, that is the responsible role for me to play for the organization and for those who report to me as long as I am here."

This activity has three rounds. Before the first round, I divide the participants into groups of three and ask the members of each triad to identify themselves as A, B, or C. When they have done so, I describe the roles and the tasks.

- A (the executive) maps out three circles on the floor and names them—*mission, belief, behavior.* She experiences the system by standing in each circle, beginning with mission, as B guides her.
- B (the guide) asks, encouraging A to be precise, "What does it look or sound like in that space?" B will continue to probe with other, more specific questions.
- C (the observer) watches A, looking for the nonverbal differences as A stands in each space, and also listens for B's questions as they help guide A's responses.

"Stepping Through" the Activity

1. The process begins when A steps into the mission circle. In response to B's question—"Is this your mission?"—A responds with the appropriate version of the mission-level choices, above. B then asks further questions, such as, "What is your experience in this place?" A responds and B probes, as necessary, until

A and B agree that the mission space has been fully explored. B asks A to step out of the mission circle and into the belief circle.

2. When A is in that circle, B asks, "Given your view of mission, what is your belief about this strategy? As you consider this strategy, what is your experience in this place of belief?" A responds with his or her position of support for the strategy, using the appropriate belief-level choices, as above. When A and B agree that the belief space has been fully explored, B invites A into the behavior circle.

3. When A steps into the behavior circle, B asks, "What happens when you act 'as though' your behaviors are in alignment with this mission? What is your experience if you feel you cannot act 'as though' you believe in the mission?" A states her or his position, and B probes.

4. While A and B are moving through these positions and questions, C is noting A's nonverbal behaviors and assessing whether A's exploration of beliefs and behaviors appear to be aligned with mission. C also observes B's ability to draw out neutrally A's experience.

5. This completes round 1. I now bring all the participants together in a circle to reflect on what they observed about themselves and each other and what they learned in the course of the exercise. At the end of the debriefing, they will continue by rotating the roles of A, B, and C. In round two B becomes the executive, C becomes the guide, and A becomes the observer.

Closure. The first debriefing helps participants learn how to do the activity with more skill. The second will focus more on content. The third helps participants generalize their learning.

Processing Tips

It is essential to clarify the roles of the experiencer, the guide, and the observer at the outset. This helps people sort among these three ways of examining their experience: as someone fully involved in an experience (A), as someone reflecting on and questioning the experience (B), or as someone even more removed, observing both the experience and the process of questioning it (C). As one moves back and forth among these ways of knowing and processing, one is developing the skills of *metaknowing*.

A is exploring a role. Once she takes on this role, she "knows" where she stands in terms of mission, belief, and behavior (each of the system levels).

B can help A explore what she thinks she knows by asking neutral and specifying questions that help A examine her experience. "What is that like for you? What does that mean to you specifically? You said 'easier'—easier than what? How is that important in this space?" B is *not* to offer A advice, his experience, or his point of view.

C may offer feedback to both A and B at the end of each round; for example, C might point out A's degree of congruity by using concrete examples from his observations of apparent dissonance; he might also report on B's effectiveness in the neutral role. C is learning to be a neutral observer.

Contributor's Commentary

The questions place the A participant in a state of disequilibrium or a state of blissful alignment and equilibrium. We sometimes find ourselves in confusing situations where we are not sure that we have choices in our behaviors. The exercise begins with the highest level, the mission. This helps A choose a stance about the organization's policy. When the exercise starts, if he is not in alignment with the policy, he is usually unclear about how he should behave. The exercise helps people recognize that they approach company strategies in different ways and that the important task is to recognize and represent how one takes on responsibility. As each person cycles through, the activity allows him or her to reach a state of equilibrium by experiencing and resolving the dissonance and disequilibrium in each place. In the course of moving among three different levels of systems thinking, the participant is also experiencing and building a capacity for metalevel insights.

If the exercise works as planned, the participants will be relieved of guilt and anxiety because it will help them understand that there is a role for them and that there are different ways to support the mission. To experience oneself as more than an isolated individual or to understand events as more than isolated happenings, it is useful to consider systems thinking. These metaknowing exercises are based on the principles of systems thinking.

Coaching for Effectiveness

Rebecca Proehl, Berkeley, California
E-mail: rproehl@stmarys-ca.edu

Rebecca Proehl is associate professor of management at Saint Mary's College of California. In addition, she facilitates leadership and team-building workshops. This activity was codeveloped with Jeri Mersky, cofounder of Risktaking Initiatives to Develop Executive Resources and Skills (RIDERS).

Developmental Intentions

    I. Toward knowing as a dialogical process.
       9. Perceiving and constructing one's reality by observing and participating.
   III. Toward being a continuous learner.
       2. Challenging oneself to learn in new realms; taking risks.
       3. Recognizing and revealing one's strengths and weaknesses as a learner and knower.
       8. Seeking authentic feedback from others.
       9. Drawing on multiple capacities for effective learning.

Context

As described, this exercise is part of a five-day retreat on a dude ranch in which the medium and challenge of horseback riding is used to develop leadership and team-building skills, primarily with corporate clients. However, the activity could focus on any challenge that is *not* directly connected to the workplace.

Description of Activity

Purpose. To help participants experience being a novice in a new learning activity, examine their own coaching style, and experience the dynamics of partnerships.

    Format-steps-process.

1. Prior to the hands-on part of the workshop, we present a minilecture on partnerships. We discuss the four requirements of partnership as well as the concept of the partner in charge, using Peter Block's (1993) *Stewardship* as the resource. This material provides a framework for the activity and adds richness to our debriefing sessions. We also present an overview of the activity, including time constraints.

2. We begin the activity by having the participants select a partner, preferably someone with whom they have had limited work experience. Occasionally, depending on the objectives of the group, we may assign partners. (For example, if the workshop is being held in-house in a corporate setting and the team has already worked together extensively, based on our interviews with and observations of the participants in other activities, we may assign as partners people who have competition or communication issues.) The training group is then divided into two smaller groups so that the partners are initially separated.

3. The next step in the process is to train each of the two groups in one particular skill. Once trained in the skills, this individual will be the "expert" and

coach for the partner. While being trained in the skill, the participants are encouraged also to observe how the wrangler is actually teaching the skill and their reactions to that teaching experience. They may approve or not approve of how they are being taught; in either case, that is a topic for reflection and later discussion. In the dude ranch retreat, one group is trained by a wrangler in how to lasso while the other group is trained in saddling. We generally take thirty minutes for this training session.

4. For the next thirty minutes, the partners once again pair up, and one of the "experts" teaches her partner the new skill she has learned. For example, they first demonstrate how to lasso and then coach their partners in that skill.

5. Next, the learners have the opportunity to demonstrate how well they have learned the skill. The coach becomes the cheerleader during this activity, but he is not allowed to coach while the partner is actually demonstrating. If the novice accomplishes the task (in this instance, lassoing the dummy steer within two minutes), the *coach* wins a prize.

6. After the demonstration, the partners debrief the experience together, primarily focusing on the learner's experience. On the dude ranch, this debriefing generally takes ten to fifteen minutes, as time has to be allowed for detailed reliving of the experience and descriptions of the challenges they faced. Learners give feedback to their coaches on the following topics:

   What worked for you as a learner?

   What did not work as well?

   What were your coach's greatest strengths?

   Greatest liabilities?

7. Then the roles are reversed, and the former experts become novices. On the dude ranch, the new experts teach their partners how to saddle. Steps 4 through 6 are repeated.

8. When both halves of the coaching experience are completed, the entire group assembles to discuss partnerships and coaching. Some of the items that we explore include

   How did it feel as a learner to depend on another person for your success?

   As the coach, how did it feel to be evaluated on how well your partner accomplished the task?

   How did the learner let the coach know what she needed?

   What are the elements of successful coaching?

   How well did you achieve the four requirements of partnership?

   What do learners need from their coaches to succeed?

   How common is it for this to happen in your organization?

Processing Tips

During the demonstration of learning in step 6, coaches are permitted only to cheer and encourage but not to continue offering advice or direction. They usually find this very difficult; however, this teaches them the importance of letting go and allowing learners to take over for themselves. In this way participants experience distinctions between coaching and micromanaging that inevitably become a focus of later discussion.

The fact that the coach, not the learner, wins the prize brings to the fore issues of investment in another's success. In the workplace, for example, supervisors may pay lip-service to the benefit of cross-functional teams, but in subtle ways may hinder their reports' participation, because it takes them away from their immediate responsibilities. However, if the system of rewards is constructed so that supervisors win acclaim when their reports are successful, that attitude changes.

This activity can focus on any new skill (or it could be modified to have the coaches teach their partners a skill that they already know). It is helpful to select skills that present some level of challenge, but are not so difficult that the learners will fail. It is important, however, to use skills that are not directly work related. This frees the participants to give honest feedback about their partner's coaching skills. Examples could include how to tie a fishing lure, play "The Saints Go Marching In" on the recorder, crochet, and so on.

Contributor's Commentary

The workshop begins with a focus on the individual, moves to partnership, and ends with a focus on teams. Through the experience of coaching and giving feedback, participants recognize that effective partnerships depend on the development of individuals and that teams are successful only when the members are willing to be partners with each other.

During the debriefing sessions, participants generally recognize that they rarely have the pleasure of *partnering* with others at work. They experience the power of the kind of support that they received in the coaching sessions (where the coaches cheered them on, gave them "high fives" when they were successful, and commiserated with them when they were not so successful) and note that such support is often missing in the workplace. The experience of providing honest feedback during the coaching sessions also powerfully brings to the fore that aspect of partnership and becomes the basis for ongoing discussion.

As Stephen Brookfield has often noted, everyone who teaches (and I would include anyone who supervises) should regularly risk learning something that they find difficult and challenging. One of the best ways to identify and understand the concerns of a learner (or novice, coachee, apprentice, trainee) is to experience that role.

Reference

Block, P. (1993). *Stewardship*. San Francisco: Berrett-Koehler Publishers.

Personal Theories of Learning

Edward W. Taylor, Harrisburg, Pennsylvania
E-mail: ewt1@psu.edu

Edward W. Taylor teaches in the School of Behavioral Sciences and Education of Pennsylvania State University, Harrisburg, and conducts research on adult teaching beliefs and related issues.

Developmental Intentions

   I. Toward knowing as a dialogical process.
     2. Surfacing and questioning assumptions underlying beliefs, ideas, actions, and positions.
     10. Tapping into and drawing on tacit knowledge.
   III. Toward being a continuous learner.
     2. Challenging oneself to learn in new realms; talking risks.
   IV. Toward self-agency and self-authorship.
     7. "Naming and claiming" what one has experienced and knows.
   V. Toward a connection with others.
     2. Experiencing oneself as part of something larger.

Context

A graduate seminar on adult learning or possibly any other course that involves an extensive review of theoretical concepts. This classroom activity would be for master's or doctoral students who are particularly resistant to traditional academic (that is, public) theories and tend to prefer the more practical application of ideas and knowledge. I usually use this activity during the first class whenever I teach a course on adult learning theory.

Description of Activity

Purpose. To help students become aware that they operate theoretically in the world.

Format-steps-process. There are three phases to this learning activity: preparation, application, and processing.

1. Preparation: To prepare for this activity the teacher needs to develop six to eight learning-dilemma centers. Each center is outfitted with a handout that describes the dilemma and poses two questions. There is also a prop to provide context for the learning dilemma. Four examples of learning dilemmas are as follows:

> Example 1. A student of yours keeps turning in her assignments late. Question A: How would you teach her to get them in on time? Question B: What does your approach to this problem say about how someone learns? Prop: a clock

> Example 2. You are helping a student write a paper for the first time on a computer. Question A: How would you *begin* to teach someone, who knew nothing about computers, how to write a class paper by using a word processing program? Question B: What does your approach say about how someone learns? Prop: A picture of a computer or an actual computer.

> Example 3. One of your students has made a racist comment during a class discussion. Question A: How would you begin to make him aware of the consequences of his actions and begin to demonstrate respect and tolerance for others? Question B: What does your approach say about how someone learns? Prop: Any picture that provokes thoughts of racism (for example, a picture of racial groups in stereotypical roles, a list of racist terms, and so forth).

> Example 4. Some students in your class are upset with the school administration for recent budget cuts in their extracurricular program. They come to you seeking assistance on how to protest these actions. Question A: How would you begin this task? Question B: What does your approach say about how someone learns? Prop: A picture of students protesting.

After the centers are set up around the room (I have all this ready before students arrive) I introduce the activity by stressing the following points:

- We all operate theoretically; our approach to teaching is a window into our theories-in-use and into the underlying assumptions, sometimes unrecognized, that guide our teaching.

- Our approach to teaching is also based on our often unconscious assumptions about how learning occurs.
- When we are faced with a learning or teaching dilemma we tend to think first of a particular teaching method without thinking of how a student might best learn in this situation. By thinking about different ways someone could learn in a particular context, along with an appropriate teaching method, we are apt to be more flexible in our practice.
- The experience of studying traditional adult learning theory (public theory) will help name and make more conscious our underlying assumptions about how we believe adults learn.

2. Application: In this phase the students begin the activity itself. Students are organized into small groups of three to four learners and encouraged to visit and discuss among themselves at least four to five centers over the next thirty to forty-five minutes. It is important to remind them that the idea is to respond to the questions at each center as they would in their own practice and describe their actions and thoughts in their own words, avoiding typical academic jargon. I usually have a handout made up with all the learning dilemmas and related questions written out as guides.

3. Processing: This is the last phase of the activity and the most crucial. First, students' responses to the various dilemmas are reviewed. This initiates an awareness of how everyone operates theoretically.

- Bring the whole class back together.
- Have two flip charts ready. One is for question A and the other is for question B of each dilemma.
- Begin reviewing the various responses students gave to each question about the different learning dilemmas; write their responses on the appropriate flip chart.
- When learners describe how they would respond to each dilemma and what they think their approach suggests about how others learn, it is important to record their own words rather than paraphrases to capture their perceptions and give credence to their own voices.
- After all learners have responded to each dilemma, encourage discussion about their reactions and connections to what is being written on the flip chart.

After discussing their reactions to the different centers, students start to become aware of their underlying assumptions about learning and how it shapes their teaching. The outcome of this activity provides great material for discussion about how learning occurs. Most significantly, as the adult learning course progresses, you can return to this material and see how the students' personal theories of learning, theories-in-use, relate to, contradict, or affirm the more public theories of adult learning.

Processing Tips

In the preparation phase, the more interesting and creative you make the learning dilemmas, the more reflection and discussion they will provoke about teaching and learning. I try to include props at some of the centers that involve a task and require students not only to be reflective, but also to teach one other something.

During the application phase I encourage students to discuss their responses to the teaching dilemmas in their small groups to help one another understand what their teaching approach to a particular dilemma says about their ideas about how someone learns. They don't have to reach consensus on the "best" approach. Each student can hold onto his or her own theory-in-use about teaching and learning. The handout can be used to record brief notes about each dilemma. Also, during the application phase, I remind students to focus their discussion not so much on the best teaching approach, but instead to spend their time discussing what various approaches reveal about how they believe someone learns.

In the processing phase, it is important to point out how their theories-in-use about learning are similar to more public theories, such as situated cognition, experiential learning, andragogy, transformative learning, and so forth. It is therefore helpful to follow this activity with an overview of these various theories in the field of adult education. In addition, as the course progresses, I encourage students to continue to reflect on their theories-in-use as they explore public theories in greater depth.

Contributor's Commentary

I have had great success with this activity, particularly with students who are fearful of a course that involves extensive review of theoretical concepts. Public theories, particularly learning theory, can be intimidating to students new to the field. This experiential and reflective activity demonstrates quite nicely how we all operate theoretically and that our approach to teaching reveals deeply help beliefs about how learning occurs. In essence, their beliefs and values about teaching are indicative of what Schön (1983) refers to as "theories-in-use." The students' theories-in-use reflect their underlying assumptions about their approach to teaching and how they believe adults learn. Furthermore, the activity encourages students to approach challenges in their classroom from a more theoretical orientation. It not only reminds them to reflect critically about how their teaching approach is based on various underlying assumptions about learning, but it also helps them take advantage of pubic theory and use it in a way that can inform their practice.

Reference

Schön, D. (1983). *The reflective practitioner: How professionals think in action.* New York: Basic Books.

Taking Multiple Perspectives

Kathleen Taylor, Berkeley, California
E-mail: ktaylor@stmarys-ca.edu

Kathleen Taylor is chair, department of portfolio development of the School of Extended Education, Saint Mary's College.

Developmental Intentions

II. Toward a dialogical relationship to oneself.
   2. Engaging the disequilibrium when one's ideas and beliefs are challenged.
III. Toward being a continuous learner.
   6. Accepting internal dissonance as part of the learning process.
IV. Toward self-agency and self-authorship.
   1. Constructing a values system that informs one's behavior.
   5. Revising aspects of oneself while maintaining continuity of other aspects.

Context

This activity has been used in a course on experiential learning portfolio development for undergraduate adult learners.

Description of Activity

Purpose. To have learners experience a different set of assumptions than their own through character role play and to discover the constructed nature of value systems.

Format-steps-process. I use the musical play *Les Miserables* partly because of the complex nature of the main characters, but also because it is possible to play taped excerpts so that learners can hear and see (and feel the emotions of) a performance.

1. I start by asking people to read a one-page synopsis of the play, which I provide (drawn from memory and the CD-liner notes). The synopsis focuses on the backgrounds of Valjean and Javert (I don't bother with the second and third plot lines). In it, I pay particular attention to the individual crisis that leads each character to sing the songs that we will focus on, "What Have I Done?" and "Javert's Suicide." For Valjean, the crisis occurs when, released from prison, he steals from a kindly priest, who then lies to the police so Valjean will not be reimprisoned. For Javert, the crisis occurs when he is freed, unharmed, by Valjean, who not only could have killed Javert, but who then risks his life to save someone else. Though I don't state it explicitly in my handouts, since I want the learners to explore these character's motivations and understandings, my interpretation is that both crises occur because these characters are shaken in their belief that it's a dog-eat-dog world in which few can be trusted and no one is selfless. I also give out the words to both songs, which I have typed side by side, so learners can compare them, line for line. Many of the phrases are similar; the learners will discover that the music is also the same.

2. We then view a performance of the songs (from a videotaped concert performance, available in many libraries or for rent at video stores—if a videotape is unavailable, audio is a distant second best).

3. Then I ask everyone to pair off and take the role of either Javert or Valjean. First, each character gets a few minutes of *uninterrupted* time to tell the other his life story. I don't allow so much time that people get bogged down by not having enough "facts." Two to three minutes per character is usually enough at this point; if after three minutes people are still going strong, the time allotment can be extended. I encourage people to embellish the story outline they have been given with made-up details, so long as the additions fit the general facts and essential character, as they understand him. For example: "What accidents of fate befell [your character]? What choices did he make? What might he have done differently?" Students are supposed to describe their experiences and beliefs, their hopes and dreams from their character's perspective.

4. When each pair has finished telling each other their individual stories, it is time to dialogue about these stories and about the experiences that bind the characters together. Each is supposed to listen carefully and respond sincerely (in character) to the other's perspective. The task is to try to understand, through discussion, why the other character feels, believes, and behaves as he does, while also explaining one's own character's motivations as clearly as possible. (This por-

tion of the activity can take twenty to thirty minutes, depending on how the conversations are going.)

5. At the end of the discussion, each person (no longer in character) writes for several minutes. I pose questions designed to encourage people to examine ways in which any aspect of themselves might resemble either of the characters, reflect on what they have discovered by taking these roles, and consider what they view differently, if anything, through "getting under the skin" of the character.

6. For closure, you may choose to facilitate a large-group discussion about any insights gained during either the role play or the subsequent reflection, and also about the exercise itself (so you will know better next time how to work it). If things go well, this can be a very rich harvest, with valuable insights about how we construct our value systems and how difficult it is to change them.

Processing Tips

I do all the time-keeping during the exercise, so people are not distracted. If you have access to technology that will let you excerpt the two songs onto another videotape, that is the best option. Otherwise it will be necessary to locate the beginning of each song on the VCR counter, in advance, and then fast-forward to each position. A word of warning: The counter on your VCR at home will rarely be the same as on the machine in the classroom.

The trick in facilitating the exercise is to give directions that will encourage people to identify strongly with the beliefs and value system of their own character and still remain open to trying to understand where the other character is "coming from." It's not helpful if people act so committed to their own position that they end up in a shouting match. However, if people get to mutual "understanding" too quickly, I suspect they are taking the "everyone is entitled to his own opinion" shortcut, and I try to stir the pot by pointing out to each of them how, by his own values, the other has behaved badly.

I walk around during the conversations, openly eavesdropping, yet from a distance, if possible, to avoid standing over the speakers. In any case, I don't stay for long, because I don't want to make people nervous or interrupt their train of thought. If listening to the conversation leads me to think an intervention will help, I have a couple of choices. I might make some observation or suggestion immediately. These are always addressed to *the character*. For example, "M. Javert, did you remember to tell M. Valjean about what it was like to grow up in a prison?" If the comment might be interpreted as criticism of what that pair is doing, I wait until I have completed that cycle of walking around, and then make a general comment to the entire class, such as, "Please try to explain to your discussion-partner not only what he has done that hurt or offended you, but *why*—how his behavior is not consistent with what you believe is good and true. Then listen carefully and discuss with him his response to your perceptions."

Contributor's Commentary

The idea is to use the role play as a way of examining the power of beliefs and values. When we are challenged about our own values, we can easily take positions. But if we are discussing values we only pretend to have, we are less vested in our "rightness" and are more likely to see that "right" and "wrong" can be a matter of interpretation. If the learners really get into their roles, they experience a sense of inner conflict. Though the other person is expressing a completely opposing view, they can see that, from his perspective (his experiences, beliefs, and values), he's "right," too!

I have used this exercise with adult undergraduates (as part of a course) and for faculty development. Most people, though not all, spoke with apparent sincerity about a sense of discovery concerning, for example, Javert's character: "He's not just an old meanie, but a prisoner of his beliefs and experiences." And many made the leap to, "*Aha!*—there are ways that I, too, may be a prisoner of *my* beliefs and experiences."

If the participants have had exposure to constructive-developmental theories, such as Kegan (1982, 1994), Kohlberg (1981), Loevinger (1976), Belenky, Clinchy, Goldberger, and Tarule (1986), or Perry (1970), another valuable discussion can focus on the developmental perspectives that Javert and Valjean appear to hold at various times. In fact, this would be a good addition to a course on developmental psychology and would help learners begin to see connections between theory and life.

References

Belenky, M. F., Clinchy, B. M., Goldberger, M. R., & Tarule, J. M. (1986). *Women's ways of knowing: The development of self, voice, and mind.* Boston: Basic Books.

Kegan, R. (1982). *The evolving self: Problem and process in human development.* Cambridge: Harvard University Press.

Kegan, R. (1994*). In over our heads: The mental demands of modern life.* Cambridge: Harvard University Press.

Kohlberg, L. (1981). *The philosophy of moral development: Moral stages and the idea of justice.* New York: Harper & Row).

Loevinger, J., with Blasi, A. (1976). *Ego development.* San Francisco: Jossey-Bass.

Mackintosh, C. (Columbia Tristar) (1996). *Les Miserables in Concert: 10th Anniversary Performance* [Video recording]. Taped in Royal Albert Hall, London.

Perry, W. G. (1970) *Forms of intellectual and moral development in the college years: A scheme.* Holt Rinehart Winston.

And Your Point Is? A Listening Experiential Exercise

Susan A. Timm, Batavia, Illinois
E-mail: stimm@niu.edu

Susan Timm is assistant director, university resources for Latinos, Northern Illinois University. She received the 1998 International Listening Association Graduate Thesis-Dissertation Award for excellence in research.

Developmental Intentions

    I. Toward knowing as a dialogical process.
        1. Inquiring into and responding openly to others' ideas.
        2. Surfacing and questioning assumptions underlying beliefs, ideas, actions, and positions.
        3. Reframing ideas or values that seem contradictory, embracing their differences, and arriving at new meanings.
   II. Toward a dialogical relationship to oneself.
        2. Engaging the disequilibrium when one's ideas and beliefs are challenged.
   V. Toward connection with others.
        3. Engaging the affective dimension when confronting differences.

Context

This exercise is effective in college courses, professional development workshops, and training seminars.

Description of Activity

Purpose. To increase participants' knowledge of the listening component of communication, aid participants in identifying effective and poor listening habits, enhance participants' understanding of listening as a component of culture and as a tool of empowerment, and improve participants' proficiency in communication by increasing their sensitivity to the conscious use of active listening skills.

Format-steps-process. Listening is one of the most important yet neglected areas of communication. When people are able to express their views and are listened to, they feel empowered and valued as individuals. This experiential exercise will enhance your active listening skills by focusing your attention on the importance of using these skills in conversations. During this exercise, you will express your points of view concerning controversial subjects during three consecutive rounds. Please read the steps for each round before beginning that round.

1. Have participants begin either by reading an overview of listening such as that described above or by completing the "What I Believe" handout (as described in step 2). The following controversial statements are examples that facilitators may include in the "What I Believe" handout. Remember to create your own controversial statements that reflect the special needs or interests of your group.

2. Instructions to participants: Read the following controversial statements and mark the intensity of your attitude toward these particular issues. Please mark the attitude that best represents how you feel at this moment. The wording of these statements in no way indicates a correct or incorrect answer. Any response that truly reflects your opinion is appropriate. You will discuss your beliefs and the reasons behind them later in small groups of three. Response options for each statement are *strongly agree, agree, so-so agree, so-so disagree, disagree, strongly disagree.*

> Marriages by gays and lesbians should be legally recognized.
>
> All high school, college, and professional athletes should be routinely drug tested.
>
> Capital punishment is justifiable and should be used more consistently.
>
> Suicide is a personal matter, and assisting people with taking their own life should not be deemed illegal.
>
> The United States should continue to provide financial and military assistance to other countries.
>
> "White" leadership in the United States has made a strong effort to help traditionally underrepresented groups.
>
> People are naïve to think that drugs are not a "race" problem.

3. Ask participants to form groups of three and to determine who will be person A, person B, and person C.

Round one: A's and B's are to examine their responses to the controversial statements listed in the "What I Believe" handout and to select one statement that reflects their disagreement with each other.

> A's express their view while B's and C's listen.
>
> After A's have completed expressing their thoughts, B's paraphrase what they heard.
>
> B's provide their own opinions after correctly paraphrasing A's comments.
>
> C's observe during this round. C's watch A's and B's to make sure that each waits her or his turn to speak and accurately paraphrases each other's comments.
>
> The group exchanges opinions about what's been said.

Round two: B's and C's talk while A's observe. B's and C's can continue discussing the same topic from round one, or they can examine their responses to another controversial statement that reflects disagreement. *Note:* The difference in this round from the first round is that B's and C's are asked not to use their hands while talking.

B's explain their views while C's and A's listen.

After B's complete their thoughts, C's paraphrase what they heard.

C's express their own opinions after correctly paraphrasing B's comments.

A's observe during round two. A's makes sure that B's and C's wait their turn to speak, appropriately paraphrase their partner's comments, and keep their hands still while talking.

The group exchanges opinions about what's been said.

Round three: This round allows participants to use their hands; B's observe during this final round. A's and C's can continue discussing the same topic, or they can examine their responses to a different controversial statement that reflects disagreement. *Note:* The difference in this round from the second round is that A's and C's will be keeping their eyes closed while talking.

C's express their views while A's and B's listen.

After C's complete their thoughts, A's paraphrase what they heard.

A's provide their own opinions after correctly paraphrasing C's comments.

B's observe during round three. B's makes sure that A's and C's wait their turn to speak, appropriately paraphrase their partner's comments, and keep their eyes closed during the round.

The group exchanges opinions about what's been said.

4. Using a worksheet that the instructor provides, ask participants to respond to the following questions about the listening exercise they just completed. Then have them discuss their thoughts concerning these questions with the other two members of their group.

What was the most difficult part of waiting to respond with your own point of view until you had paraphrased your partner's viewpoint?

Did you (or those you observed) find talking without using your (their) hands difficult? If yes, what bothered you (them) the most?

How did you (or those you observed) feel about talking with your (their) eyes closed?

What did you learn about listening from your group experience?

How can you use some of the listening techniques learned during this exercise in future interactions?

5. Have the participants discuss their insights with the large group.

Processing Tips

These are the steps to follow to facilitate this exercise successfully.

- Read the directions for each of the three rounds before participants begin so that you can make changes to the "What I Believe" page appropriate to your group, such as described in the "Contributor's Commentary."
- Make one copy of the "What I Believe" page (or a similar page that you have developed) as well as the directions for the three rounds of this exercise and a "Questions for Discussion" worksheet for each participant. In general, follow these four steps to facilitate the application of this experiential exercise.
- Divide the participants into random groups of three. (Depending on the number of participants in your session, you may need to form some groups of two.) Make sure each participant completes "What I Believe" (or a similar page you have developed).
- Have each triad discuss their opposing views concerning controversial issues following the directions given for each of the three rounds.
- Provide the "Questions for Discussion" worksheet so that each participant can respond to questions concerning their reactions to the exercise and can discuss their ideas with the other members of their group.
- Invite participants to share their insights with the rest of the class.

Contributor's Commentary

Here are some additional ways to work with this exercise.

- Create your own controversial statements for "What I Believe" that reflect the special needs or interests of your group. For example, if you are facilitating a group with health care interests, you may want to include issues related to that field, such as

    Licensed registered nurses should be able to prescribe medicines and other treatments to patients

    The government should determine the maximum amount that pharmaceutical companies can charge for every drug that they sell

- After participants have completed the first round, form small discussion groups according to the letter of the role that each participant assumed: A, B, or C. Participants can share their reactions to the role they played. Have participants record their impressions on a flip chart or other medium to compare with the other roles.
- Encourage participants to write about how or if the exercise has changed their understanding of listening.
- Develop and have participants read a summary of listening research. Many resources are available to assist you in this area. The most helpful is the International Listening Association, which promotes the study, development, and teaching of listening and the practice of effective listening skills and techniques.

Learning Activity Project

Rosemary Caffarella, Greeley, Colorado
E-mail: rscaffa@edtech.unco.edu

Rosemary Caffarella is a professor of educational leadership at University of Northern Colorado. She has written widely on issues related to adult learning and development.

Developmental Intentions

   I. Toward knowing as a dialogical process.
      4. Using one's experience to critique expert opinion and expert opinion to critique one's experience.
      9. Perceiving and constructing one's reality by observing and participating.
     10. Tapping into and drawing on tacit knowledge.
  III. Toward being a continuous learner.
      1. Reflecting on one's own and others' experiences as a guide to future behavior.
      3. Recognizing and revealing one's strengths and weaknesses as a learner and knower.

Context

I use this exercise in a graduate seminar on learning in adulthood. Most students are advanced master's or doctoral students.

Description of Activity

Purpose. To help students observe and reflect upon their own learning.

Format-steps-process. I tell participants that since we can learn a lot about the process of learning and about learning differences and preferences among adults from trying to teach someone something, they will be both a learner and a teacher in this activity.

1. I ask students to list areas that they could teach. They then choose partners based on the content they wish to learn and the ease of getting together (for example: common time schedules, geographically close).

2. I then ask students to explore further with their partners the chosen areas they want to teach. The content can be anything from life skills (such as learning how a car engine works, cooking ethnic food, surviving the teen years) to hobbies (such as music, quilting, flying, fishing, wine making) to more formal or academic knowledge (such as doing computer literature searches, learning a presentation system, understanding leadership theory). The key is to be creative.

3. As students are making the final choices about the content areas, I urge that they consider this an opportunity to challenge themselves with something that

    They have been wanting to learn for a long time,
    but haven't taken the time

    They need to know to be a better teacher, friend, parent, worker

    They have been avoiding learning for any number of reasons

4. I set out the parameter that each learning activity should total a minimum of three to five hours. That is, each student needs to prepare three to five hours of "instruction" for her or his partner, and each partner will learn something for a minimum of three to five hours. This three- to five-hour activity should be broken up into two segments with some time (at least a day, ideally longer) between the first and second segment. This break is crucial for students to reflect upon their own learning and for adjustments to be made in the teaching.

5. I also ask students to prepare a formal report that includes

    A description of the process of learning

    Reflections on what they learned about their learning through the learning and the teaching experience

    A discussion of these reflections based on the theory and research on adult learning from their readings and class interactions

A discussion of the "so what" question: What does what you have learned about yourself as a learner mean in relationship to your practice as an educator?

6. Finally, I ask students to share their papers with each other and to reflect with their partners on the learning experience. In addition, the entire class engages in group reflection and discussion about both what they learned and how they learned it.

Processing Tips

This project is spread over a full semester of work so that students have the time to complete the teaching-learning episodes and acquire broad content knowledge in which they can ground their discussions. I find that students are very excited about the process itself and what they learn from that process. The project also fosters close relationships between learners, which often translates into enhanced class interactions in general. Usually, the one area that calls on the instructor's resources is to use theory and concepts of adult learning to help explain what the students have learned through this activity.

Contributor's Commentary

I have found that students discover this activity to be especially useful in understanding how their own learning styles and ways of knowing drive the way they teach. This is especially revealing as their espoused practice prior to completing this activity is that they design learning experiences based primarily on the interests and learning styles of the learners.

This is an activity that a number of professors have used in their adult learning classes. My recollection is that Sharan Merriam, University of Georgia, first introduced the idea of the project to a number of us who teach in that area.

Reference

Merriam, S., & Caffarella, R. (1999). *Learning in adulthood: A comprehensive guide* (2nd ed.). San Francisco: Jossey-Bass.

Becoming a Mathematics Teacher:
Modeling the Teaching-Learning Interface

Barbara Jaworski, Oxford, England
E-mail: barbara.jaworski@educational-studies.ox.ac.uk

Barbara Jaworski is codirector of the Centre for Mathematics Education Research
at the University of Oxford Department of Educational Studies.

Developmental Intentions

 I. Toward knowing as a dialogical process.
   2. Surfacing and questioning assumptions underlying beliefs, ideas,
      actions, and positions.
   5. Moving between separate and connected, independent and
      interdependent ways of knowing.
 II. Toward a dialogical relationship to oneself.
   2. Engaging the disequilibrium when one's ideas and beliefs are challenged.
 III. Toward being a continuous learner.
   1. Reflecting on one's own and others' experiences as a guide to
      future behavior.
 V. Toward connection with others.
   4. Contributing one's voice to a collective endeavor.

Context

Mathematics teacher education is an internship scheme that is a partnership between a university department and a group of schools. Students (interns) are all
good mathematicians pursuing a postgraduate certificate of education (PGCE)
course. The course is designed and delivered jointly by the university and partner
schools.

The approach described here is based on the supported premise that most beginning teachers conceptualize teaching according to the way they were taught
and this is an insufficient model to provide quality mathematics education.

I use an example of teaching algebra to illustrate the general modeling approach. The interns are selected because they are very good at algebra themselves;
algebraic thinking is second nature to them and they do not think about what they
do—they just do it. The approach is designed to expose preconceptions, develop
awareness, and prepare ground for a metacognitive development of algebraic ideas.

Description of Activity

Purpose. To enable future teachers to conceptualize the teaching-learning process and to have teachers experience difficulties that students in their classes face.

Format-steps-process.

1. I set up the process by posing some guiding questions:

    How do learners learn mathematics?

    What is involved in coming to an understanding of a mathematical concept?

    What does it mean to understand?

2. The next step is to expose preconceptions of algebra by engaging in a brainstorming session on a question such as "What is algebra?" Following some individual thinking time, during which interns gather their views, perceptions, images, and knowledge, I randomly ask the interns to offer their words and phrases, which are recorded by a scribe (teacher or member of the group) on a board, avoiding implicit or explicit grouping of terms. This step is aimed at alerting interns to a wide range of elements and perspectives.

3. Next the interns engage in concept webbing. This involves taking the words and phrases from the brainstorming and linking them in some way into trees, networks, webs, and so on, all with nodes and links that represent some sort of algebraic "story." This may be done in small groups. Concept webbing provides a chance to mull over the range of perspectives from the brainstorming while trying to find links and an organizational representation of the ideas and concepts.

4. Each group presents the outcome of their webbing efforts to their colleagues. This continues the bombardment of ideas, images, and relationships. The task for each intern is to reconcile the various ideas with his or her own perceptions and make some sense of it all.

Contributor's Commentary

In this activity interns are learning the value of working with their peers—learning the advantages of stimulation from hearing other perspectives and gaining external input and of the security of not having to do it all by themselves. They can gain from listening to others. They can recognize that they are not alone in feeling nervous or threatened. They can realize that they have something to offer that others value. They can become aware of their own enhanced awareness and growth of knowledge through this activity. Later we hope they will come to a realization that these are strategies they can use in their own classrooms where students are learning mathematics. At some point we shall try to make this explicit. We recognize that we are deliberately modeling processes we hope they will use themselves in classrooms.

So far interns have been sharing knowledge and preconceptions, making sense of this sharing, and creating possibilities for new growth of knowledge. All of this has been guided and orchestrated by a teacher-educator. This teacher-educator has an agenda, and part of this agenda concerns concepts that interns need to develop. It is not a case of facilitating only. I am very concerned by the notion of teacher-as-facilitator, because it seems to imply that if only we provide the appropriate environment our students will construct what is necessary for them to know. For me, this is a fallacious interpretation of constructivist theory. As a teacher, I have responsibility to bring my students up against concepts they are going to need to know, and to provide whatever will stimulate this knowing. This is not prescriptive and for success must take account of who the students are. Ideally it involves engaging in dialogue with students in order to make judgments about the teaching approaches that have the best chance of success. This philosophy extends to our hopes for the way they will work with their own students.

For example, where the teaching of algebra is concerned, I know as a practitioner, researcher, and reader of research that there are many common errors that students make that impede their progress in algebraic learning and thinking. I could "simply" give interns a presentation of these, but I might decide to prepare the ground in some other way. For example, I may stimulate interns' imagery by asking them to solve a simple problem and then relate to the class their method of solution. Recognition of a variety of methods then opens up dialogue to an appreciation of alternative conceptions. What if these conceptions do not all fit agreed mathematical rules? What if those solving the problem have no experience of the standard rules, so that they are working on experience or intuition? What alternatives might they come up with?

Alongside interns' suggestions the teacher-educator can make further suggestions and can report from the research in this area, that is, provide input. The ground has been prepared for the input to make sense, so interns can now start to realize the importance of seeking students' images and gaining access to their experience, their alternative conceptions. We can now start to discuss this overtly. So we have moved beyond algebra into perceptions of the teaching and learning of algebra. A next step could be to start to focus on classroom strategies and activities through which, as teachers, they can create situations in which their students can develop algebraic images, challenge misconceptions, and grow toward an understanding of agreed algebraic representations.

I am constantly aware of the parallel between my own continuous on-the-spot decision making and questioning of my decisions with regard to interns' conceptualizations, and the way that I am trying to get interns to develop as teachers working with students learning mathematical concepts.

I recognize that this is multilayered because I am teaching teachers, and in some sense I am trying to get them to appreciate what I am doing and the questions I am addressing so they can learn to do and address similar questions themselves. Were I teaching mathematics, the metalevels would be different. Were I teaching my master of science students, say about learning theory, my metalevels would again be different. Were I teaching my doctoral students, again the agenda would be different. I might use brainstorming and concept webbing in all these; however, it is at the metalevels where the differences are most acute.

Reference

Jaworski, B., Wood, T., & Dawson, S. (1999). *Mathematics teacher education: Critical international perspectives.* London: Falmer Press.

Stimulating Cognitive and Ethical Development

Roberta Liebler, Aurora, Illinois
E-mail: raliebler@yahoo.com

Roberta Liebler is the director, Center for Continuing Professional Education and Center for Organizational Effectiveness, Aurora University.

Developmental Intentions

   I. Toward knowing as a dialogical process.
      2. Surfacing and questioning assumptions underlying beliefs, ideas, actions, and positions.
      3. Reframing ideas or values that seem contradictory, embracing their differences, and arriving at new meanings.
   II. Toward a dialogical relationship to oneself.
      3. Exploring life's experiences through some framework(s) of analysis.
   IV. Toward self-agency and self-authorship.
      1. Constructing a values system that informs one's behavior.
   V. Toward connection with others.
      1. Mediating boundaries between one's connection to others and one's individuality.

Context

This activity has been used in a course on global literature in a community college.

Description of Activity

Purpose. To broaden students' global literary horizons, guide them through a cognitive adventure by developing their facility for analysis, and help them observe critically and commit intellectually without dependence on certainty.

Format-steps-process. Unit structure: The syllabus organizes modern global literary readings around ethical dilemmas. At the beginning of each unit, each student writes a short personal essay answering the thematic ethical question of the unit. This essay serves as a baseline for how the student views the ethical question before the course exploration. For a unit exploring the individual's responsibility toward the needy, for example, a student might write about his response to being asked for money by a homeless person. For a unit on balancing private and public responsibilities, a mother might examine her dilemma of choosing between staying home with a sick child or making a presentation to an important client.

At the start of the next class, in small groups, students briefly share their personal viewpoints. During the unit, students will answer the same ethical question from the point of view of one character in each literary work.

Frequently I divide the class into groups, each of which views the ethical question from the perspective of a different character. Other times I bring together students with a similar perspective in order to develop a deeper understanding as a group than they could individually. All "answers" must be supported with textual material. Individually or in groups, students must support their perception with evidence from the literary work or background materials. Class discussion often focuses on groups explaining or justifying the actions of the character they are representing.

Specific exercise—role taking: This exercise assists students in considering the feelings of characters and authors. I divide the students into small groups to analyze an ethical dilemma in the literature from the perspective of different characters.

I.   Questions for the small group discussions include (fifteen minutes):
A.   What is the principal ethical issue the character faces?
B.   What are the facts?
1.   What are the claims placed on this character?
2.   How can the claims be weighed against one another?
C.   What principles are at issue (for example, justice, mercy, duty)?

D. How can the principles as formulated apply to this case? What circumstances would change the principles?

E. What are the options?

F. What choice does the character make?

  1. Why does the character select this option?

  2. What is the principle that determined this decision?

  3. Do you think the character made the "right" decision?

G. What choice would you make under these circumstances?

  1. Why did you select this option?

  2. What is the principle that determined your decision?

  3. Why did you and the character make the same (or a different) choice?

H. As a group, what is the decision you advocate?

II. Each group then reports to the whole class (two to three minutes each group, about ten minutes total) on the following questions.

A. What did your group decide was the best choice from the perspective of this character?

B. How did you arrive at your decision to act, given the situation described?

III. The whole class then engages in discussion around these questions (twenty-five minutes).

A. What was your group's ethical decision?

B. How did you arrive at your decision to act, given the situation described?

C. If members in your group agreed on the choice:

  1. What underlying principle(s) did you apply to making your decision?

  2. If more than one principle was applied in this decision, what was the connection between them?

D. If members in your group disagreed on the choice:

  1. What underlying principle(s) did you apply to making your decision?

  2. How did these underlying principles result in differing choices?

  3. Now that you understand another's perspective, can the two positions be reconciled?

Processing Tips

During the first few times students engage in this exercise, they require much encouragement. Since initially they are seeking the "right answer," they look to the instructor for verification. The instructor, however, offers help by asking questions that facilitate the students' exploration. Willingness to argue an opinion not one's own, ability to use textual support of one's argument, and appreciation of other cultural perspectives is encouraged. With practice, students become more comfortable in arguing viewpoints other than their own. Eventually, many become more articulate in arguing their own views through having learned how to explore the basis of other perspectives.

Contributor's Commentary

Though many of my students are ill prepared to face the rigors of the traditional academic regime, they respond eagerly to concepts they deem meaningful. Their lives are complex (nearly everyone holds a paying job and many have families); their academic expectations are vague (almost all are first-generation college students); and their future is indeterminate (though they hope to go on to a four-year college, they don't know how or where).

My dialectical approach emphasizes process (the how) rather than providing answers and solutions (the what). My goal is to assist students in overcoming the uncritical thinking of most undergraduates. I attempt to confront "students with the reality that experts disagree, that their finds may be studied and tested, and that one can, with effort, work one's way to some reasonable conclusions" (Plummer, 1988, p. 79). The implications of this process extend far beyond content into a different mode of thinking and perhaps living.

Reference

Plummer, T. (1988). Cognitive growth and literary analysis: A dialectical model for teaching literature. *Unterrischtspraxic, 21* (1), 79.

Encouraging a Multicultural Perspective of Ethical Dilemmas

Roberta Liebler, Aurora, Illinois
E-mail: raliebler@yahoo.com

Roberta Liebler is the director, Center for Continuing Professional Education and Center for Organizational Effectiveness, Aurora University.

Developmental Intentions

I. Toward knowing as a dialogical process.
    3. Reframing ideas or values that seem contradictory, embracing their differences, and arriving at new meanings.

II. Toward a dialogical relationship to oneself.
  2. Engaging the disequilibrium when one's ideas and beliefs are challenged.
III. Toward being a continuous a learner.
  4. Anticipating learning needed to prevent and solve problems.
IV. Toward self-agency and self-authorship.
  1. Constructing a values system that informs one's behavior.
  2. Accepting responsibility for choices one has made and will make.

Context

This exercise is presented in an undergraduate capstone course requiring creative and research exploration of a thematic concentration. The theme for this course is "Cross-Cultural Ethics." Adults take this required course at the conclusion of a program that stresses interdisciplinary connections and application of scholarly knowledge. This exercise occurs toward the end of a thirty-hour class, which has been organized to lead up to this finale.

Description of Activity

Purpose. To articulately express a cultural perspective that is not one's own, understand the underlying values and principles of a cultural perspective well enough to argue the position, support a cultural perspective in the face of opposition, search for the resolution of a conflict between viewpoints while maintaining one's own cultural values and principles, and after having argued a particular perspective, distance one's self from a perspective sufficiently to reach a workable resolution of a conflict.

Format-steps-process. Unit structure: Students read articles that address an ethical issue from several cultural perspectives. As part of the process of deep reading, each article is analyzed to uncover the values, principles, and priorities of the culture. During class discussion of each article, the learners decide which philosophical ethical model shapes the argument. After each article is thoroughly explored in this way, the class is given an application exercise to enable them to compare and contrast, analyze, and synthesize the ethical issue across cultures.

The exercise takes place during one of the final class meetings. The following two-paragraph handout is used to set the stage for the case-study simulation:

Simulating Multicultural Approaches to Environmental Ethics

A multinational corporation is presenting a proposal to the town council meeting of an economically depressed rural community. The corporation wants to buy a deserted

mine to begin removing uranium with a brand new process. The corporation presented the Chamber of Commerce and town council with a glossy brochure emphasizing how the town will benefit from the mining venture. The local Chamber of
Commerce is interested in the community development potential. The mine is on tribal
land governed by a council of uneducated and desperately poor Native Americans
who are excited about the prospect of jobs. A group of young, college-educated Native Americans oppose the mine, fearing further spiritual and ecological desecration
of their sacred lands. Most of these young people are either attending college or working away from the reservation, since the unemployment rate on the reservation is 80
percent. The small artist's colony situated ten miles out of town requested that Green-
peace send an expert to represent their position at the meeting. The Buddhist monks
who run a tiny retreat center adjacent to the artist's colony will also testify. If the proposal is not accepted in a month, the offer will be taken to another town.

In an assigned role you will be part of this deliberation. The town council will state
the issue, listen to the presenters, and make a decision. With your group, you will have
thirty minutes to clarify your position and develop your strategy. The town council is
free to structure the one-hour, forty-minute hearing. The town council may assign up
to ten minutes of break time. At the conclusion of the hearing, the town council has
ten minutes to make a decision. The council can reach a decision in any way they wish.
Participants not in the town council are to evaluate their strategy and those of the
other groups and predict the town council's decision. For the remainder of the class,
we will analyze what occurred.

I also post these times for everyone to see.

Time

   Ten minutes—class discussion of case study and assignment of roles

   Thirty minutes—groups clarify position and develop strategy

   Ninety minutes—town council hearing

   Ten minutes—break

   Ten minutes—decision making and group self-evaluation

   Thirty minutes—class analysis

1. In the previous class, articles exploring how ecological issues are viewed from
   each of the cultural perspectives were discussed and analyzed.
2. The case study is distributed and discussed with the class. The students may
   ask questions of clarification. The class is randomly assigned to role play each
   of the cultural perspectives introduced in the simulation. Assuming twenty students in the class, the number of students assigned to each group is

   Three, multinational corporation

   Four, town council

> Three, chamber of commerce
>
> Three, Native American council
>
> Two, young Native Americans
>
> Three, artist's colony and Greenpeace
>
> Two, Buddhist monks

3. Each group meets to clarify their point of view and develop their strategy. They are encouraged to use the article that discusses their viewpoint as a resource. Each student assumes a detailed persona and really "gets into character." Groups may visit each other.

4. The town council frames the question, listens to the presentation, and asks questions. During the hearing, members of all groups are in the audience. The council makes all decisions on process and content.

5. After hearing from each group, the town council must decide whether the corporation will be allowed to buy and operate the mine. Meanwhile, the other groups analyze the presentations and predict the outcome. Each group writes a brief of the outcome and supporting points.

6. The process is discussed and analyzed. Students are asked how they felt about the issue in their persona and as themselves. For example: "Has your opinion changed as a result of having gone through the experience? What did you feel during the hearing? What do you think about the process? How did the process determine the outcome? Would a different process result in a different outcome? How do you feel about the outcome? How did cultural values determine the outcome? Was the outcome fair? Was the outcome just?"

Processing Tips

Students need to be prepared for this complex and messy exercise through a series of increasingly less structured and more equivocal exercises throughout the term. The semester is organized so that students are supported as they move from certainty to relativism. The instructor is always available as a group facilitator and resource; however, by the end of the term (when this exercise occurs) students are prepared to analyze a dilemma and provide supporting information for their stand.

Contributor's Commentary

As we explore how ethical dilemmas are confronted in different societies, students investigate the interaction of innate human dispositions with cognitive and social experiences. Having enlarged their perspective to include other viewpoints, each student traces several professional, personal, and community ethical dilemmas. Finally, each student presents a coherent, individualized, ethical, decision-making model.

My role is to structure a developmental process that respects alternative viewpoints, disputes clichés and stereotypical views, cheers innovative thinking, encourages awareness of cognitive growth, and requires defensible conclusions. The fear students feel about exposing their possible error can be alleviated by a professor who acknowledges the danger, gives them permission to be fearful, and encourages learners to take the risk of asserting their viewpoint coupled with the responsibility for presenting a committed, substantiated position.

I seek to stimulate the adult development detailed by developmental psychologists such as William Perry (1970), Carol Gilligan (1982), and Robert Kegan (1982, 1994).

References

Gilligan, C. (1982). *In a different voice: Psychological theory and women's development.* Cambridge: Harvard University Press.

Kegan, R. (1982). *The evolving self: Problem and process in human development.* Cambridge: Harvard University Press.

Kegan, R. (1994). *In over our heads: The mental demands of modern life.* Cambridge: Harvard University Press.

Perry, W. G. (1970). *Forms of intellectual and moral development in the college years: A scheme.* Austin, TX: Holt Rinehart Winston.

Field Study Reflection: Two Methods for Encouraging Critical Thinking in Field Study

Don McCormick, Redlands, California
E-mail: mccormic@uor.edu

Don McCormick is an associate professor at the University of Redlands, where he teaches in the field of organization studies.

Developmental Intentions

I. Toward knowing as a dialogical process.
1. Inquiring into and responding openly to others' ideas.
2. Surfacing and questioning assumptions underlying beliefs, ideas, actions, and positions.
9. Perceiving and constructing one's reality by observing and participating.

III. Toward being a continuous learner.
2. Challenging oneself to learn in new realms; taking risks.
9. Drawing on multiple capacities for effective learning.

Context

Either of the two approaches to this activity can fit almost any context in which students are engaged in an extended experience with an organization outside the classroom.

Description of Activity

Purpose. To encourage students engaged in field study to think critically about the social systems in which they are engaged.

Format-steps-process. I draw on two methods for encouraging reflection as an integral part of engaging in field studies.

Method One (this comes from my observations of how a colleague, Cheryl Armon, helps students design internships)

1. I ask students to maintain a daily journal. In this journal, they describe the actual behavior they observe in the social system they are involved with and also describe its espoused, official values. *Example:* Students completing a field study in a day camp for children from low-income families. The camp's purpose is to promote positive interactions among the children. Students would write about the camp's goals as described by the camp personnel and what was actually occurring at the camp (how the children were interacting, the effect camp counselors have on children's interactions, and so forth).

2. Students are also asked to describe the strengths and weaknesses of the social system or organization and to write their own opinion at the end of the field study as to what else the organization could do that would help it better fulfill its goals. In the case of the camp, the student would write about how the camp could better fulfill its goal of furthering positive interactions among the children.

The journal assignment encourages critical thought because it does not ask students merely to accept the social structure and relations of the social system they are observing, but it asks them to observe, question, and evaluate them.

Method Two

Students involved in the field study write three analytic papers about the organization in which they are working. The first two papers reflect different positions in the organization—those who have more power in the system and those whom the system serves. In a social service agency, for example, this could be professionals and clients. In a business it could be management and labor, or service technicians and customers.

Paper one takes the perspective of those with relatively more power in the organization (for example, faculty in an adult BA degree completion program).

Paper two takes the perspective of the less powerful. These are often the people the organization attempts to serve (for example, students in an adult BA degree completion program).

Paper three is from the student's own point of view. In this paper, students are asked to take a stand and articulate their own position. This should take into account what they learned by looking at the agency from the point of view of the powerful and the less powerful.

This approach is adapted from an article entitled "Toward Cognitive Development Through Field Studies," by Barbara Hersh and Lenore Borzak (1979).

Processing Tips

The second method for the field study particularly pushes the student to "confront the different perspectives in systematic ways" (Hersh & Borzak, 1979, p. 69) and to assert their own opinions. Students can also be asked to discuss the strengths and weaknesses of the organizations from the three perspectives that framed the papers. This approach asks students to evaluate their internship setting in a way that can promote critical thinking.

Contributor's Commentary

The difference between classroom learning and field learning is like the difference between learning about roller coasters by watching one from across the street and learning about them while gripping the front handrail during the ride. Learning while riding is likely to be a more emotional and overwhelming experience. It is easier to be a critical thinker when contemplating information or perspectives that one learns about from a distance.

Despite the difficulty of engaging in critical analysis during a field study, it is important to develop the skill of critical thinking even when it means evaluating the more emotional information and perspectives that are learned experientially. After college, critical thinking is often called for in the middle of the metaphorical roller coaster ride.

One societal and historical context for this learning activity is the thousands-year-old tradition of liberal education. One of the central goals of liberal education is to help students learn to think for themselves, that is, to learn critical thinking. The other context is the tradition of experiential learning that goes back at least as far as the apprenticeship system of medieval times. The two educational traditions have tended to be separate. But beginning with Antioch College's innovative commitment to liberal education and cooperative education that began in the 1920s and continuing to today's burgeoning service-learning movement, those traditions have been increasingly intertwined. The assignment described here presents ways these two traditions can be more fully integrated. A theoretical context that informs these approaches to field work is covered in the work of Chris Argyris (1985) on espoused theory and theory-in-use.

The second method derives from a Piagetian, cognitive-developmental approach to human development. By asking students to examine an organization from the point of view of different groups in the organization and then forming their own opinion while incorporating these perspectives, this assignment is designed to create a certain amount of cognitive conflict that we hope will contribute to disequilibrium. There will also be a desire to reduce this disequilibrium by constructing more adequate cognitive structures—ones capable of coping with multiple perspectives. The specific cognitive-developmental theory of social perspective-taking is informed by the work of Selman (1980).

An introduction to perspective-taking and the ability to take others' perspectives in social systems is addressed in my book chapter "Listening with Empathy: Taking the Other Person's Perspective" (McCormick, 1999).

Both methods are also informed by the tradition of critical pedagogy, especially its application to organization studies. This is reflected in its examination of power relations in organizational systems and its refusal simply to accept the social structure and relations in the system in which students are engaged. A good introduction to critical pedagogy in organizational studies is Mary Boyce's article on the Web (Boyce, 1996).

References

Argyris, C. (1985). *Strategy, change, and defensive routines.* Boston: Pitman.

Boyce, M. (1996). Teaching critically as an act of praxis and resistance. In "The Electronic Journal of Radical Organisation Theory,"
http://www.mngt.waikato.ac.nz/Research/ejrot/black.asp vol. 2 (2) .

Hersh, B., & Borzak, L. (1979). Toward cognitive development through field studies. *Journal of Higher Education, 50,* 63–78.

McCormick, D. (1999). Listening with empathy: Taking the other person's perspective.
    In A. Cooke, A. Craig, B. Greig, & M. Brazzel (Eds.), *Reading book for human relations training.*
    Arlington, VA: NTL Institute.
Selman, R. L. (1980). *The growth of interpersonal understanding.* New York: Academic Press.

Being the Art Critic

Susan McGury, Chicago, Illinois
E-mail: smcgury@wppost.depaul.edu

Susan McGury is on the faculty at DePaul University's School for New Learning, where she teaches adult education, creativity, and humanities courses. She is developing a documentary film, called *Transformations: Voices of Adult Learners,* as part of her National Council of Adult Learning Fellowship.

Developmental Intentions

   I. Toward knowing as a dialogical process.
      4. Using one's experience to critique expert opinion and expert opinion to critique one's experience.
      5. Moving between separate and connected, independent and interdependent ways of knowing.
      6. Paying attention to wholes as well as the parts that comprise them.
  III. Toward being a continuous learner.
      9. Drawing on multiple capacities for effective learning.
  IV. Toward self-agency and self-authorship.
      6. Distinguishing what one has created for oneself from what is imposed by social, cultural, and other forces.

Context

I use these activities in two courses, "Art and Personal Transformation" and "Art and Cultural Transformation"; both courses are conceived of as a blend of art appreciation and self-expression across cultures and media. Most of the adult students do not describe themselves as being creative; they have not had experience with reflective journals. The usual composition of the class is a diverse mix, ethnically and racially.

    I introduce the "field trip–art critic" exercises after students have written a creative autobiography (a reflective exercise in which they look back on their early experiences with creativity and consolidate their definitions of creativity drawn from interviews, readings, and class discussions). They will also have had an extended meeting with me to identify a final project that will be personally meaningful.

Description of Activity

Purpose. To develop a self-referential basis for using or making art.

Format-steps-process.

1. The group visits an art museum and I direct their attention to works that address themes of the course that also clearly illustrate certain formal elements of art. We begin in a painting gallery with a discussion of what is usually the most straightforward visual art element, color. Observations about color's familiar emotional connections, such as the coolness of the blue in some canvases and the passion of red in others, flow easily.

2. We then move to art that illustrates elements that students feel less confident discussing, such as line. It tends to take a little longer to get at conventional associations of angularity with harshness and curves with calm, but with clear examples, we get there. *Example:* To get an emotional experience of line I take the students to an unfamiliar sculpture by Brancusi; I cover the nameplate and ask the group to provide the name of the piece—it doesn't take long to come close (it's called *Torment*). Was it just a guessing game? How did they know? Invariably, students recognize that it was the prominent arch in the child's neck and shoulder area that tells them quite clearly that the child is in pain. Whether they are drawing on their personal experience as parents or simply reading correctly a set of universal visual clues, they have had a felt experience of *that* particular curve in *that* particular sculpture that has given them an "owned" definition of the emotional qualities of line.

3. After several interactions such as this, students are given time to wander and find another unfamiliar work that draws them in. They are asked to approach the work without looking at the nameplate and to sketch it, regardless of sketching talent, to get to know it intimately.

4. I then ask them to do an anthropological-style dual-sided journal entry on the piece. On one side, they list as many objective descriptive observations as possible about the work. On the facing page, I ask them to include their reflections, impressions, feelings, and associations stimulated by those observations.

5. Once they have written their journal entries, they compare their own notes with an expert's opinion of that piece in an art text, paying particular attention to the similarities and differences between their reactions and the experts. They examine whether the differences suggest issues for their further learning. *Example:* Would the student's appreciation of the piece have been affected if he or she had known the historical event on which it was based? Or might

research into the art expert's own cultural background explain differences in interpretation?

Processing Tips

The group portion of this activity can be modified depending on the students' level of exposure to art. For intimidated beginners, I stick with the most commonsense examples, steering clear of unconventional works in which, say, red is *not* a color of passionate intensity. In a more experienced group, I may contrast a red in a representational court painting with an abstract red color wash to bring out the issue of artistic convention. With students who feel adrift without art jargon but who are in fact adrift *in* it, I have them try to translate a passage from an art history journal into their own concrete language with illustrations. With groups of quite mixed background, I vary my examples and let a more experienced student share parts of his or her creative autobiography with the group so that the others see that exposure to art comes from somewhere that they may not yet have been.

The journal portion of the exercise yields varied results, but since my assessment is individualized, this is not a problem. The one administrative difficulty that can occasionally arise is when a student chooses a very obscure work for step 4. When this happens, I sometimes have to assist the student in finding relevant expert commentary on the work (or they may have to choose another piece).

If time in the museum is limited, I allocate it so that the group experiences a few vividly felt examples in step 1, but has ample time for wandering in step 2. Once the group has felt the experience of the main elements of visual arts, such as line, color, and composition, further examples can be brought into the classroom in more traditional ways.

Contributor's Commentary

These connected activities reinforce what students have also been learning about the experiential learning cycle (Kolb, 1984). They reflect on their observations in the art museum (concrete experience, reflective observation), draw some generalizations (abstract conceptualization), compare them to others' (for example, the art critics), and apply these to the next piece of visual art they experience.

When students develop for themselves the meaning of terms used in art analysis, they tend to understand these criteria in a more substantive and transferable way than if, for example, they listen to an illustrated slide lecture on "art appreciation." The ultimate goal is for the students to learn to trust their empirical observations about art as the starting point for interpretation, rather than to focus too soon on technical terms that are easily forgotten unless grounded in the students' own context.

More generally, in the minds of pragmatic adult students, creativity and self-reflection often take a back seat as they endeavor to develop what they perceive as the more "useful" studentship skills of efficient critical reading, research, and time-management. This exercise allows students to use these practical skills in an area they initially think of as impractical. With the addition of readings and other journal assignments, most of the students come to discover that the capacity to use oneself (one's ideas, one's reactions) as a conscious reference point is, in fact, very useful and practical.

Since my course stresses the primary value of the students' *own* interpretive voice, I present material that illustrates the struggle of finding that true voice. Although this can provide a starting point for some learners to get through their *silence* (Belenky, Clinchy, Goldberger, & Tarule, 1986), this exercise does not work, educationally or developmentally, if it is based on students discussing their reactions to experts' opinions.

My overall goal as a teacher is for authentic, transformative learning. Attaining this goal requires that learners engage with a core identity that I think of as their authentic self. It is very common for returning adult students in unfamiliar fields such as art to try to figure out the "correct" answers. Conference sessions and directed journal assignments often reveal their attempts to conform to some preconceived idea of what a reflective art student *should* be. For the kind of learning I consider transformative to take place, however, their question, "What do *they* [instructors] want?" must evolve over time into "What do I have and what more do I need?" Some students lack confidence that they can enter a world that they've learned is privileged; others have lived long years being largely defined by external factors and are looking only for answers from "experts." Whatever its source, resistance to naming and claiming their own experience is my first signal that there is some important developmental work to do. This exercise gives me an entrée to students' areas of resistance so I can then structure feedback on journals and project proposals with those challenges in full view.

References

Belenky, M. F., Clinchy, B. M., Goldberger, M. R., & Tarule, J. M. (1986). *Women's ways of knowing: The development of self, voice, and mind.* Boston: Basic Books.

Kolb, D. A. (1984). *Experiential learning: Experience as the source of learning and development.* Englewood Cliffs, NJ: Prentice Hall.

Understanding Diversity and Difference

Irwin H. Siegel, Williamsport, Pennsylvania
E-mail: isiegel@pct.edu

Irwin Siegel was for many years a manager in corporate settings before becoming an assistant professor of management at the Pennsylvania College of Technology.

Developmental Intentions

I. Toward knowing as a dialogical process.
3. Reframing ideas or values that seem contradictory, embracing their differences, and arriving at new meanings.
7. Associating truth not with static fact but with contexts and relationships.
II. Toward a dialogical relationship to oneself.
2. Engaging the disequilibrium when one's ideas and beliefs are challenged.
IV. Toward self-agency and self-authorship.
1. Constructing a values system that informs one's behavior.
V. Toward connection with others.
3. Engaging the affective dimension when confronting differences.

Context

I use this activity in an undergraduate course in organizational behavior. Students are primarily, but not exclusively, pursuing business curricula.

Description of Activity

Purpose. To understand diversity by understanding difference and understand and manage diversity in the workplace through an appreciation of differences.

Format-steps-process. The overall design of the strategy is based first upon learning appropriate terminology and understanding the evolution of workforce composition over the past twenty years and into the twenty-first century. This constitutes the *what* aspect of managing diversity. The *why* aspect is addressed via the techniques described below. Finally, as a synthesis, groups of students suggest ideas relating to the *how* aspect, which they present to the class. Only afterward do I share "expert" tips from other sources on managing diversity as a basis for comparison.

1. Students are assigned a number of case studies that deal with aspects of diversity and difference. The case studies selected are designed to stimulate ideas

on understanding diversity as opposed to proscriptive rules. The case studies are selected for their ability to stimulate reflective thought, serve as a basis for class discussion, and probe stereotypes. In addition, a number of outside readings are assigned that reflect the personal feelings of those "others" who are treated differently.

2. I form small groups to address "Who to Hire?"—an experiential exercise in the Wohlberg, Gilmore, and Wolff (1998) workbook entitled *OB in Action*. This exercise explores cultural differences as well as student cultural biases. Students must individually, and then as a group, rank candidates for a position in a multinational company, all of whom come from varying ethnic and cultural backgrounds. Often students appear surprised as their own stereotypes surface.

3. Different groups are formed at the subsequent class to discuss effective means to manage diversity. Inevitably they will discover the inherent strength of recognizing and appreciating difference rather than hiding from it or attacking it. They discover the issues of power and privilege inherent within the dominant culture and become sensitized to the issues relevant to differing realities and the constructedness of truth.

4. A final reinforcing activity is the requirement that all students write an expressive paper describing some episode in their life in which they felt that they were being treated differently and how they felt as a result. The students are encouraged to link the episode they have described to the readings and class discussion.

Processing Tips

It is important that the instructor avoid having the class become entangled in legalistic arguments regarding affirmative action and reverse discrimination, but rather focus on developing the "difference" components of this unit.

Contributor's Commentary

Often students' perspectives on the more legalistic interventions will be transformed after they have explored the issues of difference, power, privileges, and the stereotypes they harbor, consciously or subconsciously.

This exercise could easily be refocused for training settings.

Reference

Wohlberg, J., Gilmore, G., & Wolff, S. (1998). *OB in action*. Boston: Houghton Mifflin.

Knowing Oneself as a Thinker and Learner

Ann V. Stanton, Montpelier, Vermont
E-mail: astanton@norwich.edu

Ann V. Stanton is a professor of liberal studies in Vermont College of Norwich University's adult degree program.

Developmental Intentions

    I. Toward knowing as a dialogical process.
        2. Surfacing and questioning assumptions underlying beliefs, ideas, actions, and positions.
  III. Toward being a continuous learner.
        1. Reflecting on one's own and other's experiences as a guide to future behavior.
        2. Challenging oneself to learn in new realms; taking risks.
        3. Recognizing and revealing one's strengths and weaknesses as a learner and knower.
        9. Drawing on multiple capacities for effective learning.

Context

These activities can be presented in many contexts. Most frequently, I use them as part of a workshop early in the semester to show students how they are thinkers and to provide them with the concrete experience of thinking in different modes.

Description of Activity

Purpose. To encourage intellectual development in students through self-reflection, develop critical thinking skills, and enable students to think about themselves as learners.

    Format-steps-process. I draw on several activities to stimulate self-reflection.

1. I use two interview questions on separate and connected knowing (Clinchy, 1997, p. 207–208). (These questions are part of the "Ways of Knowing" interview developed by Belenky, Clinchy, Goldberger, & Tarule, 1996). I ask students to pair up and interview one another regarding their reactions to the following two target statements:

"I never take anything for granted. I just tend to see the contrary. I like playing devil's advocate, arguing the opposite of what somebody is thinking, making exceptions, or thinking of a different train of thought."

"When I have an idea about something, and it differs from the way another person is thinking about it, I'll usually try to look at it from that person's point of view, see how they could say that, why they think that they are right, why it makes sense."

2. I ask students to think about which mode they prefer, why, and with what implications. I encourage students to "stretch"—to think of themselves as developing the modes that are not currently their preferred mode as they consider the advantages and drawbacks of their preferences.

3. I bring these elements together in an activity to think about and experience *critical thinking* by using the "Believing and Doubting Games" devised by Blythe Clinchy, based on Elbow (1973).

There are seven rules for playing the "Believing Game" and eight for the "Doubting Game," as follows:

Rules for the Believing Game

- The game is especially suitable for a group of players (preferably two to ten), although highly skilled players can play it fairly efficiently alone. It works best when played over a fairly long period (months, years). The only material required is a set of assertions presented orally or in writing. The assertions may be arranged in a variety of forms (for example, argument, narrative, poem).
- Take a friendly stance toward the assertions. Look for what is right about them. Try to share the experience and perceptions of the person who made the assertions. Use metaphors and analogies to help you enter the other person's skin.
- Each player acts as an advocate of the person making the assertions, trying to help the other players enter into the assertions by pointing out believable features of them, offering analogies and metaphors, and so forth.
- Use your own intuitions, experiences, and beliefs to try to project yourself into the experiences of the person making the assertions. Practice getting the feel of your self-interest so that you can sense when it is helping you to understand the assertions and when it is leading you into misunderstanding.
- Inhibit the impulse to find answers. Be patient and accepting of ambiguity, uncertainty, groping, and vagueness.
- Never argue. Do not offer assertions counter to the ones you are examining, and refrain from negative judgments.

- Believe everything that is asserted, especially statements that seem bizarre or repulsive. Remember, your belief need not be sincere or permanent (although you must try hard to pretend it is). This is only a game.

Rules for the Doubting Game

- The game is suitable for one or more players. Duration of play varies, ranging from minutes to years, but is often relatively brief. The only material required is a set of assertions (ideas, perceptions), usually written, usually arranged as a sequence of propositions.
- Take an adversarial stance toward the assertions you are examining. Put the assertions on trial. Look for what is wrong with them. Ferret out errors of fact and mistakes in reasoning, such as contradictions, loopholes in logic, and overgeneralizations. Try to disprove, disqualify, and disconfirm the author's position.
- You may find it helpful to invent an argument contrary to the one you are examining and then construct a debate between the arguments.
- Be precise, and insist that your opponent be precise.
- Use objective, impersonal criteria or rules (for example, logical consistency, clarity of definition, degree of fit between data and interpretation) in constructing and evaluating arguments, and insist that your opponent obey the same rules.
- Beware of personal bias in your own reasoning and be on the alert for bias in the propositions you are examining. As Peter Elbow (1973) says, "Weed out the self, its wishes and preoccupations." Behave like a computer, and insist that others do likewise. *Never* refer to your own experiences, feelings, beliefs, or intuitions, and rule out any such references as irrelevant if your opponents make them.
- Doubt everything that is asserted. Try especially hard to find reasons for doubting the propositions that seem most compelling.
- Remember, your doubts need not be sincere (although they must be valid). This is only a game.

4. Students read a one-page persuasive essay and then discuss the essay in groups of three or four, using first one set of rules and then the other. After each round, they discuss their responses to the "game": "Which aspects of the author's thinking were clarified and which were obscured? How was the group's process aided or hindered by each set of rules?" I, in turn, gather thoughts from the different groups and try to build a picture of how the small groups experience and react first to the "Believing Game" and then the "Doubting Game." I try to point out the advantages and disadvantages of each game, as expressed by the groups themselves.
5. After encouraging students to look at these aspects of their experience, I point out how these rules are actually procedures for engaging in critical thinking.

Then I ask them to reflect on their own routine preferences. Sometimes I ask them to do a quick free-write on this topic, that is, writing freely and spontaneously, without self-censoring ("I myself prefer the _____ game because . . . "). We discuss as a group how they might expand their thinking by employing both sets of rules.

Processing Tips

The essay chosen for students to discuss is crucial. It must raise a controversial issue that can engage both games. For example, I use one from *Newsweek* magazine, March 2, 1992, titled "A Gentle Way to Die" by Katie Letcher Lyle, a piece that learners find both engaging and plausible.

Contributor's Commentary

I think of all these techniques and practices as taking students "backstage." A tendency that is reinforced by grading systems, it is all too easy for learners to label themselves (and others) via attributes, such as "bright" or "dumb," rather than identifying with a process. This is akin to attributing the success of a play to the raw talent of the actors, disregarding all the practice, props, lighting, make-up, and other elements that go into a fine performance. Students need to become acquainted with all the elements that go into a mental-intellectual performance and realize that learning is a process and that they themselves are in process.

Overall, my strategy is to help students focus on their capacities as thinkers and knowers. I also try to set up expectations of growth that will challenge their anxieties about learning and propel them into their studies with energy and critical self-reflection. These exercises are designed to convey, right from the start, the message that they *are* thinkers while helping them experience the excitement of becoming *better* thinkers—deeper, more reflective, more critical, more understanding.

References

Belenky, M. F., Clinchy, B. M., Goldberger, N. R., & Tarule, J. M. (1996). *Women's Ways of Knowing* (2nd ed.). New York: Basic Books.

Clinchy, B. M. (1997). Connected and separate knowing: Toward a marriage of two minds. In N. R. Goldberger, J. M. Tarule, B. M. Clinchy, & M. F. Belenky (Eds.), *Knowledge, difference, and power*. New York: Basic Books.

Elbow, P. (1973). The doubting game and the believing game—an analysis of the intellectual enterprise. *Writing Without Teachers*. London: Oxford University Press.

Stanton, A. (1996). Reconfiguring teaching and knowing in the college classroom. In N. R. Goldberger, J. M. Tarule, B. M. Clinchy, & M. F. Belenky (Eds.), *Knowledge, difference, and power*. Boston: Basic Books.

Culture and Identity

Alissa Stolz, Fayetteville, North Carolina
E-mail: astolz@aol.com

Alissa Stolz has taught German language and culture to enlisted armed services personnel overseas.

Developmental Intentions

    I. Toward knowing as a dialogical process.
      2. Surfacing and questioning assumptions underlying beliefs, ideas, actions, and positions.
   III. Toward being a continuous learner.
      1. Reflecting on one's own and others' experiences as a guide to future behavior.
   IV. Toward self-agency and self-authorship.
      6. Distinguishing what one has created for oneself from what is imposed by social, cultural, and other forces.
    V. Toward connection with others.
      2. Experiencing oneself as part of something larger.
      3. Engaging the affective dimension when confronting differences.

Context

This exercise could be used effectively in any learning focused on cultural belief and bias.

Description of Activity

Purpose. To examine how cultural beliefs can shape an individual's perspective, explore some of the assumptions that create cultural imperatives (that is, how things *ought* to be), and ask learners to question what they "know" about cultural beliefs (their own and others').

Format-steps-process.

1. I ask the class what they understand culture to mean, and we spend a few minutes examining culture as a general set of societal rules. I then draw a line down the middle of a chalkboard and title one side "Germany" and the other "United States."

2. I ask the students to share briefly some of the differences they have experienced between the two cultures while I write key words on the corresponding side of the chalkboard. A comment that "bikes clog street traffic in Germany" might become "bikes as transportation" on the German side of the board and "bikes as recreation" on the American side, after I ask some leading questions about the comparison.

3. When no more examples are forthcoming, we begin to discuss a few of the cultural phenomena. I ask questions designed to get students to consider how the cultural practice may have evolved and why it might still be in existence. For example, the size of the countries, the cost of gas, the industrial base, as well as people's attitudes about pace of life, exercise, and ecology and pollution.

4. We also look for advantages and disadvantages for each difference, including both particular and more global analyses. For example: "What are the relative benefits of cheap and expensive gas? Of automobiles as a lynchpin of an economy? Of fast-paced work and personal lives?" In other words, I encourage framing the analysis in larger terms than might initially have been identified.

5. I also encourage the learners to suggest explanations for the various cultural practices, even if they do not have "facts," to make connections between what they know and some reasonable analysis. "Why is the price of gas in the U.S. half to one-third that in Germany?" We also look at the potential effects of changing some common practices. For example: "What would be the impact (locally, globally) if Germans adopted American attitudes toward cars as transportation? If Americans adopted German attitudes towards bikes as transportation?"

6. After several items have been analyzed this way, I divide the class down the middle of the room; one side is now Germany and the other, the United States. I ask each side to discuss among themselves the remaining topics from their "own" culture's perspective. I then ask them to present each issue, taking the predominant opinion of their assigned culture, regardless of what they personally believe, the same way a defense lawyer represents a client. A pair of delegates (one person from each side) debates one of the issues on the board, attempting to convince the other side of the correctness of his or her own position. For example: "Is it better to use bikes or automobiles for transportation?" Enlisting the support and assistance of others from the same side is encouraged.

7. These discussions-debates continue until all the issues on the board have been addressed. Agreement among the delegates is rare. Indeed, this exercise can stir up "nationalistic" feelings. (Given the context of young military personnel as learners, I have found a good way to end the debate is to take a break and ask people to be prepared to reflect briefly on how wars start.)

8. For closure, students form small, mixed groups of "Germans" and "Americans." They are asked to discuss what they have discovered about culture and cultural "superiority" and to share their findings with the group as a whole. They are also asked to reflect on how committed they have been to their own side of the argument, and what this implies for mutual understanding across cultures.

Processing Tips

The exercise often starts with fairly superficial observations, such as "Germans don't serve ice in beverages and their beer is warm." However, that observation can lead easily into questions of refrigerator size, hence to energy use and ecology. If such topics don't emerge, I have questions ready. It usually takes just two or three such interventions to turn the discussion to more substantive issues.

I start the cultural comparisons in step 3 slowly, focusing on the more innocuous differences. People need time to absorb the notion that culture is their own creation before they can tackle big issues. Again, if the conversation doesn't turn on its own, I have questions ready. However, once participants are more capable of putting on the lenses of each culture, the discussion becomes more and more student-idea driven. Many topics will not get the full treatment they merit, but I then encourage students to do some further research or reading of their own.

As the discussion deepens, one of the concepts that will typically emerge is *historical context*. Often, students need to discover the significance of the fact that Germany's culture has developed over several centuries, whereas the United States is relatively youthful, in terms of the life of the nation. Another useful interjection is a quick discussion of Germany's geography and changing borders. This *geographical context* is often a new perspective for students who are used to living in a country that stretches from one ocean to another.

In step 6, when the countries are assigned, I have found it useful to move desks apart along the dividing line and to have the students face across the room. They are more inclined to address each other directly in their respective debates, rather than speaking to me.

Contributor's Commentary

Students come to understand, in a very visceral way, that what they regard as "normal" is an accident of birth. Furthermore, it is an eye-opener to many that some American cultural practices do not stack up well against those of other cultures. Depending on the sophistication of the group and the purpose of the course, the exercise could focus more narrowly and deeply on certain aspects of difference, such as politics, attitudes about social and economic welfare, and so on. For example, a brainstorm of comparisons about economic issues might include the following:

Germany	*United States*
National health	Private insurance, HMO, or nothing
Shorter work week	Compulsory overtime for some
Four to six weeks vacation	One to three weeks vacation
VAT (high taxes), progressive	Low taxes, regressive
Subsidized public transportation	Little public transportation
"Onion" economy—almost all middle class; few poor or rich	"Pyramid" economy—many poor, fewer middle, fewest rich
Higher commodity prices	Lower commodity prices
More civil servants	More entrepreneurs
Stronger labor unions	Weaker labor unions

Even though the group may have no formal economic theory to draw on and few "facts," they can generate these comparisons and then make reasonable inferences about possible relationships among these factors. This could be an engaging lead-in to more formal research on the topic.

CHAPTER TEN

REFLECTING

Though closely related to *inquiring,* the learner's emphasis in *reflecting* is, "What does the question mean? How am I interpreting it?" In most cases, reflecting and inquiring will be part of the same exercise; Roberta Liebler's exercise on "Stimulating Cognitive and Ethical Development" (p. 217) is one such example. The activities are assigned to one or the other strategy according to our somewhat subjective assessment of which strategy seems to be more prominent. A number of these activities focus on reflecting on the self; see, for example, Mary Belenky's "Claiming the Powers of Voice and Mind" (p. 247) and Kathleen Taylor's "Emerging Life Patterns" (p. 261)

Activities that extend over more than one session begin with Joan Blanusa's "Using Empathic Listening as a Means of Support for Strategies Designed to Foster Adult Development" (p. 264).

◆ ◆ ◆

Myth and Metaphor, Story and Symbol: Bridges to Our Deeper Selves

Caroline Bassett, Minneapolis, Minnesota
E-mail: cbassett@wisdominst.org

Caroline Bassett is founder and president of the Wisdom Institute, which explores the higher levels of adult development, and faculty member at two distance learning universities: Walden University and Capella University.

Developmental Intentions

II. Toward a dialogical relationship to oneself.
   1. Addressing fears of losing what is familiar and safe.
   3. Exploring life's experiences through some framework(s) of analysis.
   5. Exploring and making meaning of one's life stories within contexts (for example, societal, familial, universal).
III. Toward being a continuous learner.
   9. Drawing on multiple capacities for effective learning.
IV. Toward self-agency and self-authorship.
   6. Distinguishing what one has created for oneself from what is imposed by social, cultural, and other forces.

Context

I use this exercise in graduate or undergraduate courses with a focus on adult development, adult learning, multiple intelligences, right-brain learning, or creativity.

Description of Activity

Purpose. To use myth and metaphor, symbol and story as means of deepening understanding of the self; use fictional characters, settings, and symbols as a way toward self-reflection and meaning-making; and cultivate the metaphorical mind for increasing self-knowledge.

Format-steps-process. This exercise happens on two levels. The first, and more superficial, is the actual telling of the story. The second, and deeper, level is use of the story as a way into the learner's meaning-constructive system, perhaps bypassing his or her conscious defenses and intellectualizations. Myths and metaphors are the stuff of the collective unconscious, according to Jung, and storytelling is a tool that can gain access to it.

1. I choose a story that contains aspects of the group's intentions. For example, when teaching a course on the process of transformation, I might choose a story called "Maid Maleen" that illustrates the process of coming to realize that things have changed, and you have to change, too, of going into chaos and confusion, and finally creating for yourself a new way of being (story synopsis follows).

I practice ahead of time in order to remember relevant plot details, and I may do a mild dramatization.

2. When I am actually ready to engage the class, I ask, "Do you want to hear a story?" (People's eyes usually light up and their attention shifts. The metaphorical mind is becoming activated.) I try to make the space different from the usual. I may turn out or dim the lights, go out of the room and reenter with a lit candle or a flashlight. I return, not as myself, but as "the Storyteller"—the conjuror of a world of imagination—and learners respond to this shift in perspective and reality.

3. After I have dramatized the story, emphasizing the plot lines and characters that seem most relevant to our purposes, I turn the lights back on and in other ways reestablish the learning space and myself as the instructor.

4. I then facilitate a discussion of the plot devices and symbols in the story by posing questions. The questions lead from *examination* of immediate experience through *reflection* on that experience to *abstractions.*

5. In posing the first set of questions, such as those below, I try to keep everyone involved at the experiential level before going on to deeper analysis. Some examples follow:

> Has anything like this ever happened to you?
>
> What do you like about this story; what don't you like about it?
>
> What kinds of emotions does this story evoke in you?
>
> Which character do you like best? Like least?

6. When everyone has participated, I move toward analysis. For example:

> What does [this aspect] in the story represent?
>
> Who does [a certain character] represent?
>
> Why did [certain plot devices] happen?

7. Finally, I encourage applying the analysis of aspects of the story as they may illuminate the course objectives. For example:

> Have you ever been tempted to [whatever part of the plot line, as interpreted, is relevant to the course objectives]. *Note:* Because of the intervening discussion and clarifications about the meaning of the story, this ends up being a very different question from the first one, above: "Has this ever happened to you?"
>
> How did you handle this? How did others handle this?

8. This discussion is a springboard to an assignment designed to enhance the individual learner's analysis. Depending on the course context and desired outcomes, the assignment might include

Rewriting aspects of the story, using symbols meaningful to
the learner, to achieve his or her desired ending

Exploring more deeply, in a journal, the meanings of the symbols
and characters uncovered during discussion

Retelling the story from the perspective of different characters,
other than the one with whom the learner initially identified

Processing Tips

The questions for reflective discussion depend on the kind of course, the learners' needs and intentions, and the instructor's or trainer's goals. Some instructors
(for example, in step 6) might expect or provide existing frameworks of analysis,
such as literary conventions or psychological archetypes. I am more interested
in the learners' personal reactions ("What did this character mean *to you*"), as this
exercise is about self-discovery, not literary analysis. It is therefore important to
begin with concrete reactions to the story and not to jump immediately to abstract analysis. One discovers, for example, that not everyone heard certain parts
of the story in the same way, or that people had startlingly different emotional
reactions. What one person thought was tragic, another might think was funny.
(This is often a result of people's reactions to prior experiences in their lives,
and those reactions sometimes come into the discussion. There are good opportunities here to examine the constructed nature of meaning.) If discussion begins
at the abstract level, without first getting at these differences, people may simply
take positions based on their unexplored assumptions.

If the group has had exposure to theoretical frameworks, such as models of
development, another interesting discussion can be facilitated around applying
that sort of analysis to the story and, by extension, to the learner's self-identifi-
cation within the story.

Contributor's Commentary

Stories seem to move people into another realm of consciousness, a more receptive part of themselves. Figuratively speaking, it is as though the boundaries
between the left and right brain begin to soften and ideas and images flow more
easily back and forth, with the result that there is emotional and mental resonance
to the story.

I pay attention to major myths and fairy tales, such as those told by Brothers
Grimm and Joseph Campbell, to literature, folk tales, and, because I am inter-
ested in adult development, to books by Allen Chinen (1989, 1992) and David
Whyte (1996). Certain movies are another place in which to find the kind of

complex, layered narrative that awakens self-reflection. (*Star Wars,* for example, contains many themes found in mythology.) Whether they have seen it or not, learners are intrigued to "hear" a movie in story form. If it is well-known, they are able to bring to the discussion particularly meaningful aspects of the story *to them,* even if I haven't described them in my retelling. Most people regard "going to the movies" as passive entertainment and have not asked themselves—"Is there a Darth Vader in my life? Have I ever experienced the Force? Do I believe there is a Force? How it might it become available to me and how might I use it?"—or whatever questions are likely to illuminate course objectives.

As mentioned above, "Maid Maleen" can illuminate many issues about adult development. I synopsize it here just to show how the directions about the images might work:

Maid Maleen's father shuts her up in a tower of his castle with her serving-maid for seven years so the prince can't marry her. But her provisions run low and she and her maid dig their way out only to find a desolate landscape due to a war. There is nothing at all any more—no one alive in her castle. She and the servant wander the countryside eating nettles. ("When have you 'eaten nettles'? What was that like? Can you share what the experience was about? What do nettles represent in your life journey? What happened next? How did you move beyond eating nettles to whatever came next in your life?") They finally come to another castle—the castle of her own prince, of course. But he is getting ready to marry a false bride. ("Who or what have been the 'false brides' that have seduced us?") Maid Maleen finally succeeds in getting her man, and there is fulfillment, integrity, resolution, and growth.

Most fairy tales, of course, include such gender stereotypes. However, it is not necessary to interpret the story in those ways. The "prince," for example, can be any long-desired goal; the "false bride" can be anything that deflects us from our true destiny; and so forth.

As another example of the use of the symbolic elements in a story: When Odysseus returns home in disguise after being gone for many years at war and many more years at sea, only his old dog recognizes him. ("Is there an 'old dog' in your life who knows the 'real you' whether or not you are in 'disguise'? What kind of person is this for you? What does it feel like to be recognized in this way? Can you do the same for others?") Earlier in the story, Odysseus wants to experience the enticing music of the Sirens, but hearing the Sirens leads to shipwrecks. So he tells his crew to stop up their own ears with candle wax but has them bind him, ears unstoppered, firmly to the ship's mast until the ship is safely past the danger. ("Have you ever been so curious about or seduced by an experience that you have almost destroyed yourself or others?" [Drugs, alcohol, obsessions, addictions.] "Do you have someone in your life, a friend or mentor, who can warn you about the rocks ahead so that you can find a way to avoid them? Have you been able to find a way to have the experience and still survive? What did you learn from either listening to the Sirens and going on the rocks or deciding not to because the risk was too grave?"

A well-crafted, well-told *story* can be tied to a variety of learning goals. Stories seem to be in some mysterious way much more compelling than simply reading words on a page. For people to use self-reflection in a conscious way, they need to realize that, like the roots of a tree, the parts of them that are underground provide nourishment and stability for the visible parts. Stories can provide a bridge to the metaphorical receptive mind, which works differently from our more ordinary discursive mind. Myths and the images operating within them, stories and the symbols resonating in them, can help us gain access to and use our metaphorical minds for increasing self knowledge.

References

Campbell, J. (1949/1968). *The hero with a thousand faces* (2nd ed.). Princeton, NJ: Princeton University Press.

Chinen, A. (1989). *In the ever after: Fairy tales and the second half of life.* Willamette, IL: Chiron.

Chinen, A. (1992). *Once upon a midlife: Classic stories and mythic tales to illuminate the middle years.* Los Angeles: Jeremy Tarcher.

Whyte, D. (1996). *The heart aroused: Poetry and the preservation of the soul in corporate America.* New York: Doubleday.

Claiming the Powers of Voice and Mind

Mary Field Belenky, Burlington, Vermont
E-mail: belenky@together.net

Mary Field Belenky, associate professor at the University of Vermont, is an educator and researcher who works with a variety of educational and community organizations interested in the empowerment process.

Developmental Intentions

I. Toward knowing as a dialogical process.

7. Associating truth not with static fact but with contexts and relationships.

II. Toward a dialogical relationship to oneself.

5. Exploring and making meaning of one's life stories within contexts (for example, societal, familial, universal).

III. Toward being a continuous learner.

3. Recognizing and revealing one's strengths and weaknesses as a learner and knower.

IV. Toward self-agency and self-authorship.

7. "Naming and claiming" what one has experienced and knows.

V. Toward connection with others.

5. Recognizing that collective awareness and thinking transform the sum of their parts.

Context

Undergraduate, graduate courses, and workshops for people interested in the empowerment process and the creation of collaborative learning communities.

Description of Activity

Purpose. To reflect on the kinds of experiences that enable people to cultivate more complex ways of knowing, gain a voice, and become fuller participants in the broader community, and to encourage people to seek out and develop highly creative, collaborative learning environments for themselves and others.

Format-steps-process.

1. The facilitator describes the goals and outlines the activity. If the participants do not know each other, people are asked to give a brief self-introduction.

2. The facilitator hands out "Tips for Interviewers" and "The Voice Interview." She then reads these aloud and answers any questions the participants may have about the interview process.

3. The group pairs off. First one person will interview the other; then they will switch roles. The facilitator keeps time. Depending on the time available, each interview may last from ten to twenty minutes.

4. The pairs take turns interviewing each other about their experiences of being silenced, gaining voice, and encouraging others' voices.

5. When the interview process is completed the group should reassemble to harvest what was learned. With a group of twenty people, this can easily take an hour or more.

6. Just before closing the activity, people are asked to describe any action plans they are coming away with. People who are working on similar projects or issues can be encouraged to form a mutual support system or collaborative.

Processing Tips

Asking good questions and careful listening are preconditions for creating the kind of dialogue that animates powerful learning environments. I start the harvesting process by asking people to reflect on the interview experience itself. I then collect the stories of being silenced, noting the common causes. Finally, I explore with particular care the steps that helped people gain a voice.

Meanwhile, I ask someone to record the emerging ideas on newsprint. When no new ideas are forthcoming, the group reviews the ideas that delineate the empowerment process, grouping and labeling ideas that form a cluster. Items that seem especially important might be starred. These will form a checklist that could be considered whenever one is trying to create more effective learning environments.

The time for the harvesting process is quite variable. When people are invited, perhaps for the first time, to tell their stories, it is important not to silence them once again.

Contributor's Commentary

Our ways of knowing are shaped in powerful ways by our environments—families, schools, workplaces, civic associations, and informal networks (see Belenky, Clinchy, Goldberger, & Tarule, 1996). These can be stifling places where many are silenced. People seldom talk together about what is happening. When they try to name what is going on, no one listens. Good questions are seldom asked. People fail to appreciate each other's abilities.

Other environments are mind opening for everyone. Ideas fly back and forth; questions abound. People are always drawing each other out. Plans are made and things get done (see Belenky, Bond, & Weinstock, 1997).

Building inclusive, creative, and collaborative learning environments is especially important in a highly technological era, characterized by an extraordinary rate of social change and cross-cultural exchange. Old ways no longer suffice; many aspects of life have to be reconceptualized from start to finish, again and again.

Environments where everyone is supported to become active constructors of knowledge are essential for creating and maintaining a highly democratic society. All too often we respond passively to the processes that keep people silenced at the margins of society. This work suggests we can create environments that enable many to gain a voice, claim the powers of mind, and become fuller participants in the life of their community (see Belenky, Bond, & Weinstock, 1997).

The Voice Interview (adapted from Belenky, Clinchy, Goldberger, & Tarule, 1996)

1. Describe your most powerful learning experience in or out of school.

    What stands out for you about this experience?

    Did this experience change the way you thought of yourself as a thinker? How so?

2. (*If appropriate:* You may have answered this question but let me pose it anyway, as it may bring up something more.) Describe a time when you became keenly aware of the power of your own mind, a time when you really had a voice.

    What stands out for you about this experience?

    Did this experience change the way you thought of yourself as a thinker? How so?

3. Can you recall an experience—in or out of school—of being silenced? A time when you felt voiceless, frozen, when your mind clamped down and you doubted your capacity to think?

    What stands out for you about this experience?

    Did this experience change the way you thought of yourself as a thinker? How so?

4. How did you go about reclaiming your voice?

    Who and what helped?

    What could have happened that would have facilitated the process even more?

5. Describe times when you have played a role in bringing others into voice. (Could be with friends, classmates, colleagues, children, students, etc.) What happened that was enabling?

Tips for Interviewers

- Your genuine interest in another person and their view of the world is the key to good interviewing.
- Do not assume that you know what your partner is going to say. Be really open to hear a story that is very different. Stretch yourself to hear and feel the new story.
- Be surprised to learn how many stories we have in common.
- Listen for the "growing edge," for the turning points, for the ways the person has been struggling to change his or her life. While we try not to close ourselves off to another's pain, we focus on listening for people's strengths and growth.
- The questions we have provided are a guide. You will often think of much better questions as you talk with your partner.
- Good questions are often hard to answer. Good questions help the person think

through their experience in new and different ways. Be comfortable with silences. Give your partner time.

- If you come to a question that your partner has already answered, skip it, or say, "I think you have answered this, but let me ask it again as you may have more to add." Otherwise your partner may think that you did not listen or that you did not like the answer.
- Ask lots of questions that will draw out your partner's thoughts, such as, "Can you give an example? Can you say more? How so? Why?"
- If you do not understand what your partner is saying, say so. She may be able to find different words to get the meaning across. Pretending to understand does not help your partner to get things clear.
- Try to find a place in your own experience that your partner is describing. Try to stand in her shoes and see through her eyes.
- From time to time sum up what you hear and say it back to your partner. This is the way you can check out whether you are hearing your partner's experience in the way she wants you to hear it. It also gives your partner space to reflect on her construction and make any revisions that seem helpful.
- No fancy interpretations are necessary.

References

Belenky, M. F., Bond, L., & Weinstock, J. (1997). *A tradition that has no name: Nurturing the development of people, families, and communities.* New York: Basic Books.

Belenky, M. F., Clinchy, B. M., Goldberger, N. R., & Tarule, J. M. (1996). *Women's ways of knowing: The development of self, voice, and mind* (2nd ed.). New York: Basic Books.

Goldberger, N. R., Tarule, J. M., Clinchy, B. M., & Belenky, M. F. (1996). *Knowledge, difference, and power: Essays inspired by women's ways of knowing.* New York: Basic Books.

Moral of One's Story

Catharine Farrell, Berkeley, California
E-mail: kaleki@aol.com or cfarrel@muse.sfusd.edu

Catharine Farrell conducts workshops for adults on storytelling techniques. She also teaches reentry adults in a degree-completion program.

Developmental Intentions

I. Toward knowing as a dialogical process.
   2. Surfacing and questioning assumptions underlying beliefs, ideas, actions, and positions.

    II. Toward a dialogical relationship to oneself.
        5. Exploring and making meaning of one's life stories within contexts
           (for example, societal, familial, universal).
    III. Toward being a continuous learner.
        1. Reflecting on one's own and others' experiences as a guide to
           future behavior.

Context

This activity has been used in an undergraduate course in which adult students are required to write a number of experiential learning essays to petition for college credit. It would also be effective in any course in which autobiographical self-reflection would be a valuable learning tool.

Description of Activity

Purpose. To recognize and elaborate on a meaningful theme of one's life.

Format-steps-process. I ask students to create a modern fable from their personal experience so that they can view their own life as literature. I have students assume the role of narrator to their life story. This is one of the first activities I use in teaching the class.

1. I ask students to begin by isolating one vivid incident in their lives that is still quite "charged" or evocative in their memories.
2. Students then pair with a partner and each tells the other the incident, using specific sensory details to recreate the experience. The role of the nonspeaking partner is to be an attentive listener.
3. I then ask the partners to work together to determine the "moral" to their true life stories, that is, the truism that each learned from his or her experience. The goal of the exercise is that each individual truth should be valued. Since authentic wording is important, I encourage them to avoid clichés.
4. With the moral of their story as the title of a short essay, I move students to write about how that particular truth has guided their life choices.
5. Once completed with their writing, students compare and contrast their personal truth (moral) with those in their family and in society.

Processing Tips

It is most helpful for the instructor to first model this exercise by telling a personal experience with the entire class as the active listener. In selecting an experience, choose one that has a universal appeal and one with some suspense or drama. Tell the experience in the tradition of storytelling, with an eye for compelling detail. Keep the model fable short—no more than five minutes—as I have found students will generally duplicate its length. Engage the students in a discussion of possible morals and write on the board or chart paper the one that best reflects your own belief. Indicate how you have followed this moral throughout your life. Compare and contrast your own belief to commonly held assumptions in society.

As you direct students to select their own fable, or true life story, ask them to choose one that is vivid in their memories and one that they feel safe sharing with a partner. I ask two or three partners to share a story that he or she heard with the whole group, after gaining permission from the original teller. At the very least, I ask each student in turn to share the moral of his or her fable.

Contributor's Commentary

A memory that is still emotionally charged is quite alive in conscious (and unconscious) thought. By tapping into that memory with a live audience and using sensory details in relating the incident, one can focus even more clearly on the way that meaning was constructed at that time. Working with a neutral partner will facilitate the analytic effort of meaning-making. Furthermore, the last step allows the individual to reflect on the unique character of his or her own analysis.

I have found that this is a very stimulating and lively activity. It encourages authentic voice in the writing process and is a good icebreaker for the entire class. This activity allows students to begin assessing raw experience in terms of abstractions, such as the morals or generalities they formed based on these experiences.

Developing Group Alternatives for Reconstructing Personal Behaviors

Chris Laming, Victoria, Australia
E-mail:claming@mugca.cc.monash.edu.au

Chris Laming is a social worker with the Latrobe Community Health Service in rural, southeastern Australia, where he coordinates the Men's SHED Project. (It is called the SHED Project because in Australia the shed in the backyard symbolizes the place men feel most at home, where they go to think about life, to mess around with mates, fix things, construct, reflect, change, and so on. We also use SHED as an acronym for Self-Help Ending Domestics, that is, domestic violence.)

Developmental Intentions

I. Toward knowing as a dialogical process.
   9. Perceiving and constructing one's reality by observing and participating.
II. Toward a dialogical relationship to oneself.
   2. Engaging the disequilibrium when one's ideas and beliefs are challenged.
III. Toward being a continuous learner.
   1. Reflecting on one's own and others' experiences as a guide to future behavior.
IV. Toward self-agency and self-authorship.
   2. Accepting responsibility for choices one has made and will make.
V. Toward connection with others.
   3. Engaging the affective dimension when confronting differences.

Context

I use this activity as part of the Men's Responsibility Program—a group process promoting attitudinal and behavioral change to stop family violence. This is a structured twelve-week program, which follows an ongoing intake group. Group sizes vary from six to twelve men, the majority of whom are volunteers. The rest are attending as part of a court order. Initially, resistance to learning, and to change, is high. This exercise takes place in the seventh week, though the process is applicable to a variety of situations. The program has a male and female co-facilitator and we jointly facilitate the group process. It generally takes about two hours.

Description of Activity

Purpose. To demonstrate how personal behaviors form an interrelated pattern, how behaviors can be conceptualized in a continuum, how we can create constructive alternatives to behaviors, and how we are responsible for making choices in behaviors.

   Format-steps-process.

1. Before participants enter the meeting room, we (the cofacilitators) project an overhead image of a model of the behaviors to be discussed. The participants are invited to look at it while settling down and waiting for all to take their seats. Copies of the selected model are also distributed. *Example:* With the Men's Responsibility Program (MRP), we project a conceptualized model of abusive and violent behaviors and how they are interrelated.

2. After a few minutes, we switch off the overhead and introduce the session by linking it to previous sessions. *Example:* The MRP group had previously brainstormed types of violent and abusive behavior; they cited examples that were as personal as possible. These personal examples, listed on a whiteboard, now become the focus for this session in a more structured framework.

3. We briefly get the participants to repeat the brainstorm from the previous session, describing and naming the various types of behavior and how they interlink; this is to foster recall and to synthesize the brainstorming effort. *Example:* The MRP group is encouraged to recognize how emotional abuse, threats, intimidation, and physical assault are all interlinked, controlling behaviors.

4. We next invite the participants to view a video that depicts behaviors relevant to the discussion, asking them to keep in mind the model that was projected overhead when they entered the room. We let them know that we will pause the video after a while for questions and discussion. *Example:* We show a video that depicts men behaving abusively in a number of vignettes.

5. We stop the video to discuss what we have been viewing, and encourage each participant to contribute his own recollections, insights, judgments, criticisms, reactions, and feelings about what was in the video. We also encourage them to use the photocopied sheets of the behavioral model as a reference point for the discussion. *Example:* Although there is an inclination to keep the discussion at a less-threatening, intellectual level, most of the men experience, and share, emotional reactions.

6. At the end of the video, we bring the group back to the model of behaviors, and it becomes once more the focus of discussion through questions and the relating of their own experiences. We encourage them to be as self-revealing as possible. *Example:* This is often a point where the participants start to make real connections and get an "aha" experience of suddenly having an insight into the ramifications of violent behavior on those affected.

7. We then turn to the whiteboard brainstorm and encourage participants to draw connections between the items they identified previously and the new ideas they have formed from viewing the video alongside the model of behaviors. *Example:* This is usually a very sobering time during which the men make many connections between their own types of abuse experiences and what they have seen graphically portrayed on the screen.

8. To further ground these connections, we ask the participants to stand in a line across the room, tallest at one end and shortest at the other. Next we ask them to reorganize themselves in another continuum with one man to represent a behavior listed on their whiteboard brainstorm to stand at one end, and another man representing the opposite end of that behavioral continuum to stand

at the other. (The group has to decide the continuum of behaviors.) The men are asked to identify and name the behaviors each will represent. (We point out to the group that they are not being asked in this exercise to personally identify with the behaviors, but only to participate as part of learning. Usually there is no lack of volunteers.) *Example:* The man representing the most violent behavior listed on their whiteboard brainstorm is asked to stand at one end, and another man representing the least violent behavior to stand at the other. (The men themselves have to decide the continuum of most violent behavior to least violent.) The men are asked to name and describe behaviors and identify where they belong on the continuum.

9. The group is then asked to identify and organize in a continuum the remainder of the listed behaviors and their opposites, with a man representing each. They are encouraged to discuss, debate, and challenge the placing of behaviors on the continuum, as well as the factors that might contribute to that placing. (Here we include a discussion about the effects of different types of behavior on others, including witnesses to the behavior.) *Example:* The MRP group ends up with a line of men, each of whom has "identified" with a particular behavior (not necessarily as his own, but for purposes of categorization). The grouping as a whole represents a continuum of violent behaviors, from most to least, as perceived by the group members after considerable analysis and discussion of the effects of that behavior on all who are party to it.

10. As a final step the group is asked: "What is someone like who does this behavior?" (write answers on left side of whiteboard). When they have given their answer they are further asked: "How would you describe someone who is different from that?" (write answers on opposite side of whiteboard). *Example:* The MRP group is asked these questions and also asked which they would prefer to be. (This is a platform from which further exercises emanate. For example, questions such as, "Why would you prefer to be _____ ? Why is that important to you?" And so on, followed by, "And what is someone like who is not like that?")

Processing Tips

Cofacilitation, preferably female-male, is essential. The value of the process depends on the facilitators' ability to elicit the experiences of the participants and utilize the framework of the model to help them better conceptualize their behavior.

Contributor's Commentary

This exercise is multifaceted and has the potential to be utilized with groups of high school or college students, teachers, social workers, and many others. It can focus on any activity that people engage in that they may need to recognize, observe, and challenge. Its possible applications and replications are limited only by our imagination.

This exercise reflects a dynamic, evolving process, a sort of journey to discover and develop one's personal truth in relationships. It is not an easy journey because along the way one's values, attitudes, beliefs, views, and ideas are challenged and questioned. Hence, the process is also threatening to individuals and relies on the group trust to make it happen. This requires risk taking and readiness to hear from others in the group things about oneself that might not be palatable.

However, this very process of naming difficult things in front of one's peers, and hearing hard things in the group, enables the possibility of personal growth toward truth on many levels. Personally "owning" one's behavior in a group context frees one to change in a way that public denial of that behavior does not allow. Doing so publicly also "educates" the listeners in ways that can lead to change; in this way a participant experiences being part of something larger. In sum, this group process engenders a transforming growth in collective awareness—a community education.

The Indescribable Moment

Greg J. Neimeyer, Gainesville, Florida
E-mail: neimeyer@psych.ufl.edu

Greg Neimeyer is a professor of psychology and director of training in the doctoral program in counseling psychology at the University of Florida. He has written widely on constructivist psychology.

Developmental Intentions

    I. Toward knowing as a dialogical process.
       1. Inquiring into and responding openly to others' ideas.
      10. Tapping into and drawing on tacit knowledge.
    II. Toward a dialogical relationship to oneself.
       3. Exploring life's experiences through some framework(s) of analysis.
    IV. Toward self-agency and self-authorship.
       7. "Naming and claiming" what one has experienced and knows.
    V. Toward connection with others.
       5. Recognizing that collective awareness and thinking transform
          the sum of their parts.

Context

Graduate courses in adult learning, counseling, or psychotherapy; professional development programs for practicing psychotherapists.

Description of Activity

Purpose. To explore processes of meaning-making and to illustrate the role of *languaging* in the making of meaning.

Format-steps-process. The "Indescribable Moment" involves a simple instructional set, a period of structured interaction, and a period of post-interaction reflection and processing by the participants. Participants are grouped into triads with three roles: teller, listener, and observer. The exercise ordinarily takes about forty-five to sixty minutes, depending on the number of triads and the depth of the post-interaction processing.

1. I introduce this by saying something like, "Let's take a few minutes to explore the process of meaning making." I ask the group to arrange themselves in groups of three and while they are doing this to think of a specific experience or event in each of their lives that is difficult to put into words. I ask them to consider an experience that "almost defies description—it can be a major or minor event, a pointed moment, or anything else that was personally significant but difficult to describe."

This will be the "indescribable moment." I let them know that some moments can be powerfully positive; others can be terrifying, dumbfounding, touching, or piercing. I also let them know that whatever they come up with is fine but that they will be asked to talk about it in the group, so it should be an experience they are willing to share.

2. After this setup, I give the group a few moments to consider their contribution, and meanwhile I offer a few examples: "Some people recall the birth of their first child or their earliest experience with the loss of someone they loved. One person recalled the experience of standing on the North Rim of the Grand Canyon with his toes out over the edge and feeling the force of the wind rushing up across him from the vast void beneath."

3. I then name the three roles that group members will take in turn (teller, listener, observer), and ask group members to identify who will assume each of the three roles to begin with. The group will go through the exercise three times so that everyone has a chance to do each role. Then I describe the functions of the roles:

Teller: the teller's goal is simply to try to convey the nature of his or her experience as clearly and fully as possible. "You are trying to give your listener as complete and as accurate an image of the experience as you can. We are more interested in your conveying a sense of what the experience was like for you than how you interpreted it, how it later affected you, or what significance it may have had for you. I'd like you to stay with the experience itself."

Listener: the listener's goal is to facilitate the teller's telling in whatever way(s) she or he can. Open-ended questions, requests for more detail or clarification, or emphasis on particular feelings may be helpful. Listeners can gauge their success by the teller's sense of feeling understood. "The more your tellers feel that you understand their experience, the closer you are to your goal." I add that the three things listeners should not be doing are providing interpretations ("I think that shows that you were afraid of . . ."), asking for interpretations ("What does that experience mean to you?"), or bringing the experience back to yourself ("That reminds me of an experience I had . . . "). The listener's role is to stay with the teller's experience and help facilitate its telling.

Observer: the role of the observer is to watch! Specifically, the observer is to watch for the processes of meaning-making. "Look for how meaning gets formed and conveyed. Watch the interaction between the teller and the listener; what do you see? What kinds of interaction seem to enhance the (co)construction of meaning, and what kinds seem to obstruct or derail it in some way? Can you describe these processes in any way?"

4. I start the first interaction of tellers, listeners, and observers and let it run for ten to fifteen minutes. I repeat this step twice more, after asking participants to change roles, so that all three members of the triad will have played each role.

Processing Tips

The most critical phase of this activity involves *post-interaction reflection and processing.* All participants will have had experiences in all three roles, and processing focuses on these three sets of experiences. Here are some sample questions to facilitate processing from the teller's perspective; they can be modified to fit the experience of the listener and observer:

- What was the experience of telling like for you? Did you experience any feelings, thoughts, or bodily sensations during the telling?
- Was there any "movement" for you in the telling? Did you find yourself going beyond the horizon of what you may have told before and, if so, in what way(s)?
- As a teller, what was your experience of the listener? What kinds of things did the listener say or do that were helpful in facilitating the formulation or expression of your meaning? What kinds of things were less helpful?
- How accurately or completely do you feel that you conveyed the nature of your experience to the listener? How accurately or completely do you feel that he or she understood it? How do you gauge that level of understanding?

- Are there any surprises for you in this experience? What, if anything, is striking or salient for you about your experience in this exercise?

Contributor's Commentary

The role of language in the construction of meaning is central to many constructivist traditions. Constructivist literature in psychotherapy, education, communication, and composition, among other areas, places a premium on the (trans)formation of meaning through languaging. *Languaging* can be regarded broadly as the process of symbolization. Extending well beyond the spoken and written word, languaging can include the full range of representational or expressive actions. Enactment, artistic expression, and visual representation all represent forms of languaging from this perspective insofar as they reflect the coordination of actions in relation to symbolized meanings. Many constructivist orientations acknowledge that meanings are created in the process of languaging.

There are some common experiences that I have seen emerge from the discussion that follows the exercise:

- The articulation of new meaning is difficult—as a teller and as a listener.
- Meaning-making is an emergent process; it takes time and unfolds across time.
- Meaning is co-constructed—it is not prepackaged and happens in interaction with others.

Meaning is not so much "transmitted" *to* the other as it is forged within the context of interaction *with* the other. The relational context is an important ingredient of it; greater meaning articulation is related to specific listener modes of listener participation. These include reflection ("I sensed that there was a moment of 'surprise' in there for you"), use of metaphor ("it sounds like a wake-up call, almost like a puff of air explodes in your face and your eyes spring open"), or images ("a fresh, spring-morning kind of feeling, like throwing open the curtains and finding the world suddenly in full bloom all around you"). However, description is not experience; the map is not the thing. Dimensions of experience are open to many different forms of linguistic representation; each highlights and shades different aspects of the experience, but none completely captures or exhausts it.

Describing and experiencing enjoy a dialectic relationship; each influences the other in some ways. Salient features of experience spawn particular descriptions and descriptions call attention to, clarify, or highlight selected features of experience. Careful description of experience can reinvoke that experience and thereby yield new possibilities for description.

References

Neimeyer, G., & Neimeyer, R. (Eds.) (1997). *Advances in personal construct psychology* (Vol. 4). Greenwich, CT: JAI Press.

Neimeyer, G. (Ed.) (1993). *Casebook of constructivist assessment.* Thousand Oaks, CA: Sage.

Woolum, S. (1993). *Metaphors and meaning: Understanding the theme model.* Washington, D.C.: Taylor and Francis.

Emerging Life Patterns

Kathleen Taylor, Berkeley, California
E-mail: ktaylor@stmarys-ca.edu

Kathleen Taylor is chair, department of portfolio development of the School of Extended Education, Saint Mary's College of California.

Developmental Intentions

I. Toward knowing as a dialogical process.
   4. Using one's experience to critique expert opinion and expert opinion to critique one's experience.
   9. Perceiving and constructing one's reality by observing and participating.
II. Toward a dialogical relationship to oneself.
   3. Exploring life's experiences through some framework(s) of analysis.
IV. Toward self-agency and self-authorship.
   6. Distinguishing what one has created for oneself from what is imposed by social, cultural, and other forces.

Context

I use this activity in an experiential learning portfolio development class for adult learners in a segment on adult development.

Description of Activity

Purpose. To move inductively into the study of adult development models and frameworks, and to integrate self-as-text with established theory as a way to illuminate both.

Format-steps-process. Optional: Students can start by filling in a timeline (it could be a preprinted handout with a line marked out in decades, or just a line hand-drawn horizontally across the middle of a sheet of paper) of major change events in their lives since the end of high school. I recommend that they use the space above the line for *personal* events, such as marriage, children, divorce, deaths, and below the line for *professional-educational* events, such as schooling, career and job changes, and so on. This need not take more than a few minutes; just a word or two to identify each significant year on the timeline. I don't collect this; it's to help the learner recall important events. People usually chuckle when I say, "Neatness doesn't count."

1. I arrange students into small groups (three to six people) by age and gender (for example, twenty-five to thirty-two, thirties, forties, over forty-five). The groups have twenty-five to thirty minutes to address the following questions (five to ten minutes more if necessary, usually when the group size is closer to six than three): "What was your group's main preoccupation ten years ago? Five years ago? For the last year?" (If ages of the learners warrant, I may ask about fifteen or twenty years ago, as well.)

2. I then invite the groups to report, starting with the oldest group and separating men's and women's reports. I record the responses in parallel on the whiteboard so that the class can compare the responses of men and women of roughly the same ages. I also overlap the responses, so we can compare what the group of forty-year-olds was doing when they were thirty compared to what the current thirty-year-olds are doing now.

3. After this part of the exercise, I typically present a miniframework *(lecturette)* on various (approximately five) models of development that are assigned reading for the coming week—enough background information to set some context and to whet learners' appetites for the readings.

4. The written assignment for the coming week is a paper on one model chosen by each learner as best reflecting his or her own journey of development. They are asked to use that model to examine and illuminate some aspect of their lives or some experience. At the same time, however, they are to use some experience or aspect of their lives to illuminate the theory they have chosen.

Processing Tips

The point of this exercise is to use learners' experience to bring the theories alive *before* they read the texts. In this way, adult development is no longer just an academic concept, it is a way of understanding themselves and others. If, instead, they read the text first, it can become the model for how their lives "should" be, and they lose the advantage of being able to start with what they already know.

Ideally, the age distribution in the class permits formation of groups close in age. However, when that isn't so, the fact of having or not having children can be another useful criterion for sorting. Learners who may be ten or more years apart in age but who have children tend to have more in common (at least in the present) with one another than they do with people closer in age who do not have children. I've also noticed that single career women often have life patterns that resemble men's (even married men's) patterns more than they do the patterns of women with children. Particularly when there are not enough younger learners to form single-gender groups, I sometimes create mixed-gender groups along those lines.

Given the diversity among adult learners, they rarely match across all the criteria (that is, gender, age, and family status). Cultural backgrounds are also often different. When the groups report, I therefore invite "minority reports" in which group members who have different experiences from the majority can be heard.

Contributor's Commentary

The lens of adult development theory enables people to see their experiences as part of a journey they are pleased to embark on, even if the terrain is sometimes rough going. The group report (step 2) varies with the particular experiences of the learners. Even so, the discussion can be facilitated to reveal gender and cohort differences. We approach, inductively, a lot of developmental issues that they will read about in that week's assignments.

The written assignment (step 4) is tricky, partly because it's one of the first assignments in this program since coming back to school. I struggle to find the right directions to avoid the two poles that about a third of the students usually gravitate toward: either neat mini-"reports" on the chosen model without self-reflection, or a monologue about some life experience without any connection to theory.

By contrast, learners who are successful with the assignment clearly seem to have looked at their lives and experiences in a new way. There's a noticeable "aha" in what they write, even if that word isn't there. To be honest, though, not everyone seems to get the same benefits. There are always people who entirely miss the point of the assignment, no matter how I explain it. I wonder whether I'm asking them to do something that just isn't yet within their abilities and, if so, how I could better structure this part of the exercise.

Using Empathic Listening as a Means of Support for Strategies Designed to Foster Adult Development

Joan M. Blanusa, Berkeley, California
E-mail: sgjb@vdn.com

Joan M. Blanusa is an instructor and student-teaching supervisor in a teacher preparation program at Saint Mary's College.

Developmental Intentions

   I. Toward knowing as a dialogical process.
      2. Surfacing and questioning assumptions underlying beliefs, ideas, actions, and positions.
  II. Toward a dialogical relationship to oneself.
      1. Addressing fears of losing what is familiar and safe.
      2. Engaging the disequilibrium when one's ideas and beliefs are challenged.
  IV. Toward self-agency and self-authorship.
      7. "Naming and claiming" what one has experienced and knows.
   V. Toward connection with others.
      3. Engaging the affective dimension when confronting differences.

Context

This activity can be used in courses in adult education at all levels, particularly with strategies designed to foster adult development. Students often experience moments of cognitive dissonance, emotional strife, and psychological disequilibrium as assumptions, ambiguities, and alternative viewpoints are the focus for learning.

Description of Activity

Purpose. To provide support for students coping with disconcerting, frustrating, or painful cognitive, emotional, and psychological responses evoked by a strategy or lesson; prevent students from becoming frozen or disengaged; and help instructor and students proceed toward growth at a pace commensurate with the needs of the students.

    Format-steps-process. Before the class:

1. I start by determining a strategy or exercise that I think will stimulate one or more of the developmental intentions referred to in this book.

2. With the strategy, the materials to be used, the assignments and overall purposes in mind, I reflect on and try to anticipate possible areas of cognitive, emotional, and psychological conflict for the students. This will influence the language I use in my directions, discussions, and presentations and may influence the pace at which I lead the session. I also find it useful to anticipate potential reasons for the conflict. This will influence how I present the strategy.

3. Next, I reflect on which pieces of the strategy are particularly important to me, those that I value most for which I have a special passion or fondness and to which I feel most beholden and connected. I then reflect on how I might feel when one of these pieces is challenged or criticized by a student. These will be the areas where I will be most inclined to become defensive and resistant and where it will be very difficult to "suspend my ego" and hear what the student is saying.

During the class:

4. As I implement a developmental strategy, I listen for and allow students to express conflicts they may be having with the materials, strategy, and assignments. Examples of these include

> "This article really made me angry."

> "This author is totally off base and wrong."

> "This assignment is too difficult for me—I don't know how to do this, or even where to begin."

5. When these conflicts arise, my first goal is to learn why the student thinks and feels this way, as well as to find out which aspects of the strategy are causing the most frustration and how deep the frustration goes. With this in mind and with genuine interest, I ask the student to explain. Examples of what I might say include

> "Tell me about what made you so angry. I really want to know."

> "What passage of the reading do you think is off base?"

> "Tell me anything and everything that bothers you or is difficult about this assignment." (I have found that students have a more difficult time articulating why they are having a hard time with an assignment than they do pinpointing their frustrations over readings, and thus I need to ask broader questions.)

6. While the student is explaining the reasons for his or her opinion, I carefully

> Listen for what are the key areas causing the most conflict and "pushing buttons," as well as for possibly unarticulated reasons this is so

Listen for the depth of the emotions connected to these key areas

Do not interrupt, especially not to point out where he or she may be "wrong," misinterpreting, or projecting assumptions into the essay or text

These first two areas will be key guides for the language I will use in response to the student (how sensitive I will need to be) and to help me provide adjustments and comments directly related to the particular cause of the frustration.

7. Once the student has explained the concern to his or her satisfaction, and once I feel I have a clear grasp on what in particular is causing the frustration for the student, I

Once again validate his or her feelings, by saying, for example, "Based on what you've just explained to me I can understand why you are so upset."

Paraphrase what I heard the student say, about both "facts" and feelings. If the learner indicates I've misheard something, I then ask for clarification until I can paraphrase accurately, as verified by the student.

8. In response to the student's need, I make adjustments to the assignment. Examples of adjustments might include

Asking the student to write a critique of the piece, using direct citations and messages from the essay to support his or her opinion.

Asking others in the class if they have similar impressions, and if so, ask them to elaborate (more often than not, there is more than one).

Asking the student to find a passage in the essay that corroborates their meaning-making and then ask for other students who agree to express their ideas and for those who disagree to discuss their interpretations. I then may ask the students to write a piece on how there can be these disparate interpretations.

Contributor's Commentary

Because I teach in a teacher credential and training program, I regularly discuss and teach this metastrategy with my students. Over time I have found that two or three key comments or caveats invariably arise. The first comment is always that this metastrategy is much easier than it first sounds—an observation with which I heartily concur. It is not uncommon to be put off by students' negative remarks, hostility, and resistance and to be tempted to quickly point out where such students are wrong, misinterpreting, reading unintended messages between the lines, or projecting their own issues onto the essay. This is especially true when students have made a comment in response to an essay, idea, or lesson to which one has a special attachment and fondness.

Second, it is easy for someone learning or using this metastrategy to become focused on the first part—listening empathically to the student—to the point where he or she loses sight of the second, the adult development strategy. Remember that this approach to working with adult development strategies is meant to help students stay engaged with the original material. Often when I discuss and teach this approach to future teachers, somehow the metastrategy gets misinterpreted as simply the need to listen to the student and then let the student do whatever he or she feels comfortable with, whether or not it connects to the original purpose of the session.

Although empathic listening can be effective at promoting development at every level, I have found it to be particularly complementary to the overall goal of adult development. Because this form of listening honors and validates the individual's own experience and meaning-making, it works hand in hand with the developmental aims of owning, claiming, and valuing one's feelings, thoughts, and experiences—key steps toward self-agency and self-authorship.

Reflecting on One's Beliefs and Values and Responding to Differences in Others

Laura Heid, El Sobrante, California
E-mail lsheid@aol.com

Laura Heid is an associate professor in the graduate counseling program in the School of Education at Saint Mary's College.

Developmental Intentions

    I. Toward knowing as a dialogical process.
        2. Surfacing and questioning assumptions underlying beliefs, ideas, actions, and positions.
        3. Reframing ideas or values that seem contradictory, embracing their differences, and arriving at new meanings.
    II. Toward a dialogical relationship to oneself.
        1. Addressing fears of losing what is familiar and safe.
        2. Engaging the disequilibrium when one's ideas and beliefs are challenged.

    V. Toward connection with others.
      3. Engaging the affective dimension when confronting differences.

Context

This is a multistep activity that is part of a programwide counselor training approach that emphasizes self-awareness and self-reflection and encourages the capacity to examine one's (the counselor's) own influence and impact on the counseling relationship and process. This particular activity is engaged in at the beginning of a practicum seminar course taken concurrently with students doing "real" counseling in a school or counseling agency. The practicum experience and this activity have been preceded by several foundational courses that have emphasized that development occurs within the contexts of culture, ethnicity, class, religion, gender, and history.

Description of Activity

Purposes. To have counseling trainees identify their personal beliefs and values that influence their work as counselors, recognize how one responds to others (for example, clients) based on their beliefs and values, and become more adept at handling situations in which others' beliefs and values are different from one's own.

    Format-steps-process.

- Introduction: I stress to my students that they enter the counseling relationship with a host of personal beliefs and values that will influence how they respond to and intervene with clients—this is a given. What is important is for the students to identify their significant beliefs and values and to become aware of how they function as counselors, based on these assumptions and values. I state that when the client's values and beliefs are similar to their own, they may experience less difficulty than when the client's beliefs and values are different from their own. I give examples from my own experience as a counselor that describe what I have learned are my significant values when working as a counselor, and how I have handled situations with clients whose beliefs and values were different from my own. I emphasize the personal feelings and difficulties I have had in trying to reconcile such differences, and I give a case example of conflicting values in which I had been able to respect both my own and the client's values and to proceed in counseling from there.
  - Self-reflection in writing:
    1. I ask students to write in response to the following: "What beliefs and values influence your work as a counselor? Select two or three that are most significant for you, especially in terms of your counseling work. Clearly ex-

plain each belief or value, being as specific as you can; for example, if you value education, specify what you mean by 'education.'" *Example:* Every counselor values certain aspects of the counseling process and has particular beliefs about how the client and counselor should behave and interact. Other types of beliefs and values to consider are those regarding education (including post-secondary education), work and money, parenting styles and methods of discipline, sexuality (e.g., adolescent sexuality, sexual orientation), autonomy and independence, and family relationships.

2. I then ask students to respond in writing to the following: "After defining your two or three significant beliefs or values, discuss how each one affects your work as a counselor, using case examples from your practicum experience. Be as concrete as you can and describe what you actually do or say (that is, how you verbally respond to clients and what interventions you make with clients) based on each value or belief."

• Class discussion: Following this written assignment, I engage students in a structured discussion of what they have written.

3. Students are asked to share what they have written in step 1 above. I try to have everyone participate so that the students can hear the full range of beliefs and values among themselves. Together, we identify common ones and also have students with differing values on the same topic identify how they differ with one another.

4. I then ask students to share what they have written in step 2 above. At this point, I often still need to help students see how they function as counselors based on their identified beliefs and values. I use open-ended questions first and, if needed, I provide observations from my own experience with and knowledge of the students. Examples and input from other classmates are often very useful during this discussion.

5. Although not part of the written assignment, I then elicit from students situations from their practicum experience in which clients held values and beliefs different from their own. Typically, some students present cases in which they were successful in respecting differences. Others acknowledge difficulty with clients who do not see things from the counselor's perspective. Using these case examples, I encourage students to explore their feelings, meanings, and experiences connected to a specific value or issue, particularly when a client is resistant to the difference being expressed. The ultimate aim, although not achievable in all cases and with all students (especially as this activity is taking place early in their program), is to discuss how the counselor can use these differences for the advancement of the counseling relationship.

Processing Tips

Students are most likely to bring to class those situations in which they are experiencing difficulty and confusion (and, often, frustration with the client). I can then use these case examples as a means of exploring with them how their beliefs and values are affecting the specific case.

I use a progression of questions or prompts with students to encourage them to examine their role in these challenging counseling situations. The least threatening is to ask them how they are reacting to the client in terms of their feelings toward the client, the specific attitudes or actions of the client that prompted these feelings, and the meanings that these attitudes or actions have to them (the counselors). This exploration often reveals what feelings, attitudes, or behaviors the counselors "expect" or "want the client to have." At this point, I may observe that although the counselors have certain expectations of and goals for the client, the client appears to have different values, perspectives, and personal goals; in some cases, the notion that there might be such differences was not even in the students' awareness. If needed, I will continue to ask open-ended questions of the students, such as, "What does it mean to you that this client wants to do x instead of y? How do you feel when this client expresses this particular belief or value that is so different from your own?" In other words, instead of focusing on the client, I focus on what the counselor brings to the counseling relationship and how this has an impact on the counselor's experience of the client, especially when their beliefs and values are different.

Contributor's Commentary

Although some students make the connections between their values and beliefs and their counseling responses easily, others have difficulty. They seem unable to separate themselves from their value system—a capacity that is, in my experience, fundamental to their making the necessary connections (that is, having values about their values).

During the discussion, the role of the teacher is to help students be concrete and specific about what exactly they believe or value. The discussion usually requires questioning to help students see how their counseling responses and interventions emanate from their value systems.

My ability to use these strategies effectively varies with the student's willingness, readiness, and capacity for growth; my personal feelings for and reactions to the student; and the relationship we have with one another. I have the luxury of working with most of my students over a period of two to five years. The stronger the relationship we have, the more I will take the risk of challenging the student's thinking.

I have sometimes overestimated readiness and willingness to change; other times I have been unable to demonstrate empathy for students' current feelings and perspectives. The "success" of this activity depends greatly upon the nature and strength of the relationship between my students and myself.

Occasionally, I will observe a dramatic shift in a student's perspective and ability to make personal choices about what values and beliefs they maintain and how to respect and use differences in the counseling relationship. Most often, however, I observe very small, gradual changes in the students' capacity for doing so. One or two students each year are unable (perhaps unwilling) to shift their perspectives.

This exercise could easily be adapted for a leadership-training activity by focusing on workplace rather than counseling relationships.

References

Kegan, R. (1982). *The evolving self: Problem and process in human development*. Cambridge: Harvard University Press.

Kegan, R. (1994). *In over our heads: The mental demands of modern life*. Cambridge: Harvard University Press.

Reflecting on Practice

Catherine Marienau, Oak Park, Illinois
E-mail: cmariena@wppost.depaul.edu

Catherine Marienau teaches and mentors adult learners at DePaul University's School for New Learning in individually designed, competence-based programs at undergraduate and graduate levels.

Developmental Intentions

II. Toward a dialogical relationship to oneself.
   4. Questioning critically the validity or worth of one's pursuits.
III. Toward being a continuous learner.
   3. Recognizing and revealing one's strengths and weaknesses as a learner and knower.
   4. Anticipating learning needed to prevent and solve problems.
   8. Seeking authentic feedback from others.

IV. Toward self-agency and self-authorship.
   4. Taking action toward one's potential while acknowledging one's
       limitations.

Context

This exercise would be effective in individualized graduate programs for professionals in any field of study (nonlicensure), particularly in areas not defined by existing curricula. The typical group size is fifteen.

Description of Activity

Purpose. To examine the learning dynamic between academic studies and workplace experiences, practice the process and strategies of self-assessment, perceive changes in learning and performance through iterative self-assessment, and evaluate the benefits of self-assessment for personal and professional development.

Format-steps-process. Four class sessions devoted to developing students' skills in reflecting on practice are interspersed with their ongoing seminars and independent studies at approximately five-month intervals.

Students' reflection on practice is organized around their development, application, and integration of *liberal learning skills,* which are *self-assessment* and *self-managed learning; critical, creative,* and *systemic thinking; oral* and *written communication; interpersonal relations;* and *moral reasoning.* Throughout the four assessment sessions, a *critical incident* format is used to provide a specific context from which to develop self-assessment skills and examine integration of learning in work and other situations.

Three weeks prior to each of the class meetings, I mail students an assignment that they are to prepare in writing. For purposes of this description, I first present the assignments for all four sessions, followed by the basic processing format for the sessions.

Assignments. *Session one* focuses on helping students become more aware of which *liberal learning skills* they actually use in their professional practice and plan for more intentional application of these skills.

Assignment: Select a work-related incident in which you drew upon one or more of the liberal learning skills.

1. Describe the situation, including who were the key people; what was your
    particular role; what were you trying to accomplish; and a snapshot of what

transpired, keeping the focus on what you said, did, thought, felt, and observed.

2. Analyze which liberal learning skills you used and specifically how you used them. Given that each liberal learning skill has multiple facets (descriptors), make reference to the specific facets of each liberal learning skill and identify which ones are most relevant to your experience.

3. How did you approach or handle this incident differently from how you might have in the past?

4. In retrospect, how would you have liked to respond (if differently than what you actually did)?

5. What do you need to work on to be better prepared for a similar situation in the future?

Session two focuses on helping students examine further development of their liberal learning skills and how that has occurred, and provide evidence for their assessment. Particular emphasis is given to the skill of self-assessment. Students are asked to articulate and expand upon their definitions of self-assessment and their attitudes toward it and to describe their self-assessment activities.

Assignment: Select an incident of engaging in self-assessment in your work context. What prompted you to do self-assessment? What were the actions you took or ideas you had that you are calling *self-assessment* (for example, what were the questions you asked yourself, what was your train of thought, what data did you draw on)? Did you get feedback from anyone? If so, how did you use it? What was the value, if any, of the self-assessment experience for you?

Session three focuses on students articulating significant turning points in their development of each of the liberal learning skills through their seminars to date and identifying applications in their work contexts. Continuing the discussion on self-assessment from session two, students assess changes in their reference points for evaluating performance in and outside the work setting.

Assignment:

1. Revisit your critical incident from session one in which you identified some of the liberal learning skills for further development. How, specifically, have you done this?

2. Select and describe a critical incident in your worklife that illustrates your ability to draw on the liberal learning skills as a whole.

Session four focuses on students articulating the contributions of the liberal learning skills to self-assessment, individual studies, and performance and learning in the workplace. Emphasis is given to the particular skill of *self-managed learning.*

Assignment: Write an integrating essay that addresses these questions:

1. What key abilities, areas of knowledge, attitudes, and values do you possess that allow you to be an effective learner and contributor in various settings in which you live, including work?
2. How has self-assessment contributed to these capabilities?
3. What aspects of the graduate program have been most helpful to you in developing or refining these capabilities?

In-Class Processing. When the group meets with me, we use the class time (three hours) to process students' written assignments. Feedback is provided by me and their classmates in the form of conversation, typically commenting on changes we notice from their previous report with regard to the outcomes of applying the liberal learning skills at work and with regard to these individuals' changes in how they think about and engage in self-assessment.

Typically, I ask for three volunteers to share their reflections (responses to the assignment), one at a time. I ask the group to "listen out" for which liberal learning skills they hear in someone's reflections and how they are being used, with what results. The "audience" members in the group make written or mental notes on what they hear from the presenter. In their discussions with each presenter, they share observations and pose questions based on what they heard (inferred) about the liberal learning skills. I also keep brief, private notes while someone is reporting on her reflections. Following the discussion period with each presenter, all of us then identify the liberal learning skills we've heard, and I record them on a flipchart, to be added to during the rest of the evening's conversation. After these three individuals have reported on their reflections and discussed them with the class (for about thirty to forty minutes altogether), the other students add to the conversation from their own assignments, building on what someone has already said or adding new dimensions.

Processing Tips

I also provide written feedback to students on the essays they submitted. For all students, my feedback is framed according to these criteria:

1. Specificity of their comments
2. Complexity of their analysis
3. Their awareness of self, and self in relation to context
4. Their level of contribution to the discussion and learning of the group
5. The quality of their writing

More recently, with regard to item two above, I tend to make reference to the presence or absence of four levels of complexity as described by Kolb (1984)—

symbolic, perceptual, affective, and behavioral—thus reflecting my view that meaningful learning encompasses multiple dimensions and aspects of the learner. Then, for each student, I also comment on some of their particular observations and insights.

Contributor's Commentary

This kind of iterative reflection process helps students strengthen their self-assessment skills and recognize the potentially powerful benefits that can come from ongoing reflection on their practice. It is quite inspiring to hear students talk about their self-revelations that occur during the nearly two years of the program, and about the impact that changes are having on their lives, both personally and professionally.

Reference

Kolb, D. A. (1984). *Experiential learning: Experience as the source of learning and development.* Englewood Cliffs, NJ: Prentice Hall.

Whole Person Reaction Paper

Donald McCormick, Redlands, California
E-mail: mccormic@uor.edu

Don McCormick is an associate professor at the University of Redlands, where he teaches in the field of organization studies.

Developmental Intentions

I. Toward knowing as a dialogical process.
   10. Tapping into and drawing on tacit knowledge.
III. Toward being a continuous learner.
   9. Drawing on multiple capacities for effective learning.
IV. Toward self-agency and self-authorship.
   1. Constructing a values system that informs one's behavior.
   6. Distinguishing what one has created for oneself from what is imposed by social, cultural, and other forces.

Context

I use this activity in an undergraduate course on interpersonal communication, although it can be applied to almost any reading assignment.

Description of Activity

Purpose. To learn how to "listen to yourself" and to provide practice in becoming aware of and expressing emotional responses.

Format-steps-process.

1. This activity begins with having students read the following quote from Carl Rogers (1983):

   It is often very hard for me, as for other writers, to get close to my self when I start to write. It is so easy to be distracted by the possibility of saying things that will catch approval or will look good to colleagues or make a popular appeal. How can I listen to the things that I really want to say and write? It is difficult . . . [however] the writings that I have produced on this basis turn out to be ones for which I never feel apologetic and which often communicate deeply to others. So it is a very satisfying thing when I sense that I have gotten close to me, to the feelings and hidden aspects of myself that live below the surface.

2. For each subsequent reading assignment, students write a short (about two pages) paper in which they describe their reactions to the readings with particular attention to their emotional reactions. There should be at least one written reaction to each article or book chapter that is read. I let them know that what they write can be a sentence, a page, or even two pages, but it should be something that shows that the reading engendered some response, even if only, "This is irrelevant to me."

3. A reaction piece can also be written in response to class discussion or some other learning activity; it need not focus solely on reading assignments.

4. In the written description of the assignment, I say, "A good reaction paper is one that shows that you are *engaged* with the reading—that you *care* about what the author is trying to say. Not that you agree with it, or think it is well written, but that you feel the topic is worth responding to. In recording all of these reactions, it is important to articulate the reason that you find the reading to be maddening, wonderful, boring, or whatever."

Contributor's Commentary

In the assignment description, I explain the assignment in more detail and explain why I have created it. The following is from the instructions I give the students.

There are many kinds of emotional reactions to readings. A reading may be maddening, wonderful, boring, or even make you angry. A good example of this from my own college career is the first book I was assigned to read as an undergraduate—*The Presentation of Self in Everyday Life,* by Erving Goffman. It got me so angry that I only read a few pages and then flung the book across my dorm lounge. I hated the way Goffman portrayed human nature; it went against everything I believed in. He portrayed humans as merely actors, without any central, authentic core to them. (Now, by the way, I love the book and assign sections from it in some of my classes.) Another reaction that you may have is loving the reading (or even just a line or two of it). This may happen if the reading confirms or articulates what you deeply believe.

I hope that writing papers such as these will help you become more aware of your experience. I hope that it helps you learn to do what Rogers calls learning how to listen to yourself. Congruence involves greater awareness of your physical and emotional responses. This paper should give you some practice in becoming aware of and expressing your emotional responses. Rogers says that many people are unaware of their feelings, and this exercise asks you to become aware of them. This assignment asks you to become more open to your experience. It asks you to regard feelings as friendly. It asks you to trust your feelings in the evaluation of the readings. In that sense, it gives you practice in what Rogers calls "organismic valuing." It asks you to consider yourself, not others, as your "locus of evaluation," and in this sense I hope this assignment will be empowering for you.

I created this assignment because I imagine that you have all of these reactions anyway and I want to encourage you to see them as legitimate and important. I want you to amplify these reactions so that your reactions (your own "voice," as it were) will become louder and clearer to you. It will stand out more and become more distinct if you articulate it. Writing about reactions is a way to get you to spend a little more time listening to yourself. Writing about reactions tends to get you caught up in them and encourages you to get more involved with what you are studying.

This assignment is designed to promote increased openness to experience, congruence, and internal locus of evaluation—all developmental goals defined by Rogers' person-centered theory of psychological development (1959). *Congruence* refers to the ability to be aware of what one is experiencing and the ability to communicate this to others. *An internal locus of evaluation* refers to "the source of evidence as to values" and means that each person is "the center of the valuing process" (p. 210) instead of the center residing in the judgment of others.

References

Rogers, C. R. (1959). A theory of therapy, personality, and interpersonal relationship, as developed in the client-centered framework. In S. Koch (Ed.), *Psychology: A study of a science: Vol. 3. Formulations of the person and the social context* (pp. 184–256). New York: McGraw-Hill.

Rogers, C. R. (1983). *Freedom to learn for the 80s.* Columbus: Merrill.

Structured Learning Journal

Catherine Marienau, Oak Park, Illinois
E-mail: cmariena@wppost.depaul.edu

Catherine Marienau teaches and mentors adult learners at DePaul University's School for New Learning in individually designed, competence-based programs at undergraduate and graduate levels.

Developmental Intentions

   I. Toward knowing as a dialogical process.
      4. Using one's experience to critique expert opinion and expert opinion to critique one's experience.
  II. Toward a dialogical relationship to oneself.
      2. Engaging the disequilibrium when one's ideas and beliefs are challenged.
      3. Exploring life's experiences through some framework(s) of analysis.
      5. Exploring and making meaning of one's life stories within contexts (for example, societal, familial, universal).
  III. Toward being a continuous learner.
      1. Reflecting on one's own and others' experiences as a guide to future behavior.

Context

I've used this activity in an undergraduate course for adult learners on women's psychosocial development.

Description of Activity

Purpose. To engage students in using their experiences (own and others) as text, help students connect various strands of personal experience with relevant theories and models, and help students develop competence in designated areas.

Format-process-steps. I ask students to maintain a structured learning journal throughout the course that responds to questions that I pose in weekly assignments. In general, these questions ask students to examine and reflect on their own experience in light of the course material and the particular competencies associated with the course. The progression of structured learning journal entries begins with having students describe and articulate their own experiences, then moves to drawing on the themes from their own lives to relate to ideas and theories of the material. This repetitive cycle provides students practice in giving voice to their experiences and then using existing theories and ideas to help interpret them.

1. I set up some of the themes for the journal on the first night of class by having students participate in a "life-cycle generations" exercise in age-related groups. They address questions such as

   What was going on in society during your formative years
   (major events, prevailing attitudes)?

   What are some distinguishing characteristics of your generation?

   As a woman, what do you value most about being a member of this generation? What is problematic—what would you most like to change?

   What name or metaphor would you use to represent your generation?

2. Students' reflections on this exercise are addressed in a journal assignment for the following week. I pose these questions:

   Select a period in your own life that has been especially meaningful
   for your own development.

   What period did you select, and why?

   Describe the major events or feelings that you experienced during
   this period.

   What was it about this life period that made it so meaningful for you?

   What impact did it have on your development?

3. Beginning with week three, I typically assign one set of generic journal questions as well as a set of questions specific to the areas in which students are seeking competence (for example, individual growth and development, psychological theories, issues of gender and race and class). I ask students to freewrite for twelve minutes in response to these two generic questions:

   How would you describe yourself to yourself?

   What does being a woman mean to you?

Here is an example of a competence-related question concerning individual growth and development:

Is the way you see yourself now different from the way you saw yourself in the past?

How has your sense of yourself as a woman been changing, if at all?

How do you see yourself changing in the future?

4. By week four, the journal assignments begin to focus on certain readings. Examples of competence-specific questions:

Regarding Peck's (1986) model of "women's self-definition," what are the major components of her model?

What key concepts does she draw on in her model of development and self-definition?

How is her model helpful in understanding women's self-definition?

Do you see any drawbacks in her model?

How does this model relate to the other readings we've discussed?

5. When we move into the segment on *Women's Ways of Knowing* (Belenky, Clinchy, Goldberger, & Tarule, 1986; Goldberger, Tarule, Clinchy, & Belenky, 1996) over the next several weeks, I ask students to consider this material from several vantage points:

Observe examples of separate and connected knowing in various settings and note your response to these ways of knowing.

Reflect on your own experiences as knowers using different strategies in various life contexts.

Respond to excerpts from the text (I usually identify these the first time around, after which I invite students to select their own excerpts): Explain why you chose that excerpt, write your reactions to it, and note any other reactions you might have.

6. Beginning the seventh week, students begin to prepare their synthesizing journal entry, the purposes of which are to help them pull together what they've already written in their journals with new insights from class discussions and the readings, elaborate on points already made in the journal, and refine their thinking or explore an issue in more depth. I remind students, emphatically, to make reference to the relevant readings in their discussions. An example of competence-specific questions for the synthesizing entry: Analyze your journal entries with respect to

What developmental themes are evident in your adult life?

What specific values have changed the most in your development? What circumstances prompted these changes?

What specific attitudes have changed the most in your development?

What circumstances prompted these changes?

What new understandings have you reached as a result of your developmental changes?

How would you characterize growth and development in your own life?

Processing Tips

In the fifth or sixth week, I review students' journals and give them feedback according to the criteria I will use in the final grading. Students also do a practice self-assessment with the same criteria. I then discuss any notable differences in our assessments with the individual student. At the end of the course, students use the same criteria to complete a self-assessment of their learning.

Having taught some version of this course a dozen times, I have come to recognize the need for providing more specific directions up front; hence, my questions for the journal entries have become more focused, including posing questions specific to the competencies. During each class session, students are invited to draw from their journals as they participate in discussion, sharing only what they feel comfortable with. This sharing is done in small groups and in the class as a whole so that students continue to learn from one another's experiences and see different ways that others have articulated their experiences and related them to the course material.

Contributor's Commentary

One of my goals in this course is to have students claim their own experience and their own voice in interpreting it. Theories and models can help do that by providing ideas and language, as can the experiences voiced by others. I try to keep the discussions focused on themes and topics relevant to the session at hand and to move personal storytelling into more interpretive analysis. The focus on specific competencies helps set some parameters around what is fodder for discussion. Students consistently report that learning about their own development through the lens of adult development (feminist) theories gives them new insight into their developmental paths and often sparks some area of growth, whether in improving communication with one's mother or daughter, asserting one's sense of competence at work, or deciding to move in a new direction.

References

Belenky, M. F., Clinchy, B. M., Goldberger, N. R., & Tarule, J. M. (1986). *Women's ways of knowing: The development of voice, self and mind.* New York: Basic Books.

Goldberger, N. R., Tarule, J. M., Clinchy, B. M., & Belenky, M. F. (1996). *Knowledge, difference and power.* Boston: Basic Books.

Peck, T. (1986). Women's self-definition in adulthood: From a different model? *Psychology of Women Quarterly, 10,* 74–284.

Philosophy-of-Life Paper

John Nemecek, Spring Arbor, Michigan
E-mail: Jnemecek@arbor.edu

John Nemecek is associate professor and assistant dean, School of Adult Studies, Spring Arbor College, and teaches interdisciplinary courses.

Developmental Intentions

   I. Toward knowing as a dialogical process.
      2. Surfacing and questioning assumptions underlying beliefs, ideas, actions, and positions.
      4. Using one's experience to critique expert opinion and expert opinion to critique one's experience.
  II. Toward a dialogical relationship to oneself.
      2. Engaging the disequilibrium when one's ideas and beliefs are challenged.
  IV. Toward self-agency and self-authorship.
      1. Constructing a values system that informs one's behavior.
      7. "Naming and claiming" what one has experienced and knows.

Context

This activity is the primary work product from a module titled, "Values: Personal and Social." The paper is prepared and submitted following a ten-minute oral summary given before peers at the end of a cohort-based degree completion program for adults.

Description of Activity

Students develop and present a paper on their philosophy of life (fifteen to twenty pages).

Purpose. To synthesize and integrate much of the learning that has taken place through the degree-completion program, giving evidence of higher-order learning from Bloom's cognitive and affective taxonomies, and to formulate and articulate one's philosophy of life.

Format-steps-process. To make the writing of the philosophy-of-life paper more manageable, students are encouraged to write the paper in stages as they interact with the issues and ideas raised throughout the module. Students are told that the philosophy-of-life paper should be fifteen to twenty pages in length and should address the following issues:

1. Generate a list of character traits about yourself and incorporate these into your paper. Identify your own *actual* situation versus your perception of the *ideal.* Draw some conclusions about yourself using this data. What are the gaps? How can you address them? Insights gained from instruments such as the MBTI (Myers Briggs Type Inventory) and LSI (Learning Styles Inventory) and other self-discovery activities may help you interpret your data (two to three pages).

2. Drawing on the material in the module, define and discuss your theory of truth. Examine your theory in light of the discussion of truth as objective, subjective, and relational. So that you do not abstract or generalize your discussion, be sure to use specific examples from your life experience (three to four pages).

3. In connection with Stevenson and Haberman's (1998) book, consider your basic assumptions regarding human nature. Consider how you view yourself and how you view others. Relate how the different theories of human nature inform your understanding of the nature of humanity and prescriptions for humankind's betterment (four to five pages).

4. Compare or contrast your own values with those of organizations of which you are a part. It may be helpful to consider your view of organizational values before you started your degree program and the views you now hold (two to three pages).

5. Describe your understanding of key ethical concerns in your field (one to two pages).

6. Describe the impact of your degree completion program on your personal and social values or ethical standards. To what degree has the program helped clarify your philosophy of life (one to two pages)?

7. Either as part of the discussion in other areas of the paper or as distinct sections, discuss each of the following:

   How does one find meaning in one's life? Do I possess any overriding values commitment that integrates facets of my life?

   What is of real value or importance in my life? Where does value reside? Where did I obtain my sense of value? What are my foundational principles?

   What is beauty? What criteria do I use to judge something as beautiful? What things in life do I consider beautiful?

What happens upon death? For what would I be willing to sacrifice my life? How would I like to be remembered?

8. Conclude your paper with your personal mission statement.

Processing Tips

It is important that students not simply read aloud their papers as written (except for brief portions for clarity). Instead, the oral presentation should provide a broad overview of the paper, sharing those conclusions and ideas which the student is willing to express. Time for comments and questions from the peer group and faculty can be a meaningful part of the process, especially if students have been together long enough to develop a significant degree of trust. Asking students how they use (or might use) their personal mission statement often helps emphasize the pragmatic value of the exercise. Depending upon the size of the group, some monitoring of the time (with cues to the presenting student) may be necessary.

The faculty member's written comments on the student's paper are a continuing part of the intellectual inquiry inherent in this process. Posing questions and raising additional issues can offer the opportunity for the continuation of self-discovery and the clearest possible articulation of personal mission statements.

Contributor's Commentary

The presentation of this paper before one's peers (with whom one has traveled throughout this eighteen-month program) deepens the personal impact and value of this assignment. The process of considering one's own perspective on significant life issues in contrast and comparison with major worldviews (for example, *Ten Theories of Human Nature* by Stevenson and Haberman, 1998) and in dialogue with one's peers (through classroom exercises and discussion) helps refine the articulation of learning related to the specific developmental intentions. Often some of the other developmental intentions are touched on, but the ones identified in the heading are intrinsic to the assignment and the process.

The same exercise could be used in other settings where a high level of trust has been achieved and the articulation of personal values and purpose is appropriate. The revising and editing of this paper through a tutorial process would allow for an even more personal dialogue.

References

Kolb, D. A. (1985). *Learning style inventory.* Boston: McBer.

Myers, P. B., & Myers, K. D. (1987). *Myers-Briggs Type Indicator.* Palo Alto, CA: Consulting Psychologists Press.

Stevenson, L., & Haberman, D. L. (1998). *Ten theories of human nature* (3rd ed.). New York: Oxford University Press.

The Experience-Cycle Methodology

Lindsay Oades, Wollongong, NSW, Australia
E-mail: lindsay_oades@uow.edu.au

Lindsay Oades is a clinical psychologist and research coordinator of the Illawarra Area Mental Health Service, the faculty of health and behavioral sciences, University of Wollongong.

Developmental Intentions

    I. Toward knowing as a dialogical process.
        10. Tapping into and drawing on tacit knowledge.
    II. Toward a dialogical relationship to oneself.
        3. Exploring life's experiences through some framework(s) of analysis.
    III. Toward being a continuous learner.
        1. Reflecting on one's own and others' experiences as a guide to future behavior.
    IV. Toward self-agency and self-authorship.
        7. "Naming and claiming" what one has experienced and knows.

Context

This exercise can be used for an individual or a group of adult learners.

Description of Activity

Purpose. To retrospectively describe and reflect on an experience after it is complete or to prospectively describe an experience as it occurs.

Format-steps-process. First select a discrete event that you have experienced or are about to experience. It is useful to choose significant experiences that have changed you as person or you think may have the potential to change you in the future. If this is a retrospective analysis, also focus on (1) situations in which you had fairly specific predictions about what would occur; (2) situations in which you had a significant personal investment; or (3) an experience in which you did not experience what you initially anticipated.

Examples of a discrete event to select for this exercise could range from a one-day workshop that you went to or are soon to attend to your already completed or currently unfolding experience of a degree program. The following steps take you through the cycle and are written in past tense. They may also be used in present tense for a prospective use of the cycle.

1. The first phase of the experience cycle is the *anticipation* phase, in which a prediction is formulated concerning a particular event. Questions for the learner(s):

   What things were you predicting would happen?

   What options did you see open to yourself at this time?

   Were you concerned about what others might think of you?

   About what you may think of yourself?

2. The second phase is the *investment* phase, in which the person fully involves himself or herself in this anticipation. Questions for the learner(s):

   How much did you want this prediction to come true or not to come true?

   How much did it matter to you at the time?

3. The third phase is the *encounter* phase, which consists of the person openly and actively experiencing the event. Questions for the learner(s):

   What was the context?

   Describe the actual experience of doing it.

4. The fourth phase is the *confirmation and disconfirmation* phase, which constitutes the assessment of this encounter in relation to the initial anticipation. Questions for the learner(s):

   How did things go compared to what you initially thought would happen?

   How did the prediction go?

   What feelings did you have about this?

5. In the final phase, *constructive revision*, the person reconstrues, if necessary, based on the evidence obtained during the previous four steps. Questions for the learner(s):

   In general, what did you learn from this experience that we are now processing?

6. A fresh anticipation and further cycle may then occur. Questions for the learner(s):

> In terms of a next time (or a time since the incident you described), will you or did you change as a result of this experience? For example, did or will you change the way you view things or your behavior?
>
> What things did or will you change for the next time, if there is one?
>
> What new options do you see open to you, if you were in a similar situation in the future?
>
> How do you now see the advantages and disadvantages of being in a similar situation in the future?

Contributor's Commentary

The emphasis of Kelly's (1977) cycle of experience was that individuals are involved personally in influencing the outcomes of their predictions. The experience cycle methodology was originally developed as part of my doctoral thesis that examined adolescent risk taking. In the thesis I used it retrospectively—description of experience after it is complete. I have since realized that it could be better used prospectively—description of experience as it occurs—and perhaps form part of a diary method rather than a semistructured interview format.

In an academic setting, it could also be used before writing a paper or implementing a class project; and in a workplace setting, before giving a major presentation.

References

Kelly, G. A. (1970). A brief introduction to personal construct theory. In D. Bannister (Ed.), *Perspectives in personal construct theory*. London: Academic Press.

Kelly, G. A. (1977). The psychology of the unknown. In D. Bannister (Ed.), *New perspectives in personal construct theory* (pp. 1–19). San Diego: Academic Press.

The Trading Game

Susan Toby and David Templeman, Perth, Australia
E-mail: stoby@mbox.com.au

Susan Toby and David Templeman are the principals of Growth Awareness Programmes, and seek to develop skills and enhance capabilities of individuals to help them become more effective.

Developmental Intentions

    II. Toward a dialogical relationship to oneself.
        5. Exploring and making meaning of one's life stories within contexts (for example, societal, familial, universal).
   III. Toward being a continuous learner.
        1. Reflecting on one's own and others' experiences as a guide to future behavior.
   IV. Toward self-agency and self-authorship.
        2. Accepting responsibility for choices one has made and will make.
        5. Revising aspects of oneself while maintaining continuity of other aspects.
        7. "Naming and claiming" what one has experienced and knows.

Context

This activity is used in self-actualization workshops.

Description of Activity

Purpose. To reflect and share experiences or thoughts from one's own personal bank of learning, appreciate the value of the information that one stores from experience, recognize application of stored knowledge and skills in one's daily life, and explore underlying societal issues, first by creating awareness of their existence, then by challenging established perspectives.

Format-steps-process. The trading game is based on trading stories of one's life's experiences. Participants are provided with an opportunity to explore past experiences which may influence their learning, behavior, and life decisions. Initially, these issues are dealt with informally and within a time limit. The next steps focus on the issues in greater depth.

Resources required. Questions placed on cards (see Questions on the Cards); paper and pen for a scribe in each team, white board and marker.

Trading Game (one hour)

1. Form groups of even numbers and provide each group with a set of cards (see questions below).
2. People form pairs; each chooses a card. The pairs "trade" their experiences or knowledge in relation to the questions on both cards. Allow about three minutes for each response. Each pair then trades their two cards with another pair within their group. This continues until everyone has answered all the questions.

3. During the trading, people note issues that arise. For example, when a man was a young student, he had a confrontation with a teacher that shaped his dislike of most teachers with whom he had contact.

Questions on the Cards (examples: rework to suit course objectives)

- Describe a significant experience or event with a grandparent or elderly person. Did you learn anything from this experience? How do you use that learning today?
- Describe one of your favorite teachers during your school years. What made that person special? What influence did that educator have in your future choices?
- When you were young, how did you learn about the value of money? Has that knowledge influenced how you deal with money now? If not, explain how you attained your abilities.
- Do you remember a person who was ostracized when you grew up? Why did that happen, and what was your reaction then? Given the same situation, how would you react now?
- Describe an experience where you witnessed injustice from an authoritarian figure. How did you react? Would you react the same way today? If not, what would you do differently?

Next Step(s) (time variable: one or more sessions)

1. The pairs reconvene in their small groups. People trade and reexamine salient parts of their stories; a recorder makes notes. For groups of six people, allow about forty-five minutes.
2. Then the whole group convenes. Over one or several sessions, people again trade experiences and insights gathered in the pairs and small groups. The facilitator notes themes on a whiteboard, then encourages further group exploration. For example, how has the man in the above example reacted to subsequent educational opportunities? People are also asked to consider: How can I use this information or realization to change and grow?
3. Individuals are then asked to create an action plan or set specific goals.

Contributor's Commentary

This activity centers on creating a dialogical relationship to oneself with the support of a group context. The issues and perspective discussed and shared provide the "content" for further exploration of participants' responses to issues. Challenging these perspectives, through further questions or hypothetical propositions, encourages participants really to focus on their perspective or view of the issues. For example, participants analyze their own responses in some of the following areas:

- What does this mean in terms of how I learn, function, or even possibly place impediments to my learning?
- Has this analysis confirmed my perspective? Is there an action required to re-define my perspective?
- What can I now do to change, enhance, or refine my personal goals based on the learning I've highlighted from this experience?

Finally, this can lead to action:

- What action, goal, or objective will I set to achieve this outcome?

Class Journaling

Lois J. Zachary, Phoenix, Arizona
E-mail: leadservs@aol.com

Lois J. Zachary is a specialist in adult development and learning and the principal of Leadership Development Services, a consulting firm that offers leadership education and training for corporate and not-for-profit organizations.

Developmental Intentions

   III. Toward being a continuous learner.
1. Reflecting on one's own and others' experiences as a guide to future behavior.
2. Challenging oneself to learn in new realms; taking risks.
3. Recognizing and revealing one's strengths and weakness as a learner and knower.
5. Posing and pursuing questions out of wonderment.

Context

I have found that journaling can be adapted to almost any class or workshop session. It is an important aspect of reflective practice in higher and adult education, as well as in the corporate and nonprofit sectors. This is a key component of practitioner development in teaching applied research.

Description of Activity

Purpose. To have students trace changes in their thinking and to provide a mechanism for students to hear each others' views and experiences.

Format-steps-process.

1. Toward the end of a day-long workshop or class session, I hand out NCR paper (a "carbonless" carbon paper), and ask students to respond to several questions, such as

   Identify three things you learned today.

   What stands out in your mind about what you've learned today?

   What questions remain in your mind as the day ends?

2. Each student hands in one copy of the completed sheets and keeps another copy.

3. Before the next class session, I categorize the responses to each question.

4. At the next class, I hand out a chart of the categorized responses. Students are given time to read and reflect on their earlier responses and comment in class.

5. Once this part of the exercise is complete, I provide question pages for students to add to their journal and ask them to write for ten minutes or so. Using a prefacing remark such as, "That was then [referring to the session in which their original comments were made], this is now; a lot may have happened over the week [two weeks, month]," I ask the students to reflect on their previous comments with questions such as

   Where are you right now in relation to the responses you gave last time?

   Do these still make sense to you?

   What, if anything, has changed?

6. For those students who prefer more open-ended journaling, I offer the option of having them answer their own questions.

7. I have found other helpful prompts for journaling, such as

   How are you doing spiritually?

   How are you doing emotionally?

   What is the most memorable thing you've learned so far, and how are you applying it in your life?

Progoff's stimuli of "at first . . . ," "and then . . . ," "and now . . . " are also effective prompts for this kind of journal writing.

Processing Tips

How I organize the responses is important. I try to cluster similar responses together without making value judgments about the material. I just list it all and leave spaces between categories so that students are not faced with a lot of words and no white space.

These journaling exercises take place within a larger context. In the first class session, I do an interactive presentation on journaling that sets a climate to support and encourage self-directed journaling throughout the course. I let them know that one way adults learn best and have better retention is consciously to make time to reflect on their learning. I present journaling as an opportunity to self-assess performance, gauge learning, and integrate that learning. I also provide a tip sheet that covers the following points:

- Set aside time regularly to write about your experiences.
- As you describe your learning, consider what happened and what was really going on.
- Don't get bogged down in detail. Capture a brief description and note some specifics, enough so that when you review this later on, you will be able to recall this learning experience clearly. Note your feelings at the time. That is, how were you reacting and feeling at the time?
- Remember that whatever it is that you experience or that stimulates your thinking will help you better understand your own behavior. Note these mental machinations along with frustrations, learning, curiosities, and "magic moments."
- If you get stuck, try plan B to get past it: Sit down and write *anything*, even if it is only, "I can't think of anything to write." Reflect on why that is so at this particular time. You may find that all you needed was a starting point and the rest will follow.

The regular in-class journaling exercises are meant to support the journaling that students choose to do independently. Students are encouraged to insert their originals of the NCR paper into their journals in an appropriate spot in their journal notebooks.

Contributor's Commentary

During the discussion that takes place while we are debriefing the exercise, I often hear comments such as, "When I left last time I felt like I was alone. Now I realize what I was feeling is normal." The first exercise also reminds students about topics covered in the previous class sessions. On the whole, journaling has to do with continuous reflection by utilizing one's experience and making sense from that. Actually, it builds on Tennant and Pogson's (1995) notion of naming the experience, reflecting on it, and doing something new because of it. The journal process is also a distancing and dialogue process.

At the end of the final session, I ask learners to reflect on their developmental journeys in the course or workshop through additional journal entries; that is, to journal about their journals. I encourage them first to review their previous journal entries. I take these assignments very seriously and work hard to provide feedback and suggestions about how they can continue their learning process. For example, I always end with a *next question,* one that will help push their thinking forward.

Participants report that this type of journaling—that is, journaling on their journals—assists them in integrating and processing their learning. Said one student, "It was the capstone to the [course]. Having to reflect on my own experience forced me to assess what I had learned and realize how much I have yet to learn."

References

Progoff, I. (1975). *At a journal workshop.* New York: Dialogue House Library.

Tennant, M., & Pogson, P. (1995). *Learning and change in the adult years: A developmental perspective.* San Francisco: Jossey-Bass.

Zachary, L. (2000). *The mentor's guide: Facilitating effective mentoring relationships.* San Francisco: Jossey-Bass.

PART THREE

BECOMING AN EFFECTIVE TEACHER OF ADULTS

Having described dozens of learning activities that can support development, we now take a closer look at the facilitator's role. When learning is open-ended and depends on the contributions of all participants, educators are not in control of process and content. In such learning environments, educators face unaccustomed challenges.

Chapter Eleven examines aspects of practice that emerged from our analysis of the strategies. This includes sharing power and authority, encouraging self-direction, and effectively using learners' experience. Chapter Twelve turns to how educators might grapple with these issues in ways that promote their own development, emphasizing critical self-reflection as an avenue for development. Finally, Chapter Thirteen explores some of the potential costs to adults of growth and change. It also proposes that the image of mentor as guide suggests practical ways to create the most effective environments for developmental growth.

CHAPTER ELEVEN

TEACHING AND TRAINING MATTERS

*Learning to see the structures within which we operate begins a process
of freeing ourselves from previously unseen forces and ultimately mastering
the ability to work with them and change them.*

—P. M. SENGE (1990)

In analyzing our contributors' strategies, we discovered threads of assumptions, values, and viewpoints that weave through the submissions. The way an exercise was structured, the kinds of directions provided, and the additional commentary all pointed to assumptions about the learning process and the educator's role in that process. As we considered these further, we found these assumptions raised questions in our minds. For example, if a contributor commented, "I try to _____," or "I encourage learners to ___," we wondered, *Why is ___ important? What does ___ say about how learning happens?* In order to support educators who are turning toward more experience-based approaches to learning, we will attempt to make these implicit themes explicit.

Power, Control, and Authority

Many of the contributions address the question of "Who's in charge, here?" Though we have expertise and position that automatically confer power on us, for most adult educators the goal is to share power and control. But most of us learned how to be educators in learning environments where the authority figure took responsibility for nearly every aspect of the process—what was done, how it was done, and how it was evaluated. They also controlled most of what actually occurred during the session: who spoke, when, and to whom. However, many of

the contributions imply that if our goal is to encourage deep approaches to learning, this model may no longer serve.

The other side of the power and authority issue is that many learners, even
accomplished professionals in their own fields, sometimes resist participation, as
though to say, "I'm paying good money for this, so teach me!" In some training
settings, this may grow out of compulsory attendance. Even when adults recognize their need to learn something, an implicit "or else" tends to dampen their enthusiasm. But even when learning is entirely voluntary, this reaction can result
from a lifetime of socialization "into a view of education as an authoritarian-based
transmission of information, skills, and attitudinal sets" (Brookfield, 1986, p. 296).
Or it may be that adults who are already overwhelmed with responsibility—for
work, family, and now learning—may be perfectly happy to turn over responsibility to someone else for a while. Though they want mutual respect, "Mutual
authority? Who needs it!?" When an educator faces a group of learners who have
their hands metaphorically, if not actually, folded across their chests, waiting for
illumination to occur, it takes great clarity of purpose not to respond as they wish.

> KATHLEEN: Part of encouraging shared responsibility is to help learn-
> ers reframe their assumptions about what it means to be a "good student."

Leaving aside, for the moment, simple resistance to trying something new,
some learners may not have the background, skills, or self-confidence to play under
the new rules. When required to participate, such learners may feel *more* disem-
powered and endlessly frustrated. This does not suggest to us that we give up
our intentions but that we choose cautiously, particularly at the beginning, with
an eye to how people respond and the kind of feedback we get.

Learners may have other reasons to participate less than whole-heartedly.
They may wonder whether our moves toward sharing responsibility are trustworthy. For example, David Boud's exercise (p. 63) that invites learners to set the
criteria for assessment can be used in academic courses and training workshops.
Are we confident we can rely on learners to set the bar at the appropriate level?
Or will we keep our fingers crossed, so to speak, in case we want to back out of
part or all of the agreement later on? Some educators who facilitate that exercise will reserve the right to make a suggestion if learners fail to include something they think is important; others will say that the educator's voice is never
"just another opinion," but carries implicit authority that few learners would
openly challenge.

MORRY: The instructor's power can extend to situations such as, "I'm the person who is privileged to walk around. I can pace, which suits my style, while everyone else is sitting, which may not suit theirs." So I invite learners to stand up, walk around, sit on the floor—whatever. It usually takes them several weeks to believe I mean it. When they do, they are not only more comfortable, but it subtly shifts power, too.

Meanwhile, we cannot escape the fact we are beholden to and representatives of certain institutions that expect us to maintain standards, provide a competent learning experience, evaluate learners' accomplishments, and certify the results. This suggests limits to how much or what kind of authority we can ultimately share. Freire, who is best known for his literacy work with peasants in rural Brazil (and taught them not only to read, but also to understand how they were oppressed by the existing political and economic system), distinguishes between *authority* and *authoritarianism:*

One of the mistakes we can commit in the name of freedom of the students is if I, as a teacher, would paralyze my action and my duty to teach. In the last analysis, I would leave the students by themselves, and it would be to fall into a kind of irresponsibility. At this moment, afraid of assuming authority, I lose authority. Authority is necessary to the educational process as well as necessary to the freedom of the student and my own . . . what is *not* necessary is authoritarianism. . . . The other mistake is to crush freedom and to exacerbate the authority of the teacher. Then you no longer have freedom but now you have authoritarianism, and then the teacher is the one who teaches. The teacher is the one who knows. The teacher is the one who guides. The teacher is the one who does *everything* [Horton and Freire, 1990, pp. 180–181].

At the other extreme from the educator who maintains total control, Brookfield (1990a, pp. 165–166) describes the danger of insisting on one's *lack* of expertise. In a well-meaning attempt at acknowledging their limitations, instructors may say, "I'm planning to learn a great deal from all of *you.* I don't want you to look on me as the specialist—we're all here to learn from one another." Although one certainly does not wish to overdo it in the "received wisdom" department, neither is it reassuring to learners to think their instructor is an ignoramus.

Learners are quite reasonably suspicious of the claim that "we're all equal here," when it is still the case that only the educator holds the keys to the exit door (that is, successful completion of the course). The resulting cognitive dissonance makes them anxious and can undermine movement toward whatever power-sharing is realistically possible within that environment. In addition, in certain content areas, such as computers, finance, and nursing, there are not only "right answers," but instructors may also be required to certify a level of mastery. Nevertheless, in many contexts and courses it is possible for the educator to claim, and to stick to the claim, "I'm not the authority for answers." This requires careful assessment and planning, however. Although open-ended processes always involve some element of risk, it can be hazardous for all concerned to put ill-prepared learners in a discovery learning environment and then insist on acting only as "resource person." Roberta Liebler, as she notes in her commentary on "Stimulating Cognitive and Ethical Development" (p. 217), concentrates on "asking questions that facilitate an exploration" so that students become acclimated to seeking answers from various sources, not just the instructor. This approach is also exemplified by Xenia Coulter in her "Psychology Tutorial" (p. 155).

Self-Direction and Empowerment

The notion of adults as essentially self-directed has been the subject of much controversy. Some educators claim that precisely this potential sets adults apart from younger learners (Knowles, 1973). Others point out the mixed nature of adults' capacities for self-direction (Merriam, 1994; Candy, 1991). Whereas most adults do have a clear sense of what they want to know (and by extension, what they feel is irrelevant to know) and many want to discuss ideas (rather than be incessantly lectured to), most also want the instructor's expectations spelled out *very* explicitly. How, then, do we work out the balance between "just tell me what to do," and "I'm an adult and can make my own decisions"?

Several self-directed learning strategies and techniques provide guidance. They offer learner-centered structures—individually-designed degree plans and learning contracts, for example—within which learners and educators can negotiate particulars. As with any new skill, these tasks can be quite challenging at first. They require a shift from a view of learning that is mostly authority-directed to one in which learners assume greater responsibility. Once this shift is accomplished, however, adults frequently report discovering in a new way that they are in charge not only of their learning outcomes, but also their lives.

It's that change from the idea of becoming self-reliant to experiencing an educational system that really teaches that . . . you are designing your own program that you're responsible for—it's not some counselor scratching it all on a little piece of paper and hand-

ing it to you. . . . It's that I am putting together the classes that will make my education meaningful. I'm responsible for how much meaning I get out of it. It's just so different to assume the responsibility. . . . [I'm] moving from one way of experiencing the world to a very different one—tolerating the awareness that I am ultimately responsible for myself.

Another learner analyzed the experience of designing his own degree more globally:

This is an opportunity to delve into what you're really serious about and what you might even call your purpose. . . . Never in your twelve years of structured schooling were you ever encouraged to do that, except by certain exceptional teachers.

Not all programs can support this level of self-definition. However, even within more traditionally designed degree plans or training plans, it is usually possible for learners to create individual learning contracts (Knowles, 1975). These, too, require a focus on oneself as learner that supports adults in realizing their power and in deep approaches to learning. A learner compared her experiences of self-confidence and self-discovery in a program that supported these activities to her earlier experiences of learning in more traditional environments:

[A]nd I know it wouldn't have happened if I was going to another kind of institution, because then there would be one more compartmentalized piece that I was fitting into my life rather than incorporating the process into my life. . . . [Here] you have to keep turning back to yourself. If you're going to do this, I don't see how anyone can do it without tapping into their inner resources and finding out who the hell they are and what they're gonna do in this world. I don't think it's possible.

As described in several strategies, other self-directed activities that can be incorporated in most academic or training settings include self-assessment (see Boud, "Development Through Self-Assessment," p. 63 and Marienau, "Reflecting on Practice," p. 271) and problem-focused education (see Margetson, p. 172).

Facilitating Discussion

When in our roles as teachers and trainers, if we automatically respond to each comment or question, we may without realizing it subtly reinforce the notion that we are the source of information and at the center of all interaction. We may also respond in a way that seems to say, "There, that's taken care of," and closes off further discussion. Yet as Miles Horton, founder of the Highlander Folk School, which is noted for education that empowers adults toward social activism, observed: "One of the best ways to educate is to *ask questions*. . . . [Then I] find a way in the discussion that's going on to inject that question at the right time, to get people to consider it. If they want to follow it up, then you ask more questions, growing out of that situation. You can get all your ideas across just by asking questions and at the same time you help people . . . grow and not form a dependency on you" (emphasis added, Horton and Freire, 1990, p. 147).

Brookfield's description of "critical questioning" begins to explain why a technique such as Horton's might successfully promote deep approaches to learning and developmental growth. "[It] is designed to elicit the assumptions underlying our thoughts and actions . . . it is concerned not so much with eliciting information as with prompting reflective analysis" (1989, p. 93).

As anyone who tries to shift from a question-answering mode to a critical questioning mode can attest, it takes considerable sensitivity and skill to encourage learners to openly examine their values and beliefs. If our questions are too global and abstract, learners will give formulaic, conventional responses. Brookfield (1989, pp. 94–96) begins by asking people to *reflect* on certain kinds of specific *experience*, using a "critical incident" format. He then follows up inductively on the clues they provide, in a relaxed, conversational tone, gently challenging them to think more deeply about their ideas and responses; that is, to explore new *meaning*. Gibbs (1992) also uses question posing as a way to foster deep learning approaches, though he focuses on more subject-centered questions and tasks. He also describes the challenge of posing questions at the right level of difficulty: If they are too easy, learners will not engage sufficiently; however, if the questions are too hard, learners may become discouraged.

An often overlooked facet of the question-discussion method is the time required. It needs time to develop momentum, to engage learners at deeper levels, and then to come to some resolution. A ten- or fifteen-minute "discussion" is not likely to get very far. Another time consideration concerns the difficulty most educators have if more than a few seconds of silence occurs. They tend to rush in with either another question or the "answer." Or if the question was addressed to a particular learner, the instructor may too quickly shift to someone else. Contributions that explore questioning as a vehicle for reflection and making meaning include Rob Weiner's "Interdisciplinary Tree Exercise" on p. 153, Toby Glicken's "Lifeboat Allegory" on p. 190, and Lindsay Oades' "The Experience Cycle Methodology" on p. 285.

Though not directly related to discussion method, another factor in time allocation is the intricacy of the activity selected. Recognizing the complexity of encouraging deep approaches to learning, educators may be tempted to design exercises that are overly complicated. As a result, learners' attention is diverted to figuring out how to do or manage the task, rather than focusing on the learning issues. We see in many of the contributed strategies careful attention to keeping any given task clear and relatively uncomplicated, even though the tasks may be multilayered or nested, often involving repeating cycles. For example, in Tom Hodgson's activity, "Circular Questioning in Adult Learning" (p. 165), students explore an issue from three clearly different perspectives on the way toward examining the interaction among these perspectives. In Morris Fiddler's activity, "Adding Dimensions" (p. 158), students explore relatively simple questions about the interactions of genes and environment, then move to more subtle forms of these interactions.

The question arises, however, when learners' discussion is a major, if not *the* major source of learning, how does this affect the quality of learning, and who is accountable? In academic and workplace settings, learners can be enormously rich resources for one another; perspectives are wider and more varied, examples are richer and deeper than those provided by a text or an individual instructor. Discussion as a central learning strategy can work well if learners come to the task with similar levels of maturity and responsibility, though they need not be matched with regard to depth of knowledge or experience.

Obviously, experienced individuals can benefit the less-knowledgeable by sharing the educator's role. But the learner new to the topic may also enrich the perspective of someone well versed in it through "fresh-eyed" questions that cause the "expert" to pause and think more deeply. The expert is also challenged to articulate knowledge explicitly that has probably become tacit, thus possibly exposing some gaps and areas for new or further learning.

The quality of discussion learning may be hampered by inattentive participants who, for whatever reason, are unwilling or unable to participate fully and carry their full share of the thinking and doing tasks. We sometimes hear learners' complaints about feeling somehow cheated if another learner took up too much "air time" or took a detour to another topic. This points to the need for the instructor to work with students on setting group norms with consequences. For example, students working in groups might be assessed separately for their contributions to the group as well as their individual contributions. Asking students to take turns facilitating discussion sensitizes them to the issues of discussion dynamics and tends to improve their performance when they return to their roles as participants.

Any discussion needs clearly articulated structure with accountable and assessable outcomes. Learners need to know in advance the criteria for a quality discussion so they can assess how well they are accomplishing the goal. This means carefully articulating demonstrable results that can be used as criteria; however, learners can contribute to setting these guidelines. The literature of collaborative learning may offer suggestions for such criteria, even if collaboration is not the focus of the group's work. Gail Feigenbaum's activity on "Structured Cooperative Learning" (p. 83) illustrates how students can focus on gaining comfort with a cooperative process while learning about a particular topic. Peter Reason's "Cooperative Inquiry" activity (p. 85) places collaboration at the center of the process, giving equal attention to the object of inquiry and the experience of collaboration.

CATHERINE: While the large group discussion is going on, I make mental mind maps (and sometimes written notes) of the discussion threads. Periodically, I interrupt the discussion to play back the themes I'm hearing, including ideas or questions that were dropped along the way. I also invite the students to play back what they've been hearing. This playback technique can help deepen the conversation or get it back on track, and it can make room for students' voices that have not yet been heard. Another technique I use to help keep the conversation from staying only at the level of individual storytelling is to ask students to identify the source or prompt for what they're talking about. They might be building on or responding to what someone else has said, referring to something they read in the material; sometimes, of course, they're just moved to say something, not sure what has sparked it. My intent is to have them be as thoughtful as possible about what they're contributing to the conversation.

When facilitating small group activities, some educators recommend walking around, checking in with groups to keep up their momentum. Gibbs (1992) warns, however, against falling into the expert role and answering the main questions. Learners will cease to work through the problems if they know the answers will be forthcoming (p. 49). Horton and Freire (1990) also caution that expert input can "take away the power of people to make decisions," particularly if the experts take on advocacy roles rather than just provide information (p. 130).

Brookfield, however, no longer circulates among small groups of learners engaged in discussion. He has found that his presence either intimidates, leading to a sudden hush as he joins the group, or else encourages a burst of anxious animation as people strive to be good students. He therefore allows the process to proceed uninterrupted, but actively offers himself as resource, to be called upon when needed (1989, p. 237).

The art of facilitating whole-group discussion is multifaceted and beyond the scope of a section in a single chapter (Brookfield & Preskill, 1999), but the fact that entire programs, such as the prestigious Harvard Business School's graduate degree, are built on discussion methodology, suggests that when it is done well, it is not a case of the blind leading the blind (Christensen, Garvin, & Sweet, 1991).

Disclosure

One of the more effective ways of abandoning our pedestal is to admit to being human, flawed, and still engaged in our own process of development and growth. Daloz's observations about mentoring are equally applicable to teaching and training: "[s]elf-disclosure from the mentor seems to play a crucial part in the full evolution of a mentorship from hierarchy toward symmetry. . . . [I]n the early stages of development, authority is enough, but as the student grows, his willingness to trust an authoritative mask without knowing what lies behind it dims . . . to the extent that the mentor is able to become human, the student is empowered to see more deeply" (Daloz, 1986, p. 176–177).

When, for example, an exercise calls for learners to describe aspects of their personal experience, we often begin by revealing the comparable and less than picture-perfect aspects of our own experiences. We talk openly about mistakes we have made in the past and current frustrations we have not resolved. This is not idle confessional chatter—it helps establish us as peers of adults whose experiences we share. Acknowledging to ourselves—and to learners—that we, too, are adults engaged in a life-long process of growth reduces the temptation to accept implicit designations of superiority. It may also reassure organizational leaders who are likely to come to a learning environment expecting nothing less than perfection of themselves.

> KATHLEEN: When I ask learners to do their time lines on the first night of class, I start with mine and openly discuss some of my less brilliant life choices, such as getting pregnant and married at nineteen. It breaks the ice so that they can be more relaxed about their own disclosures as the exercise continues.

Or we may admit to our own confusion or limited understanding of an author's viewpoints (among the texts for the course). We reveal parts of our personal and intellectual selves for many reasons, including, as does Kim Winkelman, in "Providing a Learning Culture" (p. 178), to "level the playing field." We hope in this way to join more readily with learners in a "culture of learning." Despite our best intentions, however, learners may experience our efforts to remove what we see as the facade of authority as yet another example of our authority.

> MORRY: The fact that I say, "I want to level the playing field," underscores who has the power. The *students* can't walk in and say, "I want to level the playing field."

In our experience, most learners appreciate our attempts and are encouraged to enter into conversation more readily. Others, however, continue to view our efforts with skepticism, perhaps wondering about our authenticity and consistency over time.

We also describe our engagement with some of the more challenging aspects of our professional work. If we hide the "imperfect processes of [our] thinking," Belenky, Clinchy, Goldberger, and Tarule (1986) tell us, only presenting the finished, polished product, learners will not see that similar accomplishments are within their reach.

Learning based in experience inevitably involves who the learner is as a person and aspects of his or her personal life. It is therefore incumbent upon us to create a safe and respectful environment within which learners can feel free to disclose and discuss. This may involve acknowledging, in advance, the difficulties it may present, and giving learners time and encouragement to approach us privately if they feel unable to participate in an exercise. It may involve ground rules for discussion—ideally, generated by the group, and not imposed by the educator— addressing issues of safety, supportiveness, inclusiveness, and civility.

> MORRY: There can be a downside to how people interpret "civility" as politeness and deference to ideas. Some ideas will trigger strong responses, some might even be offensive. But without those getting on the table, there's loss of an authentic exchange. People are holding back in deference to politeness. And there isn't necessarily the sharpening of ideas or an individual's expression of meaning that can come when things don't stay "polite."

Even with our best attempts to provide safety, some learners will be uncomfortable with discussing aspects of their personal or work lives. Although there are academically sound reasons to request that learners share personal details, we also need to ask ourselves whether any particular instance is really necessary and be exquisitely sensitive to body language and other hesitations that suggest a problem. People from other cultures, for example, may feel it is completely inappropriate to disagree with another learner's ideas or beliefs, let alone discuss issues surrounding life choices. We need at all times to be sensitive to the ethics of "requiring" self-disclosure. In certain courses, such as those designed to prepare future therapists or workshop facilitators, it may indeed be necessary. However, though we might *wish* to include learners' direct experience in, say, a course in American history, we may need to honor the decision of those—perhaps a Vietnam War veteran, for example—who do not respond to our invitation.

Coverage

For some educators, the potential advantages of encouraging more learner input are outweighed by the concern that the additional time required to learn from reflection on experience means leaving learners in the lurch by not adequately covering the material. There can be good reasons for this concern. At some level, educators bear the responsibility to preserve the continuity of knowledge. From this perspective, there is value in what Freire calls the "banking model" of education, even though it is clearly in tension with experience-based learning.

> KATHLEEN: The notion that an educator's job is to preserve knowledge by stuffing it into learners is absurd, in my view. For one thing, there's far *too much* knowledge around for that to be effective; and besides, reproductive learning has a short shelf life. For another, that's what libraries and databases are for—to hold information. As I see it, the educator's role is helping learners *locate* and *use* that information effectively. That means deep and narrow over wide and shallow. When learners really get the hang of what it means to make meaning, they can apply that understanding to many other instances not "covered" in class.

Lack of coverage can also be problematic when courses are sequenced and subsequent instructors assume a common starting point. We also recognize that some courses, such as accounting and finance, tend to focus on "mastery of content." We will not presume to wave these concerns aside. We suggest, however, that how educators define their roles and overall desired outcomes can lead to changes in practice that may reconcile some of the tensions.

> MORRY: How much "coverage" is necessary may depend on the purpose of the course or the instructor's intentions for the course. If I were teaching genetics to future geneticists, I would have to focus on getting the students to the next level of the course sequence. But when I'm teaching students mostly so they will appreciate what science is, I can focus on helping people expand their sense of themselves and of human nature and interpreting what they see differently.

For example, Gibbs (1992) reviewed studies that included "thousands of students in scores of academic departments across a wide range of academic subject areas and institutions" in Sweden, the United Kingdom, and Australia; his findings indicated that an "excessive amount of course material" and "lack of opportunity to pursue subjects in depth" were among the most salient characteristics associated with a surface approach to learning (p. 9).

> CATHERINE: I have been guilty of inundating my students with reading material, much of which is quite dense. The result, of course, has been that many don't get it all read; those who do usually aren't able to catch all the major points and nuances that I find so interesting. I need to remember that they are reading this material for the first time, while I have probably mulled it over for quite some time. I also need to remember that dealing with a few key concepts in depth, and building in time for reflection and connection to their experience and other concepts, is far more preferable than exposing them to all the content.

By contrast, one of the innovators in Gibbs's study (1992) who was successful in encouraging a deep approach to learning specifically noted that "the amount of factual material the course attempts to cover has been cut. Rather, emphasis is placed on approaching and understanding the same material from a variety of methodological positions" (p. 47). We would like to underscore the fact that Gibbs also points out "the [educator's] previous subjective experience of 'covering' the material in lectures was clearly not mirrored by students' experience of 'covering' the material!" (p. 48). This suggests that depth results from connections learners make between the material and the events and experiences of their lives.

There is no question that our responding to learners in the moment often takes us in unplanned directions. We have frequently found that attending to learners' ongoing experiences as they unfold may shift what we intended as a conceptual appetizer into the main course. However, though it is not an immediately learned skill, a skillful discussion facilitator can encourage the depth of thinking around *this* topic that might have been planned to occur around some *other* topic. A "deep [approach to] learning is more likely when students' motivation is intrinsic and when the student experiences a need to know something" (Gibbs, 1992, p. 10).

If deep approaches to learning are the goal, less may be more. "As my years [as an educator] have multiplied, I have made the paradoxical discovery that modest expectations, particularly in the realm of content, trigger more effective learning than ambitious ones. Material learned in depth—with the heart as well as the head—stays with students, but broad-based lists of facts, techniques, and theories tend to fade. . . . Thoroughness and depth compensate abundantly for the sacrifice of breadth" (Christensen, Garvin, & Sweet, 1991, p. 114).

Assessment Drives Learning

Another influential factor in encouraging a deep approach to learning is assessment. Simply put: *What we assess is what will be learned.* In his study of several innovative programs in a variety of educational settings in the United Kingdom, Gibbs (1992) found, overall, "students will be powerfully influenced by the assessment system they are working within. . . . Many conventional assessment methods, including essays, unseen exams, and laboratory reports, allow students to take a surface approach or *even implicitly encourage and reward* such an approach" (emphasis added, p. 17).

In the cases he analyzed, ways to combat this effect included, for example, involving students in the design of self-assessment (as with David Boud's exercise, "Development Through Self-Assessment," p. 63), having students educate each other and critically reflect on that process (see Rosemary Caffarella's "Learning Activity Project," p. 211), and designing assessments that depend not on memorization or rote application of procedures but that emphasize new applications or new decision making (see Catherine Marienau's "Reflecting on Practice," p. 271). In one of the programs that enjoyed the *least* success, Gibbs underscored the fact that "the assessment was largely unchanged" (1992, p. 98).

In addition to creative assessments focused on content, learning journals and self-assessments can be structured to encourage learners to focus on their process and experience as learners. (See also Phyllis Walden's exercise, "Journal Dialogue," p. 127). Learners in a program that emphasizes self-assessment report that "having to engage with the learning process so personally" makes one become "more aware of my own processes of cognition" (Marienau, 1999, p. 139).

In academic and training environments, how we assess is as important as what we assess. The traditional assessment system focuses on *summative* feedback, which is fine for generating grades but does not encourage revisiting areas of confusion to achieve greater clarity. Finding out the "right" answer after the fact is not the same thing as understanding how one might have arrived at the answer differently. More effective assessment, from a learning perspective, would incrementally build on learners' meaning-making by providing ongoing *formative* feedback. Learners would be encouraged to integrate feedback either in a revision of the same task, or in a subsequent task designed as a stepping stone to the next level of complexity. See, for example, Patricia Brewer's multiphased activity on "Learning Styles Assessment" (p. 66).

Perhaps the need to figure the *grade*—how much "off" the possible perfect score—has focused most educators' attention on what the learner did wrong or failed to do. This tends to be true even in settings where grades are not given. Unfortunately, people learn most effectively from specific attention to what they did *right*—and this implies more than just a few check marks in the margins. It requires attention to specifically why it was good, how it was well-structured or well-articulated, and so forth. Learners can then revisit the experience—the psychic and somatic imprint—that resulted in the success, and do it again, only better. When we are discussing their work, we know we have found the right key to the learners' experience when they suddenly stop frowning in concentration and say, "Oh. You mean like *that* paragraph? I can do that," because they've already done it. This is much more effective than trying somehow to impress upon them an experience they haven't had yet.

> **KATHLEEN:** Even when I focus on critical feedback, I couch that in a positive way, for example: "This is a good start, now here's how to improve." It's easy to forget how vulnerable adults can be to our feedback.

Unpredictability

When we attend to learners' ongoing experiences and respond accordingly, we must accept with as much grace as possible that we are less "in control" of the learning process than we might be with more traditional approaches. Brookfield's description of education to encourage critical thinking aptly describes the unpredictability of using developmental intentions: "When we begin to ask people to identify assumptions underlying their habitual ways of thinking and learning, we do not know exactly how they are going to respond. When we ask them to consider alternatives, we do not know which of these will be considered seriously and which will be rejected out of hand. When people are presented with counterexamples that contradict their commonly held assumptions . . . we do not know exactly what will transpire . . . *risk, surprise, and spontaneity are important and unavoidable*" (Brookfield, 1989, p. 240, emphasis added).

These unavoidable surprises can lead to the agonizing feeling, both during a class or workshop and especially afterward, when one relives the incident again and again, that one has thoroughly blown it. Paradoxically, however, learning that is a bit ragged, that reveals the lack of certainty that is the essence of knowing, and that invites learners to experience the vagaries for themselves may in the long run empower learners and contribute to deep approaches to learning.

The first time we try out any exercise, we take a deep breath and hope for the best. There is simply no surefire "recipe" for learning based in experience. We are of mixed opinion about whether to warn learners that this is the maiden voyage of this particular activity. Some learners are less than enthusiastic about being "guinea pigs," which may affect how they engage with the process. Others will be extra supportive because they have been in similar situations. In any case, we are *sure* to debrief the experience with the learners at the end, *especially* if it did not go as we imagined. However, we try not to assume, because it did not come out exactly as we imagined, that it was a "failure." Yet if something went particularly badly, we admit it. *The learners already know that.* The points we are likely to earn in the "honest, trustworthy, and real" column more than make up for the temporary loss in the "everything goes according to plan" column. At the same time, we try not to overemphasize its negative significance. What seems problematic can turn out to have unanticipated, positive side effects.

KATHLEEN: In a lively discussion that appeared to be going well, a learner suddenly said, in an aggrieved tone that sounded also at the edge of tears, "Well, excuse me for living, but that was my opinion, and I didn't need to have all of you [pointing across the room] tell me I was wrong." Everyone froze, including me. I couldn't remember any comments that might have provoked this response, yet here it was. The learner's experience and feelings had to be honored, but others did not deserved to be shamed. I bumbled my way blindly through some sort of discussion about what had happened, feeling my ineptness at every moment. Yet the learners' weekly journals revealed their *appreciation* for an environment where this kind of incident could happen! Furthermore, many reflected insightfully on ways to provide greater safety for all participants without losing the opportunity for open dialogue.

Starting Where the Learner Is

As studies have repeatedly shown (Marton & Booth, 1997), one of the more significant factors in whether students take a deep or surface approach to learning is the approach that the *educator* takes. Our first task, then, may be to explore our own assumptions that as experts in this field we already know what the issues are, how best to present the material, and what the assessment should focus on. Several notable educators suggest that we start instead by "taking the experiences of people seriously" (Horton & Freire, 1990, p. 13).

> We cannot educate if we don't start—and I said *start* and not *stay*—from [where] people perceive themselves, their relationships with others and with reality, because this is precisely what makes their knowledge. . . . The question is to know what they know and how they know, to learn how to teach them things which they don't know and want to know. The question is to know whether my knowledge is necessary, because sometimes it is not necessary. Sometimes it is necessary but the need is not yet perceived by the [learners]. Then one of the tasks of the educator is also to provoke the *discovering* of need for knowing and never to impose the knowledge whose need was not yet perceived [Horton & Freire, 1990, p. 66, original emphasis].

Nel Noddings (1984) underscores the same issue. "Suppose . . . I encounter a student who is doing poorly. . . . He tells me that he hates [this subject]. I do not begin with dazzling performances designed to intrigue him or change his attitude: I begin nearly as I can, *with the view from his eyes.* . . ." (p. 15–16, emphasis added).

Kitchener and King (1994) examine the same concerns as part of facilitating the development of reflective judgment. They recommend that educators should "informally assess students' assumptions about knowledge and how beliefs should be justified," and then use reflective journals, response papers and other assignments "through which they can view students' epistemic assumptions" (p. 240).

Though many of Ausubel's strictly cognitivist presumptions about learning and knowing have been questioned in the forty-plus years since they were introduced, the statement he claimed was the essential principle of his educational psychology still seems to hold: "The most important single factor influencing learning is what the learner already knows" (1968, p iv).

To start where learners are, we use experience they already have or else create activities based on new experiences authentic to the content. However, starting where learners are also requires that we attend to the balance they wish to strike between exploring the topic and self-exploration. Not all learners are primed and ready to engage with experience as a basis for learning. We may have to allow some warm-up time while they accustom themselves to this new approach to learning. We may also find that "where the learner is" is not immediately evident *to the learner*. Exercises that do not start off by requiring them to articulate their level of self-awareness can help such learners ease into the situation. See, for example, Toby Glicken's "Anzio Effect" (p. 100), and Chris Chiaverina's "Exploratories in Physics" (p. 93).

Limitations of Experience

Using experience as a basis for learning can be both liberating and constraining. Learners who have just begun to trust in their own *voice*—for whom knowledge formerly resided in others, including educators and authority figures—feel empowered when their experience becomes text. However, there is a crucial distinction between using one's experience as *a text* for learning, and using it as *the only text*. Someone who can view her experience only from her own perspective is rooted in the belief that truth is personal. She is, according to Belenky, Clinchy, Goldberger, and Tarule (1986), a *subjective* knower and tends to be closed to ideas that do not emanate from within herself. Given the emphasis in the strategies on students' experience as a source of learning, how can learners be helped to build on their experience, rather than get stuck in it?

CATHERINE: In my undergraduate course on women's psychosocial development, I tell students that their collective experience is one of the texts for the course, and they are each a contributing author. As with any text, it needs to be constructed and interpreted with care. As they compose their text during the course, the students are connecting their ideas and perspectives with one another, as well as with the other readings.

Depending on the learners' strategies for knowing (Goldberger, Tarule, Clinchy, & Belenky, 1996; see also Appendix B), the instructor who wishes to draw richly on students' experiences may well be mindful of certain drawbacks. Some learners will seem unwilling or unable to go outside their own experiences for ideas or perspectives. They may show little curiosity about others' ideas, from the "great" ones of history and culture to the insights of peers. They may resist exploring theories or models that don't speak directly to their own experience. If they express these perspectives loudly and often, the effect may be to shut out others from exploring various perspectives.

When participants focus solely on their experience, particularly in training environments, which are often thought of as atheoretical and experience-based, they do not develop their capacities to think beyond what they believe they already know.

Directly challenging a subjectivist is unlikely to accomplish the desired ends of having her explore new perspectives. A better strategy is asking her to "try on" other perspectives without having to commit to them or relinquish her own. For example, Roberta Liebler's "Stimulating Cognitive and Ethical Development" (p. 217), Kathleen Taylor's "Taking Multiple Perspectives" (p. 203), and Susan Munaker's "Aligning with the Organization's Mission" (p. 192) are all examples of strategies that support people temporarily suspending their views while simulating other identities. Similarly, structured journaling strategies, such as those of Phyllis Walden ("Journal Dialogue," p. 127) and Catherine Marienau ("Structured Learning Journal," p. 278), ask learners to step outside themselves to begin a broader process of critical reflection.

It is also essential, in our experience, to encourage subjectivists to air their true opinions, as some respond according to what they believe they are "supposed" to say. If we remain in the dark about what learners *really* think, we cannot see what might open the door to other possibilities.

Incorporating Experience

Deep approaches to learning tend to include or, better yet, start with learners' experience. As we have noted, however, not all students are prepared to maximize learning through their experience or that of their peers. Instructors have several choices to make in terms of when and how to use experience in the learning process. These choices are influenced by students' preparedness to work with their experiences as an entrée to exploring ideas and by the instructor's relative emphasis on students' digesting ideas versus creating them.

We therefore offer a framework—in fact, a continuum—of ways that one might use experience in the learning process. One can come into the process at any point, depending on the learners. If they are unused to working with their experiences as a source for learning, one would probably start near the beginning. If they are more adept, or if the point of the exercise is experiential learning per se, the educator might choose a later entry point. In terms of whose experience is being considered, the continuum begins "outside" the learner and ends integrated with him or her. As the learner's own experience moves to center stage, the activity begins to encourage deep approaches to learning.

Link one. This end of the continuum relies not on the learner's own experiences but on those of the authority whose text is under discussion. If, for example, the group was examining Piaget's model of child development or Taylor's model of "one right way" management, they would explore aspects of these men's lives as they might inform their models. Piaget was no doubt influenced by the social era of his time and the state of development of psychology as a field of study. Taylor wrote at the beginning of the industrial era when the workforce was uneducated and many new immigrants spoke little English.

This analysis might be accomplished by consulting biographical, historical, or other contextual material in order to ask questions of the material such as, "How did the [authority] come to these conclusions? What were some of the experiences he or she had that probably influenced their ideas and outcomes? Might one, through reflection, suggest other likely influences [experiences], even if data are not easily available to support these surmises?" This approach avoids "learning about" the topic simply by linking one abstract idea to another abstract idea, as in reproductive learning. Instead, the idea is grounded in concrete experience—even though it is not the learner's own.

Link two. As in the example above, this link also begins with the educator presenting some idea or text to the learner. However, learners are then asked to examine their own store of experiences, looking for those that help exemplify or illuminate the topic. For example, learners studying child development or management could draw on their life and work experiences that illustrate ideas in the textual material. Someone learning the concept of strategic planning for an organization might see the idea come alive through their experience of having organized a family reunion or major vacation. As in the first link, the abstract idea is followed by and grounded in experience—this time, however, the learner's own experience.

Link three. Here the learner's experience is the starting point, and the focus is less on a subject or topic and more on the learner as subject. The individual begins by examining his or her rich store of experiences, then seeks theory, text, or ideas that provide a framework to explore and illuminate selected experiences. This extends, and in some sense reverses, the previous link. Although the learner's experience is very much at the center of this exploration, the topic is not ignored.

By examining their experiences from the different perspectives offered by the textual material or subject matter, the learner is able to understand better the topic under discussion.

Link four. This link takes the previous link one step further. Once again, learners begin with their own experience, but rather than quickly moving from their own experience to text, learners stop and solidify their own understanding. The experience is examined inductively with an eye to generating theories, ideas, and generalizations. Only then do the learners consult external sources, sometimes discovering that they have substantially replicated ideas and theories devised by authorities. Even when the individual's theories are not validated in this way, this process is a major step in understanding the fundamentally constructed nature of knowledge.

Link five. When learners are able to integrate experience and text, moving effortlessly back and forth between ideas as subject and ideas as experienced, they are no longer reproducing others' ideas, but are making meaning from critical reflection on experience. This is the most complex approach to learning described in the phenomenographic literature, and the one that suggests developmental transformation: Learning as change as a person (Marton, Dall'Alba, & Beaty, 1993).

In short, the continuum is this:

1. Understanding others' ideas through examining others' experiences.
2. Illuminating others' ideas by relating them to one's own experiences.
3. Interpreting one's own experiences by using others' ideas.
4. Deriving ideas from one's own experiences.
5. Interrelating experiences and ideas of self and others.

As one moves through each step of the continuum, the potential increases for learning from experience and for developmental growth.

No Single Answer

"There is no Holy Grail," Brookfield (1989) observes, "and no one way to instructional enlightenment. Indeed, anyone who is alert will be immediately skeptical of standardized models that purport to be replicable in all possible situations. . . . Facilitators should be ready to try a range of different approaches. . . . Perfection is impossible" (pp. 233–234). The variety of strategies and commentaries from our contributors underscores the fact that though educating is an ancient human expression, it remains an imprecise, mysterious art.

CHAPTER TWELVE

OBSERVING OUR PRACTICES

Teaching, like any truly human activity, emerges from one's inwardness. . . .
Viewed from this angle, teaching holds a mirror to the soul. If I am willing
to look in that mirror and not run from what I see, I have a chance to gain
self-knowledge—and knowing myself is as crucial to good teaching as
knowing my students and my subject.

—PARKER PALMER (1998)

Educating others, as discussion of the complexities and ambiguities in Chapter Eleven suggests, is a developmental challenge. No matter how seasoned an educator we might be, all of us constantly struggle with making meaning of our teaching and training experiences and strive to learn from them. Many of us recognize that as adult educators we are also adult learners, and that engaging in critical self-reflection about our existing assumptions, values, and perspectives can further prompt our development. Development of ourselves as educators mirrors individual development in that it is always open to revision and reframing. The dynamite course that we taught last term is falling flat this time around; the training program that we conducted to acclaim in California is being harshly criticized by the employees in Vermont. These situations, and countless other experiences of successes and failures, can prompt us to question what, why, and how well we do what we do in our interactions with learners.

It may be as disconcerting to adult educators to be told "go forth and reflect critically on your experience" as it often is to our adult learners. At the same time, self-reflection is key to effective practice and ongoing development as an educator (Apps, 1991; Brookfield, 1990a; Cervero, 1988; Cranton, 1996; Mentkowski & Associates, 2000; Palmer, 1998). Useful techniques for reflection can be found in other sources. For example, Cranton (1996) and Mentkowski and Associates (2000) emphasize, in particular, engaging in dialogue with peers about the complex dimensions of one's practice. In this chapter we emphasize what adult educators might reflect upon and for what purposes so that critical self-reflection might lead to better alignment between what one thinks and what one does as an adult educator, particularly with regard to the practices described in this book.

> CATHERINE: Reflecting on my practice better equips me to take a developmental approach to teaching . . . and that is likely to have some impact on students' experiences, ones that I hope are growth-producing. Also, I can model at least part of this developmental process by communicating with students about my reflections, for example, what I'm setting out to accomplish, what I'm adapting and why—and by inviting their participation through feedback. In other words, I'm intentionally trying to do for myself what I ask them to try to do for themselves . . . be open to growth and development through reflection.

Objects of Reflection

When all the various aspects of teaching or training are in alignment, the act looks and feels simple. And participants are more likely to focus on their own learning when they don't sense or experience contradictions and inconsistencies from an educator. At those moments, we enjoy the fruits of our "knowing-in-action" (Schön, 1983)—when our deep-seated core of beliefs and values are in congruence at an unconscious level with our actions. Achieving these moments, however, can be difficult under any circumstances, even more so with adult learners who are diverse and demanding.

Over and above command of the content area(s), educators are in a role that relies on how we are and who we are in relation to the learners. The authors of the strategies in Part Two illustrate this point in varied and powerful ways. In their processing tips and commentaries, many of them remark on why they do what they do; several offer useful caution about the skills needed to pull off certain techniques; others give glimpses into their philosophy about teaching or learning; and still others emphasize the core values that guide their practice. When something works really well or when something goes awry, what does one turn to as a possible source of the success or the problem? It might be as simple as adjusting something we're doing (for example, toning down our intensity in the classroom), or one may need to examine some deep-seated beliefs—one's core knowledge (Dirkx & Prenger, 1997) before understanding successes or devising a better way to act. Each of these various aspects of teaching, then, can become sources, or objects, of reflection.

Behavior

The most usual area of self-reflection is *What actually happened? What do I actually do? What else might I have done?* Simple as it sounds, reflecting on our behaviors may be one of the most difficult things to do—we can't actually see what we are doing. In *Becoming a Critically Reflective Teacher,* Stephen Brookfield (1995) gives humorous but painful accounts of how certain of his behaviors—visiting small groups while in discussion, assigning learning contracts, doing minimal lecturing—were interpreted by his students in ways quite unlike what he intended. To achieve greater congruence between what we do (and intend to do) and what students experience, we need to imagine ourselves as the learner: *How would we, as competent adults, feel about the kind of learning environment our behaviors create?* However, since it can be difficult to put ourselves in learners' shoes, having peers observe and give feedback or asking for student feedback (as with a "One-Minute Paper" [Angelo & Cross, 1994]) can be quite useful.

Capabilities

Do I have the necessary skills and knowledge to engage learners and create environments in the way I would like? The strategies in Part Two undoubtedly grew out of the authors' capabilities; people tend to engage in those behaviors for which they are best prepared. But reflection can lead to a heightened awareness of one's existing capabilities and a plan to strengthen or develop new ones that would expand the repertoire.

CATHERINE: When I started teaching adults in classroom settings more than fifteen years ago, I avoided lecturing because I don't like to be the center of attention and I am not particularly entertaining as a presenter. But I have always been pretty good at establishing rapport with students and connecting with them through conversation. I realized I could provide minilectures to convey key ideas to help set the context for in-depth conversation. An area where I continually need to stretch (being very comfortable with abstract ideas) is providing concrete illustrations behind complex ideas.

Beliefs

What major ideas inform my teaching or training? In the previous chapters, we focused on the *practice* of educating others with developmental intentions: *what* adult educators do, *how* they do it, and some implications of both. To illustrate how reflection on beliefs can help explain practice, we turn to Merriam and Caffarella (1999), who have organized a wide array of learning theories into five major orientations to learning: *behaviorist, cognitivist, humanist, social learning,* and *constructivist.* These orientations to learning are primarily concerned with change in the individual, which may or may not be directed toward social change. In the context of our book, these orientations vary considerably in their support of educating others with developmental intentions. For example, the behaviorist creates an environment designed to elicit certain responses. The concept of meaning-making is essentially *meaningless* in this context. Humanists, at the opposite end of the spectrum, are primarily concerned with self-actualization and therefore encourage learners to set their own learning contexts as much as possible. The middle ground is occupied by cognitive-constructivists and social learning practitioners, both of whom focus on the learner's process and experiences as mediated by the social context or as filtered through various ways of processing information.

"Relationships of Dimensions of Teaching and Orientation to Learning" in Appendix D provides a more detailed examination of these learning orientations and is designed to help educators locate their own tendencies, most likely finding themselves represented by more than one orientation.

MORRY: When I consider what beliefs I hold, I realize most that the process of aligning is not hierarchical, moving only from the most abstract to the practical or vice versa. It is an ongoing dialogue and dynamic interaction among the parts, the "objects" of reflection. If I give the process enough time and intentionality, it becomes clearer that each influences another. I find myself asking, "Are there beliefs reflected in my behavior that I haven't recognized or articulated? Is there a gap in my understanding or capability of how to translate a belief into actual practice? What are some of the implications of adopting a belief that I have not thoughtfully considered?" I recently stopped short in the middle of discussion, realizing that my conversational style in the classroom reflected my belief in constructivist processes while students were grappling with curricular outcomes from a behaviorist perspective: "What should I be doing now to arrive safely at the goals at the end of the term?"

Purpose

> CATHERINE: For me, the power of thinking in terms of "developmental intentions" is that I can avoid getting boxed into any particular orientation (for example, my leanings are toward humanist and constructivist) and potentially miss helping a good portion of the students learn. In my undergraduate courses, some students are brand new to college while others are nearing completion of their programs. I encounter a wide range of academic abilities, confidence in self as learner, and understanding of the educational system. By thinking about developmental intentions, I can consider which orientations to draw upon that will be most appropriate for a given teaching situation with a given group of adult learners.

What am I trying to accomplish? A moment's reflection on this question can be invigorating—*I know where I'm headed with what I am doing*—or it can lead to an unsettling confusion. What follows may be a refreshing affirmation of one's purpose or the impetus to revisit the question: *What was or is my purpose?* It is unusual for a teacher or trainer to sustain engagement, his own or a learner's, without touching base with the purpose of the effort. In the context of this book, the developmental intentions (Chapter Three) can serve as sources for articulating one's purpose.

Environment

What are the settings or circumstances in which I help others learn? If someone has a developmental perspective, how consistent will he or she be with the norms and expectations of his or her organization, department, field, discipline, industry standard, or one's own standards? Contemplating those norms—how they are represented in espoused values and how their reality is experienced with colleagues, reward systems, and the like—can be a rich arena for reflection. It is not unusual for educators to find some degree of disjunction between their practices and the environment in which they are functioning. For example, in corporate settings, where a corporate philosophy often prescribes a way of doing things, that is, "one right way to supervise," trainers may need to compromise their learning goals or risk some type of corporate sanction (R. Proehl, 1999, personal conversation). Or reflection might affirm congruence between the norms of the environment and an educator's personal purposes(s) yet reveal difficulty in getting things done well for want of necessary capabilities.

Educators could choose any one of these discrete elements of teaching or training as an object of reflection, or they might deal with these elements more holistically. The choice is less important than engaging in an ongoing process of imagining possibilities. Either starting point can lead to "useful" reflection that, in turn, helps cultivate a reflective habit that can provide a foundation for the educator's continued personal and professional growth, change, and development. As with any habit, it needs to be practiced.

Two Kinds of Reflection

CATHERINE: Because I want to be able to design and enter almost any kind of learning situation, I need to reflect on my practice as I am experiencing it. I find it particularly helpful to draw on frameworks that can help me interpret what's going on in the moment.

I often turn quickly to Kolb's levels of complexity in the dimensions of perceptual (seeing), symbolic (understanding), affective (feeling), and behavioral (doing) because this schema can help me diagnose how a learner is attending to an experience—to what's engaged her or what she's ignoring. This helps me determine what to emphasize and how so that I'm both working with where she's at and adding in at least one other dimension for her to consider.

In another situation, I may turn to the knowing strategies of *Women's Ways of Knowing* as a guide to understanding how a learner is approaching the material and herself in relation to it. Figuring out what particular knowing strategy she seems to be using is another way to determine how best to engage her in the learning process. Conceptual frameworks, of course, aren't the whole story. For example, I need to be able to move fluidly between what I understand (symbolic) and what I do (behavioral), so that I am improvising, preferably together with the learners.

This notion of improvising is akin to what Schön (1983) calls "reflection-in-action." It is "thinking on one's feet"—the improvisational sensibility that reshapes the moment according to the needs of the participants.

Gloria: I constantly assess the way in which I communicate with students and evaluat[e] their responses . . . [and I] constantly adjust my part of our teacher-student dialogue to accommodate what I perceive to be their interest, comprehension, or resistance and noncomprehension.

Chuck: Self-reflection is important in discerning what is occurring . . . with either the individual or the group. From this I can decide upon the next or most appropriate instructional tool to use so the learning continues in a safe, yet challenging way.

Most educators probably engage in this kind of improvisation all the time, without necessarily recognizing it as reflection on their behaviors, capabilities, ideas, or purposes. However, our colleagues tell us that bringing these skills to consciousness tends to enhance their effectiveness. Mostly, reflection-in-action focuses on a better way to facilitate the next several minutes. Sometimes we may have the presence of mind to jot down a quick note to remind us to revisit and rethink an issue later; sometimes the moment comes and goes with the residue of having a little more practice and a little more awareness.

MORRY: I am standing to the side of the group as four or five of the eighteen students are talking about "territoriality" in their organizations. I am wondering about the others: Is Marty looking for an opening or unsure he understands? Is Laurie thinking about a sixteen-year-old runaway who showed up at her agency's door just before she left for class? Am I feeling satisfied that there is an animated response to a question I asked or am I holding my patience with the personal storytelling? Is Denise waiting to be invited into the discussion by her colleagues? I wonder when Sandy will talk about his teenage daughter's recent experience with a gang or doesn't he see the connection? Should I hold that conversation we had in confidence? I or somebody else in the room will make something happen in the next few minutes, but at this moment, reflecting-in-action has caught my attention.

The second kind of reflection, which Schön (1983) calls "reflection-on-action," occurs some time after a teaching engagement is over. It may be following the completion of a course, as part of a formal review, in preparation for a presentation or workshop, or in a moment's thought. This is an opportunity to look at a whole session and perhaps frame it within the context of what came before and what should come next, to draw more systematically on the "objects" of reflection. Reflection-on-action is a broader, more thorough assessment than is possible when one responds to immediate stimuli.

Mark: Was that the most important, that is, useful to the students, activity to be doing at the time? Did I give too much or not enough detail in my explanation? Did I pay attention to what I thought I learned from the last time I did this class? Did I overwhelm them with information, with the enormity of the psychological-emotional and physical challenges of producing experiential learning essays? Was I too picky in comments and feedback? Were my comments and feedback clear? In short, I second-guess myself on just about everything—*or at least wonder about it.*

Although many adult educators demand much of themselves and may gravitate to questions about "what went wrong," the heart of reflection-on-action is the room it gives for *wondering*, for the curiosity that builds on the impulse to learn more and to look at one's practice with sustained attention, that is, to contemplate. Though reexamining difficult or awkward moments may draw attention to figuring out what to do better next time, with time and experience, apparent disasters, successes, and the everyday routines can all be the triggers for reflection.

From the vantage point of longer-term reflection-on-action, some of the bigger patterns can emerge that might not have been evident in the day-to-day or week-to-week "noise" of the earlier reflections. With commitments to problem finding and solving, seeking understanding, and deliberate action (Merriam & Caffarella, 1999, p. 233), ongoing reflection provides the same bridge between experiences and meaningful learning that teaching with developmental intention offers. As Mentkowski and Associates (2000) note, reflection "is the place . . . where we can find the connections between our operational assumptions and our behaviors, decisions, and plans; where we can construct our identities and integrate different frameworks of practice" (p. 265).

The Metacontext

We have left to last one other object of reflection—*values*—because it is pivotal in a way different from the others. *What beliefs do I hold above all others?*

Although we certainly advocate educators' reflective practice being guided by whatever values they hold dear, we also wish to elevate a value that is embedded in one of the premises of this book. Adult educators enter into adults' lives and thus can have an impact on adults' development. In reflecting on this premise, we three recognize that we converge around an *ethic of care*—a value that guides each of us in our practices.

The emergence of a relational "ethic of care" in place of an individualistic "ethic of justice" may be traced to Jean Baker Miller's call for a "new psychology" based on women's experience, and to Carol Gilligan's description of hearing in women's ethical decision-making a qualitatively different approach than that which had until then been based on men's experiences. (This is further explored in Appendix C.)

Gilligan's (1982) observations led to a picture of moral development arising from conflicting responsibilities rather than from competing rights. What this means for learning is that understanding may also emerge through contextual and narrative ways of thinking and not only formal and abstract lines of reasoning. Activity arising from a predominant value of care requires an understanding of responsibility and relationships; to contrast, practices that center on fairness demand an understanding of rights and rules.

As we consider what has shaped another premise of this book—development of the individual is a worthy aim of adult education—it becomes clearer that this grows out of a belief in the importance of relationship to the emergence of the self and the value of basing important decisions in the arms of care. When we focus on what our *relationships* with learners ask of us, our professional identity is shaped by values different from those operative when we focus only on our obligations to a body of knowledge or organizational goals. But rather than experience these as "either-or" propositions, the relationship between these values becomes yet another object of reflection.

The reflective comments of the contributors in Part Two remind us that *"Good teaching cannot be reduced to technique; good teaching comes from the identity and integrity of the teacher"* (Palmer, 1998, p. 10, original emphases). *Integrity,* as Kolb (1988) sees it, is how one integrates the challenges of work (teaching) with the values to which one ascribes. Because the choices are many and personal, there is no singular formula for creating or becoming a "good teacher or trainer." We believe, however, that adult learners are more likely to adopt deep approaches to learning when they engage with educators who are authentic in aligning the various "objects of reflection" from behaviors through integrity.

Such alignment may result in development of one's authentic voice as an educator. "The discovery, honoring, and expression of an authentic voice," says Brookfield (1995), "are genuinely transformative processes" (p. 47). We strive to engender those processes in ourselves as well as our students.

CHAPTER THIRTEEN

ACCEPTING THE CHALLENGES
OF GROWTH

*When we no longer consider learning to be primarily the acquisition of knowledge,
we can no longer view teaching as the bestowal of it. If learning is about
growth and growth requires trust, then teaching is about engendering trust,
about nurturance—caring for growth.*

—LAURENT A. DALOZ (1986)

*Constructivist, active, and experiential forms of teaching and learning,
marked by high levels of uncertainty, ambiguity, contradiction, and paradox,
invite expressions of soul.*

—DIRKX (1997)

Though we have not couched it in just these terms, most of this book has been about providing the two factors essential to developmental growth: support and challenge. *Support,* in its broadest sense, is confirmation of the learner and his or her current efforts. It includes, for example, positive feedback of all kinds, clear and explicit communications and directions, affirmation of what the learner already knows, and response to the learner's perceived needs. *Challenge,* in its broadest sense, is encouragement to stretch beyond what is currently familiar and comfortable in order to achieve some new level of competence. It focuses on what remains to be done, rather than what is already accomplished. It may involve ambiguities, with the intention that the learner take a more active role in decision making. Educators may also, after appropriate consideration, challenge adults by *not* responding to certain of their expressed desires.

Most of the strategies in Part Two include supportive and challenging elements. Many of the training and teaching matters discussed in Chapter Eleven also accomplish both ends, such as sharing power and authority, encouraging self-direction, using experience as a basis for learning, and so on. We now turn to an aspect of practice not widely described in the literature of learning, though it is well represented in the literature of development: the affective dimension of growth and change and the role of the educator in what can be an emotionally charged context. The following experience of a woman in her mid-thirties is unusual only in the clarity of her articulation:

There was a time where the change was so intensive, that . . . it was going faster than I was . . . I didn't know where I was, who I was or—it's as if I was somebody who was and was trying to be somebody else—but didn't know who that other person was going to be at the end of the tunnel, and in between all of that, I wasn't anyone, myself.

As Bridges (1980) describes it, before people can transform, before they get to new beginnings, they must first endure endings, which are marked by disengagement, disidentification, disenchantment, and disorientation. If, as educators, we commit ourselves to facilitating learners' development, we may need to acknowledge that the potential for growth is often matched by a potential for disorientation. Changes of the kind described in Chapter Three of this book can mean ruptures in learners' home lives, estrangement from their communities, and alienation in their workplaces. If a learner's mate, friends, or coworkers are vested in particular ways of viewing the world, they may find it unsettling, at best, and threatening, at worst, to be challenged to see things from multiple perspectives. For that matter, learners and those who form their psychological and cultural surround may come to resent the educator who has pulled out from under them the carefully woven rug of their certainties. We may also need to be sensitive to the fact that many adult learners are facing a "double-whammy"; rather than resisting the individual's change, some modern organizations are demanding it—meanwhile their employees are adrift in the chaos of relentless organizational transition and potential loss of their livelihood.

Furthermore, certain learners or groups of learners are particularly at risk for feeling that they are committing what Brookfield (1990a) calls "cultural suicide" (p. 153). Learners with roots in communities based on political or religious fundamentalism, or in cultures where group norms are more highly valued than individualism, may be especially vulnerable. In addition, women who have focused most of their attention and care on others may feel great ambivalence about being in a position where they are required to focus care and attention (and even, perhaps, scarce family resources) on themselves. They may also face resentment and hostility from those who were formerly the primary focus of their attention. As one twenty-eight-year-old woman said, after dropping out of an educational program:

I was trying to work full time, still be the Room Mother, and still drive the kids to school, and be there on time, and feed the dog, and make sure that dinner was on the table at five o'clock. . . . There was a lot of complaining that there had to be babysitting done and I wasn't earning money at it—at what I was making him babysat for. . . . Yet when I would cry and break down and go "why aren't you supporting me?" [he'd say] "Oh yes, I still love you, yes" and "I will" and "I'm sorry" . . . Yeah, all of a sudden I wasn't giving him all the attention that he needed and that he required.

Negative reactions can come in many unexpected ways. A forty-year-old man observed that his mother focused on his new willingness to speak his mind.

I guess before I was more quiet. And as time went along she kept telling me or kept asking me, "What's going on with you? Shut up!" [Laughter.]. . . . If something bugs me, [I] speak out now. Before, I held it inside. It kinda carried over to my daughter. I told her the same thing. "If something bugs you, say it. Don't hold it inside." So my mom—I think this is one thing that bugs my mom. Seems like as time goes along, I tend to speak out more.

Though they may be uncomfortable at the discomfort of those around them, many learners in these circumstances nevertheless feel good about learning to trust themselves and their own ideas in a new way. A thirty-six-year-old woman changed careers and also changed the way she presented herself to others.

I know who I am now. . . . There's no need for me to keep trying to [to conform]. That's one thing I would have done before: "OK, maybe if I were thinner, or if I looked like this, *or [wore] my hair like* that, *maybe then—" But now this is who I am. . . . I don't feel the need to put down who I am, and a lot of times [in the past] I would—you know, how bright I was, or how metaphysical that I am. I would shut a lot of that down . . . in order to make [others] feel comfortable.*

As encouraging as it is for educators to hear these reports of self-discovery and increased self-confidence, it is important not to lose sight of the fact that such growth is rarely achieved without cost. Daloz (1986) claims that an educator who provides appropriate support through these upheavals is a *mentor* and, furthermore, that the "capacity to provide emotional support when it is needed are hallmarks that distinguish the good mentor from the mediocre teacher" (p. 33).

Role of the Mentor

The workplace has long valued mentors. They are likely to be senior or seasoned colleagues who know the ropes, see the bigger picture, and understand the culture of the organization. They care about their protégés' progress and sometimes intend that their protégés succeed to their place at some future time. Educational mentors occupy much the same niche. Given the ages of adult learners, educational mentors may not literally be senior, but they are seasoned in the ways of educational environments and expectations. They understand the culture of learning and care about their learners' progress. They may also hope that their learners will take their place at some future time, not necessarily in their roles as educators, but in their roles as facilitators of others' development and growth.

There are no simple directions for this kind of mentoring—that is, attending to and caring for another's experience of growth. The closest thing educators have to a "text" on this subject is Daloz's *Mentor: Guiding the Journey of Adult Learners* (1999). In descriptions that reveal the "special kind of empathy" (Kegan, 1982) that can help another human being toward a new way of perceiving and understanding, Daloz characterizes a mentor as someone who supports others in "progressively taking apart and putting together the structures that give [their] lives meaning" (1999, p. 243). His graceful accounts of his work with learners provide memorable models of caring for growth.

As we indicated earlier, the essence of mentorship is a certain kind of relationship. Based on reflection on our most deeply held values about learning, we three have, over time, developed metaphors that inform our way of thinking about the kind of relationship we seek to create with adult learners.

KATHLEEN: The image that works for me is *journeyman architect*. I think of a journeyman as someone who teaches by example, and in this way guides the less experienced apprentice toward developing his or her own way of working at their craft. An architect is also someone who designs for construction; in this instance, the construction is meaning. So my goal for an *educator-as-journeyman architect* is to help learners develop the skills, criteria, and vision to see patterns, recognize flaws, and construct meaning that is sturdy, flexible, and esthetically pleasing. Journeymen see themselves not as "masters," but as fellow travelers on a life-long journey of self-improvement, working always toward bettering their own and others' understanding and execution of their craft.

MORRY: As I've thought about the best teachers I've experienced and those I've learned the most from, my clearest insight is that I left each with a clear sense of understanding—only to return at some later point to an idea or subject or an insight into myself that I connect with them to realize my understanding then was but a wonderful illusion that provided a point of departure for continued learning. If people who have worked with me look back at some point in the course of revisiting and reconstructing their knowledge with an appreciative recognition of their illusion of understanding while learning with me, I've succeeded. An "illusionist." And if I can find the ways for each student to come to that point then I must be a bit of a "chameleon" as well to have adapted to their learning.

CATHERINE: I see myself as a guide on someone else's journey. The destination point is theirs to set and I do my best to help them get there, though sometimes we end up at a different place than either of us anticipated. When we are exploring relatively uncharted territory, I assist in navigating the unfamiliar landscape; when the path is more familiar, I may challenge the journeyer to explore a new byway. My trustiest navigational instrument is my store of learning from guiding hundreds of fellow travelers on similar quests, aided also by theories and models from adult learning and development.

Mentor as Guide

Daloz (1999) also relies on the image of mentor as guide. Though some people succeed in growing and changing without such a guide, it is a much lonelier and more difficult process, and like any challenging journey undertaken alone, more prone to missteps, injury, and losing one's way. Drawing further on this metaphor, we will provide some practical suggestions for being a more effective mentor:

Prepare the Learner Adequately for the Journey. A guide is not a travel agent. Setting out on a new and challenging trail is more than just sun and fun; there may be unexpected detours and delays and some hard trekking where the goal seems to recede rather than come closer. A good guide acknowledges rather than downplays the difficulties of the journey while keeping up the traveler's enthusiasm, even when the going gets tough. Guides can also attest to the magnificent view at trail's end. This is encouraging, because the mountain looks tallest from the bottom, and most people are not willing to start out on a challenging quest that may not be worth the effort they will have had to expend.

Blaze the Trail. A guide outlines several possible pathways toward the learner's goals and then helps him or her mark the stages as they are accomplished. As one woman in her late thirties observed about a mentor's acknowledgement:

Knowing that there [were] people that kind of felt what I was doing was OK [was important to me]. You know, we all look for validation. We say we don't but we all do. When you're young, you get it from your parents all the time, but you think, "Well, they['re] my parents. They're my family, so they gotta say that kind of stuff." When you get it from the outside world, "It's ok you did this. It's ok what you did."—That was real important for me.

Provide a Map. Understanding their process of change and growth supports learners through the emotional ups and downs. Adults who have some familiarity with models of development are much more likely to take charge of their process, rather than be overwhelmed by unexpected, unexplained feelings. When the course content lends itself to such exploration, introduction of development theories as a springboard to self-reflection can greatly facilitate adults' process of growth (Taylor 1995b), as these learners' observations suggest:

I've learned that the people I have relationships with are also going through changes in their lives. This class made me realize it is "normal" to be afraid of changes and that my transitional "stuck" stages are a pivot for a new change.

All the models of development have meaning for me. I feel like I now have a guidebook that will help me during my bouts of despair. The good news is that we really do reinvent ourselves by totally dismantling our lives, discarding the pieces that don't work, keeping the ones that do and putting new pieces in place that create the new, rebuilt, self.

Looking at this model, I can easily see how my life pattern followed a very typical, normal course as I matured through life. To me, however, it seemed anything but normal as each stage was experienced. As I lived through each stage, I believed that my experiences were unique. This made me feel quite alone at the time. . . . [W]hy didn't I hear about [these theories] while I was going through it? Could I have changed the course of these events if I had been better informed?

Several activities in this book include some focus on understanding one's process of growth. See, for example, Chris Michael's "Developing Students' Edu-Autobiographies" (p. 74), Carolyn Clark and Deborah Kilgore's "Educational Autobiographies" (p. 69); also Mary Belenky's "Claiming the Powers of Voice and Mind" (p. 247), Laura Heid's "Reflecting on One's Beliefs and Values and Responding to Differences in Others" (p. 267), and Kathleen Taylor's "Emerging Life Patterns" (p. 261). Parts of these exercises could be worked into various courses or training sessions. Furthermore, many adult-focused programs include orientation sessions in which a block of time could be devoted to examining adults' developmental growth patterns. Ideally this would be interactive, since adults are reassured to know that they are not alone in experiencing the challenges of growth: "Learning conversations which take place about a person's construct system (whether it be in a group, on a one-to-one basis . . . , or in a reflective mode, alone) . . . [are] an important part in allowing them to change (i.e. to learn)" (Candy, 1982, p. 64). In any case, articles or other information about development could be included in almost any course or training handouts.

Allow the Learner to Set the Pace. However much we, as educators, may value development, not everyone can or should follow our lead. For some, the costs of growth are too dear (Daloz, 1988). It is therefore up to the learner to decide when or whether to move forward, developmentally speaking. It may be frustrating to the guide if the goals change en route or if the learner stops just before the summit, but a good guide knows that the learner whose decision has been honored may return to try again some other day.

Provide a Lifeline. The guide may be the only person in the learner's environment who fully understands the challenges of examining cherished assumptions, questioning values, and establishing new behaviors and beliefs. It is therefore important to be available and to listen without judgment or advice to the emotional content of the learner's experience. When the learner stumbles and threatens to fall, a lifeline can save the situation.

Colleagues new to this concept of mentoring sometimes ask us if these are appropriate concerns for educators: Aren't anxieties about loss of one's sense of self or fear of change the domain of a therapist or counselor? As we see it, if we educate with developmental intentions, we need also to provide support for the changes that may ensue. At the very least, this means acknowledging the learner's feelings—whether despair or exultation—in an authentic manner.

> KATHLEEN: Given the congruity between perspective change as described in the literature of adult learning and transformation as described in the literature of adult development, some outcomes of educating with developmental intentions may be comparable to those accomplished in psychological therapy. Even so, educators should not attempt to "do therapy" (because that is not our training, or if it is, that is not our responsibility when we are in our roles as teachers or trainers). However, if adults in our classes or workshops happen to make the kinds of self-discoveries that would ordinarily happen in therapy—heck, that's not *our* fault!

Support and Challenge. Paradoxically, perhaps, learners who receive this high level of mentoring and support often grow beyond needing it. In recounting changes in her anxiety about her ability to learn, a former woman executive in her mid-thirties described her experience of growth toward self-agency and self-authorship:

[A] significant change [in me] . . . was that I was looking less and less toward others and external resources to make me feel OK about myself. What happened was, I started to be able to reinforce myself and that was a wonderful change for me. . . . I've constantly been working for external acknowledgment [but] . . . I started to get internal acknowl-

edgement and was less reliant on others. . . . I think what mainly impacted on these changes was the support . . . that who I was, was OK. The belief in me that I could do it.

But support is only half the story. Essential though it may be, too much support is enervating. Developmental growth also requires challenge. People need to be pushed, prodded, and encouraged past the point that feels comfortable and safe. Unfortunately, many educational environments are long on challenge and short on the necessary balance between the two. For example, high expectations are appropriately challenging when the environment *also* provides adequate guidance toward meeting those expectations. Informing learners that they have not yet met course or workshop objectives is appropriately challenging if they are *also* acknowledged for their good work and supported toward improvement. In other words, supporting growth does not mean giving up standards. The challenge to do better quality work is important, but the *combination* of support and challenge is known to be *most* effective in supporting development. Critical feedback is not a problem if the educator has also focused on what the learner did right. "*Emphasize positive movement,*" Daloz (1986) emphasizes, "underline it, restate it, praise it" (p. 127).

It may be difficult for an educator to realize the enormity of asking learners to reexamine their core values and beliefs. Facing down established ways of thinking is a developmental *challenge* that shakes an individual's sense of self. As we play devil's advocate or ask learners to engage with both sides of a question where they may have deep emotional attachments to one perspective, we must provide *support* for "dismantling of old structures and construction of new" (Daloz, 1986, p. 150). Before adults can experience a new sense of self and new ways of looking at the world around them, they must give up the sense of self that they have labored since adolescence to construct. We must not underestimate the magnitude of this transformation and the extent of this challenge. "We do not," William More (1974) observes in *Emotions and Adult Learning,* "pay sufficient heed to the loneliness of learning" (p. 108). When someone begins to question the way she has looked at the world, she begins to leave that world. Though this can be an empowering and exhilarating journey, most travelers heading off to some new, unknown land are understandably anxious about what awaits them. The support of the mentor-guide, and of peers who lately trod this path, can be essential.

Three Caveats

This book is about the possibility for teachers and trainers to contribute to the developmental growth of adult learners. This chapter, in particular, describes the importance of a "holding environment" (Kegan, 1992, 1994) to promote transformational, not only informational, learning. However, the first caveat is that we cannot say with certainty that developmental *intentions* will necessarily achieve developmental *outcomes.* Significant change takes time, far more time than brief training courses or individual class sessions can offer, and perhaps even more than an entire program of courses or workshops.

Second, no educator has the right to decide that someone else's worldview should change (Daloz, 1988). We nevertheless hope that this book has clarified the potential benefits of educating in ways that are informed and influenced by development theory.

Third, even if learners do grow in the ways described by the developmental intentions, this increasingly self-authored and empowered version of self may be insufficient in the *postmodern* world. Merriam and Caffarella (1999) point to the "multiple, ever changing, and, some say, fragmented" nature of the self, which is no longer "the unified, integrated, authentic self of modern times" (p. 357). In other words, the changes we are trying to support may be necessary and useful but may not represent all the growth that is desirable. We agree. Nevertheless, we have focused on developmental intentions as described to us by experienced adult educators. They appear to support Kegan's contention that "the central curricular focus for a majority of contemporary adults is still that of mastering the . . . mental burden of *modern* life" (original emphasis, 1994, p. 350). Furthermore, developmental theory suggests that people cannot achieve more sophisticated levels of development until they have successfully traversed all the steps that come before.

A Shared Journey

Acknowledging the importance of development in the lives of adult learners may imply that we need also to recognize ourselves as developing adults. Indeed, we may have to face similar challenges as our learners do, even as we try to facilitate this process for others. In *The Evolving Self,* Robert Kegan (1982) writes: "Who comes into a person's life may be the single greatest factor of influence to what that life becomes" (p. 19). With few exceptions, when educators come into their learners' lives, these adults are at the threshold of change. To facilitate that change may ultimately require that we move toward our learners, as persons on an equal footing, open to the possibility that we will learn as much as they do.

For those of us accustomed to literature framed by the positivist paradigm, it can be oddly disconcerting to see professional articles, chapters, and even whole books on "spirit" and "soul." But on closer inspection, we may find they speak to aspects of education for development that are not otherwise addressed. John

Dirkx (1997), for example, describes the reemergence of *mythos* after centuries in which *logos* was in the ascendant. "Learning through soul," he suggests, "giv[es] voice in a deep and powerful way to imaginative and poetic expressions of self and the world" (p. 80). Harrison Owen, who facilitates transformational change in organizations, also points to the contextual nature of *mythos* as the lens through which we perceive "reality" and underscores the "moving quality of the human Spirit as it seeks to become whatever it was supposed to be" (1987, p. 11). Parker Palmer (1990) reflects on spirituality and leadership and describes aspects of facilitating another's inner work, which could well be a synonym for developmental growth. In *Learning as a Way of Being*, Peter Vaill (1996) suggests that "genuine spirituality . . . is the willingness to enter into a process of dialogue about meaning" (p. 180).

If, as we have claimed in this book, the fundamental human need to make meaning is the well-spring of development, we may also have to accept that the quality of change we encourage—change in one's very way of being in the world—requires not only cleverly constructed exercises, opportunities for reflection, and encouragement to make one's own meaning, but an act of transcendence. As we come into the lives of adult learners, our best and greatest influence may be our willingness to travel with them on that journey.

APPENDIX A
AN EXPERIENTIAL THEORY
OF DEVELOPMENT

The attributes of meaning-making, an essential element of adults' development, emerge in a progressively higher-order process that David Kolb refers to as "integrative development." His model of development derives from his theory of experiential learning.

Kolb (1984) synthesized three models of learning—from Lewin, Dewey, and Piaget—recognizing that all three described learning as emerging from the resolution of conflicting ways of dealing with the world. For Lewin, the conflicts are between experiencing something concretely and conceptualizing abstractly, and between observing and acting; for Dewey, the conflict is between the "impulse that gives ideas their moving force" (1938/1963, p. 35) and reason that gives direction to desires; in Piaget's view, it is the tension between accommodating ideas to an external world and assimilating experience into an individual's existing conceptual structures that drives experiential learning and cognitive development.

Kolb's interpretation of these models as having dialectic relationships is the foundation for his theory of experiential learning. The higher-order processes that emerge when these conflicting orientations to learning confront each other drives an ongoing, internal, metaphorical dialogue with oneself. Expanding on the premise that learning is the process by which "knowing" is converted to knowledge, Kolb suggested that "learning is . . . the process whereby development occurs" (p. 132)—a relatively novel connection in the literature of development at the time.

Kolb used a dialectic lens to shape an experiential theory of development, focusing on the transactions between internal characteristics of personal knowledge and external circumstances of social knowledge and codes. His image of the developing individual is one of a reflective person acting on the world in order to change it; learning is a proactive adaptation to the repeated transactions in which one participates throughout life.

Dialectical processes are a cornerstone of Kolb's ideas; they also serve as a useful, interpretive lens for other models and theories we draw on in this book. As we noted earlier, Daloz, Keen, Keen, and Parks (1996) use the term "dialectical thought" as the "ability to recognize and work effectively with contradictions, either by resisting closure or by reframing one's response in order to compose a more inclusive synthesis." Because knowledge is not static and seems to grow out of our interactions with the world around us, our adaptation through viable representations of reality is a process that repeats itself over and over. This is a theme through much of the literature on meaning-making and adult development, including Kolb's work.

Kolb's research led him to theorize that development is marked by progressive and increasing differentiation accompanied by hierarchic integration of functioning. The "backing and forthing" between differentiation and interaction grows up out of the dialectics of experiential learning. In language similar to that used by developmental biologists, Kolb suggests that differentiation is marked by an increasing complexity of categories of experience along with a decreasing interdependence of these facets of experience. As an infant develops, undifferentiated excitement is refined first to distress and delight and then to fear, disgust, anxiety, joy, affection, and other emotions (Bridges, 1932, as cited by Kolb, 1984).

Differentiation leads to increasing complexity that we organize through integrative processes. These may include levels of rules from the simple (good versus bad) to the interpretive, which generate a multiplicity of alternative possibilities. Higher levels of integration generate interrelationships among our experiences and concepts, making complexity, and facility with it, qualities of development.

The dual processes of differentiation and integration are another set of paired responses that we can understand as a dialectic that rises and resolves repeatedly through life. Kolb's designation of four dimensions of experiential learning—affective complexity, perceptual complexity, symbolic complexity, and behavioral complexity—offer markers to pay attention to as we observe, encourage, or simply try to understand the evolving meaning-making process. Each dimension differentiates—toward greater ranges of emotions, increased awareness and capacity to "see," more sophisticated conceptualization schemes, and a more refined repertoire of behaviors—as the individual interacts with challenges of life and the environment. The integration of these four learning modes marks the course of development. And the capacity for meaning-making shifts from a state of immersion in the world around the individual toward a self that is first marked by what it knows and then by how it transacts with the world and draws on itself to adapt and transform it.

The reiterative application of the four modes of learning can help to explain progressions of development, characterize the nature of individual differences and variation in meaning making, and offer a basis for predicting what we may expect of ourselves and others. Kolb (1984) suggests that progress along any one of the "four dimensions can occur with relative independence from the others" (p. 140). Emotional maturity—a state of differentiated feelings, integrated by both internal and external guides of social appropriateness and personal effectiveness—can emerge without a parallel level of sophistication of cognitive capabilities. Development in one mode, however, tends to contribute to development of the others. The capacity to hold the complexities, resolve the multiple tensions and contributions that each makes to the self, and integrate the dialectic conflicts that arise among the four dimensions marks the developing adults' movement toward proactive adaptation, growth, and creativity.

The differences in the states of differentiation and integration of each dimension as well as among the four seem to influence how individual adults translate their experiences into meaning and action. As though they were spotlights on experiences, what one pays attention to, as well as interprets, may be highlighted by the level of development and integration of the four dimensions of learning. And, if we can assess the relative states of development of each, it can point to areas one might anticipate greatest internal conflict.

The interrelationships among experiences and these dimensions of learning define the person and characterize the complexity with which he or she constructs knowledge and appreciates the nature of life itself. Kolb extends his theory of development to the nature of consciousness and the evolution of one's stance toward life contexts. As we develop in adulthood, we continue to raise the stakes of the dialectic process, seeking to resolve yet even higher-order conflicts between the meanings we make and the relevance of our choices in real-life circumstances, and between the value judgments that determine what we explore or pay attention to and what we know about realities. His theory of development ultimately sets the pinnacle of development as integrity—the unity of goals, ideas, purpose, and communication (Bennis, 1981–1982). "Integrity as a way of knowing embraces the future and the unknown . . . to stand at the interface between social knowledge and the ever-novel predicaments and dilemmas we find ourselves in . . . [to] make some new contribution to the data bank of social knowledge for generations to come"

(Kolb, 1984, p. 225). For this driver of development, his theory holds, we turn to courage, love, wisdom, and justice to resolve the highest-order dialectics of life.

APPENDIX B

CONSTRUCTIVE-DEVELOPMENTAL
THEORIES

Development is one way of describing the processes of change and growth that we experience throughout our lifetimes. Constructive-development theories posit that *how we know is who we are.* In this group of theories, the "rules" or frameworks that guide us as we make meaning change throughout our lives. We will examine three theories of particular importance to educators of adults: Perry's cognitively oriented scheme (1970), strategies for *Women's Ways of Knowing* (Belenky, Clinchy, Goldberger, & Tarule, 1986), and Kegan's "transformation of consciousness" (1994).

The Perry Scheme

Nearly forty years ago, William Perry studied changes in patterns (or *forms*) of thinking and reasoning as people move from late adolescence into adulthood. Though his research sample was drawn from middle-upper class, white male undergraduates at Harvard, his findings are still considered landmark research and continue to be widely cited by psychologists and educators. Many mark his as the first constructive-developmental analysis of *adult* thinking. Perry's "scheme" describes movement through a sequence of nine steps or stages in thinking and values-based decision making (Exhibit B.1).

Exhibit B.1. Perry's Model of Cognitive and Ethical Development.

Dualism modified	Position 1	Authorities know, and if we work hard, read every word, and learn Right Answers, all will be well.
	Transition	But what about those Others I hear about? And different opinions? And Uncertainties? Some of our own Authorities disagree with each other and don't seem to know, and some give us problems instead of Answers.
	Position 2	True Authorities must be Right; the others are frauds. We remain Right. Others must be different and Wrong. Good Authorities give us problems so we can learn to find the Right Answer by our own independent thought.
	Transition	But even Good Authorities admit they don't know all the answers *yet!*
	Position 3	Then some uncertainties and different opinions are real and legitimate *temporarily,* even for Authorities. They're working on them to get to the Truth.
	Transition	But there are so *many* things they don't know the Answers to! And they won't for a long time.
	Position 4a	Where Authorities don't know the Right Answers, everyone has a right to his own opinion; no one is wrong!
Relativism discovered	Transition *(and/or)*	But some of my friends ask me to support my opinions with facts and reasons.
	Transition	Then what right have They to grade us? About what?
	Position 4b	In certain courses Authorities are not asking for the Right Answer; They want us to *think* about some things in a certain way, *supporting* opinion with data. That's what they grade us on.
	Transition	But this "way" seems to *work* in most courses, and even outside them.
	Position 5	Then *all* thinking must be like this, even for Them. Everything is relative but not equally valid. You have to understand how each context works. Theories are not Truth but metaphors to interpret data with. You have to think about your thinking.
	Transition	But if everything is relative, am I relative too? How can I know I'm making the Right Choice?
Commitments in Relativism developed	Position 6	I see I'm going to have to make my own decisions in an uncertain world with no one to tell me I'm Right.
	Transition	I'm lost if I don't. When I decide on my career (or marriage or values) everything will straighten out.
	Position 7	Well, I've made my first Commitment!
	Transition	Why didn't that settle everything?
	Position 8	I've made several commitments. I've got to balance them—how many, how deep? How certain, how tentative?
	Transition	Things are getting contradictory. I can't make logical sense out of life's dilemmas.
	Position 9	This is how life will be. I must be wholehearted while tentative, fight for my values yet respect others, believe my deepest values right yet be ready to learn. I see that I shall be retracing this whole journey over and over— but, I hope, more wisely.

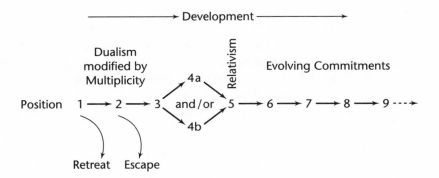

Dualism	Division of meaning into two realms—Good versus Bad, Right versus Wrong, We versus They, All that is not Success is Failure, and the like. Right Answers exist *somewhere* for every problem, and Authorities know them. Right Answers are to be memorized by hard work. Knowledge is quantitative. Agency is experienced as "out there" in Authority, test scores, the Right job.
Multiplicity	Diversity of opinion and values is recognized as legitimate in areas where right answers are not yet known. Opinions remain atomistic without pattern or system. No judgments can be made among them so "everyone has a right to his own opinion; none can be called wrong."
Relativism	Diversity of opinion, values, and judgment derived from coherent sources, evidence, logics, systems, and patterns allowing for analysis and comparison. Some opinions may be found worthless, while there will remain matters about which reasonable people will reasonably disagree. Knowledge is qualitative, dependent on contexts.
Commitment (uppercase C)	An affirmation, choice, or decision (career, values, politics, personal relationship) made in the awareness of Relativism (distinct from lowercase *c* of commitments never questioned). Agency is experienced as within the individual.
Temporizing	Postponement of movement for a year or more.
Escape	Alienation, abandonment of responsibility. Exploitation of Multiplicity and Relativism for avoidance of Commitment.
Retreat	Avoidance of complexity and ambivalence by regression to Dualism colored by hatred of otherness.

Source: Perry, 1981. Used by permission.

The scheme can be divided into three over-arching categories: dualism, multiplicity-relativism, and commitment. Those initially embedded in dualistic positions see the world in dichotomous, absolutist terms: right-wrong, black-white, we-they. Teachers are viewed as Authorities who have Answers, and students as responsible to figure out which answers teachers are "looking for."

As they progress, dualists increasingly acknowledge the possibility of more than one perspective, though they are not yet able to deal with the potential conflicts or contradictions between opposing points of view. They may be able to maintain what they perceive as clarity about the rightness of solutions to mathematics or computer problems, for example, but having to interpret poems or function in a leaderless team may open the floodgates of doubt. Some multiplists regard such assignments as an elaborate ruse, designed to encourage them to figure out "what They (teachers/authorities) really want." Others become frustrated with what they see as insufficient guidance toward the desired outcome ("Why don't They tell us what They want?"), and question the fairness of authorities' evaluations under these circumstances.

When the dam finally breaks, the realization that there can be more than one answer to most questions washes away the clarity of dualism. However, the multiplist has little sense of how to discriminate among what now appears to be an almost infinite array of choices, or even that such discrimination is possible. The anthem of this position is, "Everyone is entitled to his own opinion." By taking this stance, the individual remains protected from having to engage with the conflicts or contradictions that would otherwise ensue.

Authorities are no longer perceived as having Answers, but as having developed criteria that support them in discrimination among academic or work products. However, students and employees who study these criteria so that they will do better when evaluated initially perceive that they are "doing what They want" and do not yet understand how these criteria relate to the ongoing construction of knowledge.

The next move more firmly establishes the inherent grayness of what was formerly a black-and-white world; there may still be a few areas in which authority and answers prevail, but generally, the move to relativism acknowledges that individual perspectives and beliefs affect nearly all perceptions and decisions. With further development, the individual recognizes that every decision is not as good as every other, and that some ideas will have to be embraced and others rejected. This becomes a move to commitment within relativism, a statement of belief and purpose based not on authority or certainty, but tentative affirmation of choices made and choices forgone. These individuals must confront contradictions in ideas and values, within themselves and between themselves and others. They must endeavor to reframe and, perhaps, to reconcile multiple perspectives, and if that cannot happen, to accept complexity and contradiction with a sense not of resignation, but of possibility.

In the final stages of the scheme, an individual realizes the enormity of the challenge and accepts this responsibility as inherent to the human process: to make life decisions without any certainty that they are right, commit to ideas and act on those commitments, and yet be open to reexamining them at some future time.

Perry also identified departures from this progression. Some students find multiplicity too unsettling and *retreat* to the simpler world of duality. This may be expressed as rebellion against authorities' demands or as reactionism and self-righteous condemnation of all who acknowledge the possibility of other perspectives.

Escape is another departure. These individuals accept multiplicity-relativism but deny or reject the need also for commitment: Everything is relative; anything goes. They may make effective arguments for any value-based decision, but only as an intellectual exercise, not as a statement of commitment or as a spur to action.

Women's Ways of Knowing

Perry's research had focused on young, privileged male undergraduates. Four women psychologists subsequently undertook a similar study with women of diverse backgrounds in school and community settings. The *Women's Ways of Knowing* (WWK) model originally consisted of five *positions*, rather than *stages*, since the authors were reluctant to declare an unvarying, linear progression (Belenky, Clinchy, Goldberger, & Tarule, 1986). In the decade following publication of that work, they reframed the positions as *strategies for knowing* (1996). More fully developed individuals have a broader repertoire of knowing strategies to choose among in response to different situations; those with less developed capacities have fewer options, even in situations that warrant more flexible response. The five positions or strategies are *silence, received knowing, subjective knowing, procedural knowing*, and *constructed knowing* (see Exhibit B.2).

Although this model parallels Perry's in many respects, significant differences can be noted. In both models, development involves increasingly complex ways of viewing oneself and the world, and both describe movement from depending on knowledge that someone else constructs to including oneself as a co-constructor of knowledge. However, the young men in Perry's research tended to describe knowing and learning in terms of "looking" and "seeing," whereas women in the WWK study tended to use metaphors of "hearing" and "speaking."

Exhibit B.2. Women's Ways of Knowing.

Silence (knowing-in-action)

Knowledge: Gets knowledge through concrete experience, not words.
Mind: Sees self as "deaf and dumb" with little ability to think.
Mode: Survives by obedience to powerful, punitive Authority.
Voice: Little awareness of power of language for sharing thoughts, insights, and so on.

Received knowing

Knowledge: Knowledge received from Authorities.
Mind: Sees self as capable/efficient learner; soaks up information.
Mode: Good listener; remembers and reproduces knowledge; seeks/invents strategies for remembering.
Voice: Intent on listening; seldom speaks up or gives opinions.

Subjective knowing

Knowledge: Springs from inner sources; legitimate ideas need to feel right; analysis may destroy knowledge.
Mind: Own opinions are unique, valued; fascinated with exploring different points of view; not concerned about correspondence between own truth and external reality.
Mode: Listens to inner voice for the truth that's right for her.
Voice: Speaks from her feelings/experience with heart; journals; listens, needs others to listen, without judging.

Procedural knowing

Knowledge: Recognizes different frameworks, realms of knowledge; realizes positive role of analysis, other procedures for evaluating, creating knowledge.
Mind: Aims to see world as it "really is"—suspicious of unexamined subjective knowledge.
Mode:
(Separate): Logic, analysis, debate.
(Connected): Empathy, collaboration, careful listening.
Voice:
(Separate): Aims for accuracy, precision; modulates voice to fit standards of logic or discipline.
(Connected): Aims for dialogue where self and others are clearly and accurately understood, even where different.

Constructed knowing

Knowledge: Integrates strengths of previous positions; systems of thought can be examined, shaped, and shared.
Mind: Full two-way dialogue with both heart and mind: seeks truth through questioning and dialogue.
Mode: Integration of separate and connected modes.
Voice: Adept at marshaling/critiquing arguments as well as empathic listening and understanding; speaks/listens with confidence, balance, and care.

Source: Stanton (1996). Used by permission.

This important distinction appears to focus on the potential distance between the knower and the known. Seeing is best done by stepping back to get the whole picture or to see things "objectively." Speaking and listening, by contrast, require being close enough to hear another's voice, and suggest more interaction. Furthermore, having a "voice"—knowing one has worthwhile ideas and the right to express them—and being able to speak out, speak up, and speak for oneself are related to women's construction of identity and intellect.

The two models also differ with the discovery, in WWK, of the position of *silence*. A silent woman does not believe that she knows anything or has a right to claim any voice. In the WWK research, this occurred only in women who were subject to extreme sex-role stereotyping and isolation. Such women are literally "seen and not heard." They feel dumb, in the sense of both unintelligent and unable to speak; it is hardly surprising that Perry did not find a comparable position in his study of Harvard undergraduates. Though teachers and trainers of adults are not likely to find truly silent women in learning environments, we find the notion of silence useful to describe those who, by virtue of race, class, culture, educational background, and occupational status, are effectively ignored and therefore silenced by the society at large.

However, silence, as Goldberger, Tarule, Clinchy, and Belenky (1996) point out, may be much more complicated than that. Their recent inquiries suggest that in some cultures women's silence may reflect culturally appropriate behavior (for example, Native American cultures). In other instances, it may be the tactical or strategic silence of those who, by virtue of their bicultural identity, must negotiate life in white communities or workplaces (p. 345).

WWK's second strategy, *received knowing,* appears to correspond to dualism in Perry's model. In both instances, the source of knowledge is other people. In Perry's model, these are authorities from whom men expect to get the knowledge that will ultimately turn them into authorities. In the WWK model, received knowers also rely on authorities, but do not have the same expectation of someday becoming authorities. Received knowers turn to everyone else for information and knowledge and tend to conform to the ideas and beliefs of the group. By contrast, those in Perry's early stages are much less concerned with being a member of the group than with identifying with the authority who is leading the parade.

The third strategy, *subjective knowing,* shares characteristics with Perry's multiplists. Both multiplicity and subjective knowing emerge when absolute truth is no longer vested in external authorities. However, when truth becomes a matter of opinion, the multiplist's perspective becomes, "My opinion is as good as yours or anyone's." Subjective knowers, by contrast, discover their "inner voice"—truth that is personal and based on experience. Their perspective becomes, "That may be true for you but it isn't true for me." Some women, in fact, close their ears to ideas that do not emanate from within themselves. Though this seems similar to the dualistic perspective, particularly in terms of the nonengagement with conflicting views, a major difference is the source of authority. For dualists, Authority resides in those whom they hope someday to become. For a subjectivist woman, she is her own authority—without a capital A because she does not conceive of her authority as being Right, only being right for *her.*

The authors of WWK found that received knowers often made the transition to subjectivism after a failure of some masculine authority—for example, a cheating boyfriend, a spouse who did not follow through in some important way. Once received knowers realize they can no longer believe in authority, they begin to sense the "gut feelings" that become the basis of their new subjectivist epistemology.

In Perry's scheme, as people move through multiplicity, they eventually begin to develop criteria for determining which among the many opinions and ideas swirling around them are worthy of commitment. Similarly, when WWK's subjectivists start to learn methods, procedures, and rules of thought that enable them to evaluate ideas from a formally reasoned, rather than simply intuited, perspective, they become procedural knowers.

The fourth strategy, *procedural knowing*, recognizes that different frameworks exist and that there are appropriate methods and criteria for creating and evaluating knowledge. Procedural knowing contains a dialectic in the form of *separate* and *connected* modes of knowing. This quotation captures the essence of *separate* knowing: "I never take anything for granted. I just tend to see the contrary. I like playing devil's advocate, arguing the opposite of what somebody's saying, thinking at exceptions to what the person has said, or thinking of a different train of thought." This quote provides the flavor of *connected* knowing: "When I have an idea about something, and it differs from the way another person is thinking about it, I'll usually try to look at it from that person's point of view, see how they could say that, why they think that they're right, why it makes sense" Belenky, Clinchy, Goldberger, & Tarule, 1986, p. 100).

Both separate and connected knowing are rational approaches but with different frames of reference. In the separate mode, knowing is organized around logic, analysis, and debate, whereas the connected mode emphasizes empathy, collaboration, and careful listening. The "voice" in separate knowing can marshal arguments whereas the connected voice aims for dialogue (Stanton, 1996, p. 31).

In *constructed knowing*, the final strategy, the separate-connected dialectic is resolved as the individual is able to integrate the strengths of the previous positions; she can "hold a full two-way dialogue with both heart and mind" (Stanton, 1996, p. 31) and can seek truth and understanding through questioning-critique and interchange-dialogue. The voice of the constructed knower is firm and empathic; she knows when to speak clearly and with conviction and when to be quiet so that other voices can be listened to and heard.

Those individuals who develop commitment within relativism (Perry) and those who develop as constructed knowers (WWK) recognize that the "rightness" or "correctness" of ideas and actions is a matter of interpretation, and that different situations may require reinterpretation of experience. They also recognize that to live effective, meaningful lives, they have to make choices, take responsibility, resolve conflicts and reconcile contradictions, and commit to certain frameworks for living.

The WWK model offers useful perspectives on the evolution of self in the knowing process: from the muted self in silence to the externally defined and validated self of the received knower to the private and isolated self of the subjective knower to the self of the procedural knower that is either distanced or affiliated to the self of the constructed knower that is at once stable and dynamic. The resolution of the dialectic is seen in the balance that is sought and sustained by the constructed knower.

Moral decision making follows a similar path. In the position of silence, blind obedience is the way to keep out of trouble. Received knowers' moral judgments conform with convention; occasionally, they may give themselves over to the highly nonconventional, such as, for example, a cult leader. Subjective knowers "just know" they are morally correct, whatever anyone else may say. Separate procedural knowers base their morality on impartial rules and laws and an ethic of justice and fairness; connected procedural knowers' morality is based on human circumstance and an ethic of care and mercy. Finally, constructed knowers' moral decisions are motivated by a deep sense of responsibility that translates into caring actions (Kramp & Roth, 1987).

Though we have continued to speak as though Perry's scheme describes only men and WWK describes only women, in fact no such gender-specificity is intended or warranted. Though women may be more *likely* than men to exhibit certain characteristics, this is a cultural phenomenon. Hence, both models are understood to describe men and women as learners and knowers.

Transformation of Consciousness

Robert Kegan's model also describes changes in how people think and know and may be considered a metamodel to Perry's scheme and WWK. Kegan's model is concerned with three things: (1) meaning—that which the human organism organizes, also that which gives significance or purpose; (2) transformation—changing (going beyond, outside of, or on the other side of) form; and (3) consciousness—the state or fact of being mentally aware.

We are, according to Kegan, makers of meaning; indeed, "it is not that a person makes meaning, as much as that the activity of being a person is the activity of meaning-making" (1982, p. 11). From our earliest moments, and continuing throughout life, we seek to make sense of what goes on around and within us. As we learn and grow, however, the process of that sense-making changes; it takes on new, more complex, forms. We do not merely gain knowledge as we mature (the informational explanation for change and growth), but we also know in a different way (the transformational explanation).

Transformation (Latin) or metamorphosis (Greek) is a tricky business, however. Metamorphosis is a change that takes us beyond or outside of the previous form. As we change how we know, we take on a new, larger form of knowing. It is interesting to note that this was a focus of educational philosophy long before psychology, let alone developmental psychology, existed. Newman, for example, in *The Idea of a University,* described "that true enlargement of mind which is the power of viewing things at once as one whole, of referring them severally to their true place in the universal system, of understanding their respective values and determining their mutual dependence" (1852/1898, p. 136).

Each time we know in this larger way, we become aware for the first time of the smaller, less complex but more rigid form that no longer confines (or defines) us. In Kegan's terms, what we were once *subject* to now becomes *object* to us. We cannot take a similar perspective on our current self, because we are subject to that self. Eventually, perhaps, we will once again experience a qualitative shift in our complexity and flexibility of thought, at which point we will be able to see what will then have become our former limitations.

Kegan's model describes five such transformations throughout the life span. The first, the shift in consciousness from infancy to childhood, we will not explore; nor will we examine the fifth, since empirical studies suggest it is still only rarely achieved (1994, p. 195). We will begin with the second shift, from adolescence to young adulthood, as a springboard to a more focused view of the major transformation of adults in modern Western society from third-order to fourth-order consciousness.

The end of adolescence, from a developmental standpoint, occurs when the young person's perspective shifts from self-absorption to absorption of what Kegan calls the "psychological surround"—that is, the young person assimilates the collective voice of those who define what it means to be an adult in that society or community. Exhibit B.3 details this shift.

Exhibit B.3. Second- and Third-Order Consciousness.

Second-Order Consciousness	Third-Order Consciousness
Others (relationships) are seen and valued in terms of what they can provide.	Is in relationship with others who are seen and valued in terms of the connection they represent.
Social contract based on self-interest; maintains own point of view; unempathetic.	Social contract based on mutuality; internalizes others' points of view; empathetic.
Moral and ethical code: "My needs are primary. If I concern myself with your needs, it is only to the extent that they don't conflict with mine. I have no guilt about meeting my needs at your expense."	Moral and ethical code includes guilt and hyperawareness of others' needs, even those unstated or imagined: "I am responsible for your feelings; you are responsible for mine."
Descriptive identity, for example, gender, perhaps family association; the adult concept of identity is meaningless.	Identifies (not necessarily consciously) as member of group, family, culture, race, religion, etc.; also identified by job, relationships, affiliations.

Source: Taylor and Marienau (1997). Used by permission.

From society's perspective, this is an essential transformation—narcissism gives way to empathy, self-interest to mutuality, and amorality to the possibility of guilt. If it does *not* happen, there is increased likelihood of sociopathic attitudes and behaviors (Kegan, 1986). As adult educators, however, we are more focused on the *next* transformation. The young adult, having made this transition to what Kegan calls *traditional* consciousness, goes along for a while—and in some instances for quite a while—blithely unaware that "there is no feeling, no experience, no thought, no perception, independent of a meaning-making context in which it *becomes* a feeling, an experience, a thought, a perception" and that it is our construction of this meaning that makes us who we are, "because we *are* the meaning-making context" (1982, p. 11, original emphasis).

For many adults, learning holds the potential to transform this awareness, or nonawareness. Environments that challenge individuals' deeply held, if invisible beliefs, that bring people into contact with otherwise apparently reasonable people who unaccountably hold views completely different from their own, and that ask them to examine how they know what they think they know—such learning experiences can stretch existing forms of knowing beyond their tensile strength. If this expansion takes place and if there is also enough support to balance the challenge, these adults may develop the larger and more flexible forms of knowing that Kegan identifies as the transformation to fourth-order consciousness (see Exhibit B.4).

Exhibit B.4. Third- and Fourth-Order Consciousness.

Third-Order Consciousness	Fourth-Order Consciousness
In relationship with others; the level of mutuality and empathy approaches fusion; differences are perceived as threatening.	In relationship *to relationships;* can set limits and boundaries; differences respected, even valued.
Values, morals, ethics based on group, family, cultural imperatives; norms, assumptions are invisible and unquestioned.	Has values *about values;* they are perceived as contextual, situational, and constructed; former assumptions can be surfaced, examined, accepted, or rejected.
(Early) "I know what I've heard" (knowledge comes from others; Received Knowing).* (Late) "I know what I know" (knowledge comes from the self; Subjective Knowing).*	Has ideas *about ideas;* explores where knowledge comes from, who is responsible for it, how and by whom it is constructed; "authorizes" knowledge, critically evaluates own and others' ideas.
Identity constructed by and through others; others responsible for own feelings; self responsible for others' feelings and states of mind.	Identity self-constructed; aware of and sensitive to others, but not responsible for others' states of mind or feelings; others not responsible for own.
Looks out through others' eyes.**	Sees self through own eyes; dialogical relationship to self.***

Source: Taylor and Marienau (1997). Used with permission.

*These epistemological positions are further described by Belenky, Clinchy, Goldberger, and Tarule (1986) in their model of *Women's Ways of Knowing.*

**As described by Koller (1982) in *An Unknown Woman: A Journal of Self-Discovery.*

***As described by Basseches (1988) in *Dialectical Thinking and Development.*

This shift echoes aspects of the Perry model, for example, the discovery that one's earlier perceptions were not truth, and that authorities have few, if any, answers. It also echoes *Women's Ways of Knowing*, in the realization that one is responsible to co-construct, or "authorize" knowledge, rather than to absorb it from others or to listen solely to one's "gut feelings." There is even an echo of the relational models, as those who have moved toward the fourth order can engage in *connected autonomy* that honors both their individuality and their need for community and relationship (Taylor, 1999).

APPENDIX C

RELATIONAL MODELS OF DEVELOPMENT AND THE ETHIC OF CARE

Though we have referred only in passing (Chapter Twelve) to relational models of development, they significantly influence our thinking in two ways. First, relational models offer distinct ways to understand adults' experiences and meaning-making processes. Second, they provide a lens through which educators may examine the nature of their professional identity. We juxtapose relational models of development with comments about the ethic of care because of their overlapping values.

Research on women's development suggests that relationships are central to women's sense of self. "The deepest sense of one's being is continuously formed in connection to others and is inextricably tied to relational formation . . . empathic responsiveness in the context of interpersonal mutuality" (Jordan, 1997, p. 15). This theme of *self in relation* is one of the dialectic tensions described in most models as a challenge of development toward an autonomous self. However, many relational models question whether autonomy should be a universal developmental goal, as its history is traced to models of identity development drawn from research with men that was later extrapolated to women (Gilligan, 1982). In relational models, by contrast, connection to others contributes to development of identity. Rather than separation-individuation, developmental growth is described in terms of relationship-differentiation—a dynamic process that encompasses increasing levels of complexity, structure, and articulation within the context of human bonds and attachments (Miller, 1991).

The ethic of care is common to models of relational development and models of moral development. Daloz, Keen, Keen, and Parks (1996) effectively describe the ethic of care as acting for the common good; it is also linked to honoring each person's dignity by acknowledging his or her authentic individuality. The ethic of care and relational models of development both hold that "one becomes whole only when functioning with others" (Merriam & Caffarella, 1999, p. 174). Meaning is derived from how ethical dilemmas are defined and resolved.

Gilligan (1982) observed that women were more likely to identify with an ethic of care than were men, who focused more on an ethic of justice. In the care orientation, moral problems arise from conflicting responsibilities and are resolved contextually. In the justice orientation, moral problems arise from competing rights and are resolved through abstract reasoning. Moral decision making based on care focuses on responsibility and relationships; in contrast, moral decision making based on fairness and justice focuses on rights and rules. Someone operating from an ethic of care and from the "autonomous" level of development in Loevinger and Blasi's (1976) model would be concerned to do *enough*, but not *too much*—to "modulat[e] an excessive sense of responsibility through the recognition that other people have responsibility for their own destiny" (Gilligan, 1982, p. 21).

Relational development theory and other feminist psychological research has revealed the psychological bias of assuming that "men" meant "all people." Furthermore, the relationally based concept of the ethic of care has helped us understand morality less as a dichotomous choice (that is, justice *or* mercy) and more as a search for resolution of a dialectic (for example, needs *and* responsibilities, rights *and* obligations, justice *and* desserts).

As adult educators, we find that the basic premise of this book—development of the individual as a worthy aim of education—implies a belief in the importance of relationship and the provision of care. When our responsibility to learners focuses on *care*, we hold a different professional identity than when our primary responsibility is to a body of knowledge. The importance of relationships and connectedness to the learning process, and of valuing interactions among one's experience and ideas and those of others, has been highlighted in the literature on women's development and feminist pedagogy (Merriam & Caffarella, 1999; p. 111; Fiddler & Marienau, 1995).

APPENDIX D

ORIENTATIONS TO TEACHING AND LEARNING

Clearly, not all approaches to teaching and learning lead to change and the potential for personal development. Rote learning, for example, offers little toward challenging adult learners' values, beliefs, and assumptions (Ausubel, 1968). Merriam and Cafferella's (1999) organization of a wide array of learning theories into five *orientations to learning*—behaviorist, cognitivist, humanist, social learning, and constructivist—also vary in their support of developmental outcomes. Merriam and Cafferella's exploration of these approaches (1999, pp. 248-266) underscores the complexity of the teaching and learning enterprise, which is not easily captured by any one perspective. They also note that these orientations to learning are primarily concerned with change in the individual, which may or may not be directed toward social change. Thus, they do not explicitly capture other perspectives that also may inform adult learning, including Marxism, critical theory, critical pedagogy, multiculturalism, postmodernism, and feminist pedagogy. These perspectives are seen in a "power relations" framework (Merriam and Cafferella, p. 340), focusing on sociocultural contexts where learning takes place. Issues such as power, oppression, interactions of gender, race and class, access to knowledge, and privileged knowledge occupy center stage for teachers and students to critique and challenge contextual influences on learning (Foley, 1995).

As adult educators, when we see a list of named orientations, we tend to start by identifying with one or the other, based on what we know of our own

Exhibit D.1. Relationships of Dimensions of Teaching and Orientation to Learning.

When Your Belief that the Locus of Learning Is	*Your Orientation to Learning Is Predominantly*
Stimuli in external environment	Behaviorist
Internal cognitive structuring	Cognitivist
Affective and cognitive needs	Humanist
Interaction of person, behavior, and environment	Social learning
Internal construction of reality by individual	Constructivist

When You Identify the Purpose of Education as	
Producing change in desired direction	Behaviorist
Develop capacity and skills to learn better	Cognitivist
Becoming self-actualized, autonomous	Humanist
Modeling new roles and behavior	Social learning
Constructing knowledge	Constructivist

When You View Your Role as a Teacher Is to	
Arrange environment to elicit desired response	Behaviorist
Structure content of learning activity	Cognitivist
Facilitate development of the whole person	Humanist
Model and guide new roles and behavior	Social learning
Facilitate learners' negotiation of meaning	Constructivist

When Your View of the Learning Process Is	
Changes in behavior	Behaviorist
Internal mental processes	Cognitivist
A personal act to fulfill potential	Humanist
Interaction with and observation of others in a social context	Social learning
Construction of meaning from experience	Constructivist

When Your Efforts with Adults Are	
Toward meeting behavioral objectives	Behaviorist
Competency-based	Behaviorist
Toward skill development and training	Behaviorist
Toward cognitive development	Cognitivist
Learning how to learn	Cognitivist
Correlating with intelligence, learning, and memory with age	Cognitivist
Framed by andragogy	Humanist
Toward self-directed learning	Humanist and constructivist
Toward socialization and social roles	Social learning
Framed by mentoring	Social learning
Oriented to the locus of control	Social learning
Framed by experiential learning	Constructivist
Toward perspective transformation	Constructivist
Toward reflective practice	Constructivist

Source: Adapted fromMerriam and Caffarella (1999). Used by permission.

philosophical and attitudinal bent. Although it is valuable to have such a "home base" for thinking about one's practice, we find that this can lead to an unnecessarily narrowed focus. We have therefore restructured Merriam and Caffarella's chart to show how one's existing beliefs and practices may actually fit several theoretical stances (Exhibit D.1).

For example, when we see our role as *facilitating development of the whole person,* we are leaning toward a humanist perspective. If the view of the learning process focuses specifically on *changes in learners' behaviors,* we are emphasizing behaviorist intentions. When teaching adults centers on *learning how to learn,* the orientation is predominantly cognitivist. When the emphasis is on *mentoring* and *modeling,* social learning is the core approach. If the overriding concern is making meaning to encourage *perspective transformation,* we are taking a constructivist stance. With this overview in mind, we will reexamine these orientations toward learning, paying particular attention to their potential to support adult development.

The concept *locus of learning* might be restated as *where does learning happen,* or *what is learning centered around?* From the behaviorist point of view, learning happens in response to stimuli. Behaviorists focus on stimuli and the effectiveness of the reinforcements needed to achieve measurable behavioral change. Learning environments based on rewards for increments of desired change, currently used most often with learners who have limited cognitive skills, draw on behavioral theory. However, since behaviorists define learning solely in terms of changed behavior, they intentionally *ignore* what goes on inside the learner. A typical example would be programmed instruction, or a training session on how to use software.

Cognitivists (Ausubel, 1968), by comparison, focus almost exclusively on what is happening inside the learner and on preexisting mental models as they affect the possibility of new learning. By changing these models, or cognitive structures, the cognitivist seeks to enable increasingly effective symbolic processing and problem-solving abilities—cognitivist goals for meaningful learning. For example, an instructor following good cognitivist practice would begin with a carefully structured overview, intending in this way to provide learners with adequate "anchors" for the new knowledge to follow.

Constructivists (Piaget, 1972) focus on learners' self-construction of meaning and define knowledge as "temporary, developmental, socially and culturally mediated, and thus nonobjective" (Brooks & Brooks, 1993, p vii), whereas cognitivists think of knowledge as absolute and transmissible (Marton & Booth, 1997). A constructivist educator is likely to create situations for "discovery" learning, as in certain kinds of laboratory or field work.

Social learning theory (Bandura, 1986) situates learning in the interaction of the individual with a "real" setting or context, leading toward modeling new roles and behavior. Social learning theory incorporates some aspects of behaviorist and cognitive frameworks. It differs from strict behaviorism in its presumption of a reciprocal relationship, where each affects the other, rather than a stimulus applied to the learner with the intention of producing a desired response. Working in groups is one expression of social learning theory.

The humanist (Rogers, 1960) sees the individual person's needs and desires, both cognitive and affective, as primary, leading toward self-actualization. This is also among the goals of many psychological models of development (Maslow, 1968; Erikson, 1959). Humanist educators offer highly individualized attention and are likely to consider the learner's process as content.

Clearly, the role of the adult educator changes as these assumptions and intentions change. For example, the behaviorist instructor—usually a "trainer"—first sets up behavioral objectives described in terms of competencies. Then she or he provides appropriate stimuli and reinforcements toward eliciting the specified responses. A concept of meaningful learning is meaningless from the behaviorist standpoint. In fact, "if the learner [is] active in constructing meaning and interpreting experience, knowledge and truth [are] compromised" (Pratt, 1993, p. 16). In this orientation, the instructor-trainer designs the goals and the methods of their implementation.

By contrast, the humanist who seeks development of the self-actualized individual posits the learner's *self*-direction as the ultimate goal. The instructor, therefore, acts as facilitator within an adult learner-centered framework. The learner's desires and potential will determine the outcomes of the learning process. Research suggests that the capacities required for self-directed learning overlap those necessary for meaningful learning (Taylor, 1987; Kegan, 1994).

In terms of the educator's assumed control over the learning environment, humanists are probably at the opposite end of the spectrum from behaviorists. Social learning theorists might be somewhere nearer the middle, with their focus on the *interaction* of instructor (or mentor) and the learner (and others in the social context) and toward socialization and changed social roles.

Situated somewhere between instructor-focused and learner-focused orientations, cognitivists pay greater attention than social learning theorists to the internal mental processes of learners. They also structure the content of learning activities to improve learners' information-processing abilities to affect future learning. Though cognitivists emphasize the importance of meaningful, as opposed to rote, learning (Ausubel, 1968, p. 38), early cognitive theory stressed the educational value of verbally presented material and content coverage over problem solving and "discovery" (experience-based) learning techniques. In recent years, however, cognitivists have embraced the constructive emphasis on the learner's process (Garrison, 1991), paying special attention to facilitating the construction of *meaning*. This includes the constructivist focus on the social and cultural mediation of learning (Brooks & Brooks, 1993) and on making meaning through discourse and critical reflection on experience (Mezirow, 1996). Constructivists do not stress learners' information-processing capacities as much as cognitivists do, but pay more attention to enabling learners to develop increasingly effective representations of their experiential world (von Glasersfeld, 1996). Cognitivists stress the significance of developing metacognitive processes to enhance future learning (Garrison, 1991). According to Peter Cooper (1993), "The move from behaviorism through cognitivism to constructivism represents shifts in emphasis away from an external view to an internal view. To the behaviorist, the internal processing is of no interest; to the cognitivist, the internal process is only of importance to the extent to which it explains how external reality is understood. In contrast, the constructivist views the mind as a builder of symbols— the tools used to represent the knower's reality" (p. 16).

Though it may not be so much an orientation to learning as a "philosophical stance with regard to the purposes of adult education and the relationship of the individual to society" (Pratt, 1993, p 22), no discussion of approaches to teaching adults would be complete without mention of *andragogy*—that is, education for the man (or adult) in place of *pedagogy*, meaning education for the child. This approach, developed by Knowles (1975, 1973) following the insights of Lindeman (1961), combines aspects of humanist, constructivist, and cognitivist orientations toward learning. Knowles described ways in which adult learners were different from younger students and identified "(1) self-concept, (2) prior experience, (3) readiness to learn, (4) learning orientation, and (5) motivation to learn." Knowles's emphasis on self-direction, his concern for development of the individual toward autonomy and full potential, and his description of the caring, authentic, facilitative role of the instructor align him with humanist philosophy and practice. He also shows some constructivist tendencies in his acknowledgement that "learning is not . . . the discovery of an independent, preexisting world outside as much as it is the construction of meaning through experience" (Pratt, 1993, p. 16). Cognitive theorists may also recognize themselves in Knowles's concern for the role of prior experience in how learners approach new learning tasks.

Most educators will find aspects of their practice described across several of these orientations. In our own practice, we three find that whatever our philosophical starting point, we actually move frequently and fluidly among them, as circumstances warrant. One of our own adult programs, for example, stresses self-directed learning within a competency-based outcomes framework. At the same time, it focuses on constructing meaning from experience and developing metacognitive skills toward becoming life-long learners.

APPENDIX E
TYPOLOGY OF LEARNING

Peter Jarvis's (1992) typology of learning (Table E.1) proposes that there are nine possible types of responses to an experience, which can be grouped into three overarching categories (see left-hand column, "Category of responses to experience"). Each category involves three types of learning or nonlearning (see right-hand column).

Table E.1. A Typology of Learning.

Category of responses to experience	Type of learning/nonlearning
Nonlearning	Presumption Nonconsideration Rejection
Nonreflective learning	Preconscious learning Skills learning Memorization
Reflective learning	Contemplation Reflective skills learning Experimental learning

Source: Jarvis (1992). Used by permission.

Nonlearning

People don't learn from their experiences.

Presumption: People believe that things will stay the same, so there is no need to question or to learn anything new (p. 72).

Nonconsideration: People do not respond to a potential learning experience because it does not capture their attention (for instance, they are too busy to think about it, fearful of the outcome, or not able to understand the situation) (p. 73).

Rejection: People are not willing to change their opinions, attitudes, or beliefs about something because they are sure they are right in this situation (p. 73).

Nonreflective Learning

Common forms of learning that do not involve reflectivity.

Preconscious learning: A learning process that passes into the mind without the learner's conscious awareness and usually not involving the communicative mode of experience (p. 75).

Skills learning: Learning of simple, short procedures, such as work on an assembly line, occurring in the action mode of experience, rather than the communicative mode (p. 75).

Memorization: Experience and information that is stored in memory and recalled for later use (p. 76).

Reflective Learning

People are able to stand back, make decisions, and evaluate their learning.

Contemplation: The process of thinking about an experience and reaching a conclusion about it without necessarily referring to the wider social reality (p. 77).

Reflective skills learning: Involves not only learning a skill but also learning the concepts that undergird the practice (p. 77).

Experimental learning: A theory is tried out in practice, resulting in a new form of knowledge that captures social reality (pp. 77–78).

REFERENCES

Aisenberg, N., & Harrington, M. (1988). *Women of academe: Outsiders in the sacred grove.* Amherst: University of Massachusetts Press.

Angelo, T. A., & Cross, K. P. (1994). *Classroom assessment techniques: A handbook for college teachers* (2nd ed.). San Francisco: Jossey-Bass.

Apps, J. W. (1991). *Mastering the teaching of adults,* Malabar, FL: Krieger.

Argyris, C. (1985). *Strategy, change and defensive routines.* Boston: Pitman.

Armstrong, A. K. (1977). *Masters of their own destiny: A comparison of the thought of Coady and Freire.* Occasional Papers in Continuing Education No. 13. Vancouver: Centre for Continuing Education, University of British Columbia.

Aronson, E., Blaney, N., Stephin, C., Sikes, J., & Snapp, M. (1978). *The jigsaw classroom.* Beverly Hills, CA: Sage.

Association for Supervision and Curriculum Development. (1997). *A conversation with Howard Gardner: Exploring our multiple intelligences* [CD-ROM]. Alexandria, VA: Author.

Ausubel, D. P. (1968). *Educational psychology: A cognitive view.* Austin, TX: Holt, Rinehart and Winston.

Bandura, A. (1986). *Social foundations of thought and action: A social cognitive theory.* Englewood Cliffs, NJ: Prentice Hall.

Bassaches, M. (1985). *Dialectical thinking and adult development.* Norwood, NJ: Ablex.

Bateson, G. (1979). *Mind and nature: A necessary unity.* New York: Dutton.

Belenky, M. F., Bond, L., & Weinstock, J. (1997). *A tradition that has no name: Nurturing the development of people, families, and communities.* New York: Basic Books.

Belenky, M. F., Clinchy, B. M., Goldberger, M. R., & Tarule, J. M. (1986). *Women's ways of knowing: The development of self, voice, and mind.* New York: Basic Books.

Belenky, M. F., Clinchy, B. M., Goldberger, M. R., & Tarule, J. M. (1996). *Women's ways of knowing: The development of self, voice, and mind* (2nd ed.). New York: Basic Books.

Bennis, W. G. (1981–82). A goal for the Eighties: Organizational integrity. *New Jersey Bell Journal, 4* (4), pp. 1–8.

Bennis, W. G., & Goldsmith, J. (1994). *Learning to lead: A workbook on becoming a leader.* Reading, MA: Addison-Wesley.

Bergquist, W. (1993). *The postmodern organization: Mastering the art of irreversible change.* San Francisco: Jossey-Bass.

Biagi, S., & Kern-Foxworth, M. (1997). *Facing differences: Race, gender, and mass media.* Thousand Oaks, CA: Pine Forge Press.

Block, P. (1993). *Stewardship.* San Francisco: Berrett-Koehler.

Botkin, J., Elmandjra, M., & Malitz, M. (1979). *No limits to learning: Bridging the human gap.* New York: Pergamon.

Boud, D. (1989). Some competing traditions in experiential learning. In S. W. Weil & I. McGill, I. (Eds.), *Making sense of experiential learning: Diversity in theory and practice.* Milton Keynes, U.K.: Society for Research into Higher Education and Open University Press.

Boud, D. (1995). *Enhancing learning through self-assessment.* London: Kogan Page.

Boud, D., Cohen, R., & Walker, D. (1993). *Using experience for learning.* Buckingham, U.K.: Society for Research into Higher Education and Open University Press.

Boud, D., & Feletti, G. (Eds.). (1997). *The challenge of problem-based learning* (2nd ed.). New York: St. Martin's Press.

Boud, D., Keogh, R., & Walker, D. (Eds.) (1985). *Reflection: Turning experience into learning.* London: Kogan Page.

Boud, D., Keogh, R., & Walker, D. (1996). Promoting reflection in learning: A model. In R. Edwards, A. Hanson, and P. Raggett (Eds.), *Boundaries of adult learning.* New York: Routledge.

Boud, D., & Miller, N. (Eds.) (1996). *Working with experience: Animating learning.* London: Routledge.

Boyce, M. (1996). Teaching critically as an act of praxis and resistance. In "The Electronic Journal of Radical Organisation Theory," http://www.mngt.waikato.ac.nz/Research/ejrot/back.asp vol. 2.

Bridges, K. (1932). Emotional development in early infancy. *Child Development, 3,* 340.

Bridges, W. (1980). *Transitions: Making sense of life's changes.* Reading, MA: Perseus Books.

Bridges, W. (1988). *Surviving corporate transition.* New York: Doubleday.

Bridges, W. (1993). *The character of organizations.* Palo Alto, CA: Consulting Psychologists Press.

Bridges, W. (1994). *Jobshift.* Reading, MA: Addison-Wesley.

Bright, B. (1986*). Adult development, learning, and teaching.* Newland Papers No. 12. Hull, U.K.: University of Hull, Department of Adult and Continuing Education.

Brookfield, S. D. (1985). Self-directed learning: From theory to practice. *New Directions for Continuing Education,* no. 25. San Francisco: Jossey-Bass.

Brookfield, S. D. (1986). *Understanding and facilitating adult learning.* San Francisco: Jossey-Bass.

Brookfield, S. D. (1987). *Learning democracy: Eduard Lindeman on adult education and social change.* London: Croom Helm.

Brookfield, S. D. (1989). *Developing critical thinkers: Challenging adults to explore alternative ways of thinking and acting.* San Francisco: Jossey-Bass.

Brookfield, S. D. (1990a). *The skillful teacher.* San Francisco: Jossey-Bass.

Brookfield, S. (1990b). Using critical incidents to explore learners' assumptions. In J. Mezirow & Associates, *Fostering critical reflection in adulthood: A guide to transformative and emancipatory learning* (pp. 173–93). San Francisco: Jossey-Bass.

Brookfield, S. D. (1998). Against naïve romanticism: From celebration to the critical analysis of experience. *Studies in Continuing Education, 20*(2).

Brookfield, S. D., & Preskill, S. (1999). *Discussion as a way of teaching: Tools and techniques for a democratic classroom.* San Francisco: Jossey-Bass.

Brooks, J., & Brooks, M. G. (1993). *In search of understanding: The case for constructivist classrooms.* Alexandria, VA: Association for Supervisor and Curriculum Development.

Campbell, J. (1987). *The hero with a thousand faces.* Princeton: Princeton University Press.

Candy, P. C. (1980, August). *Adult Learners' Views of Adult Learning: Report of a Pilot Study.* Paper presented at a national workshop on Working with Adults: Strategies for Adult Learning, Macquarie University, New South Wales, Australia.

Candy, P. C. (1981). Mirrors of the mind: Personal construct theory in the training of adult educators. *Manchester Monograph* No. 16. Manchester: Department of Adult Education, University of Manchester.

Candy, P. C. (1982). Personal constructs and personal paradigms: Elaboration, modification, and transformation. *Interchange in Educational Policy, 13*(4), 56-69.

Candy, P. C. (1990). Repertory grids: Playing verbal chess. In J. Mezirow & Associates (Eds.), *Fostering critical reflection in adulthood: A guide to transformative and emancipatory learning.* San Francisco: Jossey-Bass.

Candy, P. C. (1991). *Self-direction for lifelong learning: A comprehensive guide to theory and practice.* San Francisco: Jossey-Bass.

Carbo, M. (1987). *Increasing reading achievement.* Alexandria, VA: National Association of Secondary School Principals.

Cervero, R. (1988). *Effective continuing education for professionals.* San Francisco: Jossey-Bass.

Chickering, A. W. & Associates. (1981). *The modern American college.* San Francisco: Jossey-Bass.

Chinen, A. (1989). *In the ever after: Fairy tales and the second half of life.* Wilmette, IL: Chiron.

Chinen, A. (1992). *Once upon a midlife: Classic stories and mythic tales to illuminate the middle years.* Los Angeles: Jeremy Tarcher.

Chisom, R., & Washington, M. (1997). *Undoing racism.* New Orleans, LA: People's Institute Press.

Christensen, C. R., Garvin, D. A., & Sweet, A. (1991). *Education for judgment: The artistry of discussion leadership.* Boston: Harvard Business School Press.

Clinchy, B. M. (1996). Connected and separate knowing: Toward a marriage of two minds. In N. Goldberger, J. Tarule, B. Clinchy, & M. Belenky (Eds.), *Knowledge, difference, and power.* New York: Basic Books.

Cooper, P. A. (1993). Paradigm shifts in designed instruction: From behaviorism to cognitivism to constructivism. *Educational Technology, 33*(5), 12-19.

Cranton, P. (1994). *Understanding and promoting transformative learning.* San Francisco: Jossey-Bass.

Cranton, P. (1996). *Professional development as transformative learning.* San Francisco: Jossey-Bass.

Dahlgren, L. (1984). Outcomes of learning. In F. Marton, D. Hounsell, & N. Entwistle (Eds.), *The experience of learning.* Edinburgh: Scottish Academic Press.

Daloz, L. A. (1986). *Effective teaching and mentoring.* San Francisco: Jossey-Bass.

Daloz, L. A. (1988). The story of Gladys who refused to grow: A morality tale for mentors. *Lifelong Learning: An Omnibus of Practice and Research,* 11(4).

Daloz, L. A. (1999). *Mentor: Guiding the journey of adult learners.* San Francisco: Jossey-Bass.

Daloz, L. A., Keen, C., Keen, J., & Parks, S. (1996). *Common fire: Leading lives of commitment in a complex world.* Boston: Beacon Press.

Dewey, J. (1938/1963). *Experience and education.* New York: Collier.

Dewey, J. (1944). *Democracy and education.* New York: The Free Press.

Dirkx, J. M. (1997). Nurturing soul in adult learning. In P. Cranton (Ed.), *Transformative learning in action.* New Directions for Adult and Continuing Education, No. 74. San Francisco: Jossey-Bass.

Dirkx, J., & Prenger, S. (1977). *A guide for implementing instruction for adults: A theme-based approach.* San Francisco: Jossey-Bass.

Elbow, P. (1973). The doubting game and the believing game—an analysis of the intellectual enterprise. In *Writing without teachers.* London: Oxford University Press.

Entwistle, N. (1984). Contrasting perspectives on learning. In F. Marton, D. Hounsell, & N. Entwistle (Eds.), *The experience of learning.* Edinburgh: Scottish Academic Press.

Erikson, E. (1959). *Identity and the life-cycle.* New York: International Universities Press.

Fiddler, M., & Marienau, C. (1995). Linking learning, teaching, and development. In K. Taylor & C. Marienau (Eds.), *Learning environments for women's adult development: Bridges toward change.* New Directions for Adult and Continuing Education, No. 65. San Francisco: Jossey-Bass.

Foley, G. (1995). *Understanding adult education and training.* St. Leonards, Australia: Allen and Unwin.

Fowler, J. (1981). *Stages of faith: The psychology of human development and the quest for meaning.* New York: Harper Collins.

Fransella, F., & Bannister, D. (1977). *A manual for repertory grid technique.* London: Academic Press.

Freire, P. (1986). *Politics of education.* Greenwich, CT: Brunner/Mazel.

Freire, P. (1992). *Pedagogy of the oppressed.* New York: Continuum.

Frye, N. (1963/1993). The educated imagination. *Massey Lectures* (p. 28). Toronto: Canadian Broadcasting Corporation.

Gardner, H. (1993). *Frames of the mind: The theory of multiple intelligences.* New York: Basic Books.

Garrison, D. R. (1991). Critical thinking and self-directed learning in adult education: An analysis of responsibility and control issues. *Adult Education Quarterly, 42,* 136-148.

Gelb, M. (1998). *How to think like Leonardo da Vinci: Seven steps to genius every day.* New York: Delacorte Press.

Gibbs, G. (1992). *Improving the quality of student learning.* Bristol, U.K.: Technical and Educational Services.

Gibbs, G., Morgan, A. R., & Taylor E. (1980). A review of the research of Ference Marton and the Goteborg Group, *Institute of Education Technology, The Open University, Study Methods Group.* No. 2.

Gilligan, C. (1982). *In a different voice: Psychological theory and women's development.* Cambridge: Harvard University Press.

Goldberger, N. R., Tarule, J. M., Clinchy, B. M., & Belenky, M. F. (1996). *Knowledge, difference, and power.* Boston: Basic Books.

Habermas, J. (1984/1987). *The theory of communicative action. Vol. 1: Reason and the rationalization of society Vol. 2: Lifeworld and system: A critique of functionalist reason* (Trans. Thomas McCarthy). Boston: Beacon Press.

Hayes, R. L., & Oppenheim, R. (1997). Constructionism: Reality is what you make it. In T. Sexton & B. Griffin (Eds.), *Constructivist thinking in counseling practice, research, and training.* New York: Teachers College Press.

Hersh, B., & Borzak, L. (1979). Toward cognitive development through field studies. *Journal of Higher Education, 50,* 63–78.

Horton, M., & Freire, P. (1990). *We make the road by walking: Conversations on education and social change.* Philadelphia: Temple University Press.

Hounsell, D. (1984). Understanding teaching and teaching for understanding. In F. Marton, D. Hounsell, & N. Entwistle (Eds.), *The experience of learning.* Edinburgh: Scottish Academic Press.

Jarvis, P. (1987a). Meaningful and meaningless experience: Towards an analysis of learning from life. *Adult Education Quarterly, 37* (3), 164–172.

Jarvis, P. (Ed.). (1987b). *Twentieth century thinkers in adult education.* London: Croom Helm.

Jarvis, P. (1992). *Paradoxes of learning: On becoming an individual in society.* San Francisco: Jossey-Bass.

Jaworski, B., Wood, T., & Dawson, S. (1999). *Mathematics teacher education: Critical international perspectives.* London: Falmer Press.

Jordan, J. V. (Ed.) (1997). *Women's growth in diversity: More writings from the Stone Center.* New York: Guilford Press.

Jordan, J. V., Kaplan, A. G., Miller, J. B., Stiver, I. P., and Surrey, J. L. (1991). *Women's growth in connection.* New York: Guilford Press.

Kassis, J. (1987). Personal communication. Family Therapy Training Program: Crossroads Community Growth Center, Holyoke, MA.

Kegan, R. (1982). *The evolving self: Problem and process in human development.* Cambridge: Harvard University Press.

Kegan, R. (1986). The child behind the mask: Sociopathology as developmental delay. In W. D. Reid, J. W. Bonner III, D. Dorr, & J. I Walker (Eds.), *Unmasking the psychopath.* New York: Norton.

Kegan, R. (1994). *In over our heads: The mental demands of modern life.* Cambridge: Harvard University Press.

Kegan, R. (2000). What "form" transforms? A constructive-developmental approach to transformative learning. In J. Mezirow (Ed.), *Learning as transformation.* San Francisco: Jossey-Bass.

Kelly, G. A. (1955). *The psychology of personal constructs* (2 vols). New York: Norton.

Kelly, G. A. (1970). A brief introduction to personal construct theory. In D. Bannister (Ed.), *Perspectives in personal construct theory.* London: Academic Press.

Kelly, G. A. (1977). The psychology of the unknown. In D. Bannister (Ed.), *New perspectives in personal construct theory* (pp. 1–19). San Diego: Academic Press.

Kitchener, K. S., & King, P. (1994). *Developing reflective judgment.* San Francisco: Jossey-Bass.

Knowles, M. (1973). *The adult learner: A neglected species* (2nd. ed.). Houston: Gulf.

Knowles, M. (1975). *Self-directed learning.* Chicago: Association Press, Follett.

Kohlberg, L. (1981). T*he philosophy of moral development: Moral stages and the idea of justice.* New York: Harper & Row.

Kolb, D. A. (1985). *Learning style inventory.* Boston: McBer Company.

Kolb, D. A. (1984). *Experiential learning: Experience as the source of learning and development.* Englewood Cliffs, NJ: Prentice Hall.

Kolb, D. A. (1988). Integrity, advanced professional development, and learning (p. 68–88). In S. Srivastava & Associates (Eds.), *Executive integrity.* San Francisco: Jossey-Bass.

Koller, A. (1981). *An unknown woman: A journey of self-discovery.* New York: Holt, Rinehart and Winston.

Kotter, J. P. (1996). *Leading change.* Cambridge, MA: Harvard Business School Press.

Kramp, M. K., & Roth, J. (1987). *Women's Ways of Knowing: Working notes for educators.* Milwaukee, WI: Alverno College.

Levinson, D., & Associates. (1978). *The seasons of a man's life.* New York: Knopf.

Lindeman, E. (1961). *The meaning of adult education.* Montreal: Harvest House.

Loevinger, J., with Blasi, A. (1976). *Ego development.* San Francisco: Jossey-Bass.

Luft, J. (1969). *Of human interaction: The Johari awareness model.* Mountain View, CA: Mayfield.

Luft, J. (1984). *Group processes: An introduction to group dynamics* (3rd ed.). Mountain View, CA: Mayfield.

Mackintosh, C. (Columbia Tristar) (1996). *Les Miserables in concert* [Video recording]. Produced by and taped in Royal Albert Hall, London.

Margetson, D. B. (1994). Current educational reform and the significance of problem-based learning. *Studies in Higher Education, 19*(1), 5–19.

Margetson, D. B. (1996). Beginning with the essentials: Why problem-based learning begins with problems. *Education for Health: Change in Training and Practice, 9*(1), 61–69.

Margetson, D. B. (1998). What counts as problem-based learning? *Education for Health: Change in Training and Practice, 11* (2), 93–201.

Margetson, D. B. (1999). The relation between understanding and practice in problem-based medical education. *Medical Education, 33* (5), 359–364.

Marienau, C. (1999). Self-assessment at work: Outcomes of adult learners' reflections on practice. *Adult Education Quarterly, 49* (3), 135–146.

Marsick, V. J., Cederholm, L., Turner, E., & Pearson, T. (1992). Action-reflection learning. *Training and Development, 46*(8), 63–66.

Marton, F., & Booth, S. (1997). *Learning and awareness.* Mahwah, NJ: Erlbaum.

Marton, F., Dall'Alba, G., & Beaty, E. (1993). Conceptions of learning. *International Journal of Educational Research 19,* 277–300.

Maslow, A. H. (1968). *Toward a psychology of being* (2nd ed.). New York: Van Nostrand Reinhold.

McCormick, D. (1999). Listening with empathy: Taking the other person's perspective. In A. Cooke, A. Craig, B. Greig, & M. Brazzel, M. (Eds.), *Reading book for human relations training.* Arlington, VA: NTL Institute.

Mentkowski, M., & Associates. (2000). *Learning that lasts: Integrating learning, development, and performance in college and beyond.* San Francisco: Jossey-Bass.

Merriam, S. (1994). Learning and life experience: The connection in adulthood. In J. Sinnott (Ed.), *Interdisciplinary handbook of adult lifespan learning.* Westport, CT: Greenwood Press.

Merriam, S., & Caffarella, R. (1999). *Learning in adulthood: A comprehensive guide* (2nd ed.) San Francisco: Jossey-Bass.

Merriam, S., & Yang, B. (1996). A longitudinal study of adult life experiences and developmental outcomes. *Adult Education Quarterly, 46* (2), 62–81.

Mezirow, J. (1985). A critical theory of self-directed learning. In S. Brookfield (Ed.), *Self-directed learning: From theory to practice.* New Directions for Continuing Education, no. 25. San Francisco: Jossey-Bass.

Mezirow, J. (1990). *Fostering critical reflection in adulthood: A guide to transformative and emancipatory learning.* San Francisco: Jossey Bass.

Mezirow, J. (1991). *Transformative dimensions of adult learning.* San Francisco: Jossey-Bass.

Mezirow, J. (1996). Contemporary paradigms of learning. *Adult Education Quarterly, 44*(3), 158–173.

Mezirow, J. (2000). *Learning as transformation: Critical perspectives on a theory in progress.* San Francisco: Jossey-Bass.

Michael, C., & Young, N. (1999). New traditions of the calling: Progressive practitioner education in Vermont college's graduate program. *Cael Forum and News, 22*(3), 9–10, 24.

Middleton, S. (1993). *Educating feminists: Life histories and pedagogy.* New York: Teachers College Press.

Miller, J. B. (1976). *Toward a new psychology of women.* Boston: Beacon.

Miller, J. B. (1991). The development of women's sense of self. In J. V. Jordan, A. G. Kaplan, J. B. Miller, I. P. Stiver, & J. L. Surrey (Eds.), *Women's growth in connection.* New York: Guilford Press.

More, W. S. (1974). *Emotions and adult learning.* Lexington, MA: Lexington Books.

Morgan, G. (1997). *Imaginization: The art of creative management.* San Francisco: Berrett-Koehler.

Morgan, G. (1999). *Images of organizations* (2nd ed.). Newbury Park, CA: Sage.

Myers, P. B., Myers, K. D. (1987). *Myers-Briggs Type Indicator.* Palo Alto, CA: Consulting Psychologists Press.

Naparestek, B. (1994). *Staying well with guided imagery.* New York: Warner.

Neimeyer, G. (Ed.) (1993). *Casebook of constructivist assessment.* Thousand Oaks, CA: Sage.

Neimeyer, G., & Neimeyer, R. A. (Eds.) (1997). *Advances in personal construct psychology* (Vol. 4). Greenwich, CT: JAI Press.

Neimeyer, R. A. (1979, July). *The structure and meaningfulness of tacit construing.* Paper presented at the Third International Congress on Personal Construct Psychology, Breukelen, Netherlands.

Nemiroff, R., & Colarusso, C. (Eds.). (1990). *New dimensions in adult development.* New York: Basic Books.

Nelson, T. S., Fleuridas, C., & Rosenthal, D. (1986). The evolution of circular questions: Training family therapists. *Journal of Marital and Family Therapy,* 12(2), 113–117.

Newman, J. H. (1852/1898). *The idea of a university.* New York: Longmans, Green.

Noddings, N. (1984) *Caring.* Berkeley, CA: University of California Press.

Norman, D. (1982). *Learning and memory.* San Francisco: Freeman.

O'Neil, J. A. (1999). *The role of the learning advisor in action learning.* Unpublished doctoral dissertation, Teachers College, Columbia University, New York.

O'Neil, J. A., & Dilworth, L. (1999). Issues in the design and implementation of an action learning initiative. In L. Yorks, J. O'Neil, & V. J. Marsick (Eds.), *Management, development, and organizational learning through action learning* (pp. 41–70). San Francisco: Berrett-Koehler.

O'Neil, J. A., & Marsick, V. J. (1994). Becoming critically reflective through action reflection learning. In A. Brooks & K. Watkins (Eds.), *The emerging power of action inquiry technologies* (pp. 17–30). New Directions for Adult and Continuing Education No. 63. San Francisco: Jossey-Bass.

Owen, H. (1987). *Spirit: Transformation and development in organizations.* Potomac, MD: Abbott Publishing.

Palazzoli Selvini, M., Boscolo, L., Cecchin, G., & Prata, G. (1980). Hypothesizing-circularity-neutrality: Three guidelines for the conductor of the session. *Family Process, 19,* 3–12.

Palmer, P. J. (1990, March). Leading from within: Reflections on spirituality and leadership (Address given at the Annual Celebration Dinner of the Indiana Office for Campus Ministries). Washington, DC: The Servant Leadership School.

Palmer, P. J. (1998). *The courage to teach: Exploring the inner landscape of a teacher's life.* San Francisco: Jossey-Bass.

Peck, T. A. (1986). Women's self-definition: From a different model? *Psychology of Women Quarterly, 10,* 274–284.

Penn, P. (1982). Circular questioning. *Family Process, 21,* 267–280.

Perry, W. G. (1970). *Forms of intellectual and moral development in the college years: A scheme.* Austin, TX: Holt, Rinehart and Winston.

Perry, W. G. (1981). Cognitive and ethical growth: The making of meaning. In A. W. Chickering & Associates, *The Modern American College* (pp. 76–116). San Francisco: Jossey-Bass.

Piaget, J. (1954). *The construction of reality in the child.* New York: Basic Books.

Piaget, J. (1972). Intellectual evolution from adolescent to adulthood. *Human Development, 16,* 346-370.

Plummer, T. (1988). *Cognitive growth and literary analysis: A dialectical model for teaching literature.* Unterrischtspraxic, *21* (1), p. 79.

Pratt, D. D. (1993). Andragogy after twenty-five years. In S. B. Merriam (Ed.), *An update on adult learning theory.* New Directions for Adult and Continuing Education, no. 57. San Francisco: Jossey-Bass.

Pratt, D. D., & Candy, P. C. (1985, March*). The repertory grid in group oriented learning situations: Construing the constructions of others.* Paper presented at the Twenty-sixth Annual Adult Education Research Conference, Arizona State University.

Progoff, I. (1975). *At a journal workshop.* New York: Dialogue House Library.

Prosser, K., & Trigwell, M. (1997). Relations between perceptions of the teaching environment and approaches to learning. *British Journal of Educational Psychology 67,* 23–35.

Reason, P. (1988). *Human inquiry in action.* Thousand Oaks, CA: Sage.

Reason, P. (1995). *Participation in human inquiry.* Thousand Oaks, CA: Sage.

Reason, P., & Rowan, J. (1981). *Human inquiry.* Chicester, U.K.: Wiley.

Richardson, J.T.E. (1999). The concepts and methods of phenomenographic research. *Review of Educational Research, 69* (1), 53–82.

Rogers, C. R. (1959). A theory of therapy, personality, and interpersonal relationship, as developed in the client-centered framework. In S. Koch (Ed.), *Psychology: A study of a science: Vol. 3. Formulations of the person and the social context* (pp. 184–256). New York: McGraw-Hill.

Rogers, C. R. (1960). *Freedom to learn: A view of what education might become.* Columbus, OH: Merrill.

Rogers, C. R. (1983). *Freedom to learn for the 80s.* Columbus, OH: Merrill.

Säljö, R. (1982). *Learning and understanding: A study of differences in constructing meaning from text.* Goteburg Studies in Educational Science, 41. Acta Universitatis Gothoburgensis.

Samples, R. (1976). *The metaphoric mind: A celebration of creative consciousness.* Reading, MA: Addison Wesley.

Schneps, M. H. (Director) (1989). *Private universe: misconceptions that block learning.* Santa Monica: Pyramid Film & Video.

Schommer, M. The role of adults' beliefs about knowledge in school, work, and everyday life. In M.C. Smith & T. Pourchot (Eds.), *Adult learning and development.* Hillsdale, NJ: Erlbaum.

Schön, D. (1983). *The reflective practitioner: How professionals think in action.* New York: Basic Books.

Selman, R. L. (1989). *The growth of interpersonal understanding.* New York: Academic Press.

Senge, P. M. (1990). *The fifth discipline: The art and practice of the learning organization.* New York: Doubleday.

Sexton, T. L. (1997). Constructivist thinking within the history of ideas: The challenge of a new paradigm. In T. L. Sexton & B. Griffin (Eds.), *Constructivist thinking in counseling practice, research, and training.* New York: Teachers College Press.

Sheckley, B. (1989). Experiential learning theory: Implications for workplace learning. Philadelphia: CAEL International Assembly.

Spencer, L. J. (1989). *Winning through participation: Meeting the challenge of corporate change with the Technology of Participation.* Dubuque, IA: Kendall-Hunt. (Also available from the Institute of Cultural Affairs at www.ica-use.org.)

Stanfield, B. (Ed.) (1997). *The Art of Focused Conversation: 100 Ways to Access Group Wisdom in the Workplace.* Toronto, CA: Institute of Cultural Affairs. (Available from the Institute of Cultural Affairs at www.ica-usa.org or www.web.net/~icacan.)

Stanton, A. (1996). Reconfiguring teaching and knowing in the college classroom. In N. R. Goldberger, J. M. Tarule, B. M. Clinchy, & M. F. Belenky (Eds.), *Knowledge, difference, and power.* New York: Basic Books.

Stevenson, L., & Haberman, D. L. (1998). *Ten theories of human nature* (3rd ed.). New York: Oxford University Press.

Tarule, J. M. (1980). The process of transformation: Steps toward change (pp. 23–34). New Directions for Higher Education, No. 29. San Francisco: Jossey-Bass.

Taylor, K. (1995a). Sitting beside herself: Self-assessment and women's adult development. In K. Taylor & C. Marienau, (Eds.), *Learning environments for women's adult development: Bridges toward change.* New Directions in Adult and Continuing Education, No. 65. San Francisco: Jossey-Bass.

Taylor, K. (1995b). Teaching adult development to developing adults. *Research and Reflection, 1*(2). http://www.gonzaga.edu/rr/v1n2/taylor.htm

Taylor, K. (1999). Development as separation and connection: Finding a balance. In M. C. Clark & R. Caffarella (Eds.), *An update on adult development theory: New ways of thinking about the life course.* New Directions for Adult and Continuing Education, No. 84, pp. 59–66.

Taylor, K., & Marienau, C. (1997). Constructive-developmental theory as a framework for assessment in higher education. *Assessment and Evaluation in Higher Education, 22*(2), 233-243.

Taylor, M. (1987). Self-directed learning: More than meets the observer's eye. In D. Boud & V. Griffin (Eds.), *Appreciating adults learning: From the learner's perspective.* London: Kogan Page.

Tennant, M. (1997). *Psychology and adult learning* (2nd ed.). London: Routledge.

Tennant, M., and Pogson, P. (1995). *Learning and change in the adult years.* San Francisco: Jossey-Bass.

Thomas, L. F., & Harri-Augstein, E. S. (1985). *Self-organised learning: Foundations for a conversational science of psychology.* London: Routledge & Kegan Paul.

Tishman, S., & Andrade, A. (1997). *Critical squares: Games of critical thinking and understanding.* Englewood, CO: Teacher Ideas Press.

Usher, R., Bryant, I., & Johnston, R. (1997). *Adult education and the postmodern challenge: Learning beyond the limits.* London: Routledge.

Vaill, P. (1996). *Learning as a way of being.* San Francisco: Jossey-Bass.

von Glasersfeld, E. (1984). An introduction to radical constructivism. In P. Watzlawick (Ed.), *The invented reality.* New York: Norton.

von Glasersfeld, E. (1996). Introduction: Aspects of constructivism. In C. T. Fosnot (Ed.), *Constructivism: Theory, perspectives, and practice* (pp. 3–7). New York: Teachers College Press.

Vygotsky, L. (1978). *Mind in society: The development of higher psychological processes.* Cambridge, MA: Harvard University Press.

Wah, L. M. (Producer and Director), & Hunter, M. (Co-producer) (1994). *The color of fear* (1994). Oakland, CA: Stir-Fry Productions.

Watzlawick, P. (1984) *The invented reality.* New York: Norton.

Weathersby, R., & Tarule, J. (1980). *Adult development: Implications for higher education.* (AAHE-ERIC/Higher Education Research Report No. 4.) Washington, DC: American Association for Higher Education.

Wheatley, M. (1992). *Leadership and the new science: Discovering order in a chaotic world* (2nd ed.). San Francisco: Berrett-Koehler.

Whyte, D. (1996). *The heart aroused: Poetry and the preservation of the soul in corporate America.* New York: Doubleday.

Wildemeersch, D. (1989). The principle meaning of dialogue for the construction and transformation of reality. In S. Warner Weil & I. McGill (Eds.), *Making sense of experiential learning.* Milton Keynes, U.K.: Society for Research into Higher Education and Open University Press.

Wohlberg, J., Gilmore, G., & Wolff, S. (1998). *OB in action.* Boston: Houghton Mifflin.

Woolum, S. (1993). *Metaphors and meaning: Understanding the theme model.* Washington, DC: Taylor and Francis.

Zachary, L. (2000). *The mentor's guide to facilitating effective mentoring relationships.* San Francisco: Jossey-Bass.

Index of Strategies

374

Developmental Intentions	Name of Activity	Strategy	Contributor	Page
3. Reframing ideas or values that seem contradictory, embracing their differences, and arriving at new meanings	Repertory Grids	Assessing	Candy	49
	Executive Coaching Practice	Simulating	Cashman	187
	Anzio Effect	Imagining	Glicken	100
	Reflecting on Beliefs & Values	Reflecting	Heid	267
	Circular Questioning in Adult Learning	Inquiring	Hodgson	165
	Cognitive & Ethical Development	Simulating	Liebler	217
	Multicultural Ethical Dilemmas	Simulating	Liebler	220
	Clustering	Imagining	Melamed	104
	Aligning with the Mission	Simulating	Munaker	192
	Examining Your Paradigms	Imagining	Proehl	119
	Understanding Diversity & Difference	Simulating	Siegel	232
	Listening Activity	Simulating	Timm	207
4. Using one's experience to critique expert opinion and expert opinion to critique one's experience	Learning Circles	Collaborating	Bishop & Gibson	80
	Critique Expert Opinion	Inquiring	Brookfield	130
	Learning Activity Project	Simulating-Performing	Caffarella	211
	Executive Coaching Practice	Simulating	Cashman	187
	Educational Autobiographies	Assessing	Clark & Kilgore	69
	Psychology Tutorial	Inquiring	Coulter	155
	Structured Learning Journal	Reflecting	Marienau	278
	Being the Art Critic	Simulating	McGury	228
	Philosophy-of-Life Paper	Reflecting	Nemecek	282
	Drawing Theory	Imagining	Stenersen	125
	Emerging Life Patterns	Reflecting	Taylor, K.	261
5. Moving between separate and connected, independent and interdependent ways of knowing	Demystifying Inquiry	Inquiring	Firestone	161
	Circular Questioning in Adult Learning	Inquiring	Hodgson	165
	Modeling Teaching-Learning	Simulating	Jaworski	214
	Being the Art Critic	Simulating	McGury	228
	Aligning with the Mission	Simulating	Munaker	192
	ICA Kaleidoscope	Imagining	Packard	114
6. Pay attention to wholes as well as the parts that comprise them	Learning Styles Assessment	Assessment	Brewer	66
	Adding Dimensions	Inquiring	Fiddler	158
	Demystifying Inquiry	Inquiring	Firestone	161
	Through Another's Eyes	Inquiring	Horvath-Neimeyer	170
	Problem-Focused Education	Inquiring	Margetson	172
	Being the Art Critic	Simulating	McGury	228
	Clustering	Imagining	Melamed	104
	Critical Thinking Tic-Tac-Toe	Inquiring	Newell	140
	ICA Kaleidoscope	Imagining	Packard	114

Developmental Intentions	Name of Activity	Strategy	Contributor	Page
7. Associating truth not with static fact but with contexts and relationships	Claiming Power of Voice & Mind	Reflecting	Belenky	247
	Western Town	Simulating	Bergquist	183
	Psychology Tutorial	Inquiring	Coulter	155
	Structured Cooperative Learning	Collaborating	Feigenbaum	83
	Clustering	Imagining	Melamed	104
	Understanding Diversity & Difference	Simulating	Siegel	232
	Parents as Experts	Inquiring	Stahl	150
	Journal Dialogue	Imagining	Walden	127
	Interdisciplinary Tree	Inquiring	Weiner	153
8. Pursuing the possibility of objective truth	Exploratories in Physics	Experimenting	Chiaverina	93
	DNA Modeling	Experimenting	Fiddler	90
	Demystifying Inquiry	Inquiring	Firestone	161
9. Perceiving and constructing one's reality by observing and participating	Learning Activity Project	Performing-Simulating	Caffarella	211
	Exploratories in Physics	Experimenting	Chiaverina	93
	Structured Cooperative Learning	Collaborating	Feigenbaum	83
	Anzio Effect	Imagining	Glicken	100
	Symbols Circle	Imagining	Hicks	102
	Circular Questioning in Adult Learning	Inquiring	Hodgson	165
	Reconstructing Behaviors	Reflecting	Laming	253
	Insight by Surprise	Inquiring	Luft	137
	Field Study Reflection	Performing	McCormick	224
	Perspective Shift	Imagining	Munaker	111
	Coaching for Effectiveness	Performing-Simulating	Proehl	195
	Cooperative Inquiry	Collaborating	Reason	85
	Emerging Life Patterns	Reflecting	Taylor, K.	261
10. Tapping into and drawing on tacit knowledge	Learning Activity Project	Performing-Simulating	Caffarella	211
	Executive Coaching Practice	Simulating	Cashman	187
	ORID Discussion	Inquiring	Dunn	133
	Problem-Focused Education	Inquiring	Margetson	172
	Whole Person Reaction Paper	Reflecting	McCormick	275
	Clustering	Imagining	Melamed	104
	Critical Thinking Tic-Tac-Toe	Inquiring	Newell	140
	Indescribable Moment	Reflecting	Neimeyer	257
	Experience-Cycle Methodology	Reflecting	Oades	285
	Personal Theories of Learning	Simulating	Taylor, E.	199
	Providing a Learning Culture	Inquiring	Winkelman	178

Developmental Intentions	Name of Activity	Strategy	Contributor	Page

II. Toward a dialogical relationship to oneself

Developmental Intentions	Name of Activity	Strategy	Contributor	Page
1. Addressing fears of losing what is familiar and safe	Myth & Metaphor	Reflecting	Bassett	242
	Using Empathic Listening	Reflecting	Blanusa	264
	Contradictions Workshop	Assessing	Dunn	55
	Translating Experience	Assessing	Eive	71
	Reflecting on Beliefs & Values	Reflecting	Heid	267
	Developing Edu-autobiographies	Assessing	Michael	74
	Seeing Your Emerging Future	Imagining	Morton	107
	Parents as Experts	Inquiring	Stahl	150
2. Engaging the disequilibrium when one's ideas and beliefs are challenged	Using Empathic Listening	Reflecting	Blanusa	264
	Repertory Grids	Assessing	Candy	49
	Reflecting on Beliefs & Values	Reflecting	Heid	267
	Modeling Teaching-Learning	Simulating	Jaworski	214
	Reconstructing Behaviors	Reflecting	Laming	253
	Multicultural Ethical Dilemmas	Simulating	Liebler	220
	Structured Learning Journal	Reflecting	Marienau	278
	Seeing Your Emerging Future	Imagining	Morton	107
	Philosophy-of-Life Paper	Reflecting	Nemecek	282
	Understanding Diversity & Difference	Simulating	Siegel	232
	Taking Multiple Perspectives	Simulating	Taylor, K.	203
	Rotating Groups	Collaborating	Tennant	78
	Listening Activity	Simulating	Timm	207
	Interdisciplinary Tree	Inquiring	Weiner	153
3. Exploring life's experiences through some framework(s) of analysis	Myth & Metaphor	Reflecting	Bassett	242
	Critique Expert Opinion	Inquiring	Brookfield	130
	Learning Styles Assessment	Assessing	Brewer	66
	Exploratories in Physics	Experimenting	Chiaverina	93
	Educational Autobiographies	Assessing	Clark & Kilgore	69
	Contradictions Workshop	Assessing	Dunn	55
	Adding Dimensions	Inquiring	Fiddler	158
	Novice to Expert	Assessing	Fiddler	59
	Anzio Effect	Imagining	Glicken	100
	Symbols Circle	Imagining	Hicks	102
	Circular Questioning in Adult Learning	Inquiring	Hodgson	165
	Cognitive & Ethical Development	Simulating	Liebler	217
	Structured Learning Journal	Reflecting	Marienau	278
	Indescribable Moment	Reflecting	Neimeyer	257
	Experience-Cycle Methodology	Reflecting	Oades	285

III. Toward being a continuous learner

Developmental Intentions	Name of Activity	Strategy	Contributor	Page
	Structured Learning Journal	Reflecting	Marienau	278
	Developing Edu-autobiographies	Assessing	Michael	74
	Critical Thinking Tic-Tac-Toe	Inquiring	Newell	140
	Experience-Cycle Methodology	Reflecting	Oades	285
	Action Learning	Imagining	O'Neil & Marsick	96
	Cultural Economic Values	Inquiring	Smith	147
	Knowing Oneself as a Thinker	Simulating	Stanton	234
	Culture & Identity	Simulating	Stolz	238
	Rotating Groups	Collaborating	Tennant	78
	Trading Game	Reflecting	Toby & Templeman	287
	Class Journaling	Reflecting	Zachary	290
2. Challenging oneself to learn in new realms; taking risks	Psychology Tutorial	Inquiring	Coulter	155
	Demystifying Inquiry	Inquiring	Firestone	161
	Through Another's Eyes	Inquiring	Horvath-Neimeyer	
	Field Study Reflection	Performing	McCormick	224
	Coaching for Effectiveness	Performing-Simulating	Proehl	195
	Knowing Oneself as a Thinker	Simulating	Stanton	234
	Developing Media Literacy	Inquiring	Taylor, A.	175
	Personal Theories of Learning	Simulating	Taylor, E.	199
	Class Journaling	Reflecting	Zachary	290
3. Recognizing and revealing one's strengths and weaknesses as a learner and knower	Claiming Power of Voice & Mind	Reflecting	Belenky	247
	Developing Through Self-Assessment	Assessing	Boud	63
	Learning Styles Assessment	Assessing	Brewer	66
	Learning Activity Project	Performing-Simulating	Caffarella	211
	Reflecting on Practice	Assessing	Marienau	271
	Developing Edu-autobiographies	Assessing	Michael	74
	Coaching for Effectiveness	Performing-Simulating	Proehl	195
	Knowing Oneself as a Thinker	Simulating	Stanton	234
	Class Journaling	Reflecting	Zachary	290
4. Anticipating learning needed to prevent and solve problems	Adding Dimensions	Inquiring	Fiddler	158
	Multicultural Ethical Dilemmas	Simulating	Liebler	220
	Reflecting on Practice	Assessing	Marienau	271

Developmental Intentions	Name of Activity	Strategy	Contributor	Page
5. Posing and pursuing questions out of wonderment	Exploratories in Physics	Experimenting	Chiaverina	93
	ORID Discussion	Inquiring	Dunn	133
	Interdisciplinary Tree	Inquiring	Weiner	153
	Class Journaling	Reflecting	Zachary	290
6. Accepting internal dissonance as part of the learning process	Developing Edu-autobiographies	Assessing	Michael	74
	Aligning with the Mission	Simulating	Munaker	192
	Perspective Shift	Imagining	Munaker	111
	Action Learning	Imagining	O'Neil & Marsick	96
	Taking Multiple Perspectives	Simulating	Taylor, K.	203
	Journal Dialogue	Imagining	Walden	127
7. Setting one's own learning goals, being goal-directed, and being habitual in learning	Learning Styles Assessment	Assessing	Brewer	66
	Psychology Tutorial	Inquiring	Coulter	155
	Novice to Expert	Assessing	Fiddler	59
	Problem-Focused Education	Inquiring	Margetson	172
	Perspective Shift	Imagining	Munaker	111
	Critical Thinking Tic-Tac-Toe	Inquiring	Newell	140
	Action Learning	Imagining	O'Neil & Marsick	96
	Cooperative Inquiry	Collaborating	Reason	85
8. Seeking authentic feedback from others	Developing through Self-Assessment	Assessing	Boud	63
	Executive Coaching Practice	Simulating	Cashman	187
	Educational Autobiographies	Assessing	Clark & Kilgore	69
	Translating Experiences	Assessing	Eive	71
	Novice to Expert	Assessing	Fiddler	59
	Symbols Circle	Imagining	Hicks	102
	Reflecting on Practice	Assessing	Marienau	271
	Action Learning	Imagining	O'Neil & Marsick	96
	Coaching for Effectiveness	Performing-Simulating	Proehl	195
9. Drawing on multiple capacities for effective learning	Myth & Metaphor	Reflecting	Bassett	242
	Western Town	Simulation	Bergquist	183
	DNA Modeling	Experimenting	Fiddler	90
	Demystifying Inquiry	Inquiring	Firestone	161
	Field Study Reflection	Performing	McCormick	224
	Whole Person Reaction Paper	Reflecting	McCormick	275
	Being the Art Critic	Simulating	McGury	228
	Seeing Your Emerging Future	Imagining	Morton	107
	Perspective Shift	Imagining	Munaker	111
	ICA Kaleidoscope	Inquiring	Packard	114
	Coaching for Effectiveness	Performing-Simulating	Proehl	195
	Knowing Oneself as a Thinker	Simulating	Stanton	234
	Drawing Theory	Imagining	Stenersen	125

Developmental Intentions	Name of Activity	Strategy	Contributor	Page
IV. Toward self-agency and self-authorship				
1. Constructing a values system that informs one's behavior	Critique Expert Opinion	Inquiring	Brookfield	130
	Repertory Grids	Assessing	Candy	49
	Cognitive & Ethical Development	Simulating	Liebler	217
	Multicultural Ethical Dilemmas	Simulating	Liebler	220
	Insight by Surprise	Inquiring	Luft	137
	Whole Person Reaction Paper	Reflecting	McCormick	275
	Philosophy-of-Life Paper	Reflecting	Nemecek	282
	Understanding Diversity & Difference	Simulating	Siegel	232
	Cooperative Inquiry	Collaborating	Reason	85
	Taking Multiple Perspectives	Simulating	Taylor, K.	203
2. Accepting responsibility for choices one has made and will make	Developing Through Self-Assessing	Assessing	Boud	63
	Novice to Expert	Assessing	Fiddler	59
	Reconstructing Behaviors	Reflecting	Laming	253
	Multicultural Ethical Dilemmas	Simulating	Liebler	220
	Discovering True Perceptions	Imagining	Morton	109
	Trading Game	Reflecting	Toby & Templeman	287
	Providing a Learning Culture	Inquiring	Winkelman	178
3. Risking action on behalf of one's beliefs and commitments	Cooperative Inquiry	Collaborating	Reason	85
	Creating a Shared Vision	Imagining	Proehl	122
4. Taking action toward one's potential while acknowledging one's limitations	Reflecting on Practice	Assessing	Marienau	271
5. Revising aspects of oneself while maintaining continuity of other aspects	Translating Experiences	Assessing	Eive	71
	Seeing Your Emerging Future	Imagining	Morton	107
	Discovering True Perceptions	Imagining	Morton	109
	Taking Multiple Perspectives	Simulating	Taylor, K.	203
	Trading Game	Reflecting	Toby & Templeman	287

Developmental Intentions	Name of Activity	Strategy	Contributor	Page
6. Distinguishing what one has created for oneself from what is imposed by social, cultural, and other forces	Myth & Metaphor	Reflecting	Bassett	242
	Educational Autobiographies	Assessing	Clark & Kilgore	69
	Lifeboat Allegory	Simulating	Glicken	190
	Symbols Circle	Imagining	Hicks	102
	Insight by Surprise	Inquiring	Luft	137
	Whole Person Reaction Paper	Reflecting	McCormick	275
	Being the Art Critic	Simulating	McGury	228
	Discovering True Perceptions	Imagining	Morton	109
	Examining Your Paradigms	Imagining	Proehl	119
	Cultural Economic Values	Inquiring	Smith	147
	Culture & Identity	Simulating	Stolz	238
	Emerging Life Patterns	Reflecting	Taylor, K.	261
	Providing a Learning Culture	Inquiring	Winkelman	178
7. "Naming and claiming" what one has experienced and knows	Claiming Power of Voice & Mind	Reflecting	Belenky	247
	Using Empathic Listening	Reflecting	Blanusa	264
	Developing Through Self-Assessing	Assessing	Boud	63
	Educational Autobiographies	Assessing	Clark & Kilgore	69
	Structured Cooperative Learning	Collaborating	Feigenbaum	83
	Symbols Circle	Imagining	Hicks	102
	Philosophy-of-Life Paper	Reflecting	Nemecek	282
	Indescribable Moment	Reflecting	Neimeyer	257
	Experience-Cycle Methodology	Reflecting	Oades	285
	Exploring Culture	Inquiring	Parish	143
	Developing Media Literacy	Inquiring	Taylor, A.	175
	Personal Theories of Learning	Simulating	Taylor, E.	199
	Trading Game	Reflecting	Toby & Templeman	287

V. Toward connection with others

1. Mediating boundaries between one's connection to others and one's individuality	Western Town	Simulating	Bergquist	183
	Cognitive & Ethical Development	Simulating	Liebler	217
	Through Another's Eyes	Inquiring	Horvath-Neimeyer	170
	Aligning with the Mission	Simulating	Munaker	192
	Creating a Shared Vision	Imagining	Proehl	122
2. Experiencing oneself as part of something larger	Contradictions Workshop	Assessing	Dunn	55
	Structured Cooperative Learning	Collaborating	Feigenbaum	83
	Aligning with the Mission	Simulating	Munaker	192
	Creating a Shared Vision	Imagining	Proehl	122
	Culture & Identity	Simulating	Stolz	238

Developmental Intentions	Name of Activity	Strategy	Contributor	Page
	Personal Theories of Learning	Simulating	Taylor, E.	199
	Rotating Groups	Collaborating	Tennant	78
3. Engaging the affective dimension when confronting differences	Using Empathic Listening	Reflecting	Blanusa	264
	Reflecting on Beliefs & Values	Reflecting	Heid	267
	Reconstructing Behaviors	Reflecting	Laming	253
	Understanding Diversity & Difference	Simulating	Siegel	232
	Parents as Experts	Inquiring	Stahl	150
	Culture & Identity	Simulating	Stolz	238
	Listening Activity	Simulating	Timm	207
	Journal Dialogue	Imagining	Walden	127
4. Contributing one's voice to a collective endeavor	Western Town	Simulating	Bergquist	183
	Learning Circles	Collaborating	Bishop & Gibson	80
	Contradictions Workshop	Assessing	Dunn	55
	ORID Discussion	Inquiring	Dunn	133
	DNA Modeling	Experimenting	Fiddler	90
	Lifeboat Allegory	Simulating	Glicken	190
	Modeling Teaching-Learning	Simulating	Jaworski	214
	Perspective Shift	Imagining	Munaker	111
	Creating a Shared Vision	Imagining	Proehl	122
	Rotating Groups	Collaborating	Tennant	78
	Interdisciplinary Tree	Inquiring	Weiner	153
	Providing a Learning Culture	Inquiring	Winkelman	178
5. Recognizing that collective awareness and thinking transform the sum of their parts	Claiming Power of Voice & Mind	Reflecting	Belenky	247
	Western Town	Simulating	Bergquist	183
	Learning Circles	Collaborating	Bishop & Gibson	80
	Exploratories in Physics	Experimenting	Chiaverina	93
	Contradictions Workshop	Assessing	Dunn	55
	Structured Cooperative Learning	Collaborating	Feigenbaum	83
	Problem-Focused Education	Inquiring	Margetson	172
	Clustering	Imagining	Melamed	104
	Indescribable Moment	Reflecting	Neimeyer	257
	ICA Kaleidoscope	Imagining	Packard	114
	Exploring Culture	Inquiring	Parish	143
	Creating a Shared Vision	Imagining	Proehl	122
	Cooperative Inquiry	Collaborating	Reason	85
	Developing Media Literacy	Inquiring	Taylor, A.	175
	Interdisciplinary Tree	Inquiring	Weiner	153

Name Index

A

Aisenberg, N., 70, 71
Andrade, A., 143
Angelo, T. A., 319
Apps, J. W., 317
Argyris, C., 227
Armon, C., 225
Armstrong, A. K., 54, 55
Aronson, E., 85
Association for Supervision and
    Curriculum Development, 68
Ausubel, D. P., 313, 355, 357, 358

B

Bandura, A., 357
Bannister, D., 55
Bateson, G., 166, 169
Beaty, E., 26, 316
Belenky, M. F., 8, 16, 20, 21, 22,
    37, 70, 71, 206, 231, 234, 237,
    249, 250, 251, 280, 281, 282,
    306, 313, 314, 331, 341, 345,
    347, 348
Bennis, W. G., xii, 71, 339
Bergquist, W., 187

Biagi, S., 176, 178
Blaney, N., 85
Blasi, A., 20, 206, 354
Block, P., 196, 199
Bond, L., 249, 251
Booth, S., 14, 17, 26, 30, 312, 357
Borzak, L., 226, 227
Botkin, J., 39
Boud, D., 27, 28, 30, 42, 66, 175,
    298, 301, 309
Boyce, M., 227
Brewer, P., 310
Bridges, W., xi, 9, 37, 38, 327
Brookfield, S. D., 7, 25, 27, 29, 35,
    36, 42, 76, 77, 131, 132, 133,
    149, 198, 298, 299, 302, 304,
    310, 311, 316, 317, 319, 325, 327
Brooks, A., 357, 359

C

Caffarella, R., 28, 213, 309, 320,
    324, 334, 354, 355
Campbell, J., 245, 247
Candy, P. C., 19, 39, 55, 300, 331
Carbo, M., 68
Cederholm, L., 97, 100

Cervero, R., 317
Chiaverina, C., 313
Chickering, A. W., 16
Chinen, A., 245, 247
Chisom, R., 176, 178
Christensen, C. R., 305, 309
Clark, C., 47, 331
Clinchy, B. M., 8, 20, 21, 22, 37,
    70, 71, 206, 231, 234, 235, 237,
    249, 250, 280, 281, 282, 306,
    313, 314, 341, 345, 347, 348
Cohen, R., 66
Colarusso, C., 10
Cooper, P., 359
Coulter, X., 300
Cranton, P., 29, 40, 317
Cross, K. P., 319

D

Dahlgren, L., 39
Dall'Alba, G., 26, 316
Daloz, L. A., 3, 16, 37, 42, 305,
    326, 328, 329, 330, 332, 333,
    334, 338, 354
Dawson, S., 217
Dewey, J., 11, 19, 26, 27, 38, 337

Subject Index

A

Accomodation, 11

Action learning 82; process of 97, 99–100.

Action research, 88

Activities. *See* Index of Strategies, 373

Adult development: and adult learning theories, 22–25; defined, 10; differentiation and integration cycle and, 11; as dynamic process, 33–43; educational environment influence on, 16; environmental interactions and, 11; four aspects of, 10–11; reframing experience and, 12; relational models of, 353–354; transformations throughout, 350–352t, 351t; transformative learning and, 12–13; variable process of, 11–12. *See also* Constructive-developmental theories; Developmental intentions

Adult learners: adult educators as, 317, 334; assessment drives learning of, 309–310; challenges of working with, 8–9; changes experienced by, 9–10; characteristics of, 4–9; coverage of material issues for, 307–309; diversity of, 3; facilitating discussion by, 301–305; power, control, and authority issues for, 297–300; problematic experiences with learning by, 6; relationship between teacher and, 325, 327, 329–332; risk of cultural suicide by, 327–328; self-direction and empowerment issues for, 300–301; shared journey of teacher and, 334–335; subjectivist perceptions of, 314–315. *See also* Experience; Learning; Teachers of adults

Adult learning theories: constructive-development, 341–352; developmental dimensions of, 22–25; and experience, 25–26;

Jarvis's typology of learning, 361–362; Kolb's experiential theory of development, 337–340; and meaning-making, 29–30; orientations to teaching and learning, 355–359; and reflection, 26–29; relational models of development/ethic of care, 353–354. *See also* Constructive- developmental theories; Deep approaches to learning; Learning

Adulthood transformations, 13–14, 21–22, 357

Andragogy, 359

Assessment. *See* Deep approaches to learning; Self-assessment

Authority: of adult learner, 40–41; vs. authoritarianism, 299; façade of, 306; for knowledge, 341–348; and self-disclosure of mentor, 305; as teaching issue, 297–300; of text vs. experience, 315.

Autonomy, 40–42: and connection, 352; vs. self in relation, 353